D1523028

CONSTRUCTING ALLIED COOPERATION

To Bob,

With deep admiration for you and your work,

Marina

Berlin, Oct 2019

CONSTRUCTING ALLIED COOPERATION

Diplomacy, Payments, and Power in Multilateral Military Coalitions

Marina E. Henke

CORNELL UNIVERSITY PRESS   **ITHACA AND LONDON**

Cornell University Press gratefully acknowledges receipt of a grant from the Alice Kaplan Institute for the Humanities, Northwestern University, which aided in the publication of this book.

First published 2019 by Cornell University Press

Library of Congress Cataloging-in-Publication Data

Names: Henke, Marina E., 1982– author.
Title: Constructing allied cooperation : diplomacy, payments, and power in multilateral military coalitions / Marina E. Henke.
Description: Ithaca : Cornell University Press, 2019. | Includes bibliographical references and index.
Identifiers: LCCN 2018053745 (print) | LCCN 2018054967 (ebook) | ISBN 9781501739705 (pdf) | ISBN 9781501739712 (epub/mobi) | ISBN 9781501739699 | ISBN 9781501739699– (cloth: -alk. paper)
Subjects: LCSH: Combined operations (Military science)—Political aspects. | Intervention (International law)—Political aspects. | Security, International—International cooperation. | International relations—Political aspects.
Classification: LCC U260 (ebook) | LCC U260. H44 2019 (print) | DDC 355/.031—dc23
LC record available at https://lccn.loc.gov/2018053745

For my parents

But man has almost constant occasion for the help of his brethren, and it is in vain for him to expect it from their benevolence only. He will be more likely to prevail if he can interest their self-love in his favour, and show them that it is for their own advantage to do for him what he requires of them. Whoever offers to another a bargain of any kind, proposes to do this. Give me that which I want, and you shall have this which you want, is the meaning of every such offer; and it is in this manner that we obtain from one another the far greater part of those good offices which we stand in need of.

Adam Smith, *Wealth of Nations*

Contents

Figures and Tables

Figures

Tables

Acknowledgments

Every book has its own story. Mine begins in early 2008, when I stumbled upon the EU deployment to Chad and the Central African Republic. I was captivated to understand how EU member states were able to field this operation despite the political controversy surrounding it. As a graduate student, I had the time to set out and investigate. The result is this book: a study of the construction of cooperation in security and defense affairs—in Europe, America, and worldwide.

The journey of writing this book took me once around the world. It started at Princeton under the guidance of Robert Keohane, Andrew Moravcsik, Tom Christensen, and Christina Davis. Their academic brilliance provided me with intellectual roots when I most needed them. Their belief in me and this project gave me wings. Time and again they inspired me to think harder, dig deeper, and push further. I could not be more grateful. Especially, Robert Keohane was a mentor that any grad student can only dream of.

Lamis Abdelaaty, Omar Bashir, Torben Behmer, Elisa Burchert, Sarah Bush, Jeff Colgan, Adrien Desgeorges, Rex Douglass, Andrea Everett, Andi Fuchs, Salla Garzky, Tom Hale, David Hsu, Alex Lanoszka, Oriana Mastro, Jason McMann, Alex Ovodenko, Tom Scherer, and Meredith Wilf contributed greatly to my time in New Jersey. They read numerous draft chapters, listened patiently to my presentations, and invited me out for coffee, lunch, and dinner when "dissertating" was overtaking my life. I also greatly benefited from kind academic and personal guidance from Aaron Friedberg, Jim Gadsden, John Ikenberry, Sophie Meunier, and Ezra Suleiman.

Starting in 2013, I found a new intellectual home at Northwestern. I am particularly grateful to Karen Alter, Ana Ajona, Loubna El Amine, Dan Galvin, Laurel Hardbridge-Yong, Beth Hurd, Ian Hurd, Daniel Krcmaric, Michael Loriaux, Steve Nelson, Sara Monoson, Tom Ogorzalek, Wendy Pearlman, Will Reno, Rachel Riedl, Andrew Roberts, Jason Seawright, Hendrik Spruyt, and Alvin Tillery for their intellectual creativity and personal support. Pamela Straw, Jill Decremer, John Robert Mocek, Stephen Monteiro, and Courtney Syskowski helped me keep my head above water by providing magnificent administrative support.

During the final stages of this book, I called the European University Institute in Florence my home. I am grateful to Richard Bellamy, Frederica Bicchi, Ulrich Krotz, Rich Maher, Jennifer Welsh, and my formidable cohort of Max Weber fellows—especially Matt Canfield, Jeanne Commault, Mirjam Dageförde, Chiara

Destri, Valentin Jentsch, Hanna Kleider, Robin Markwica, Hugo Meijer, Cyrille Thibault, Paul van Hooft, Anna Wallerman, and Aydin Yildirim—for a fantastic year in Tuscany.

Along the way many people have helped me with and commented on this work—at conferences or workshops or in reviews of my research. They include Austin Carson, Jon Caverley, Bridget Coggins, Katharina Coleman, Kyle Breadsley, Adam Dean, Nisha Fazal, Benjamin Fordham, Erik Gartzke, Heidi Hardt, Stephanie Hofmann, Michael Horowitz, Sarah Kreps, Tobias Lenz, Charles Lipson, Roland Marchal, Jonathan Markowitz, Pat McDonald, John Mearsheimer, Jonathan Monten, Dan Nexon, Paul Poast, Robert Pape, Vincent Pouliot, Stefano Recchia, Paul Staniland, Alexander Thompson, Stephanie von Hlatky, Srdjan Vucetic, Jessica Weeks, Alex Weisiger, Krista Wiegand, Paul Williams, Scott Wohlforth, and Amy Yuen. I am particularly grateful to Steve Brooks, who propelled this project forward when it needed an urgent boost.

I have learned a tremendous amount from and am grateful to Deborah Avant, Dick Betts, Steve Biddle, Maria Carrasquilla, Nancy Chaarani-Meza, Mai'a Cross Davis, Nancy Duong, Andrea Gilli, Mauro Gilli, Jim Goldgeier, Carla Henke, Lise Howard, Bruce Jentleson, Kelly Kadera, Zuli Majeed, Sarah Mitchell, Sarah Samis, Anne-Marie Slaughter, Caitlin Talmadge, and Rudolf Templer.

Anyone who has done field research knows the huge debts one accumulates in the process. I feel particularly grateful to Karen Beashel, my lovely host in Australia; Ayo Abogan, whose parents took me in like their own daughter in Nigeria; Florent de Bodman, Laurence and Pierre Sabatié-Garat, who opened so many doors for me in Paris; Lili Cole, who graciously arranged that I could spend a month at the USIP in Washington, D.C.; Jenn Keser, who made London much more fun; Errol Levy, whose guest room became my home in Brussels; and the one and only Başak Yavçan, whose talent to arrange interviews in Turkey will forever remain unmatched.

Many more people took time out of their busy schedules to answer my questions and put me in touch with colleagues, friends, and family around the globe. Your willingness to help, your readiness to disclose potentially sensitive information, and your interest in my work touched me profoundly. I thank you all.

A number of research assistants have played a key role in developing this book, especially Joe Baka, James Crisafulli, Evan Frohman, Julian Gerez, Jamie Golinkoff, Esther Li, Hansen Ong, Simone Rivera, Amelia Strauss, and Jules Villa.

I have also been the lucky recipient of a number of grants and fellowships that supported my research. Heartfelt thanks go to the National Science Foundation, the Bradley Foundation, the United States Institute of Peace, the Princeton Institute for International and Regional Studies, Princeton's Woodrow Wilson School, Princeton's Center for International Security Studies, Northwestern University,

Northwestern's Buffett Institute, Northwestern's French Interdisciplinary Group, Northwestern's Kellogg School of Management Dispute Resolution Research Center, and the European University Institute.

At Cornell University Press, Roger Haydon has been an excellent guide in the process of writing this book. Every book has its ups and downs, and Roger managed them with grace and dedication. I thank the two external reviewers for their careful comments on the manuscript.

I dedicate this book to my parents, Lucie and Hartmut Henke. Their stories about their work and life in faraway places, their respect and love for this world and its peoples in all their diversity instilled in me a curiosity to discover and understand myself—a desire that lies at the very heart of this work.

An online appendix of additional data can be found on my website at www.marinahenke.com under the "Research" link.

CONSTRUCTING ALLIED COOPERATION

1

THE PUZZLE OF ORGANIZING
COLLECTIVE ACTION

On June 25, 1950, North Korea launched an attack across the 38th parallel. The aggression rattled the government of U.S. president Harry S. Truman. Mao Zedong's communist forces had defeated the American-backed Kuomintang on the Chinese mainland only a few months earlier, in December 1949, and critics of the Truman administration had portrayed this "loss of China" as a colossal catastrophe. Weary of the claim of weakness, Truman's advisers quickly formed a consensus: This time around, communist aggression had to be faced head on—the world would unite behind U.S. leadership. The U.S. government called the United Nations (UN) into action, and for the very first time since the creation of that global institution, UN member states were asked to mobilize military forces and uphold the principle of collective security. UN resolution 83 (1950) requested UN member states to "furnish . . . assistance to the Republic of Korea . . . to repel the armed attack and to restore international peace and security in the area."[1] Although many UN members voiced political support for the U.S. endeavor, their enthusiasm for sending troops to Korea was decidedly limited. U.S. goals in Korea were not theirs, and "feeding their people" had priority over "putting chains on Communists around the world."[2] Still, the U.S. government insisted that a multilateral coalition should be deployed. As U.S. secretary of state Dean Acheson put it: "We are to do *everything possible* to encourage offers of actual military forces from other countries" to join the Korean War.[3] Thus began the construction process of the Korean War coalition.

From 1950 to 1952, U.S. government officials worked tirelessly to recruit states to deploy to the Korean Peninsula. They cajoled, bargained, and intimidated. They used flattery, side payments, and coercive threats. In the end, they recruited over twenty states to join the Korean War. U.S. secretary of defense George Marshall presciently suggested in September 1950 that the process by which the Korean coalition was formed would set "a pattern for future collective military action."[4] He could hardly have been closer to the truth. Not only did U.S. techniques for the Korean War set a pattern for all future U.S.-led military coalitions, but other countries such as France, Great Britain, Australia, Russia, Nigeria, and even Saudi Arabia would adopt similar ways of persuading states to join military interventions. Moreover, the same patterns influenced coalitions constructed under the auspices of the UN, the North Atlantic Treaty Organization (NATO), the European Union (EU), the African Union (AU), and most other international security organizations.

In this book, I use a social-institutional theory and evidence from over eighty multilateral military coalitions to explain these coalition-building practices. At the heart of the theory lies the belief that coalitions seldom emerge "naturally" due to common interests, norms, values, or alliance commitments. Rather, coalitions are purposefully constructed by individual states. The states that organize these efforts—pivotal states—instrumentalize preexisting institutional and social ties to bargain fellow states into a specific coalition. This process involves arguing, persuasion, and often also side payments. Bilateral and multilateral networks, which include civilian as well as military ties, constitute an invaluable resource in this process. These ties give pivotal states access to private information about the deployment preferences of potential participants. Moreover, they facilitate issue linkages and side payments and allow states to overcome problems of credible commitments. Finally, pivotal states can use common institutional contacts as cooperation brokers and can convert common institutional venues into fora for coalition negotiations.

The evidence presented in this book requires us to revisit the conventional wisdom about how collective action in the security sphere is achieved. It also generates new insights with respect to who is most likely to join a given multilateral intervention and what factors influence the strength and capacity of particular coalitions. Moreover, as the Trump administration promotes an "America First" policy and withdraws from international agreements and the U.K. negotiates Brexit, this book is an important reminder that international security cannot be delinked from more mundane forms of cooperation; multilateral military coalitions thrive or fail depending on the breadth and depth of existing social and diplomatic networks.

Why Does It Matter How Multilateral Coalitions Are Built?

The puzzle of collective mobilization lies at the root of all politics.[5] Studying the construction of multilateral military coalitions trains this puzzle on the context of international security—the one area of international cooperation that has traditionally been perceived as the most difficult to sustain a cooperative equilibrium.[6] How can states overcome problems of collective action in the face of human atrocities, terrorism, and the threat of weapons of mass destruction? What cooperative constellations are used to topple governments, deter aggressors, or build peace? What does international burden-sharing in this context look like between the rich and the poor or the big and the small? Who holds agency and what constitutes power in these processes that profoundly affect international security and stability? What is the role of international organizations and diplomacy? How do ideas, interests, cooption, and coercion interact? This book advances our understanding of all of these questions and adds new perspectives and insights on the central political phenomenon that is international cooperation.

Moreover, the specific techniques used to build multilateral military coalitions affect how wars are fought. On the battlefield, coalition operations are supposedly more successful than non-coalition endeavors.[7] What explains this success? Multilateral coalitions enhance the perceived legitimacy of the operation and thus public support—domestically as well as internationally. They facilitate inter-agency bargaining and bargaining with third-party states over (for example) landing and basing rights. Multilateral coalitions can also have a deterrent effect on the target state and offer cover for compromises. That said, strategic or coercive coalition building can undermine war-fighting effectiveness; military forces that are not intrinsically motivated to join a given intervention have gained a reputation for a less reliable commitment. They also have a record of being discouraged by setbacks and casualties and of being less willing to follow through when a situation goes sour.[8] Furthermore, the recruitment of forces for political motives can generate cumbersome command structures, introduce complex interoperability challenges, and affect coalition cohesion, agility, and discipline.[9] Beyond the battlefield, such techniques can trigger social unrest, mutinies, and even coups d'état.[10]

Multilateral coalition building also affects the prospect for peace. Most peace-keeping deployments today are coalition endeavors, and research suggests that the stronger their participants, particularly in terms of personnel numbers and equipment, the more effective the missions are likely to be.[11] In the same vein, coalition participants can influence peace negotiations, postwar stabilization, and state-building efforts. By participating in these practices, such states become local stakeholders: they contribute resources, ideas, and legitimacy. But can politically constructed peacekeeping cooperation really achieve successful and sustainable peace? Are coalition participants under these circumstances willing to give their all? Or do they restrict their involvement to whatever is needed to maintain their relationship with the pivotal state? Might they even be tempted to manipulate their engagement to extract further concessions from the pivotal state?

Finally, coalitions unleash important socialization dynamics among participating states. They create common battle experiences and shape threat perceptions, military doctrine, and strategy for years to come. Sometimes, participation in a coalition can radically change a country's political trajectory. Turkey's participation in the Korean War, for instance, led to its membership in NATO, and Thailand's participation in the same war led to its alignment with the United States during the Cold War. More recently, Pakistan's deployment to Somalia arguably influenced the U.S. decision to remove economic sanctions imposed on Pakistan as a result of the country's nuclear program. Poland, in turn, influenced the EU Lisbon Treaty negotiations by deploying forces to Chad in 2008. These examples indicate that countries can convert their coalition deployments into a fungible, tradable power asset. Multilateral coalition building allows these states to reap political and economic benefits that other areas of international cooperation do not offer. Indeed, a large number of states no longer calibrate their military involvements to their security interests. Instead, they are willing to trade their coalition contribution for cash or a concession on another international issue.

The Limits of Existing Explanations

Most research on multilateral interventions takes coalition building as a given. Research that offers explanations of how this process unfolds takes three broad approaches; they focus on alliance ties; hegemonic order and related economic and political coercion; or interest convergence among coalition participants. This body of literature is rich, but it suffers from several important limitations.

Alliance theory proposes that alliance partners share threat perceptions, norms, and values and therefore are likely to join the same military coalitions. Moreover, the "Alliance Security Dilemma" holds that alliance partners support each other even if their interests and values do not converge.[12] Rather, by joining forces, alliance partners intend to signal the credibility of their mutual commitment. Cox and O'Connor argue, for example, that such a motive explains

Australia's participation in the Iraq War coalition in 2003; Davidson makes the same argument for the involvement of Italy and the U.K. in the same conflict.[13] Weitsman, in turn, suggests that "institutions of interstate violence serve as ready mechanisms for employing force" in multilateral coalitions.[14] But while alliances are undoubtedly important, they do not generate coalition contributions automatically: roughly three quarters of coalitions that intervened in crises during the late twentieth and early twenty-first centuries involved no allied states, and of those coalitions that did involve allies, most also included non-allied partners (e.g., the Gulf War, the Iraq War, Afghanistan, Libya). Theories of alliances and alignment thus cannot predict who participates in multilateral military coalitions.[15]

A more recent wave of research argues that hegemonic orders and related economic or political dependencies better explain coalition contributions. Powerful states *coerce* other countries into cooperation. Two types of coercive mechanisms are at play. In the first one, a pivotal state uses or threatens to use its superior power capabilities to get a third party to join a coalition.[16] Newnham, for instance, writes that the United States "found it especially easy to influence countries" to contribute troops to the Iraq invasion that "were already dependent on U.S. aid."[17] In the second one, a pivotal state commands a third party to join an operation, and the latter chooses to comply out of "subordination" to the superior power capabilities of the pivotal state.[18] The subordinate state finds the coalition demand legitimate given the existing power hierarchy. Lake indeed suggests that the latter logic was prevalent during the Iraq War. He writes: "It appears that states participated in the war as a costly signal of support for the United States and an acknowledgment of its authority."[19] There are certainly cases that support this argument, but many instances contradict the logic. Instead of obliging to coercive threats or demonstrating submissiveness, countries receive generous compensation for joining a coalition. Examples include Thailand, South Africa, and Ethiopia in the Korean War; Poland and Bulgaria in the Iraq War; and Turkey and Syria in the Gulf War—to name just a few.

The third explanation focuses on preference convergence among coalition partners irrespective of alliance concerns. States join coalitions for a range of idiosyncratic reasons. Countries may be driven by normative rationales or identity motivations, by civil-military relations, or by other types of political and economic motives such as prestige or financial reimbursements. Such motivations push coalition partners to coalesce or, as Ward and Dorussen put it, most such deployments constitute "a collective response of a coalition of countries that perceive a common interest to intervene in a particular situation."[20] Many of these accounts do acknowledge the existence of a diplomatic process of some sort coordinating coalition participation. Nevertheless, this process remains largely undertheorized. This constitutes a glaring oversight. Any type of cooperation requires organization. It entails an adjustment of policies, which does not just happen automatically. On top of this, collective action problems need to be overcome. Furthermore, the convergence of intrinsic preferences in many coalitions is doubtful. What seems more likely is that a spectrum of preference intensities exists with regard to the launch of a particular intervention. Some states feel very strongly about a situation, whereas others care less.

There are two more general problems with existing research. First, the literature on coalition building has focused almost exclusively on categorical causes (e.g., alliance concerns, normative motivations, threat perceptions, economic interests) to explain decisions to join an operation. It pays little to no attention to *how* multilateral military coalitions are actually built. But political processes matter: they can determine election outcomes, peace negotiations, and incarceration rates. They affect the selection of job candidates, mortgage fees, and construction permits. They can affect a particular outcome at least as much as individual preferences and actions.[21] Second, the literature provides little understanding of the bargaining nature of coalition building.[22] Who holds agency in coalition negotiations, and how does agency affect the outcomes? Who holds power in these negotiations and why? Does the bargaining process for ad hoc coalitions differ from negotiations conducted under the umbrella of the UN or NATO?

Constructing Cooperation

This book offers a social-institutional theory for how multilateral military coalitions are built. Most coalitions do not emerge naturally; they are not the result of alliance commitments or convergent preferences. Rather, pivotal states deliberately build coalitions. They develop operational plans and provide incentives for suitable third parties to join. To bargain these states into joining the coalition, pivotal states purposefully instrumentalize their bilateral and multilateral diplomatic connections, what I term *diplomatic embeddedness,* as a resource.[23] These connections provide information on deployment preferences, create trust, and facilitate side payments and issue linkages. Moreover, shared contacts serve as cooperation brokers and shared institutional venues as negotiation fora.

I define diplomatic embeddedness as the cumulative number of bilateral and multilateral diplomatic ties that connect a country dyad. Most of these ties are the result of bilateral or multilateral agreements that a country pair entertains. Each one of these agreements requires government officials to interact with their foreign counterparts. They have to talk, exchange letters or emails, and meet at bilateral or multilateral summits and other types of gatherings. Each agreement creates an identifiable institutional network.[24] A pivotal state can exploit these networks when constructing a multilateral military coalition. These ties turn into a state capability to engage others in collective action.

First, these networks provide trust and credible commitments. Without these attributes, cooperative agreements, especially in military affairs, are less likely to succeed. Second, these networks provide information. Coalition participants are often substitutable, and pivotal states must pre-select a group of states that they deem worthy to engage in coalition negotiations. To whittle down the numbers, pivotal states need to know (1) what can a state contribute to the operation; (2) how much does a state intrinsically care to be a member, and (3) what external incentives could a pivotal state offer to make that state join the coalition. The latter two criteria in particular are fundamentally subjective political considerations. Without access to private information, pivotal states cannot fully determine these factors. Thus, they revert to diplomatic networks for such information. Via these ties, U.S. diplomats learned, for instance, that Nigerian president Olusegun Obasanjo was privately panicking that his key policy objective—debt relief for Nigeria—was slipping through his fingers. During the construction of the peacekeeping coalition that deployed to Darfur, the U.S. government used this information to bargain Nigeria into the coalition. Third, diplomatic embeddedness allows pivotal states to link issues and channel side payments through preexisting ties (e.g., existing aid budgets, the UN, the World Bank), thus lowering transaction costs and avoiding public scrutiny. For example, to fund the contributions of South Korea and the Philippines to the Vietnam War coalition, the United States used the "Food for Peace" program to channel subsidies to both governments. The U.S. government shipped rice and other bulk foods to these two countries with the *explicit* understanding that the food could be resold and the proceeds could be used to help meet Vietnam expenses.[25] Fourth, pivotal states often ask common institutional contacts, such as officials at international organizations (IOs), to serve as cooperation brokers. Using their own networks, these brokers can help pivotal states collect information on deployment preferences and sway states to join a coalition—especially if these brokers can bridge "structural holes," that is, connect a pivotal state to a largely unknown third party.[26] Fifth, common institutional fora, such as bilateral and multilateral summits, often serve as negotiation venues. Face-to-face interactions can help pivotal states in their recruitment. Finally, of course, diplomatic embeddedness can also play an important role in coercing cooperation by increasing the range of negative linkage opportunities. The more bilateral and multilateral ties exist, the greater the range of linkages and also the greater their credibility.[27] Pivotal states can thus use these ties to exert leverage over reluctant coalition participants.[28]

Many people recognize the advantages of being "networked" in their daily lives. These connections can lead to better jobs, loans, and concert tickets. This book suggests that for states it is no different: if used purposefully by pivotal states, extensive diplomatic networks can provide for reliable and rapid collective action. Diplomatic embeddedness constitutes a strategic capability to organize collective mobilization. Bilateral and multilateral connections thus provide benefits to states that go way past the specific purposes the individual institutions were created for; institutional relationships matter beyond what they were set out to achieve. Notably, they help in the construction of cooperation. These are novel insights. International Relations (IR) theory has not focused thus far on the aggregate effects of institutional connections.

My focus in this book is the building of military coalitions. Nevertheless, some of my findings are likely to apply to coalitions in other issue areas, notably human rights, the environment, economic sanctions, trade, financial regulation, and arms control. One of the principal weaknesses of existing research on international cooperation is its implicit assumption of *automaticity,* the idea that like-minded states coalesce "naturally" to address a common problem—or at least the neglect of diplomatic processes that enable such cooperation.[29] Thus, the techniques involved in building military coalitions examined in this book might be useful for a wide audience.

Scope Conditions

I define a multilateral military coalition as an ad hoc understanding between two or more states to deploy military and/or police forces in pursuit of a specific security-related mission. The understanding dissolves once that mission is complete.[30] Such coalitions can be led by individual states or operate under the umbrella of an international organization.[31] Missions include humanitarian, peacekeeping, and peace enforcement as well as regime change operations in a third state. I exclude the creation of military alliances that are intended to last beyond a specific mission. Following Morey, I believe that alliances and coalitions are distinct creatures.[32] Alliances are promises to provide aid or take particular actions in the case of conflict. Coalitions, on the other hand, represent active foreign engagement. There can, of course, be a relationship between alliances and coalitions, as allied states may become members of the same coalition. That said, the transition is never automatic. Alliance partners can opt out of coalition deployments, whereas coalitions can form between states with no prior alliance commitments.

Empirical Approach

This book uses an integrative mixed-method research design to test the theory of military coalition building introduced above. I combine large-N regression analysis, in-depth elite interviews, and archival research to support a unified causal narrative. I use each method for what it is especially suited: large-N regression analysis to produce statistical inferences and case study research to illustrate key assumptions about causal interactions and pathways. This approach yields a more robust outcome than either triangulation or a single-method approach.[33]

The large-N regression analysis tests which social, normative, political, and economic factors have the greatest influence on who joins a multilateral coalition with a pivotal state. I constructed an original dataset to conduct the analysis. The dataset includes eighty-two multilateral coalitions established between 1990 and 2005. I coded various new variables to assemble the dataset, notably the exact number of troops deployed per coalition as well as the pivotal states by mission. This analysis sheds light on the macro-factors determining efforts to build multilateral military coalitions. In particular, it permits us to determine quantitatively to what degree diplomatic embeddedness can predict coalition participation.

The case studies, in turn, serve to illustrate in detail the causal mechanisms that underpin the concept of diplomatic embeddedness.[34] Moreover, via detailed process-tracing, I also corroborate that there is no confounding between different causal pathways.[35]

Case Selection

I chose as cases the coalition-building processes for the Korean War, the UN-AU deployment to Darfur (UNAMID), the Australian-led intervention in East Timor (INTERFET), and the EU intervention in Chad and the Central African Republic (EUFOR Chad-CAR). These cases provide extreme factorial variation, which allows me to portray the consistency of the stipulated causal mechanisms across a wide range of coalition characteristics. The Korean War coalition deployed in 1950 at the very beginning of the Cold War to counter communist aggression. The coalition was the first military operation ever to be assembled under the UN flag. Nevertheless, the United States very quickly took over all operational aspects of the deployment. INTERFET deployed almost sixty years later. It was an Australian-led intervention to address the outbreak of violence in the aftermath of an independence referendum in East Timor. UNAMID, in turn, was a humanitarian operation that set out to address ethnic cleansing and other types of atrocities in Darfur, a region in Sudan. UNAMID deployed in 2007 and was the first operation that was jointly conducted by the UN and the AU. Finally, EUFOR

Chad-CAR, which deployed in 2008 and was mandated to protect civilians in refugee camps, was a coalition that formed under the umbrella of the EU.

To reconstruct the coalition-building processes for these four interventions, I relied on both archival research and elite interviews. In total, I consulted archival documents related to military coalition building since 1950 at the National Archives in Washington, D.C., the National Security Archives in Washington, D.C., the George H. W. Bush Presidential Library Archives, the Lyndon B. Johnson Presidential Library Archives, the Mudd Library in Princeton, and the Truman Presidential Library Archives. To gain insights on current practices and to complement the archival research, I conducted over 150 in-depth interviews over eight years in Nigeria, India, Jordan, Turkey, Australia, Belgium, Austria, Ireland, Germany, France, the United Kingdom, and the United States. In each country, I interviewed a broad range of government actors: military officers, generals, diplomats, ambassadors, ministers, and even heads of state. Due to the delicate information exchanged, many interviews were conducted "on background" (that is, my interview partners granted me permission to use the information, but they asked me not to identify them by name in this book).

CONSTRUCTING MULTILATERAL MILITARY COALITIONS

How do countries build multilateral military coalitions? This chapter argues that diplomatic networks provide critical underpinnings for multilateral coalition-building efforts. States that are most interested in seeing a given coalition deploy, develop operational plans of how the mission should look, and instrumentalize existing bilateral and multilateral connections to recruit fitting coalition contributors. The trust, information, and facility to construct issue linkages and side payments embedded in these networks help these states in their coalition-building endeavor. Moreover, these states ask common institutional contacts to serve as cooperation brokers and use institutional venues as coalition negotiation fora. In short, diplomatic embeddedness serves as a resource, a strategic capability that states use to bargain third parties into joining a coalition.

Pivotal States

It is always states (not institutions) that are the ultimate decision-makers in coalition-building processes, regardless of whether a multilateral military coalition is constructed ad hoc or under the umbrella of a regional or international security organization. Pivotal states, in particular, play a critical role in this process.[1] In relative terms, these states hold the strongest preference intensity with regard to the formation of a particular coalition. These states organize the coalition-building process: they want other states to join the coalition.[2] They are "political entrepreneurs" who are willing to pay disproportionate costs to organize collective mobilization: they make issues and stakes more salient, scan possible participants, and attract and push these states into coalitions through persuasion and other forms of incentive.[3] For some coalitions, one single state takes on the entire organizational process; for other coalitions, a small number of states share among themselves these responsibilities. If no pivotal states exist, effective coalitions are highly unlikely to emerge.[4]

Pivotal states do not exist on a permanent basis, and no single variable can explain why countries turn into pivotal states in specific coalition-building efforts. Rather, it is a combination of structural and domestic factors that motivate pivotal states to take on this role. Most pivotal states are powerful and wealthy—characteristics that certainly facilitate leadership.[5] Per my own analysis, the most frequent pivotal states in recent years have been the United States, France, the United Kingdom, Italy, Germany, Australia, and Russia.[6] U.S. leadership in the construction of the military coalition that ultimately intervened in Darfur in 2007 was largely the result of intense lobbying efforts by a domestic mass movement, the Save Darfur Coalition (for details, see chapter 5). Australian leadership on East Timor in 1999, in turn, was the result of geography and ad hoc domestic factors. Australia neighbors East Timor to the south. Moreover, a coalition of left- and right-wing elements of Australian society was collectively able to pressure the Howard government to engage in the first large-scale military intervention that Australia had ever launched on its own (for details, see chapter 6).

While pivotal states feel an urge to launch an intervention abroad, most other states do not—or at least not to the same degree.[7] Figure 2.1 tries to capture this variance in preferences among states in the international community with regard to one particular military intervention. The figure presents a hypothetical distribution of preferences held by states A–Z.[8] Every state gets a number based on how much it is interested in the launch of a multilateral military operation. A numerical value of ten means the intervention constitutes a top policy priority, while zero signifies indifference; negative values indicate opposition. States that are marked A, B, and C are intensively interested in the launch of a particular operation.[9] States D–Z, in turn, hold less intense preferences: States D–S value the intervention slightly, states T–U are indifferent, and states V–Z are opposed to the intervention. They hold negative preference intensities.

Visualizing this preference diversity among international actors is important. Its underlying logic puts into doubt the notion of "free riding," which is often used to explain lack of engagement in multilateral coalition-building processes.[10] Collective action theory assumes that all countries equally desire a certain action/outcome to occur. Nevertheless, some countries try to free ride to save costs if they think that the collective act will occur even without their individual

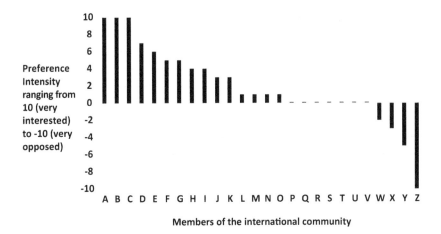

FIGURE 2.1   Hypothetical distribution of preference intensities among members of the international community regarding the launch of a specific intervention

contribution.[11] The concept of diverse preference intensities presented here suggests instead that some countries simply care less about a specific outcome than others and therefore do not contribute to the collective output. I argue that this latter assumption of diverse preferences and preference intensities is more appropriate when it comes to military intervention decisions. Indeed, I consider it a stretch to treat military interventions, including UN operations, as a "pure" public good equally valued by all members of the international community.[12] Rather, some states benefit or expect to benefit more than others based on threat perceptions, normative motivations, political interests, and so forth. All these factors are unique to each individual state. They depend, among others, on a state's distance from the conflict theater,[13] its normative identity, its civil society makeup,[14] civil-military relations,[15] and socioeconomic structures[16]—to name just a few. Moreover, there are financial cost concerns. For many countries around the world, foreign deployments might look appealing, but, given their financial constraints, they simply cannot afford them; other areas have greater priority.[17] These preferences thus put states on a spectrum—from intensively motivated (that is, pivotal states) to indifferent to opposed to the intervention (see figure 2.1).[18] For example, Brazilian president Getúlio Vargas's answer to whether he was interested in deploying to Korea in 1950 was not a simple yes or no. Rather, he argued that while he saw the benefits of such intervention, his top policy priority at the time was "feeding his people."[19] Similarly, Nigeria showed some, but not enthusiastic, interest in a deployment to Darfur. Nigerian president Olusegun Obasanjo had a personal stake in the conflict. Nevertheless, what the U.S. administration requested from Nigeria in 2006 was more than Obasanjo was willing to volunteer on his own initiative (for details, see chapter 5). Many countries also simply lack precise intervention preferences. They do not pursue a global foreign policy, have little foreign policy staff, and thus do not know what their position ought to be with regard even to large political issues around the world.[20]

Planning Coalition Interventions

When conceiving of a multilateral military coalition, pivotal states (often in cooperation with international organizations) develop plans of what the mission should look like: how many troops need to be deployed, what kind of equipment is required, what kind of logistical obstacles need to be overcome, and what kind of political challenges await the operation. Based on these factors, pivotal states then develop plans involving coalition composition: which states in particular can help in overcoming the military-strategic, logistical, or political problems the intervention faces. Some coalition-building projects thereby aim to build the smallest operation necessary (many UN operations, for instance); others strive, for political reasons, to create the largest coalition possible (as in the Gulf War).[21]

For many interventions, political motives largely determine these coalition planning strategies. In these cases, pivotal states dispose of all the required military assets necessary to launch the mission. However, by building a multilateral coalition, they try to boost the legitimacy of the operation.[22] For the Korean War, for instance, U.S. secretary of state Dean Acheson, who drove the decision-making process,[23] doubted that a coalition could render "effective [military] assistance."[24] Rather, Acheson was eager to prove, in particular to the Soviet Union, that U.S. policies in Korea were broadly supported by the international community and were therefore legitimate.[25] In addition, Acheson hoped that building a multilateral coalition would quell isolationist sentiments in the United States.[26] Similarly, U.S. president Lyndon B. Johnson sought coalition participants for the Vietnam War to strengthen the international legitimacy of the war and dampen domestic and international criticism of the intervention.[27] Johnson was thereby especially keen to have Asian countries serve in the coalition to prevent the war from looking like a "white man's club."[28] U.S. secretary of state James Baker, in turn, made an extra effort to recruit Arab and Muslim countries to join the Gulf War intervention to attenuate the skepticism of a large number of citizens in the Arab world toward the intervention.[29]

For other interventions, however, pivotal states do take strategic-military considerations into account. A select number of states is deemed critical to join the mission, for instance because they are neighboring states to the conflict theater or possess indispensable military or intelligence capabilities. During the coalition-building process for Darfur, for example, the United States desperately sought coalition participants that could provide strategic transport assets such as helicopters. On March 7, 2008, the U.S. State Department thus sent out an "action request" to U.S. embassies in Bangladesh, India, Pakistan, and Angola requesting those assets.[30] On May 9, 2008, a similar cable went out to Sri Lanka, Bangladesh, Jordan, Pakistan, and Ukraine. The cable mentioned that the U.S. government "must exhaust all efforts to secure these assets for UNAMID."[31] Similarly, France was eager to find coalition participants that could provide strategic "enablers" (tactical air transport, medical facilities, and other logistical support) for EUFOR Chad-CAR.[32] In other cases, pivotal states want to split the costs and political responsibility of the coalition deployment and/or the reconstruction phase in the interventions' aftermath by bringing additional parties on board.[33] Under these circumstances, pivotal states do look for coalition participants that have sufficient military and political capabilities to perform the required tasks.[34]

Once these plans have been developed, pivotal states (again, often with help from international organizations) issue calls for coalition participation. States then react. Some are eager to join the intervention: they agree with the strategic objectives or see other direct benefits in participating in the coalition. Alternatively, they might also feel compelled to participate due to alliance pressures or other socialization dynamics.[35] Either way, they join the coalition voluntarily. I thus call this group "bandwagoneers."[36]

A second set of states signals to pivotal states their interest in deploying but conditions this interest with a set of demands. These demands usually range from financial subsidies or material donations (for instance, transport to the mission theater; equipment to be used in the mission theater;[37] allowances/deployment bonuses; health, disability, and life insurances; and pre-deployment military training)[38] to political side payments or issue linkages unrelated to the military operation per se (foreign or military aid, debt relief, sanction relief, loan or trade agreements, military equipment deals, or other political favors). I call this second group "self-starters," as they self-initiate coalition negotiations with the pivotal states.

Lastly, there are "coalition recruits." These states do not volunteer to join a mission but are actively drafted by pivotal states. The empirical analysis in the chapters to come will show that this group outnumbers the other two. Irrespective of coalition type, very few states are proactive coalition-joiners.[39] As a result, the remainder of this chapter will focus on how pivotal states organize the recruitment processes of this latter group of states. How are they able to engage third parties in collective action? How do they construct military cooperation?

Searching for Coalition Participants

Based on operational plans and related personnel and capability needs, pivotal states engage in a deliberate search for suitable coalition participants: they pre-select a number of states that they deem as worthy to engage in detailed recruitment negotiations.[40] In this process, pivotal states tend to establish prospect lists. The following three criteria largely determine which countries make that list.

Criterion 1: What Can a State Contribute to the Coalition?

Depending on the specific coalition to be constructed, political or military-strategic factors influence the relative value of the potential coalition contribution to the pivotal states. These factors are determined by the pivotal states on a case-by-case basis and are usually grounded in the following: First, the size of the contingent a state can contribute matters. Many pivotal states tend to prefer larger contingents if possible. When searching for coalition contributions to the U.S.-led Somalia intervention in 1992 (UNITAF), U.S. admiral David E. Jeremiah, who served as the vice chairman of the Joint Chiefs of Staff, for instance, stated: "We want a coalition of forces between company and battalion size that are self-sustaining. Mostly countries that would give large numbers."[41] Second, the quality of troops is of value. The U.S. government vigorously pursued Nigeria to deploy troops to the UN-AU mission in Darfur because it possessed one of Africa's best-trained and -equipped military forces (for details, see chapter 5). Third, in certain situations, specific military assets (reconnaissance aircraft, mine-sweepers, decontamination units) carry weight. Fourth, geography factors into the search. Pivotal states sometimes search for states that are located close to the operational theater; Turkey during the Gulf War is one example. The United States wanted to use Turkish military bases and airspace for coalition operations targeting Iraq and Kuwait. Finally, political, ideological, or religious characteristics of third parties can affect a pivotal state's search criteria. For the UN operation in Lebanon (UNIFIL II), a deliberate attempt was made to recruit Middle Eastern states because "the force could not be composed entirely of Europeans."[42] Australia, in turn, was eager to recruit Asian countries for its coalition to intervene in East Timor in 1999.[43]

Criterion 2: How Much Is a State Intrinsically Motivated to Join the Coalition?

The second criterion focuses on how much a potential participant cares to be a member of a specific coalition.[44] This factor is much harder to assess than criterion 1. Figure 2.1 showed a hypothetical depiction of preference intensities among a group of members of the international community. In reality, such depictions are very difficult to come by.[45] As mentioned earlier, preferences held by individual states with regard to a particular intervention are the result of a litany of factors (security interests, public opinion, and so on). The combination of these factors determines whether a state considers a deployment to be a top priority or a medium priority, regards it with indifference or with opposition. Moreover, a potential participant may have an interest in keeping its exact preference intensity secret (or even downplay it) to increase the bargaining power it holds in potential coalition negotiations.[46] This complicates even further, of course, any assessment of intrinsic interests by the pivotal states.

Criterion 3: What External Incentives Might Exist That Could Be Offered to Make a Country Join a Particular Coalition?

Finally, pivotal states consider what external incentives could be offered to make a particular country join a specific coalition. The range of external incentives that pivotal states can offer (and have offered) is almost infinite. Most often they contain financial incentives and military equipment. However, at times, quite curious quid pro quos are constructed. The Bulgarian government, for instance, desired, in exchange for its contribution to the U.S.-led intervention in Iraq, that the U.S. Commerce Department designate Bulgaria a "market-based economy."[47] Overall, the value of these external incentives is tied to how intrinsically interested a potential coalition participant appears to be in the coalition and what type of military-strategic value its coalition contribution holds: the less intrinsically interested (but deemed highly valuable), the greater the external incentive.[48]

A conversation that occurred in 1965 during the coalition-building process for the Vietnam War illustrates the importance, in practice, of these three criteria. McGeorge Bundy, the U.S. national security advisor in the Lyndon B. Johnson administration, asked John T. McNaughton, the U.S. assistant secretary of defense for international security affairs, to suggest where the United States could obtain combat forces for Vietnam. In response, McNaughton came up with three categories of states that might be potential coalition contributors. The first category listed three states that already had combat troops in Vietnam: South Korea, Australia, and New Zealand. McNaughton noted, among other things, that it would be possible to obtain two more battalions (two thousand troops) from Australia without "cumshaw" (external incentives), since it had enough capability and intrinsic motivation to do so. The second category then listed states that had the necessary capabilities but only very limited intrinsic interest and thus required some cumshaw. McNaughton even estimated a possible dollar amount: $300–500 million. These countries included Greece, Taiwan, the Philippines, and Thailand. Finally, the third category included states with sufficient capabilities but no motivation to join the coalition; for such states, it would involve "selling our souls and raising hob in various ways" to encourage these states to commit. The latter group included Germany, Israel, Spain, Turkey, and the United Kingdom.[49]

As the Vietnam anecdote illustrates, the search criteria elaborated above can be viewed as a three-layered filtering process (see also figure 2.2). The first criterion is thereby objectively measurable: depending on the coalition to be formed, a pivotal state can self-assess what another state can bring to the table. The second and third criteria, however, are purely subjective political calculations. They are critical factors for the pivotal states to know. However, due to information asymmetries and incentives to dissimulate, pivotal states cannot access this information publicly. Indeed, it remains unclear from the memo above how McNaughton was able to determine that Greece and the Philippines would require only some cumshaw, while Spain and Israel a considerable amount of it to join the Vietnam War. What technique did McNaughton use to make this assessment? Moreover, how could McNaughton come up with precise dollar figures to determine the size of the external incentive these states would require to join the coalition? Were these just random guesses? Or rather, did McNaughton rely on a heuristic to make these assessments? Do pivotal states use specific tools to organize these transactions and thus engage third parties in collective action?

I argue that they do and it is called diplomatic embeddedness: states instrumentalize preexisting bilateral and multilateral connections to structure coalition recruitment processes. Operational requirements form a first filter. For some (few) coalitions this is a very firm baseline: recruits have to meet certain specific criteria. For most others, however, these criteria are malleable or loose or cast a wide net of potential recruits (it may be that all that matters is that a state comes

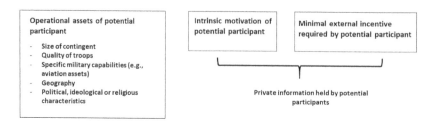

FIGURE 2.2 Factors impacting search process

Diplomatic embeddedness

Pivotal States

Extract resources from diplomatic embeddedness
to bargain third parties into a given coalition

Coalition contributions

FIGURE 2.3   Proposed causal mechanism

from a certain world region). Among these suitable candidates, pivotal states then pre-select those for further negotiations with which they are the most diplomatically embedded. Why? The trust, information, and facility to construct issue linkages and side payments embedded in these diplomatic networks increases the chances of bargaining success.

The Role of Diplomatic Embeddedness in Coalition Building

I define diplomatic embeddedness as the cumulative number of bilateral and multilateral diplomatic ties that connect a country dyad.[50] Most of these ties are the result of bilateral or multilateral agreements that a country dyad entertains. These agreements can relate to politics, economics, security, or any other area of international cooperation. Each tie connects people.[51] Most of these people work in official government positions: they are elected officials, bureaucrats, diplomats, or military officers. Each tie also creates practices:[52] because of the agreements in place, these government officials are compelled to interact with their foreign counterparts. They are required to talk, exchange letters or emails, and meet at bilateral or multilateral summits or other gatherings. Interdependencies and routines of interactions arise.[53] Not all ties have, of course, the same impact. Some may be limited to an official function; others involve social transactions. Some may be friendly; others indifferent or downright hostile. Some trigger repeated and intense interactions; others prompt only irregular or fleeting exchanges, thus creating strong or weak ties, respectively.[54] In the aggregate, however, these ties generate structural opportunities. They provide pivotal states with resources that can be exploited to pursue collective action; they constitute the most fundamental capability to engage other states in collective mobilization.

What are these resources? I count five of them, which I describe in detail in the following section.

Information

Diplomatic embeddedness provides access to information.[55] Much of this information inheres in social relations. Diplomats and military officers who reside in foreign countries and have regular interactions with their local counterparts are often able to gather information on highly specific and ephemeral social and political constellations.[56] This information contains the views, constraints, and policy preferences of a country's political and military leadership: knowledge of personalities and their parochial personal interests and positions in the local power hierarchies,[57] as well as the political and economic limits under which they act and how far they can potentially be pushed.[58] Moreover, diplomatic embeddedness reveals working methods, prevailing cultural currencies, and other types of micro-level data such as which people to select as coalition negotiation interlocutors, how to approach these interlocutors, how to orient the discussions, and how to phrase the coalition request.[59] Often this information gets picked up using interstate relations that are maintained for other purposes.[60] For example, diplomats in residence in a foreign country can learn about intra-party rivalries affecting their host state's government while attending a bilateral meeting on environmental safety, and military officers can study their foreign counterparts' threat perceptions while engaging in common training exercises.[61] Outside of the bilateral context, multilateral summits and other types of gatherings also represent formidable information collection opportunities.[62] On these occasions, many governments implicitly or explicitly reveal private information: On which topics do they speak up? When do they stand on the sidelines? How do they interact with other members? These summits also represent opportunities for face-to-face interactions that usually improve the quality of information exchanged.[63] This information cannot be matched by any other source—especially not the public media.[64]

Using this information, government officials in pivotal states can build up new knowledge or sort out rumors from the truth.[65] In the context of multilateral coalition building, such detailed information collection helps, in particular, in assessing deployment preferences of potential coalition participants: how much a country intrinsically desires to be a member of the coalition and what external incentives might be interesting for a particular country. The information gathering process for both questions works in parallel. When interacting and observing partner countries in bilateral or multilateral settings, pivotal states not only learn about the preferences third parties hold regarding the area of intervention but also other areas of interest. This information can then come in handy when thinking of a good argument of why a third party should join a given coalition. Indeed, as Risse has suggested, choosing the appropriate narrative can be critical in persuasion efforts.[66] Moreover, such information can help produce ideas of extrinsic incentives that might motivate a specific state to join a particular coalition. In short, diplomatic embeddedness constitutes an invaluable resource to collect private information that affects third party deployment decisions.[67]

Two empirical examples illustrate how this phenomenon works in practice. In November 2009, the U.S. government was in the midst of recruiting states to participate in the Afghanistan "surge." The Netherlands was a key target that the U.S. government wanted to draft, and yet it faced stern opposition. In particular, Dutch finance minister Wouter Bos was most opposed to such deployment. To turn Bos, the U.S. government sought advice from its NATO ambassador, Ivo Daalder. Daalder recommended that "it would be useful for the United States to make the issue personal for him. . . . Bos would respond well to the idea that remaining in Afghanistan is an issue of leadership for a Deputy Prime Minister of a party with a proud history. . . . Bos has future ambitions, and the United States should point out that he should not lose international credibility by insisting on the Dutch withdrawal from Afghanistan at this critical moment."[68] Daalder was able to make such suggestions because he had been relentlessly collecting private information on Dutch political actors by instrumentalizing diplomatic embeddedness.[69] No public accounts at the time revealed the same information in such detail.

The second example illustrates how important diplomatic embeddedness was in persuading Turkey to join the Gulf War coalition. The account is from a 1995 book written by former U.S. secretary of state James Baker. He writes:

> I'd known [the Turkish president] Turgut Ozal since my years at [the U.S.] Treasury. . . . Turkey's psychological needs were in many ways more important than its economic requirements. For years, Turkey had chafed at what it considered a lack of respect from some of its colleagues in the North Atlantic Treaty Organization. It was anxious to be treated more as a full NATO partner. . . . I told Ozal that I had already consulted with key NATO allies and was authorized to reaffirm the alliance's treaty obligations to Turkey's defense. . . .[70]

The quotation illustrates the importance of two different diplomatic ties in opening information channels: ties established between Baker and Ozal while both were working as finance ministers in their respective countries, and diplomatic ties via NATO. Without these two connections, it would have been almost impossible for Baker to know about the "psychological needs" of Turkey (and Ozal personally).

Credible Commitments

Cooperation in military coalitions bears risks—especially cooperation that is not intrinsically motivated but induced by external incentives.[71] Pivotal states need to worry about whether the coalition participants fulfill their cooperation promise. Why not pocket cash or other incentives and then limit the coalition commitment to the absolute minimum? Diplomatic embeddedness reduces these credible commitment problems via three mechanisms: punishment, information, and trust.[72] First, extensive diplomatic ties increase the range of possible "retaliatory linkage" opportunities and thus maximize the costs of reneging on an agreement by transforming single shot games into iterated games with a longer time horizon. This logic has been elaborated elsewhere.[73] Second, diplomatic embeddedness increases the information of "cooperation types." Perhaps the simplest possible argument about trust and trustworthy behavior is that a potential trustor tries to gather information on whether the interests of the trustee would lead her to be trustworthy.[74] Such information can be gained either through direct experience or by examining potential trustees' previous histories of interaction via institutional and social ties. Third, diplomatic embeddedness can build affection and friendship leading to compliance.[75] Deeply embedded actors might feel an emotional urge to behave in prescribed ways so as not to hurt a "friend," or as Granovetter puts it: "I may deal fairly with you not only because it is in my interest, . . . but because we have been close for so long that we expect this of one another, and I would be mortified and distressed to have cheated you even if you did not find out (though all the more so if you did)."[76] In the same vein, March and Olsen have suggested that embedded actors often seek "to fulfill the obligations encapsulated in a role, an identity, a membership in a political community or group, and the ethos, practices, and expectations of its institutions"[77]—and thus might not want to cheat in coalition operations.

Cooperation Brokers

Diplomatic embeddedness multiplies the number of available cooperation brokers—actors that can serve as intermediaries between pivotal states and potential coalition participants and help construct collective mobilization. What do these brokers do? They use their own knowledge, material resources, technical skills, and social-institutional networks to help pivotal states in their recruitment efforts. IO officials fall squarely into this category. UN under-secretary-general for peacekeeping Jean-Marie Guéhenno, for instance, fulfilled a formidable brokerage function during the coalition-building process for the Darfur intervention. In November 2007, he met with U.S. deputy secretary of state John Negroponte. At that time, the United States was desperately looking for aviation assets. Using his own wide network of contacts, Guéhenno was able to recommend that the United States approach South Africa, Nigeria, Poland, the Czech Republic, Ukraine, and Brazil for potential coalition contributions. Guéhenno, however, also warned that "only South Africa and Nigeria have a direct interest in the conflict" (for details, see chapter 5)—all of the others had no or minimal intrinsic interests in the operation and thus might require steep external incentives to deploy. Similarly, UN secretary-general Boutros Boutros-Ghali helped the U.S. government locate coalition contributions for UNITAF,[78] and during the Korean War, UN secretary-general Trygve Lie was able to serve as a "post office."[79] His "official" task was to transmit information on deployment preferences of UN member states to the U.S. government.[80] Outside of the UN context, officials of regional organizations (such as the EU or NATO) often play similar roles (for details, see chapter 7).

At times, these brokerage roles can also be taken on by friendly states that can bridge "structural holes" or, in other words, connect a pivotal state to a largely unknown third party.[81] Egyptian prime minister Hosni Mubarak, for example, served exactly in this function when he helped the U.S. government to bring Syria on board for the Gulf War coalition, as the following quotation from U.S. secretary of state James Baker's private papers illustrates:

> Mubarak was critical in building the coalition. He established good relationships with [Syrian president] Assad early on . . . he was very, very supportive throughout and was a strong leader. My first exposure to him was as the chief of staff–designate of the Reagan White House in 1980 after the election, when he came to Washington and he asked to see me. He was the vice president of Egypt, and I remember him coming into the room and saying, "Where are my tanks?" First thing he said to me—you've promised me some tanks, they're not here, we need those tanks. [laughs] And of course it was all new to me at the time. . . . [Later on] every time I would go to Cairo—not every time, but at least two or three times, he would simply pick up the phone . . . and call Assad and say, "Now Jim Baker's coming, and you must be prepared to do such and such and such, it's really important." So he's sorta paved the way, and then he would send his national security adviser often times in advance of my going to Damascus.[82]

Payment Flexibility

Diplomatic embeddedness facilitates the construction of issue linkages and side payments, which I define, following Friman, as "compensatory exchanges between functionally unrelated issues aimed at facilitating agreement between two negotiating parties."[83] In the context of coalition building, these transactions come in many forms and shapes. Some exchanges entail direct monetary transfers; others focus on military equipment deals; still others involve indirect compensation in the form of material or political concessions or promises on other issues.[84] Many scholars have noted that negotiating such side payments and issue linkages is tricky.[85] Bargaining actors risk being cheated either during the negotiation phase or the enforcement phase.[86] Moreover, side payment negotiations frequently fail because of domestic opposition to the deal.[87] Side payments may arouse domestic opposition as money needs to be shifted from one area of preoccupation to another. The same holds true for issue linkages. Any issue linkage is likely to bring about increased benefits for some domestic interest groups but losses for others, and the losers are likely to be more vocal about their losses than the winners are about their gains.[88]

Diplomatic embeddedness can minimize these difficulties. As mentioned earlier, social and institutional ties reduce credible commitment problems. Moreover, diplomatic embeddedness provides for what I term "payment flexibility." First, already existing bilateral or multilateral networks (e.g., existing aid budgets, the UN, or the World Bank) can be used to channel side payments or construct issue linkages.[89] This minimizes public scrutiny and the necessity to create new budget lines, which often requires specific legislative and other public political approval. Second, such networks allow for the divvying up of transactions. This entails that the conditions of the side payments and issue linkages are not explicitly spelled out at the time of coalition negotiations but rather are banked in the "goodwill account" of the partner country. This also works in the other direction, in that pivotal states can invoke favors they had previously provided to other countries when asking them to join a particular coalition.[90]

The following two examples illustrate this technique: First, to fund the contributions of South Korea and the Philippines to the Vietnam War coalition, the United States used the "Food for Peace" program to funnel money to both governments. The original intent of the program, as mandated by U.S. Congress, was to donate U.S. agricultural commodities to the Philippines and South Korea. In the context of the Vietnam War, however, the U.S. government used this program to provide rice and other bulk foods to these two governments with the explicit understanding that the food could be resold once inside the country, with the proceeds earmarked to help meet these countries' Vietnam expenses.[91] Why did the U.S government resort to this technique? It arguably provided payment flexibility. Channeling these side payments through existing ties avoided public scrutiny and the release of "fresh" money.

Second, to persuade Thailand to participate in the Australian-led coalition that deployed to East Timor (INTERFET) in 1999, Australia made use of its goodwill account with Thailand. Approximately a year prior to INTERFET, in the wake of the Asian financial crisis, Australia had provided a $1 billion loan to Thailand.[92] In addition, just months prior to INTERFET, Australia had maintained staunch support for Thailand's candidate, Supachai Panitchpakdi, as the new head of the World Trade Organization (WTO).[93] When constructing the coalition to intervene in East Timor, the Australian government was aware that both of these diplomatic actions had generated considerable goodwill toward Australia in Thailand and that it could use that goodwill to induce Thailand to join the INTERFET coalition.[94] Australia could have certainly found a different type of side payment or issue linkage to bring Thailand on board of INTERFET. Nevertheless, the deal described above, using existing institutional ties, enabled Australia to minimize transaction costs.

Negotiation Venues

Diplomatic embeddedness creates negotiation venues. Why does this matter? Coalition negotiations are often conducted at the highest levels of government (by heads of state, foreign or defense ministers, and the like). These government actors are usually the only state actors who can construct complex issue linkages and side payments.[95] Often these actors prefer to conduct delicate negotiations in person rather than over the phone or via email. It might sound impratical, but in such situations personal contact matters. Social psychologists have found that solidarity and cooperation are often intensified by face-to-face interaction.[96] Moreover, interpersonal interactions allow leaders to "exchange information not only through the content of what they say but also via a myriad of other channels. These include facial expressions, attitude, body language, tone of voice, and even unconscious movements or reactions."[97] This extra information is highly valuable in a risk-prone and information-scarce environment such as coalition negotiations.

To arrange for such face-to-face interactions, diplomatic embeddedness is helpful. Indeed, diplomatic embeddedness enables pivotal states to convert regularly scheduled bilateral meetings and even multilateral summits into venues for coalition negotiations. These events allow key players to schedule meetings at the margins of the office program, or as Devin put it: "Between solemn opening and closing ceremonies [summits] comprise a set of uncontrolled interactions—unofficial gatherings, corridor meetings, shared meals,"[98] each one of which can be used to persuade reluctant states to join a given coalition. The actual topic of the event as well as its official agenda are thereby completely secondary, and lines between security, economic, and military channels are often completely blurred.[99] Australian prime minister John Howard, for example, used the Asia-Pacific Economic Community (APEC) summit as a key venue to recruit coalition

participants for INTERFET.[100] APEC does not deal with security issues. Nevertheless, during that summit, Howard was able to schedule bilateral meetings with
APEC heads of state and gain numerous "in principle" promises of military support for INTERFET. He recalls that the APEC meeting was "another example of
how the occasion of international meetings provided the opportunity for leaders
to resolve issues in separate 'corridor' discussions, often quite unrelated to the
formal agenda of the meeting."[101] Similarly, U.S. secretary of state Colin Powell
used the UN General Assembly in New York City to negotiate with South Korean
foreign minister Yoon Young-kwan the terms of a Korean deployment to Iraq.[102]
Powell also made use of the World Economic Forum in Davos to meet Turkish
prime minister Abdullah Gül and discuss a possible Turkish participation in the
Iraq war coalition.[103]

In summary, the embeddedness approach described above highlights the diplomatic
nature of military coalition building. The approach doubts the existence of coalition-
building strategies that ignore the social-institutional context in which the process
takes place (for example, theories that suggest that issue linkages and side payments
do not necessitate access to private information or trust and can be easily constructed
irrespective of diplomatic embeddedness). However, it also questions that social-
institutional connections necessarily lead to a convergence of interests and values—a
view that has been propagated widely by constructivist scholars.[104] Rather, it suggests
that successful coalition building hinges on the instrumentalization of diplomatic
connections. Diplomatic embeddedness constitutes a strategic state capability in
coalition-building processes. This capability is built on material assets. Only wealthy
states have the means to entertain embassies around the world, train competent diplomats and military attachés, attend and organize international summits, finance
international institutions, and maintain large military-to-military training programs.

> Diplomatic embeddedness, if
> instrumentalized, constitutes a state resource.
> It provides for:
>
> 1. Trust and credible commitments
> 2. Access to private information
> 3. Opportunities for issue linkages and side
>   payments
> 4. Cooperation brokers
> 5. Negotiation venues

FIGURE 2.4   What is diplomatic embeddedness?

Moreover, material assets allow pivotal states to provide issue linkages and side payments to reluctant coalition participants and also to benefit from a higher status and standing (or pecking order, as Pouliot calls it) in the institutional arena.[105] They also often determine the composition of a state's network and thus the resources it can extract from it (that is, what type of states it can mobilize).[106] A prominent billionaire has a different set of connections than the average middle-class person, and for states the situation is no different: G-7 states tend to be embedded with one another and not necessarily with the bottom 2 percent.

Nevertheless, the embeddedness approach also suggests that *having* these material assets is not enough. It is not enough to simply dispose of a large diplomatic core, multiple IO memberships, and intelligence agencies. Rather, all these material assets need to be exploited in order to unlock their true power potential. For social-institutional networks to act as a concrete power resource to organize collective action, these networks need to be activated; they need to be instrumentalized. In other words, the embeddedness approach makes a deliberate attempt to disentangle the possession of diplomatic assets and to use these assets to construct cooperation. It suggests that turning structural assets into power requires constant work. It does not happen automatically.[107] This fact becomes particularly apparent in the case studies on the Korean War, INTERFET, and EUFOR Chad-CAR. Each time, it was not changes to the structural composition of U.S., French, or Australian diplomatic networks that improved the recruitment results. Rather, it was the instrumentalization of the latter networks that led to the desired recruitment outcomes. U.S., French, and Australian government officials learned to see social-institutional connections as a fungible asset.

The embeddedness approach thus advances our understanding of the relationship between diplomacy and power. How do diplomatic ties translate into actual influence? How can structural assets be turned into power in practice—power as in the ability to engage others in collective mobilization?[108] By answering these questions, the objective of the theory elaborated above is not to dismiss the importance of material assets in international politics but rather to open the "black box" of power and highlight the panoply (and interaction) of sources from which states can draw power. The theory suggests that these sources of power are not only of a material nature but also reside in the mobilization of social and institutional connections.

Coercion in Coalition Building

A critic of the social-institutional account above might ask: why is coercion not more frequently used in coalition building? Why don't pivotal states simply use their superior power capabilities and force subordinate countries to join a military coalition? Such an account, however, misunderstands the distribution of bargaining power in most coalition negotiations. Indeed, in coalition negotiations (as in any type of negotiation) two types of power matter. The first type is material power, such as wealth and military capabilities. The second type of power derives from having a beneficial no-agreement alternative to fall back on—a good "best alternative to a negotiated agreement," also known as a good BATNA.[109] If a state has a good BATNA, it does not necessarily need to reach an agreement and therefore has considerable leverage to shape the outcome of negotiations. Contrary to this, if a state has a poor BATNA, reaching an agreement—*any* agreement—is critically important to its interests, for the state has little leverage to influence the final settlement.

In coalition negotiations, pivotal states are most often more eager to see a coalition deploy and succeed than are their bargaining partners. Often their preference for intervention is widely known: Even prior to the start of the recruitment process, pivotal states invest political capital to launch the endeavor (for example, they seek IO approval of the intervention and attract and push other states to support the proposal). Once the recruitment process is under way, pivotal state officials ranging from ambassadors to the head of state undertake diplomatic démarches, make phone calls and set up meetings on the sidelines of summits to woo countries into a specific coalition. As a result, *a priori* pivotal states have a worse BATNA going into the negotiations than do their counterparts. Nevertheless, given their often-superior power capabilities, they can worsen the BATNA of their bargaining partners. They can link external issues to the coalition negotiations. For instance, they can make foreign aid payments or trade benefits conditional on participation in the coalition. Such a move has the potential to change the third party's preference ranking: a deployment that by itself looks uninteresting suddenly becomes a political necessity. In a competitive coalition-building environment, in an environment in which potential coalition contributors are plentiful and thus easily substitutable, such a strategy is very powerful. Under these circumstances, a pivotal state can easily drop and punish a state (that is, enforce the coercive threat) if it does not agree to the offered terms.[110] Nevertheless, most coalition-building environments are not competitive. Rather, coalition contributions are scarce: the demand for contributions in most cases exceeds the supply.[111] Under these circumstances, coercive threats in coalition negotiations are much less credible. The cost of implementing the threat to the pivotal state is high: there are effectively very few (if any) countries that could serve as substitutes in the coalition.[112] As a result, potential participants can drive a hard bargain: they know that pivotal states desperately want and need their contribution and thus might be willing to agree to further concessions. Alternatively, coalition participants can increase their bargaining leverage once they have deployed to the theater of operation. They can threaten to reduce or withdraw their forces if their negotiation demands are not met. Indeed, coalition negotiations might be one of the few instances in which the most powerful states find themselves quite weak and relatively weak states can dominate negotiations, thus reversing traditional hierarchies in international affairs.[113]

In the chapters that follow, many incidences describe these power dynamics. Chapter 4 shows, for example, how South Africa utilized its BATNA when negotiating with the United States during the Korean War. In early 1952 it threatened to withdraw its air squadron from the coalition if the United States did not provide it with new jet aircraft. Worried that the South African withdrawal from South Korea might start a chain reaction in the reduction of forces of other countries in Korea with "attendant weakening of UN position and encouragement" of the enemy, the United States quickly reacted to the threat.[114] Similarly, in September 1967, Thailand offered an additional 8,500 men to serve in the Vietnam War but requested an exorbitant reward: $149 million.[115] Sure enough, the United States obliged out of fear, as U.S. national security advisor Walt Rostow explained: if Washington decided that the price was too high and chose "to forget the whole thing," then Bangkok might become less willing to make Thai "real estate" available to the United States "for a broad range of Vietnam-related projects," such as bombing missions and logistical support.[116] South Korea also drove a hard bargain during the U.S.-led coalition-building process for the Iraq War despite its apparent dependence on the U.S. security umbrella. When asked for a substantive contribution to the coalition, South Korean president Roh Moo-hyun insisted that such a deployment could only occur if the United States changed its position in the six-party talks on the North Korean nuclear issue.[117] Roh disagreed with the harsh stance the United States had taken on North Korea, and he wanted the United States to engage North Korea and not punish it any further.[118] After some delicate negotiations, South Korea in essence got its way.[119]

In addition to these bargaining power dynamics, it appears that the costs of coercion also sometimes prevent pivotal states from enacting coercive strategies.[120] President Lyndon B. Johnson, for instance, was furious that America's "best ally," Great Britain, refused to send troops to Vietnam. In mid-1965 a number of White House advisers thus developed the idea of conditioning U.S. financial support for the pound sterling, which suffered periodic crises or "runs" that required American bailouts, on Great Britain sending soldiers to Vietnam. Nevertheless, the Johnson government quickly realized that if the British agreed to send troops to Vietnam only under duress and the world found out about it, the national and international controversy over America's standing and desperation to find troops would only inflame, leading to a public relations disaster.[121]

The Limits of Preference Convergence

Other critics might point out that diplomatic embeddedness cannot be disentangled from preference convergence: only states that share preferences form diplomatic relationships. As a result, diplomatic embeddedness simply serves as a proxy for homogeneous interests. I largely disagree with this assessment. As mentioned above, I reject the idea that social-institutional connections automatically lead to convergent interests no matter the issue area (that is, common interests in trade relations lead to common intervention preferences). Indeed, intervention preferences are very peculiar. They are rooted in geography, history, economic, and other societal characteristics of individual states. They are also often deeply infused by ad hoc domestic political dynamics. Just think of why the United States intervened in Iraq or Vietnam or even took the lead in organizing the coalition-building process for the UN-AU operation in Darfur (for details, see chapter 5). In each of these cases, a very specific set of preferences and political dynamics drove the U.S. intervention decision. In the case of Iraq, neoconservative ideas, the experience of 9/11, and bureaucratic politics in the George W. Bush White House played an important role.[122] In the case of Vietnam, President Johnson's peculiar personal characteristics, party politics, and Catholic interest groups had a major impact on the intervention decisions.[123] No other country was exposed to these dynamics to an equal degree and, frankly, it is highly unlikely that these preferences "spilled over" via diplomatic embeddedness into other countries and thus led to quasi-homogeneous preferences with regard to the intervention proposals. As a result, it is highly doubtful that diplomatic embeddedness serves as a mere placeholder for convergent preferences among embedded states on each individual intervention proposal. Two countries can cooperate intensely on economic, environmental, and even security issues and still have very different preferences with regard to a particular intervention. Thus, it is not homogeneous preferences that lead to coalition participation. Rather, pivotal states use diplomatic embeddedness as a resource to bring other states on board.

Research Methodology

In what follows I employ an integrative mixed-method research design to test the social-institutional theory of multilateral military coalition building presented above. I combine large-N regression analysis, in-depth elite interviews, and archival research and thereby exploit the strength of each method: large-N regression analysis to produce statistical inferences and case study research to illustrate key assumptions about causal interactions and pathways.[124]

Macro-Case Selection

The multilateral military operations I will focus on are the Korean War coalition, the UN-AU deployment to Darfur, the Australian-led coalition that intervened in East Timor and the EU intervention in Chad and the Central African Republic. I selected these four cases because of their extreme factorial variation. This variation allows portraying the consistency of the stipulated causal mechanisms across a wide range of coalitions. The four operations indeed could not be more different, as table 2.1 below illustrates. The four coalitions vary by target nation, organizational structure, coalition objective, operational intensity, pivotal state, and time of deployment. All of these variables have been said to impact coalition commitments. For instance, scholars have suggested that states are more likely to commit troops to low-intensity operations than high-intensity operations. Similarly, UN operations are said to be more attractive than non-UN operations because of the legitimacy and the financial incentives the UN can provide to troop contributors.[125] Thus, if I find that the same causal pathways operate in each case, I can be confident that the pathways are robust across a wide array of coalitions. Indeed, thus far the research on coalition building and burden-sharing is deeply divided between U.S.-led and non-U.S.-led operations; between operations conducted under the umbrella of the UN and other regional organizations such as the European Union; and between alliance (e.g., NATO) and non-alliance operations. My aim is to illustrate that these distinctions are exaggerated. Rather, a common logic undergirds coalition-building processes across this wide spectrum of operations and institutions.

TABLE 2.1 Macro-case variation

OPERATION	TARGET NATION	ORGANIZATIONAL STRUCTURE	COALITION OBJECTIVE	OPERATIONAL INTENSITY	PIVOTAL STATE	COLD WAR
EUFOR Chad/CAR	Chad/CAR	EU	Refugee crisis	Medium	France	No
INTERFET	East Timor	ad hoc	Mass killing after secession	High	Australia	No
UNAMID	Sudan	UN-AU	Ethnic cleansing/ genocide	Low-medium	USA	No
Korean War	Korea	U.S./UN	Repel aggression	High	USA	Yes

TABLE 2.2 Micro-case variation

OPERATION	KOREAN WAR	UNAMID	INTERFET	EUFOR CHAD/CAR
Top three coalition contributors (based	UK	Nigeria	Thailand	Ireland
on size of contingent and excluding	Canada	Rwanda	Jordan	Poland
the pivotal state)	Turkey	Egypt	Philippines	Sweden
Low Diplomatic Embeddedness score	South Africa	Thailand	Brazil	Russia
High Diplomatic Embeddedness score	Philippines	Germany	Canada	Austria

Micro-Case Selection

A range of countries participated in each of the four coalitions presented above. Due to space constraints, it is impossible to trace the recruitment process of each individual participant. Thus, I selected specific recruitment cases based on extreme values of both the dependent variable of the study (troop commitments to a particular coalition) and the independent variable (diplomatic embeddedness with the pivotal state). Seawright suggests that if one of the key goals of the case study research is to discover confounding variables (in this instance, convergent preferences and coercion), extreme-case selection on the dependent variable has greatest value.[126] Thus, I look at the recruitment process of the three largest coalition contributors (excluding the pivotal state) of each one of the four operations presented above. Moreover, Seawright suggests that to demonstrate the existence of a specific causal pathway, extreme-case selection on the independent variable is most helpful. As a result, I pick a second set of recruitment cases based on how they score with regard to diplomatic embeddedness: for each one of the four operations, I pick one state that is deeply diplomatically embedded with the pivotal state and one case that has a low diplomatic embeddedness score (see table 2.2). To select these states, I use the data I collected on diplomatic embeddedness, which I will explain in greater detail in the next chapter.

I do not specifically select cases to examine bargaining failure. I have analyzed this phenomenon elsewhere.[127] Still, the integrated research design combining large-N regression analysis and in-depth case studies allows me to avoid selecting on the dependent variable: the dataset I use for the regression analyses in chapter 3 contains many instances of states *not* joining a given military operation.

Structure of Case Studies and Key Theoretical Expectations

Every case study chapter follows a similar structure. First, I explain the factors that drove the pivotal states to take on a leadership role with regard to the deployment of a multilateral military coalition. While I do not try to develop a theory of why states turn into pivotal states, I thought it important that the reader dispose of this information as background knowledge.[128] Second, each chapter takes a bird's-eye perspective and describes the overall intervention planning, search, and negotiation strategy adopted by pivotal states. Third, each case study dives into individual instances of coalition negotiations (see above for the selection of micro-cases) and tries to understand what factors influenced these negotiations and led to negotiation success. With each chapter, my goal is to demonstrate the following key elements of multilateral military coalition building: First, few states hold convergent preferences with regard to the launch of a military coalition. Thus, coalitions do not form naturally. Rather, they are constructed by pivotal states who bargain third parties into participating in a military intervention. Second, pivotal states follow a systematic recruitment process: they develop operational plans of how the mission should look and issue calls for participation, and some states do volunteer (conditionally or unconditionally) to join the operation. I call these latter states "bandwagoneers" and "self-starters," respectively. To fill the remaining gaps in the coalition lineup, which are usually plentiful, pivotal states then instrumentalize diplomatic ties and use them to recruit the necessary and fitting coalition contributors. In other words, I hypothesize that diplomatic embeddedness determines the likelihood of states joining a military coalition given operational constraints: if a range of states can offer roughly the same operational assets (political, military, or other), pivotal states recruit those states most successfully with which they are the most diplomatically embedded. As a corollary, diplomatic embeddedness impacts substantive military contributions in the same way as token contributions made mostly for legitimating purposes.[129] If a pivotal state intends to recruit a substantive force, it uses diplomatic embeddedness to assess which states among those that could contribute such force are most likely to oblige; if it seeks merely symbolic contributions, it uses diplomatic embeddedness to achieve the latter aim. Overall, I expect that states that are deeply embedded with the pivotal states form the bulk of coalition recruits (that is, states that are drafted into the coalition by pivotal states). States that are weakly diplomatically embedded, on the other hand (for instance, those states with a low diplomatic embeddedness score in table 2.3), should join a given coalition for reasons other than diplomatic embeddedness (i.e., they are bandwagoneers or self-starters).

TABLE 2.3 Summary of theoretical expectations

	DEEPLY EMBEDDED WITH PIVOTAL STATE	WEAKLY EMBEDDED WITH PIVOTAL STATE
Bandwagoneer		x
Self-starter		x
Coalition recruit	x	

Observable Implications

In more detailed terms, what should we observe if the social-institutional theory I advance is correct? To assess the exact causal mechanisms at play, I propose to analyze the empirical evidence presented in the case studies along four different dimensions. These dimensions serve as "diagnostic pieces of evidence that yield insight into causal connections and mechanisms, providing leverage for adjudicating among hypotheses."[130]

Preference Structure

I term the first dimension "preference structure." Observations that account for the preferences potential coalition participants hold prior to joining the operation fall into this category. If most multilateral military coalitions are indeed the construction of pivotal states, we should see a clear difference in preferences and preference intensities between pivotal states and other members of the international community with respect to a particular intervention proposal. Pivotal states stand out by being intensely interested in launching a multilateral deployment. Few other states share this intense preference. Many scholars believe that alliance structures lead to an automatic convergence of preferences. This dimension thus also serves to test whether this claim is true.

Agency

The second dimension focuses on agency. I expect that given the above described preference divergence, pivotal states take the lead in organizing the coalition-building process. Pivotal states introduce an intervention proposal either in an ad hoc manner or via an international organization. In parallel, pivotal states approach third parties in search of coalition contributions. Archival records and interviews, for instance, should indicate that pivotal states undertook diplomatic démarches asking third parties to contribute troops to a specific coalition. I also expect pivotal states to ask IO officials and friendly allies to act as "cooperation brokers." Pivotal states should approach these actors and request their help (notably with the provision of information) in the coalition-building process. Countervailing evidence instead would show that states largely join coalitions on their own accord with little influence (or nagging) by a pivotal state.

Search Process

The third dimension looks at the search process for coalition participants. In deciding which states to approach for troop contributions, I expect pivotal states to act systematically. Instead of randomly asking countries to join a given coalition, I expect them to think strategically of how to best search for suitable recruits. Overall, the search criteria should include the following three factors: (1) What can a state bring to the fight given operational necessities? (2) How much does that state care to be a member of a coalition? and (3) If the state is not entirely intrinsically motivated, what can the pivotal state offer to attract the participation of that state? Based on these criteria, I expect pivotal states to come up with "prospect lists." These lists include countries that constitute ideal targets for direct bilateral participation appeals. In the drafting process of these lists, I expect pivotal states to instrumentalize diplomatic embeddedness. In other words, officials representing the pivotal state should purposefully exploit diplomatic networks to access information on the criteria listed above. In concrete terms, I expect pivotal states to (1) instruct diplomats and military attachés to collect information on deployment preferences of their host states; (2) instruct military officers involved in training foreign military contingents to report on the deployment preferences of their trainees; (3) approach foreign diplomats and other officials at bilateral or multilateral gatherings and ask for their views on a particular deployment; (4) request information from foreign alums of military training academies, joint training exercises, or joint operations; (5) ask IO officials notably at the UN, NATO, the AU, or the EU for recruitment information; and (6) ask friendly states for information and advice. I also expect officials representing the pivotal state to hold regular "interagency" meetings to circulate information between different branches of the government with regard to the criteria listed above. Archival resources should provide evidence of such interagency discussions. Similarly, interviews should confirm that pivotal states systematically go about searching for potential coalition partners, as described above.

Countervailing evidence would suggest instead that pivotal states do not purposefully and systematically exploit their social and institutional networks. Rather, pivotal states engage in quasi–ad hoc maneuvers to recruit coalition participants—they ask states randomly to join a given coalition or alternatively ask every member of the international community to join.

Negotiation Process

The fourth dimension focuses on the coalition negotiation process. I expect intense bargaining between coalition participants and pivotal states. During these negotiations, I expect pivotal states to use diplomatic embeddedness to construct issue linkages and side payments. For example, I expect to observe that diplomatic ties are used to channel payments through preexisting bilateral or multilateral institutions. In other words, payments are made via the World Bank, the United Nations, or other already existing aid programs instead of creating "new budget lines." Similarly, I also expect pivotal states to make use of "goodwill accounts," that is, remind potential coalition participants of the help they were provided by the pivotal state in the recent past. Moreover, I also expect diplomatic embeddedness to offer negotiation venues. Pivotal states should hold coalition negotiations at the sideline of the UN General Assembly, APEC summits, EU summits, and the like. Finally, I expect that the coalition negotiation outcome is not entirely determined by material power but rather by how much each state cares to conclude a coalition cooperation agreement. Weaker and subordinate states can sometimes dominate the negotiations because they know how eager the pivotal state is to reach an agreement. How do they know? Pivotal states reveal their intense preferences by organizing the intervention proposal and approaching third parties to ask for troop contributions.

Overall, I expect that pivotal states deliberately use diplomatic embeddedness as a resource. In this regard, I explicitly distinguish between "routine diplomacy" (routine activities of diplomatic personnel, intelligence agencies, and military officials) and explicit attempts to exploit diplomatic networks for coalition-building purposes. In other words, I discriminate between having diplomatic assets and activating them to organize collective action. For the latter to occur, the empirical evidence needs to show purposive actions by pivotal state actors. For instance, information on deployment preferences and potential side payments is not "routinely" transmitted. Rather, it is requested explicitly by the political leadership in the pivotal state for coalition-building purposes. Potential coalition contributors are not "routinely" met. Rather, meetings are explicitly set up to negotiate coalition contributions, and so forth. The degree of deliberate usage of diplomatic embeddedness might vary, of course, based on the practice the pivotal state has with multilateral coalition building. If a state routinely engages in coalition building, exploiting diplomatic networks might have turned into a practicality: it's tacit, inarticulate, and automatic.[131]

Alternative Explanations

I propose two alternative accounts that can also explain multilateral military coalition building. In this section, I will present the causal mechanisms that undergird these alternative explanations. I also develop detailed observable implications for each one of these theories. I summarize these implications in table 2.4. All empirical case studies presented in chapters 4 through 7 engage in these alternative explanations and thus allow the reader to weigh the evidence in favor of each.

Preference Convergence Drives Multilateral Military Coalition Building

The theory laid out above suggests that a small number of countries join coalitions on their own accord. Their intervention preferences converge with those of the pivotal state. Sometimes, they even aid the pivotal state in constructing the operation. I call these states "bandwagoneers." Nevertheless, conventional wisdom in international relations thus far suggests that the large majority of states fall into that category: states coalesce instinctively because of common interests, institutions, threat perceptions, political ideologies, norms, and values. Alliances thereby play a particularly important role in this preference convergence process.[132] Most scholars working in this tradition acknowledge the existence of a diplomatic process of some sort coordinating coalition participants. Nevertheless, this process remains largely undertheorized.[133] As a result, from this viewpoint, diplomatic embeddedness largely serves as a proxy for homogeneous preferences and socialization processes. States that are similar to one another are more likely to form diplomatic ties, and once these ties are formed a snowball effect ensues: socialization leads to even more homogenous interests.[134]

If preference convergence is indeed the underlying force of multilateral military coalition building and diplomatic embeddedness serves only as a placeholder for convergent preferences, what would we be able to observe? First, with regard to the preference structure, most coalition participants should be "like-minded"; they should hold convergent preferences and similar preference intensities with regard to the intervention proposal. In other words, one coalition partner can pursue geostrategic objectives, the other financial or normative motivations. Nevertheless, all assign about the same level of importance to the cooperative outcome; for all participants, the operation is a top foreign policy priority. When interviewed, decision-makers should be able to describe the preference structure underlying their country's troop deployment. They should emphasize its political priority compared to other preferences in their set of foreign policy objectives. For instance, decision-makers should be able to explain which branches of the government favor participation and for what reasons. They should also be able to explain why this particular conflict gained the attention of the government as opposed to any others.

Second, as to agency, I expect that pivotal states take on a far less intensive role than under the social-institutional model. Especially for operations conducted under the umbrella of military alliances or international organizations such as NATO, the UN, the AU, or the EU, the role of pivotal states should be minimal to nonexistent. Rather, IO officials from these institutions should be in charge of organizing and coordinating coalition participation.

Third, with regard to the search process, no explicit search is conducted. Rather, most coalition partners coalesce naturally due to convergent interests. However, preferences for specific states joining or not joining the coalition based on operational plans might exist, thus requiring some kind of selection process. Archival resources should provide evidence of such scenarios. The large majority of states should join coalitions on their own accord without any (or only little) influence from a pivotal state. Similarly, interviews should confirm that pivotal states play only a small role in selecting, prompting, and cajoling coalition contributions.

Finally, with regard to the negotiation process, coalition negotiations under the "preference convergence model" should resemble a coincidence or coordination game.[135] Agreements are determined by distributional consequences.[136] Cooperating partners are averse to an absence of policy coordination. Nevertheless, they may have trouble determining where "to settle on the Pareto-frontier"[137] (for instance, what type of military strategy to pursue or what type of forces to employ). Under this model, negotiations thus succeed if cooperating partners manage to agree on an equilibrium point at which to settle (whether to use air or ground forces or the like). Negotiations fail if the potential distributional consequences for an individual bargaining partner are too high to settle on a compromise. Once a cooperative equilibrium is found, cooperation partners have no incentive to defect from it.[138] Archival resources should provide evidence of such negotiations. Similarly, interviews should confirm that coalition negotiation is focused on policy coordination. Side payments and issue linkages should be discussed as little as possible. Given a common spirit of joint problem-solving, I do not expect that coalition participants risk jeopardizing the operation by holding private information about their willingness to join hostage in an attempt to extract concessions unrelated to the operation from the pivotal state.

Coercion Is the Underlying Coalition-Building Force

The second alternative explanation borrows from hegemonic power theory.[139] It contends that state behavior that appears cooperative is, in fact, usually the result of coercion by a major power or hegemon. Coercion thereby can take on two primary forms.[140] In "brute" coercion, a major power uses or threatens to use its superior power capabilities (military, economic, or other) to get a third party to alter its actions (for instance, via negative linkages).[141] In "implicit" coercion (also called "political authority"), a major power asks a third party to alter its actions. The latter then chooses to comply out of "submissiveness" or "subordination" to the major power.[142] Either way, under such a theoretical framework, participation in multilateral military coalitions is less voluntary than the social-institutional theory assumes. While the embeddedness framework previously laid out suggests that pivotal states can sometimes construct negative linkages and thus put pressure on third parties to join a coalition, the coercion model argues that coercive strategies are the dominant way of constructing cooperation. Moreover, material power capabilities determine coalition negotiation outcomes, or as François de Callières put it: "when a prince or state is powerful enough to dictate to his neighbors, the art of negotiation loses its value, for then there is need for nothing but a mere statement of the prince's will."[143] Given this causal pathway, the observable implications are as follows.

First, with regard to state preferences, the coercion model predicts the same as the social-institutional model. We should see a clear distinction between pivotal states and other members of the international community. Second, with regard to agency, the coercion model predicts that major powers or hegemons take the lead. They develop and introduce an intervention proposal. In parallel, they approach third parties in search for coalition contributions. Third, with regards to the search process, I expect major powers or hegemons to choose coalition candidates based on the amount of unexploited bargaining power in the existing bilateral relationships. This is arguably most easily done by looking at costly bilateral dependencies such as alliance dependence, foreign aid, military assistance, loans, and so on.[144] If manipulated, such asymmetrical flows can lower the "bottom line" of potential cooperating partners.[145] When asked why certain countries were approached for coalition contributions, officials should indicate that they knew that these countries were the most "dependent" or "subordinate" in security, aid, or trade terms, and that is why they were expected to oblige most easily. Archival resources should provide evidence for such a strategy. I expect to come across transcripts that mention the vulnerability and dependence of states and thus their relative attractiveness as potential coalition participants.

Finally, with regard to the negotiation process, I expect that officials representing the major power adopt a take-it-or-leave-it negotiation strategy toward the potential coalition participant, which often involves "negative linkages"—threats to cut foreign or military aid and so forth.[146] The potential coalition participant, in turn, feels obligated to accept the proposal for two reasons: (1) any other move would be very costly or (2) as Lake suggests, "states do genuflect toward authority. . . . This implies that subordinates may comply . . . with commands not only out of shared interests or threatened punishments but also because they respect and comply with the authority of the dominant state."[147] Overall, the hegemon, due to its superior material power, should always come out on top of the coalition negotiations. Archival resources and interviews should provide evidence for such power discrepancies and thus the bargaining advantage of the hegemon. They should illustrate that the potential coalition participant is aware of its precarious bargaining situation. When interviewed, officials representing the potential coalition participant should recall feeling stress, fear, and anxiety during the coalition negotiations.[148] At the conclusion of the negotiations, they

TABLE 2.4 Summary of observable implications

DIMENSIONS	SOCIAL-INSTITUTIONAL FRAMEWORK	PREFERENCE CONVERGENCE THEORY	COERCION THEORY
Preference structure	Dissimilar intrinsic preferences/preference intensities among coalition participants.	Convergent intrinsic preferences and common preference intensities among coalition participants.	Dissimilar intrinsic preferences/preference intensities among coalition participants.
Agency	Pivotal states act as coalition organizers.	Pivotal states take on a smaller role, especially in coalition operations conducted under the umbrella of IOs.	Major powers/hegemons act as coalition organizers.
Search process	Pivotal states instrumentalize diplomatic embeddedness to determine deployment preferences and possible side-payments of potential coalition partners. States on which no such information is available are approached last or not at all. Common institutional contacts serve as cooperation brokers.	No explicit search (though preferences for specific states joining the coalition based on operational plans might exist).	Pivotal states approach countries that they think are the most vulnerable to pressure. Non-vulnerable countries are not approached or approached as a last resort.
Negotiation process	Intense negotiations often involving side payments or issue linkages. Diplomatic embeddedness provides payment flexibility, trust, and negotiation venues. Preference intensities determine bargaining outcome.	Focus on policy coordination.	Coalition participants are induced into cooperation using "negative linkages." States might also "genuflect" toward the authority of the dominant state. Material power determines negotiation outcome.

should perceive that they are in a less advantageous position, even if they accede to the coercion out of a sense of self-interest.[149]

By December 3, 1992, President George H. W. Bush had called eleven heads of state to ask for troop contributions for the U.S.-led intervention in Somalia (UNITAF), which led Admiral Jonathan Howe, who was serving as deputy national security advisor in the first Bush administration, to remark that "his calls made all the difference."[150] One might wonder why that was. This chapter has provided the reader with an answer. Multilateral military coalition building does not happen automatically. Instead, each coalition is the creation of a pivotal state. In relative terms, these states are most interested in seeing the formation of a multilateral military coalition. Thus, these states are willing to expend the necessary costs to organize the coalition-building process. What does such organization entail? Operational plans of how the mission should look need to be developed; calls for participation need to be issued; and if not enough coalition volunteers exists, potential coalition participants need to be located. In addition, coalition negotiations need to be conducted to determine the exact conditions of each individual deployment. In short, coalition building involves three phases: a planning phase, a search phase, and a bargaining phase. To reduce the transaction costs that occur in the second and third phases, pivotal states use diplomatic embeddedness as a resource. By instrumentalizing diplomatic embeddedness, these states gain benefits, most notably trust, access to private information, a facility to negotiate side payments and issue linkages, cooperation brokers, and negotiation venues. Thus, diplomatic networks provide critical underpinnings for multilateral coalition-building efforts. Diplomatic embeddedness constitutes a strategic state capability to engage other states in collective mobilization. This capability is built on material assets. It takes a lot of money to entertain embassies around the world and finance international institutions and similar organizations. Nevertheless, material power alone often cannot explain the coalition negotiation outcomes we observe. Pivotal states often cannot dominate coalition negotiations because potential participants know how eager they are to clinch a deal.

The following chapters shift to detailed empirical research that assesses how well this social-institutional theory explains multilateral coalition building. Each chapter attempts to clarify agency and process in multilateral military coalition building. Each case examines various answers to the following questions: What preferences do states hold when joining multilateral interventions? Who organizes the coalition-building process? Is there an explicit search process for coalition participants? If so, what factors structure this process? And how does this process affect the outcome we observe? What types of power matter in coalition negotiation? Each chapter tests the theoretical frameworks presented above in an attempt to better understand how states manage to cooperate in modern militarized conflict. My overall objective is, of course, not to prove all existing theories wrong. Rather, I aim to illustrate the added value of the social-institutional framework. Coalition building is a complicated endeavor, and I expect multiple dynamics to matter simultaneously.

A QUANTITATIVE TEST

What Factors Influence Multilateral Military Coalition Building?

This book proposes that most multilateral military coalitions are political constructions. They do not emerge naturally but are the creation of individual states. Without the existence of these states, very few coalitions would be built. This is, of course, true for coalitions that are constructed ad hoc but also for those constructed under the umbrella of international organizations (UN, NATO, EU, and so on). I call these states that construct multilateral military coalitions pivotal states. The key task these pivotal states must perform is persuading third parties to join a given coalition. During this process, diplomatic embeddedness plays an important role. If purposefully exploited, it provides access to information, trust, and a facility to construct issue linkages and side payments. As a result, extensive diplomatic embeddedness between pivotal states and third parties is likely to increase the likelihood of coalition contributions.[1] This chapter sets out to quantitatively test the theoretical premises of this theory. To do so, I construct statistical models that include the concept of diplomatic embeddedness. Moreover, I control in these models for the alternative explanations that I have laid out in the preceding chapters. To remind the reader, these explanations are as follows:

Alternative Explanations

1. The Preference Convergence Theory

Most existing accounts of military coalition building focus on preference convergence. Alliance theory thereby constitutes one of the dominant theoretical paradigms explaining how such convergent preferences emerge.[2] Alliance scholars often suggest that states form multilateral coalitions to balance the most imminent threat (e.g., threats to territorial integrity, citizens' safety, natural resources, or other economic necessities).[3] Nevertheless, the impact of alliances also extends beyond capability aggregation. Alliance partners often provide each other with military support despite divergent threat perceptions. They engage in reciprocal burden sharing to signal mutual appreciation for the overall alliance relationship. In addition to alliances, scholars have advanced normative motivations and related state identities to explain preference convergence.[4] Some countries self-identify as "good Samaritans." They feel compelled to act in the case of large-scale human suffering or genocide.[5] Others intend to demonstrate "good international citizenship," spread democracy, or garner international prestige and legitimacy via international deployments.[6] Next, scholars have suggested that civil-military relations and other domestic political concerns can drive preferences in deployment matters. Some governments are said to see foreign deployments as a way of keeping their armed forces occupied outside of the country rather than having them plan domestic coups.[7] Finally, the literature also suggests that a variety of geopolitical, economic, and other ad hoc political interests related to the theater of operation can drive convergent deployment decisions. For example, countries are more likely to intervene in a conflict closer to home because they fear negative conflict spillovers from the conflict theater such as refugee flows.[8] Moreover, states participate in military interventions because of economic interests. An intervention can result in preferential access to natural resources or other trade opportunities, including reconstruction projects.[9] Finally, linguistic, colonial, and religious ties have also been noted to explain intervention decisions.

2. The Coercion Theory

A different set of arguments explaining military coalition formation focuses on hegemonic orders and related economic or other institutional dependencies that facilitate coercion, which I define, following Thompson, as "efforts to convince a target to take a certain course of action . . . by imposing or threatening to impose costs."[10] These efforts can involve the use of brute force (that is, explicit threats of punishment if certain actions are not taken). Newnham suggests in this regard that the United States used the threat of withdrawing U.S. aid payments to influence countries to contribute troops to the 2003 U.S.-led Iraq invasion.[11] Alternatively, coercive diplomacy can take on more subtle forms. Lake, for instance, suggests that both economic and security "hierarchy" influences a state's decision to contribute troops to a U.S.-led operation. He argues that states that are "subordinate" to the United States provide troops to these operations as acts of symbolic obeisance, which he defines as "collective displays of submission that acknowledge and affirm the authority of the ruler."[12]

Evaluation Strategy

In each statistical analysis that follows, I will test the explanatory power of the concept of diplomatic embeddedness. Moreover, I try to systematically control for the two alternative explanations described above using an array of different proxy variables. In addition, most models will include a small number of control variables that might also influence coalition contributions. Nevertheless, they are of less overall theoretical interest. Such factors include, among others, the availability of military and other capabilities accessible to potential participants, the type of operation (ad hoc, UN, NATO, or other), the type of pivotal state, and so forth.

   The precise question that the statistical models that follow attempt to address is: Given the existence of pivotal states that attempt to raise a peacekeeping force, which states are most likely to join the operation? The analysis does not try to examine how operational plans are written. Rather, its aim is to test the *overall* impact of diplomatic embeddedness on coalition participation irrespective of operational requirements. Moreover, the analysis does not control for the instrumentalization of diplomatic embeddedness. Instead it operates under the assumption that if such ties exist, states are more likely to exploit them in the case of coalition building—though such exploitation can, of course, not be taken for granted.

Replicating Lake (2009)

My first statistical analysis replicates a study conducted by David Lake. Lake, building on Atsushi Tago's work, focuses exclusively on U.S.-led multilateral coalitions. His dataset includes fifteen U.S.-led interventions conducted between 1950 and 2000.[13] The focus of Lake's analysis is to test how economic and security "hierarchy" affects coalition contributions to U.S.-led interventions. In what follows, I first replicate Lake's regressions and then modify his model to test for the influence of diplomatic embeddedness on coalition contributions.

Description of Variables

Lake uses *Coalition Participation* as the dependent variable in his analysis. It has a binary value, that is, 0 (= no participation) or 1 (= participation). Lake's independent variables roughly correspond to the theoretical arguments presented above. To test for the coercion theory, Lake uses two "hierarchy indices," which attempt to measure how dependent a state is on the United States. The first index, the "security hierarchy index," measures a state's dependence on the U.S. security umbrella. The second index, the "economic hierarchy index," intends to capture a state's economic dependence on the United States. Each index is composed of two indicators. For the "security hierarchy index," the index components are (1) an indicator that measures the presence of U.S. forces on the territory of the potential coalition participant and (2) the number of non-U.S. or "independent" alliances possessed by the potential coalition contributor.[14] For the "economic hierarchy index," the index components are (1) an indicator that measures monetary dependence on the United States and (2) an indicator measuring the relative trade dependence of the potential coalition participant on the United States. To control for the preference convergence theory, Lake uses geographical contiguity of the potential participant and the target of the intervention, joint primary language (as a proxy for cultural affinities), joint regime type (as a proxy for normative affinities), and joint alliance with the United States. As control variables, Lake uses involvement in an enduring rivalry, major power status of the potential participant, and the potential participant's annual military expenditure. He also utilizes proxy variables to test whether the potential participant faces an internal government crisis at the moment of deployment and includes variables to test whether the type of coalition matters: Is it a "war" (a military action against at least one sovereign state with more than one thousand battle deaths) or a domestic intervention (a military intervention that takes place inside a country's territory without the consent of the government)? And does the coalition operate under a UN or regional mandate?[15]

I now add to this range of independent variables a new variable: diplomatic embeddedness. I operationalize diplomatic embeddedness by counting all bilateral and multilateral institutional ties the United States has established with a foreign country at the date of intervention. As mentioned in the preceding chapter, I define diplomatic embeddedness as the cumulative number of bilateral and multilateral diplomatic ties that connect a country dyad. Since most of these ties are the result of bilateral or multilateral agreements that a country dyad entertains, such a coding choice seems reasonable. Data on cumulative joint international organization membership come from the International Governmental Organization (IGO) Dataset.[16] Data on cumulative bilateral cooperation treaties come from the World Treaty Index.[17]

Model Specifications

I adopt Lake's model specifications in their entirety. I run logit regression models and employ panel-corrected standard errors to mitigate possible heteroscedasticity. I also use a lagged dependent variable and an AR (1) correction to address problems of serial autocorrelation.[18]

Statistical Results

The statistical results of this first test are shown in table 3.1. For comparison purposes, Model 1 represents the exact replication of Lake's study. Model 2 shows the results when the variable of diplomatic embeddedness is added to the analysis. We can see that diplomatic embeddedness is positively correlated with troop contributions and highly statistically significant. One other noticeable change compared to Model 1 is the loss of statistical significance of the "security hierarchy index." All other results remain essentially the same. Model 3 now disaggregates the indexes into their individual components. The changes are as follows: Diplomatic embeddedness remains positively correlated with coalition contributions and highly statistically significant. The variable *Exchange Rate Regime* is also strongly positively correlated with coalition contributions at the 0.01 level. The variable *Independent Alliances* is positively correlated at the 0.05 level. All other variables do not change substantially compared to the two previous models. Overall, this first statistical analysis thus provides preliminary evidence of the importance of diplomatic embeddedness in U.S. coalition-building efforts. In addition, it illustrates that exchange rate regimes affect coalition contributions, whereas trade dependence does not appear to be critical. Alliance dependence also influences coalition contributions, but to a lesser degree. The presence of U.S. troops on the territory of a potential contributor does not seem to matter. Finally, we learn that the coercion theory alone might not be able to explain the entirety of coalition contributions we observe.

Expanding the Universe of U.S.-Led Multilateral Coalitions

The second statistical analysis I conduct uses an original and much larger dataset of forty-one U.S.-led coalitions conducted between 1990 and 2005. To construct this dataset, I use a broader definition of U.S.-led coalitions than Lake does. Lake requires a U.S.-led coalition to be commanded by a U.S. general and to be primarily staffed by U.S. soldiers (that is, the United States needs to contribute the largest national coalition contingent). Both criteria significantly limit the universe of cases. Moreover, such a definition does not fully account for the type of U.S. leadership in multilateral military coalition building we observe, especially

TABLE 3.1 Regression results: Lake (2009) replication

	(1)	(2)	(3)
	Lake (2009) regression	Lake (2009) regression modified	Lake (2009) with index components
Diplomatic embeddedness		0.025***	0.022***
		(0.002)	(0.003)
Coercion theory			
Index of security hierarchy	0.823**	0.350	
	(0.021)	(0.442)	
Independent alliances			0.650**
			(0.026)
Military personnel			−0.370
			(0.481)
Index of economic hierarchy	1.315***	1.257***	
	(0.001)	(0.003)	
Relative trade dependence			−0.187
			(0.789)
Exchange rate regime			0.954***
			(0.005)
Preference convergence theory			
Same region	1.893***	1.950***	1.971***
	(0.000)	(0.000)	(0.000)
Joint primary language	1.092***	1.022***	1.029***
	(0.001)	(0.002)	(0.000)
Joint democracy	0.455	0.255	0.217
	(0.103)	(0.383)	(0.414)
Controls			
Major power status	0.033	0.097	0.049
	(0.975)	(0.927)	(0.962)
Military expenditures (log)	0.210***	0.110**	0.106***
	(0.000)	(0.028)	(0.010)
Involvement in enduring rivalry	−0.352	−0.390	−0.435
	(0.380)	(0.340)	(0.251)
Government crisis	0.304*	0.309*	0.280
	(0.092)	(0.090)	(0.113)
Coalition war operation	0.364	0.149	0.248
	(0.300)	(0.683)	(0.479)
Coalition intervention in domestic affairs	−0.524	−0.914**	−0.872**
	(0.200)	(0.038)	(0.035)
UN legitimation	1.888***	2.006***	2.103***
	(0.000)	(0.000)	(0.000)
Regional legitimation	0.085	0.121	0.075
	(0.819)	(0.746)	(0.834)
Constant	−7.592***	−7.131***	−7.068***
	(0.000)	(0.000)	(0.000)
Observations	1,525	1,525	2,015

Notes: Robust p-values are in parentheses. Time series logit (xtlogit). Standard Errors clustered by potential coalition participant. Estimation performed using Stata 14. *** p<0.01, ** p<0.05, * p<0.1

after the U.S.-led Somalia intervention (UNITAF) in 1993. The tragic death of U.S. soldiers in this intervention led to the drafting of U.S. Presidential Decision Directive 25.[19] It decreed that U.S. troop deployments, in particular, to peacekeeping and humanitarian operations had to be kept to a strict minimum. The United States thus changed to a new mode of multilateral military coalition building. Instead of sending U.S. soldiers abroad, successive U.S. administrations reverted to orchestrating the political aspects of multilateral military deployments, often via international institutions such as the UN or NATO.

As the case studies in this book will show, such political management also involved the recruitment of non-U.S. troops to serve in the latter type of operations. Thus, to take account of this policy change, I include in the new dataset both types of coalitions: those which were commanded by the United States and those in which the U.S. government politically initiated and orchestrated the setup of the coalition. To code coalitions which were politically initiated and orchestrated by the United States, I use two techniques. First, I look at public statements by U.S. government officials (notably in the UN Security Council) that indicate that the United States took on a leadership role in launching a particular deployment. Moreover, to corroborate that the United States put its money where its mouth is, I also examined U.S. involvement in actively orchestrating the political processes that led to the establishment of a particular operation. For instance, I examine whether the United States brokered the peace and/or ceasefire negotiations that preceded the deployment. I also look at the relative financial contributions the U.S. government made to resolve a particular conflict.[20]

Description of Variables

Lake uses "coalition participation"—a binary variable—as the dependent variable. In this new analysis, I attempt to provide greater detail. Therefore, I use three dependent variables: (1) a binary variable set to one if a country participated at all in a specific U.S.-led coalition; (2) a binary variable set to one if a country deployed at least a company-sized contingent (minimum one hundred troops); and (3) a continuous variable accounting for the exact number of troops deployed by a given country to a specific U.S.-led coalition. While the first dependent variable examines overall participation, the second dependent variable focuses on substantive contributions, thus excluding symbolic or token contributions. The third dependent variable captures the exact level of troop commitment. Like Lake, I include all countries in the international system that dispose of military forces as a potential force contributor to each U.S.-led coalition. Data for operation participation and troop contributions comes from the International Institute for Strategic Studies (IISS) journal *The Military Balance* (years 1990–2006), the United Nations Peacekeeping Department (UNDPKO), the Réseau Francophone de Recherche sur les Opérations de Paix (ROP), and the Stockholm International Peace Research Institute (SIPRI), as well as other secondary sources.

The key independent variable of this extended quantitative study of U.S. coalition participation is, of course, dyadic diplomatic embeddedness. I use it to test whether diplomatic embeddedness between a potential coalition participant and the United States increases the likelihood of coalition participation and/or the likelihood of sending a larger number of troops to a U.S.-led operation. To control for the coercion theory, I use the potential coalition participant's dependence (that is, hierarchy) on the United States in terms of dyadic trade and aid flows. I divide these flows by the potential participant's GDP to control for the relative importance of such flows to the participant.[21] To test the explanatory power of the preference convergence theory, I use (1) formal alliance agreements between the United States and potential coalition participants (as a proxy for shared threat perceptions); (2) interest affinity between the United States and the potential coalition participant;[22] (3) potential coalition participant–target state contiguity and potential coalition participant and target state common regional membership; (4) the potential coalition participant's diplomatic, trade, and aid ties with the target state of the intervention (as a proxy for intrinsic motivation);[23] and (5) regime type of the potential participant.[24] As control variables I use the potential coalition participant's level of economic development (in terms of GDP per capita);[25] and the potential coalition participant's Composite Index of National Capability (CINC) score (as a statistical measure of national power).[26] I also control for whether the potential coalition participant is involved in other disputes at the time of the intervention (as a proxy for equipment and troop availability).[27]

Model Specification

I use the new dataset to run five statistical models (see table 3.2). Regarding the model specifications, I stick very closely to Lake's analysis above. Models 1 and 2 are both logit regression models. Model 1 uses a binary dependent variable set to one if a country participated at all in a specific military operation. Model 2 uses a binary dependent variable set to one if a country participated with at least one hundred troops in the same operation.[28] Both models estimate robust standard errors clustered by target state to control for intra-class correlation among cross sections.[29] I thus assume that observations are not independent within one specific conflict theater. Several target states receive multiple operations (for instance, Haiti). A country which participates in the first operation to a specific target state might be more likely to stay on and participate in all subsequent operations. Clustering standard errors by target state controls for such scenarios.[30] Both models also include year dummies and control variables for whether the operation is conducted ad hoc or under a NATO or UN umbrella. Model 3 now changes these statistical specifications. It employs a zero-inflated Poisson regression model. It uses a count variable as the dependent variable (that is, the log transformed number of troops deployed per country/operation). It thus controls for an over-dispersed distribution of the dependent variable. In other words, the dependent variable includes "excess zeros," countries that are counted as potential troop contributors but in actuality are not approached by the United States to serve in a specific coalition. I argue that diplomatically embedded states are more likely to be approached by the United States for troop contributions. I therefore use diplomatic embeddedness to predict the excess zeros among the potential participants. All other model specifications stay exactly the same as in the previous models (that is, all but time-static independent variables are lagged by one year). Finally, Models 4 and 5 are fixed effects models. Model 4 uses the binary dependent variable set to one if a country participated at all in a specific military operation, while Model 5 uses a binary dependent variable set to one if a country participated with at least one hundred troops in the same operation. There is a small likelihood that all prior models suffer under an omitted variable bias. Indeed, one could argue that an unobserved factor—let's call it homogenous preferences or homophily—biases previous estimations. In other words, diplomatic embeddedness, alliance agreements, interest affinity, and even coalition participation does not occur randomly but could be the result of a U.S. tendency to associate and bond with states that are similar to itself. The problem is that this variable cannot be measured. Nevertheless, if such a tendency indeed exists, it does not change over time.[31] As a result, a fixed effects model can provide remedy. It produces unbiased estimates by using each variable's difference from its within-individual mean. Time-invariant variables, including an unobserved one such as homophily, thus drop out of the model.[32] Models 4 and 5 hence serve as important robustness checks.

Statistical Results

The statistical results using the expanded dataset of U.S.-led coalitions are shown in table 3.2. The results lend further probability to the claim that diplomatic embeddedness between the United States and potential coalition participants strongly influences troop deployments. Across all five different statistical models, using three different dependent variables and a very diverse set of model specifications, the variable diplomatic embeddedness is the only independent variable that is consistently positively correlated with coalition contributions and highly

TABLE 3.2 Regression results: New dataset

	(1)	(2)	(3)	(4)	(5)
	Logit	Logit (min 100 troops)	Zero-inflated Poisson	Fixed effects	Fixed effects (min 100 troops)
Diplomatic	0.010***	0.011***	0.002***	0.011***	0.011***
embeddedness$_{t-1}$	(0.000)	(0.000)	(0.000)	(0.000)	(0.000)
Preference conver- gence theory					
US alliance $_{t-1}$	−0.573***	−0.451***	0.000	−0.590***	−0.442***
	(0.000)	(0.003)	(0.997)	(0.000)	(0.005)
US affinity score $_{t-1}$	0.327	1.005*	−0.222	0.389*	1.074***
	(0.500)	(0.052)	(0.126)	(0.087)	(0.002)
Participant–target	−0.142	0.197	−0.006	−0.172	0.191
nation contiguity	(0.652)	(0.563)	(0.950)	(0.413)	(0.495)
Participant–target	0.582**	0.552**	0.077	0.632***	0.738***
nation same region	(0.045)	(0.047)	(0.165)	(0.000)	(0.000)
Participant has dip-	1.039***	1.010*	0.215**	0.636***	0.623**
lomatic represen- tation in target nation$_{t-1}$	(0.000)	(0.060)	(0.013)	(0.000)	(0.040)
Participant–target	−0.008	−0.021	−0.004	−0.026***	−0.047***
nation trade $_{t-1}$	(0.555)	(0.326)	(0.223)	(0.001)	(0.000)
Participant–target	−0.018	−0.036*	−0.005	−0.052***	−0.078***
nation aid $_{t-1}$	(0.276)	(0.075)	(0.246)	(0.000)	(0.000)
Participant polity2 $_{t-1}$	0.069***	0.045***	0.004	0.073***	0.050***
	(0.000)	(0.001)	(0.377)	(0.000)	(0.000)
Coercion theory					
US-participant aid $_{t-1}$	0.007*	−0.004	−0.002	0.006	−0.006
	(0.091)	(0.647)	(0.505)	(0.251)	(0.445)
US-participant	−0.066***	−0.132***	−0.033	−0.069**	−0.133***
trade $_{t-1}$	(0.007)	(0.001)	(0.179)	(0.013)	(0.004)
Controls					
Participant MID $_{t-1}$	−0.494***	−0.518***	−0.007	−0.498***	−0.516***
	(0.001)	(0.009)	(0.898)	(0.000)	(0.003)
Participant–target	0.283	0.858*	0.167**	0.353*	0.882***
nation common language	(0.494)	(0.073)	(0.029)	(0.061)	(0.001)
Participant CINC$_{t-1}$	2.721	2.668	1.593	3.946	4.640
	(0.503)	(0.580)	(0.186)	(0.208)	(0.277)
Participant GDP	0.031	−0.013	−0.022	0.019	−0.025
p.c. $_{t-1}$	(0.680)	(0.908)	(0.293)	(0.607)	(0.670)
Constant	−5.698***	−9.651***	−0.139		
	(0.000)	(0.000)	(0.810)		
Inflate (diplomatic			0.009***		
embeddedness)			(0.000)		
Observations	4,966	4,966	4,909	4,966	4,476

Notes: Robust p-values are in parentheses. Standard Errors are clustered by target state. Estimation includes year and IO dummies. Estimation performed using Stata 14. *** p<0.01, ** p<0.05, * p<0.1

statistically significant. The proxy variables accounting for the coercion theory and preference convergence theory do less well. Alliance ties, a key proxy for the preference convergence model, for instance, do not appear to matter at all.[33] Indeed, in four of the five models presented in table 3.2, they are negatively correlated with coalition contributions. UN affinity, another key proxy of the latter model, is positively correlated with coalitions contributions (at the 0.01 level) only in one of the five models depicted in table 3.2. Nevertheless, the democracy score, also a proxy for the preference convergence theory, does seem to be a fairly good predictor of a country's decision to participate in a U.S.-led coalition. In addition, countries that are involved in another conflict at the time of the U.S. coalition-building effort are highly unlikely to join a U.S.-led coalition.[34] The same effect occurs for dependence on trade with the United States.

Substantive Effects

Figure 3.1 presents the predicted effects of diplomatic embeddedness on the probability of participating in a U.S.-led coalition while holding all other variables at their means.[35] The filled triangles show the impact of diplomatic embeddedness on the probability of participating at all in a U.S.-led operation. This probability amounts to roughly 15 percent at the mean of diplomatic embeddedness (corresponding to about 71 bilateral and multilateral ties), 25 percent when we look at one standard deviation above the mean (about 130 ties), and 38 percent at two standard deviations (about 189 ties) above the mean. The empty triangles illustrate the probability of contributing at least a company-sized contingent (minimum 100 troops) to a U.S.-led coalition. This probability amounts to roughly 3 percent at the mean of diplomatic embeddedness. It increases to 6 percent when we look at one standard deviation above the mean, and to roughly 11 percent at two standard deviations above the mean.

Robustness Checks[36]

To control for the possibility that the UN interferes in U.S.-led coalition-building processes, I split the new dataset into UN and non-UN operations. The results indicate that for both UN-only and non-UN operations, diplomatic embeddedness is positively associated with troop contributions and highly statistically significant: for UN-only operations at the 0.01 level, for non-UN operations at the 0.01 level for deployments of minimum one hundred troops, and at the 0.05 level for all sizes of deployments. For only UN operations, the alliance coefficient is strongly negatively correlated with troop contributions.[37] For only non-UN interventions, the alliance variable is no longer statistically significant. In

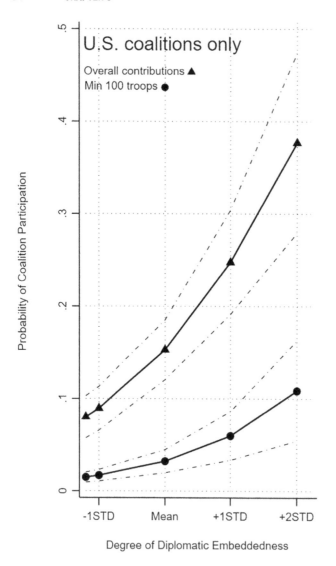

FIGURE 3.1 Substantive effects of statistical analysis (U.S. coalitions only)

addition, I test my results for multicollinearity. I find that diplomatic embedded-ness and the Index of Security Hierarchy (table 3.1) are correlated at 0.3, while diplomatic embeddedness and U.S. alliances (table 3.2) are correlated at 0.6, thus dampening multicollinearity concerns. Both a VIF test and a Collin test further corroborate that multicollinearity does not affect the regression results.

Overall, these statistical results strongly suggest that diplomatic embeddedness influences U.S. coalition-building efforts. Using a range of proxy variables to control for the coercion theory and the preference convergence theory and employing a diverse assortment of statistical models, diplomatic embeddedness is consistently positively correlated with coalition contributions. These correlations across all models are also highly statistically significant. Both alternative explanations fare decidedly less well in their overall explanatory power of the phenomenon under investigation.

Expanding the Universe to All Multilateral Coalitions

To corroborate the findings above, my next regression analysis looks at all multilateral military coalitions—U.S.-led and non-U.S.-led combined. Between 1990 and 2005, I count eighty-two such coalitions. These coalitions are either conducted ad hoc or under the umbrella of the UN, EU, NATO, AU, the Commonwealth of Independent States (CIS), the Economic Community of West African States (ECOWAS), or the Southern African Development Community (SADC).[38]

Coding of Pivotal States

As mentioned earlier, no international or regional organization is by itself capable of launching a multilateral coalition. Thus, any coalition requires states to act as political organizers behind the launch of a deployment. I call these pivotal states. For the purpose of this data analysis, I code the pivotal states for each one of the coalitions included in the dataset. To do so, I use the following coding criteria: First, I use the UN Index to Speeches[39] to count the number of times a country speaks in the UN Security Council (UNSC) on the topic of a specific coalition deployment. Most coalitions are discussed prior to their deployment in the UNSC even if these operations are ultimately conducted under the umbrella of an international organization other than the UN.[40] Second, I examine the willingness of these states to put their words into action; that is, I code whether these states are also involved in initiating and orchestrating the political processes that lead up to the establishment of a particular coalition. Such actions regularly include being involved in peace and/or ceasefire negotiations that most often precede the deployment of a specific coalition. Only states that fulfill both criteria (speaking and acting) are coded pivotal states of a specific coalition. My coding process wielded the pivotal states for the major international conflicts as shown in table 3.3.[41]

TABLE 3.3 Pivotal states in select conflict theaters

CONFLICT THEATER	OPERATIONS	PIVOTAL STATES
Angola	UNAVEM II, UNAVEM III, MONUA	USA, USSR/Russia, Portugal
Afghanistan	ISAF	USA
Cambodia	UNAMIC, UNTAC	France, Japan, USA Indonesia, Australia
Cote d'Ivoire	ECOMICI, UNOCI	France
Ethiopia and Eritrea	UNMEE	USA
East Timor	INTERFET, UNTAET, UNMISET	Australia
Haiti (1990s)	UNMIH, Operation Uphold Democracy, UNSMIH, UNT-MIH, MIPONUH	USA
Haiti (2004–)	MIFH, MINUSTAH	USA, France
Kuwait/Iraq	Operation Desert Storm, UNIKOM	USA
Liberia (1990s)	ECOMOG-Liberia, UNOMIL	USA, Nigeria
Liberia (2003–)	ECOMIL, UNMIL	USA
Georgia	UNOMIG, CIS Peacekeeping Forces in Georgia, CSCE/OSCE Mission to Georgia	Russia
Ex-Yugoslavia (until 1995)	UNPROFOR	France, U.K.
Ex-Yugoslavia (1995–)	IFOR, SFOR, UNMIBH, UNPRE-DEP, UNTAES	USA, Russia, U.K., France, Germany, Italy
Kosovo	Operation Allied Harbor, KFOR, Operation Essential Harvest	USA, U.K., France, Germany, Italy
Sierra Leone	ECOMOG-Sierra Leone, UNOM-SIL, UNAMSIL	U.K., USA, Nigeria
Somalia	UNOSOM I, UNOSOM II, UNITAF	USA
Sudan	AMIS, UNMIS	USA

Description of Variables

The data analysis again uses three dependent variables: (1) a binary dependent variable set to one if a country participated at all in a specific coalition, (2) a binary dependent variable set to one if a country deployed at least a company-sized contingent (min. 100 troops), and (3) a continuous variable accounting for the exact number of troops deployed per country/coalition. Each country that has participated at least once in a multilateral military coalition between 1990 and 2005 is considered a potential force contributor for each coalition, as it has shown that it is in practice capable and willing to deploy troops abroad.[42] Pivotal states and target states of individual operations are excluded from the list of potential coalition partners. The unit of analysis of the study is potential participant/coalition.[43] The key independent variable of this study is, of course, diplomatic embeddedness. Identical to the analyses above, I measure diplomatic embeddedness by counting all bilateral as well as multilateral ties pivotal states have established with potential coalition partners.

To control for the coercion theory, I use the potential coalition participant's dependence (that is, hierarchy) in aid and trade terms on all pivotal states. I divide these flows by the potential participant's GDP to control for the relative importance of such flows to the participant.[44] To control for the preference convergence theory, I include in the data analysis (1) formal alliance memberships between all pivotal states and potential coalition participants;[45] (2) interest affinity between pivotal states and potential coalition participants using the UN affinity score; (3) potential coalition participant-target state contiguity[46] and potential coalition participant and target state common regional membership[47]; (4) potential coalition participant-target state common language usage; (5) the potential coalition participant's diplomatic, trade, and aid ties with the target state of the intervention (as a proxy for intrinsic motivation);[48] and (5) regime type of the potential participant.[49] Finally, as control variables, I use a continuous variable accounting for the number of a country's simultaneous military deployments (greater than 100 troops) in a given year. In addition, I use the potential coalition participant's level of economic development (in terms of GDP per capita);[50] the potential coalition participant's CINC score;[51] and potential coalition participant involvement in a dispute at the time of the intervention.[52]

I lag all time-varying independent variables by one year to avoid simultanity problems. Outlier problems are addressed by expressing aid and trade flows in log form. In cases featuring multiple pivotal states, the analysis uses the aggregate aid and trade flows between all pivotal states and the potential participants as well as the aggregate number of all diplomatic ties shared between all pivotal states and the potential participants. I coded missing data on aid and trade flows as zero under the assumption that levels between states with missing data were negligible.[53]

Model Specifications

Using the data accounting for all multilateral military coalitions, I run seven different statistical models. Similar to the analyses above, I pursue a dyadic (instead of a network) research design. During my empirical analysis of this topic, notably the in-depth case studies, I did not come across any evidence of interactions between potential coalition participants prior to their joining the coalition. The vast majority of negotiations unfolded in a hub-and-spokes system in which the pivotal states constitute the hub and potential participants the spokes. As a result, I consider a dyadic approach more appropriate given that a network approach operates under the assumption that most of the nodes are connected.

To control for problems of intra-class correlation,[54] I use multilevel regression models as well as models with clustered standard errors. More specifically,

Models 1 and 2 in table 3.4 are xtlogit regression models controlling for intra-class correlation by coalition.[55] Model 1 uses a binary dependent variable set to one if a country participated at all in a specific coalition. Model 2 uses a binary dependent variable set to one if a country participated with at least 100 troops in the same coalition. It thus excludes all token contributions. Both models also include year, pivotal state, and umbrella organization dummies. Models 3 and 4 employ a regular logit regression model with standard errors clustered by coalition. Both models thus serve as a robustness check for Models 1 and 2. Model 5 uses a count variable as the dependent variable: the exact number of troops deployed per country/coalition. In addition, the model employs a zero-inflated negative binomial regression model. It thus attempts to control for the over-dispersion of the dependent variable (that is, the dependent variable includes "excess zeros," countries that are counted as potential troop contributors but in practice are not approached by the pivotal states to serve in a specific coalition). Similar to the analyses above, I use diplomatic embeddedness to predict the excess zeros among the potential participants. All other model specifications again stay exactly the same as in the previous models. Finally, Models 6 and 7 are fixed effects models. They try to control for a potentially unobserved factor (that is, homophily) that might bias the estimates (see above).

Statistical Results

The results of the regressions are presented in table 3.4. The variable diplomatic embeddedness is positively correlated with coalition contributions and highly statistically significant (at the 0.01 level) across all seven models. This result again speaks to the importance of diplomatic embeddedness in the process of constructing multilateral military coalitions irrespective of which countries serve as pivotal states and irrespective of whether the coalitions are constructed ad hoc or under the umbrella of an international institution. Nevertheless, diplomatic embeddedness is not the only variable that matters when looking at all multilateral military coalitions combined. If a state is situated in the region of the operation, its likelihood of coalition participation significantly increases. Similarly, democracies are more likely to commit coalition contributions. Having diplomatic representation in the target countries also affects coalition contributions, although to a less consistent degree. All three of these findings speak to the relevance of certain aspects of the preference convergence theory. Finally, the number of simultaneous troop deployments also matters: it appears that some countries have a special penchant to serve in multilateral military coalitions without being inhibited by military capability and troop overstretch. With regard to the factors that negatively influence coalition contributions, trade dependence between pivotal states and potential coalition contributors stands out. Across the seven models, this variable is consistently negatively correlated (at the 0.01 level) with coalition contributions. Parallel conflict involvement also negatively correlates with troop commitments in six models. Alliance ties, in turn, negatively correlate with coalition contributions in three models (at the 0.01 level).

Substantive Effects

Figures 3.2 and 3.3 present the predicted effects of diplomatic embeddedness between pivotal states and potential participants on the probability of a potential participant to join a coalition. The analysis varies the values of diplomatic embeddedness while holding all other variables at their means. Figure 3.2 looks at all coalition contributions. At the mean of diplomatic embeddedness (roughly 118 ties), the probability of participating in a UN operation amounts to 15 percent, the probability of participating in a non-UN operations amounts to 2.4 percent, and the probability of participating in both types of operations amounts to 8 percent. At one standard deviation above the mean of diplomatic embeddedness (roughly 235 ties) this probability doubles in almost all instances. It increases to 32 percent for UN operations, 4 percent for non-UN operations, and 15 percent for all types of operations. Figure 3.3 now excludes token contributions. At the mean of diplomatic embeddedness, the probability of deploying a minimum of 100 troops in a UN operation amounts to 3 percent, in a non-UN operation to 0.6 percent, and in both types of operations to 2 percent. At one standard deviation above the mean of diplomatic embeddedness, this probability again substantively increases for each type of operation, rising to 6.5 percent for UN operations, 1.4 percent for non-UN operations, and 4 percent for all types of operations.

Robustness Checks[56]

To further assess the robustness of the results presented above, I conducted a battery of robustness checks. First, the statistical research design presented above assumes that multilateral coalitions are random events (that is, pivotal states select intervention targets randomly). Such an assumption does not necessarily coincide with reality. Nevertheless, I cannot identify a satisfactory selection function that would incorporate the plethora of domestic and international factors influencing a pivotal state's decision to take the lead in a specific operation. However, based on the assumption that no single factor exists influencing the decision-making process to lead a security operation, I conducted robustness checks with a multitude of randomly sampled subsets of the data. The results using those randomly sampled

TABLE 3.4 Regression results: All multilateral coalitions

	(1) XTLOGIT (ALL CONTRIBUTIONS)	(2) XTLOGIT (MIN. 100 TROOPS)	(3) LOGIT (ALL CONTRIBUTIONS)	(4) LOGIT (MIN. 100 TROOPS)
Diplomatic embeddedness$_{t-1}$	0.007***	0.006***	0.006***	0.005***
	(0.000)	(0.000)	(0.000)	(0.000)
Preference convergence theory				
Pivotal states–potential participant shared alliances $_{t-1}$	−0.166***	−0.058	−0.128	−0.028
	(0.002)	(0.398)	(0.102)	(0.703)
Pivotal states–potential participant UN affinity$_{t-1}$	0.952***	0.525*	0.033	−0.239
	(0.000)	(0.057)	(0.911)	(0.551)
Potential participant–target nation contiguity	0.033	0.421**	0.129	0.520**
	(0.834)	(0.031)	(0.494)	(0.023)
Potential participant–target nation same region	1.176***	1.357***	1.082***	1.243***
	(0.000)	(0.000)	(0.000)	(0.000)
Potential participant diplomatic representation in target nation $_{t-1}$	0.622***	0.579**	0.876***	0.657***
	(0.000)	(0.046)	(0.000)	(0.002)
Potential participant–target nation trade flows $_{t-1}$	−0.011**	−0.011	−0.005	−0.004
	(0.045)	(0.169)	(0.590)	(0.722)
Potential participant-target nation aid flows$_{t-1}$	−0.034***	−0.035***	−0.031***	−0.036**
	(0.000)	(0.000)	(0.009)	(0.016)
Potential participant polity2 $_{t-1}$	0.047***	0.040***	0.054***	0.045***
	(0.000)	(0.000)	(0.000)	(0.000)
Coercion theory				
Pivotal states–potential participant aid flows$_{t-1}$	−0.007**	−0.010*	−0.005	−0.008
	(0.045)	(0.069)	(0.284)	(0.119)
Pivotal states–participant trade flows$_{t-1}$	−0.027***	−0.045***	−0.031***	−0.048***
	(0.000)	(0.000)	(0.000)	(0.000)
Controls				
Potential participant simultaneous deployments $_{t-1}$	0.415***	0.416***	0.398***	0.416***
	(0.000)	(0.000)	(0.000)	(0.000)
Potential participant MID $_{t-1}$	−0.422***	−0.382***	−0.408***	−0.371***
	(0.000)	(0.002)	(0.000)	(0.000)
Potential participant–target nation common language	0.319**	0.584***	0.234	0.502**
	(0.016)	(0.001)	(0.250)	(0.019)
Potential participant CINC$_{t-1}$	2.111	3.714	1.577	3.623
	(0.319)	(0.199)	(0.458)	(0.160)
Potential participant GDP$_{t-1}$	−0.067**	−0.050	−0.001	0.023
	(0.021)	(0.256)	(0.985)	(0.743)
Constant	−5.185***	−7.387***	−4.741***	−6.991***
	(0.000)	(0.000)	(0.000)	(0.000)
Observations	11,521	11,521	11,521	11,521

Notes: Robust p-values are in parentheses. All models include pivotal states, year and IO dummies. Estimation performed using STATA14. *** p<0.01, ** p<0.05, * p<0.1.

	(5) ZERO-INFLATED NEGATIVE BINOMIAL	(6) FIXED EFFECTS (ALL CONTRIBUTIONS)	(7) FIXED EFFECTS (MIN. 100 TROOPS)
Diplomatic embeddedness$_{t-1}$	0.010***	0.007***	0.006***
	(0.000)	(0.000)	(0.000)
Preference convergence theory			
Pivotal states–potential participant shared alliances $_{t-1}$	−0.362***	−0.169***	−0.064
	(0.001)	(0.001)	(0.365)
Pivotal states–potential participant UN affinity $_{t-1}$	−0.999**	1.115***	0.672**
	(0.014)	(0.000)	(0.017)
Potential participant–target nation contiguity	0.901**	0.017	0.408**
	(0.017)	(0.911)	(0.037)
Potential participant–target nation same region	2.924***	1.177***	1.362***
	(0.000)	(0.000)	(0.000)
Potential participant diplomatic representation in target nation $_{t-1}$	1.356***	0.562***	0.552*
	(0.000)	(0.001)	(0.059)
Potential participant–target nation trade flows $_{t-1}$	0.007	−0.011**	−0.011
	(0.532)	(0.036)	(0.167)
Potential participant–target nation aid flows $_{t-1}$	−0.016	−0.035***	−0.034***
	(0.347)	(0.000)	(0.001)
Potential participant polity2 $_{t-1}$	0.016	0.045***	0.038***
	(0.226)	(0.000)	(0.000)
Coercion theory			
Pivotal states–potential participant aid flows $_{t-1}$	−0.008	−0.008**	−0.010*
	(0.323)	(0.034)	(0.064)
Pivotal states–participant trade flows $_{t-1}$	−0.054***	−0.025***	−0.043***
	(0.001)	(0.000)	(0.000)
Controls			
Potential participant simultaneous deployments$_{t-1}$	0.882***	0.416***	0.411***
	(0.000)	(0.000)	(0.000)
Potential participant MID$_{t-1}$	−0.286*	−0.420***	−0.381***
	0.096)	(0.000)	(0.002)
Potential participant–target nation common language	0.269	0.337**	0.575***
	(0.379)	(0.011)	(0.001)
Potential participant CINC$_{t-1}$	4.325	2.181	3.650
	(0.325)	(0.306)	(0.212)
Potential participant GDP p.c.$_{t-1}$	0.173***	−0.079***	−0.067
	(0.004)	(0.007)	(0.137)
Inflate (diplomatic embeddedness $_{t-1}$)	−0.021***		
	(0.000)		
Constant	−2.678***		
	(0.003)		
Observations	11,384	11,379	9,853

Notes: Robust p-values are in parentheses. Model (5) includes pivotal states, year and IO dummies. Estimation performed using STATA14. *** p<0.01, ** p<0.05, * p<0.1.

subsets do not alter the key findings described above. Second, I ran the key models described above with a reduced number of potential participants. Instead of including all of the countries that participated at least once in one operation between 1990 and 2005, potential participants were required to meet a specific CINC score threshold (one standard deviation above the mean) to qualify for participation. Again, the results do not affect the principal findings shown above.

This chapter's objective was to highlight the macro-factors determining multilateral military coalition-building. The dependent variable of the chapter was coalition participation. I tried to find out what factors affect countries' decisions to join multilateral military coalitions. The results of the quantitative analysis are as follows: yes, diplomatic embeddedness matters in multilateral coalition-building process whether the United States served the role of pivotal state or other states filled that position. Moreover, the results hold for coalitions that are constructed ad hoc as well as those built under the umbrella of international organizations. In addition, the results are robust across a wide range of different statistical models and using three different dependent variables. In each case, diplomatic embeddedness is positively correlated with coalition contributions at high levels of statistical significance ($p < 0.01$). The substantive impact of diplomatic embeddedness on coalition contributions is large as well. In the context of U.S.-led coalitions, the probability of joining such coalitions amounts to 15 percent at the mean of diplomatic embeddedness. It increases to 25 percent when we look at one standard deviation above the mean. With regard to large troop contributions, the results are similar: at the mean of diplomatic embeddedness, the probability amounts to 3 percent. It increases to 6 percent when we look at one standard deviation above the mean. The results are even more impressive when we look at all multilateral coalitions. At one standard deviation above the mean of diplomatic embeddedness with the pivotal state, the probability of joining such a multilateral coalition doubles in almost all instances. It increases from 15 percent to 32 percent for UN operations, from 2.4 percent to 4 percent for non-UN operations, and from 8 percent to 15 percent for all types of operations. The substantive impact is even more impressive when token coalition contributions (that is, coalition contributions smaller than 100 troops) are excluded from the calculations. Indeed, at one standard deviation above the mean of diplomatic embeddedness, the probability of deploying a minimum of 100 troops at least doubles for all types of operations: it rises from 3 percent to 6 percent for UN operations, from 0.6 percent to 1.4 percent for non-UN operations, and from 2 percent to 4 percent for all types of operations.

    Diplomatic embeddedness is, however, not the only factor influencing troop deployments. When it comes to U.S.-led coalitions, some proxy variables for the preference convergence theory (that is, regime type, diplomatic representation, and regional membership) matter equally, although, arguably less consistently than diplomatic embeddedness. The same is true for multilateral coalitions (U.S.-led and non-U.S.-led). Here, being located in the region of operation has a strong and consistently positive effect on the probability of deploying forces.

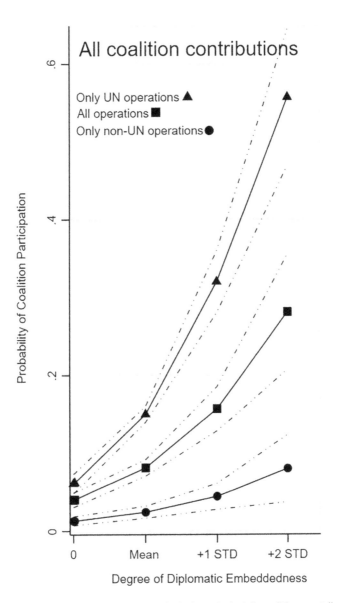

FIGURE 3.2   Substantive effects of statistical analysis (all coalition contributions)

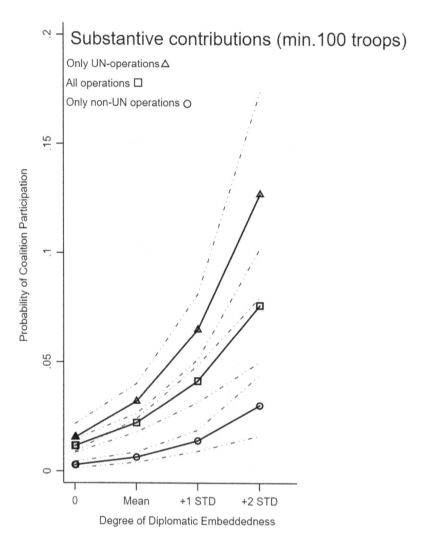

FIGURE 3.3   Substantive effects excluding token contributions

In addition, democracies are more likely to join such multilateral coalitions. Moreover, simultaneous deployments increase the likelihood of coalition participation. This indicates that a particular set of countries has a special penchant to deploy military forces abroad, even simultaneously in different theaters. The regression results also hint at factors that do not positively correlate with coalition contributions; most importantly, trade dependence between pivotal states and potential coalition participants negatively affects a potential participant's likelihood to send troops to a pivotal state's coalition. This puts in doubt the explanatory power of certain aspects of the coercion theory, notably its focus on asymmetrical trade dependence as an efficient coalition-building tool.

In summary, diplomatic embeddedness matters greatly. Nevertheless, the analysis above does not exclude the possibility that other factors equally impact coalition participation. Moreover, the analysis reveals very little about the causal mechanisms that actually undergird diplomatic embeddedness. As a result, we now turn to the case-study analysis to resolve these questions.

4

CHAINING COMMUNISTS
The Korean War (1950–1953)

The Korean War began in the predawn hours of June 25, 1950. At around 4 a.m., North Korean units launched an artillery attack across the 38th parallel and amphibious landings in two areas of South Korea's eastern coast. The attack came as a complete surprise.[1] Korea had been divided into two zones ever since the surrender of the Japanese forces that controlled the country between 1910 and 1945. In 1945, the Soviet Union accepted the Japanese surrender in the North; the Americans in the South. In December 1945, U.S. secretary of state James F. Byrnes and Soviet foreign minister Vyacheslav Molotov worked out an agreement that foresaw a joint UN commission to reunify the two zones and bring independence to Korea. The commission, however, made very little progress, and by 1947 the United States had grown weary of the Korean problem. In September 1947, U.S. president Harry S Truman thus suggested to the UN General Assembly (UNGA) that UN-monitored elections be held in Korea. Truman believed that elections would help establish a new independent and unified Korean government, which, in turn, would allow for the withdrawal of all foreign forces from the peninsula. The Soviet Union agreed to the withdrawal proposal but rejected the idea of UN-supervised elections. Consequently, on May 10, 1948, elections were held, but only in the U.S.-controlled South. In August 1948, the American military government in Korea officially ceased its operations, and by June 1949 most U.S. troops had left South Korea, leaving behind only a small training mission.[2] Soviet troops in the North had also largely withdrawn from the peninsula by mid-1949. Kim Il-sung, a former anti-Japanese guerrilla leader whom the Soviets had installed as chairman of the northern branch of the Korean Communist Party in December 1945, was left in charge of the country—and it was he who ordered the attack on South Korea on June 25, 1950.

The Korean War was a war of numerous firsts. It was the first "limited war" conducted under the shadow of two nuclear powers. It was also the first time that the United Nations countered aggression by deploying military forces. Most importantly, however, at least for the purposes of this book, the Korean War constituted the first instance of multilateral military coalition building in the post–World War II era. The U.S. government served as the pivotal state in this coalition-building effort. The U.S. government was able to recruit the following countries to participate in the Korean War: the United Kingdom (14,198 troops), Canada (6,146 troops), Turkey (5,453 troops), Australia (2,282 troops), the Philippines (1,496 troops), New Zealand (1,385 troops), Ethiopia (1,271 troops), Greece (1,263 troops), Thailand (1,204 troops), France (1,119 troops), Colombia (1,068 troops), Belgium (900 troops), South Africa (826 troops), the Netherlands (819 troops), and Luxembourg (44 troops). India contributed a field hospital, and Denmark, Norway, Italy, and Sweden provided other medical services.[3] Despite the Cold War atmosphere surrounding the Korean War and the UN mandate that authorized the intervention, most of these countries only joined the coalition after intense U.S. negotiations. Many countries around the world did not consider the Korean War "their war"; as a U.S. State Department official said: "The main reason we do not have more foreign troops in Korea is that other peoples are not sure that we are fighting for goals of equal importance to them."[4] The United States thus had to conduct an explicit recruitment process, in which U.S. diplomatic networks played an indispensable role. These networks provided the U.S. government with information on deployment preferences and trust. They also facilitated the construction of issue linkages and side payments.

This chapter focuses on the deployment decisions of the three largest troop-contributing countries: the United Kingdom, Canada, and Turkey; the Philippines, a deeply embedded state with the United States in 1950; and South Africa, a weakly embedded state with the United States in 1950.[5] The chapter shows that the deployment decisions of the U.K. and Canada were the result of intense U.S. prodding involving a mixture of personal appeals, incentives, and threats. In this process, the U.S. government instrumentalized diplomatic networks to the greatest extent possible. These ties provided U.S. diplomats with critical information on how best to cajole, tease, and bully their British and Canadian counterparts and with refined opportunities to link issues that were functionally unrelated to the intervention per se. Interestingly, alliance considerations, especially NATO, played only a minor role in both negotiation processes. Turkey, the third-largest contributor (and much less embedded with the United States in 1950), can be considered a "self-starter." It offered to serve in the Korean War in exchange for membership in NATO. The Philippines, a deeply embedded country with the United States in 1950, was lured into the coalition via U.S. diplomatic embeddedness. The U.S. government had occupied the Philippines until 1946—only four years prior to the war. In 1950, the U.S. government was able to exploit the extensive ties it still had with the country to coax it into joining the coalition. Finally, in the case of South Africa, a country weakly embedded with the United States, diplomatic embeddedness played no direct role. Rather, South Africa perceived the Korean War as an opportunity to gain from the United States long-desired military equipment, in particular military aircraft. Alongside Turkey, it can thus also be considered a "self-starter."

Origins of U.S. Involvement in the Korean War

In hindsight, the U.S.-led deployment to Korea that left almost 180,000 dead, 30,000 missing, and 570,000 wounded seems to have been a folly—a non-rational choice of war.[6] So what motivated U.S. officials to wage war in Korea? U.S. secretary of state Dean Acheson, who dominated the decision-making process,[7] justified the decision in his memoir the following way: "To back away [from Korea] . . . would [have been] highly destructive of the power and prestige of the United States. By prestige I mean the shadow cast by power, which is of great deterrent importance."[8] In other words, a strong stance on Korea was necessary to discourage similar Soviet actions elsewhere.[9] The Soviet blockade of Berlin, which lasted from June 24, 1948 to May 12, 1949, and other Soviet-related developments had induced in Washington a "chill of fear of Russian intentions and ruthlessness"[10] and a desire to contain Soviet influence.[11] President Truman picked up on a similar theme in his memoir. He argued that the North Korean attack was another case in which "the strong attacked the weak." If the Communist leaders were to be appeased, then the scale of violence and the number of participating states would gradually increase to global dimensions. A third world war between Communist and non-Communist states would inevitably ensue.[12] Nevertheless, it is impossible to fully understand U.S. engagement in the Korean War without also looking at the domestic context that surrounded the U.S. decision-making process. South Korea came under attack when the Truman administration faced ferocious Republican criticism regarding the Communist conquest of China, which had occurred just a year earlier, in 1949. Voices charging the State Department of Communist subversion grew louder each day.[13] The criticisms were all the more powerful, as a midterm election was on the horizon. Dean Acheson was under particular scrutiny because of his close relationship with Alger Hiss, a State Department official who in January 1950 had been convicted of perjury in a Communist espionage case.[14] As a result, the Truman government's decision-making on Korea was certainly at least a partial attempt to avoid "losing" another country to the communist camp and thus evade further Republican criticism.[15]

In formulating a response to the North Korean attack, Dean Acheson quickly reached out to the United Nations to authorize an international response to the invasion. Moreover, Acheson immediately expressed a strong desire to construct a multinational coalition to repel the aggression. Acheson doubted that such a coalition could render "effective [military] assistance" to the Korean War effort.[16] Rather, the purpose of it was highly political. Acheson was eager to prove, in particular to the Soviet Union, that U.S. policies in Korea were broadly supported by the international community and therefore legitimate.[17] In addition, Acheson also hoped that building a multilateral coalition would bolster U.S. domestic public approval of the operation. He allegedly remarked to his Canadian counterpart that "if the United States had to do all the fighting in Korea, there was a real danger that [domestic] public opinion . . . would favour preparing in isolation for the larger conflict ahead and writing allies off."[18] U.S. senators were also eager for the United States not to "go it alone." On July 11, 1950, Senator Robert A. Taft and Senator Willis Smith explicitly mentioned to John Foster Dulles, who was serving as a consultant to President Truman, that an "increased effort should be made to bring contingents from other United Nations members into the fighting in Korea and, if possible, into the ground fighting."[19] U.S. government officials also thought that the Korean War represented a unique opportunity to weld UN member states "more closely together in opposition to Communism wherever it may occur."[20] They considered the Korean War to be a mobilizing tool—a wakeup call for U.S. allies that the Communist threat was real and had to be actively confronted. This desire concerned, in particular, Western Europe and Latin America.[21] With regard to Latin America, State Department official John C. Dreier argued that

> the political advantage of active participation by Latin American forces in the UN action in Korea . . . would be enormous. The Latin American peoples as a whole are relatively remote from the Asian scene and they are tempted by the thought, which is encouraged by Communist propaganda, that the present crisis is merely a struggle for power between the USA and USSR. If, however, Latin American troops participate with the UN forces, the nationalism and patriotism of the Latin American people will be aroused in support of the entire UN action against Communist aggression. The Latin countries will be accordingly more closely

than ever lined with the position of the United States in the world at large, and more directly committed to the UN.[22]

Initially, the U.S. military did not like the idea of building a multilateral coalition to intervene in Korea. They objected, in particular, to any UN interference in the planning and execution of the operation and preferred to leave both solely in the hands of the United States.[23] Nevertheless, when the casualties in Korea shot up, beginning in late November 1950, the U.S. military became the loudest advocate for recruiting additional non-U.S. forces.[24]

Planning for Coalition Intervention

At the request of the United States, UN secretary-general Trygve Lie officially launched the coalition-building process for the Korean War. On June 27, 1950, Lie sent a letter addressed to all UN member states recommending that "the members of the UN furnish . . . assistance to the Republic of Korea as may be necessary to repel the armed attack and to restore international peace and security in the area," paraphrasing UN Resolution 83 the UN Security Council had passed the same day.[25]

Since the Korean intervention was the first time that the United Nations acted in a military manner, no official process existed that streamlined the recruitment of coalition forces. As a result, almost immediately after the passage of UN Resolution 83, U.S. State Department officials discussed with their UN counterparts how this process should be handled. Among both groups, a consensus existed that "there should be some official machinery with the United Nations label which could coordinate these offers of military assistance."[26] U.S. and UN officials did not, however, agree on much else. Andrew Cordier, the executive assistant to the UN secretary-general, proposed that a "Security Council Committee" should be in charge of the process. This committee would meet in private and decide which coalition offers could be accepted.[27] U.S. officials, however, largely disagreed with this idea. They felt that it was "not practical for the United Nations to get into the actual use and control of [military] assistance . . . and it was unthinkable to use the [UN] Military Staff Committee in any way." Rather, the UN and, in particular, Secretary-General Lie should operate as no more than a "post office."[28] They would transmit to the United States information submitted to them by UN member states about their deployment preferences. Essentially, the United States would be the "operating agent" of the process and all the heavy lifting would be done bilaterally, or as Dean Acheson formulated it in a telegram[29] to the U.S. mission to the UN on July 12, 1950: "Immediately following [the secretary-general's] circular a [U.S.] bilateral approach will be initiated with the countries that we consider in a position to offer effective economic or military assistance, particularly combat forces."[30]

The final recruitment procedure that both parties eventually agreed upon reflected mostly American ideas. It put the U.S.-led Unified Command in charge of all military planning and execution. It also left all important recruitment decisions in the hands of the U.S. government. It included among others the following provisions:

1. Offers of military assistance from member governments will be transmitted to the Secretary-General of the United Nations who, in turn, will transmit the offers to the Unified Command (USG) through the United States Mission to the United Nations. Requests from the Unified Command (USG) for additional effective assistance in Korea will be transmitted to the Secretary-General for communication to the permanent delegations of member governments.
2. Upon receipt of the offer Unified Command (USG) will enter into direct negotiations with the member government concerned regarding the details of the offer and its utilization. The Unified Command (USG) will keep the Secretary-General periodically informed of the status of these negotiations.
3. Upon the completion of direct negotiations, the Unified Command (USG) will inform the Secretary-General of their results. The Secretary-General will transmit this information to the delegation of the member government concerned and, in consultation with the Unified Command (USG) and the delegation concerned, will release this information to the press.[31]

There can thus be no doubt that the United States—as the pivotal state of the intervention—was in charge of planning the mission, including the recruitment of coalition forces. UN officials were de facto sidelined.

In the early days of the operation, the Pentagon took full responsibility for all the tasks that were required to launch the war. The Joint Chiefs of Staff were left in charge of determining what military forces were needed and what kinds of offers were suitable. In contrast to Acheson, the Pentagon was eager to build a coalition that was of at least some military utility to the United States. Its recruitment strategy did not state any geographical preferences—troops were welcome from any UN member state—but it focused very heavily on the military suitability of troop contributions. On July 15, 1950, for instance, General Douglas McArthur recommended that the United States accept only ground units comprised of at least 1,000 men capable of arriving in Korea by themselves and with supplies, ammunition, and arms sufficient to last for sixty days.[32] On September 25, he again made it clear that "all offers of military assistance should conform as far as practicable with the general criteria of useful military assistance."[33] In a memorandum dated July 19, 1950, sent to Assistant Secretary of State for Far Eastern Affairs Dean Rusk by his deputy, Livingston Merchant, the latter also noted that the Joint Chiefs of Staff would likely turn down some countries that were considering deploying to Korea due to their lack of qualified troops, difficulties related to logistics, lack of weapons standardization, or language barriers. Such difficulties would render certain national units "unsuitable or a hindrance" and would create "problems greater than their military contribution," the Joint Chiefs of Staff reckoned.[34] Overall, an attitude permeated the Pentagon that if foreign troops were accepted, "military convenience" would be "overriding political considerations."[35]

The Pentagon's dominance of the coalition-building process was, however, very short-lived. Its coalition-building criteria trained on military suitability were very quickly sidelined. Indeed, by early August 1950 the Soviet Union had launched an impressive propaganda machine denouncing the intervention in Korea as lacking any substantive international support. Speaking at the UN in New York, Soviet ambassador to the United Nations Yakov Malik publicly exploited the fact that exceedingly few countries had signed up to serve in the Korean War coalition, and Malik was right. Despite a political outburst of UN member support for the intervention, very few countries had shown any interest in joining the United States in Korea.[36] This alarmed Dean Acheson and his colleagues. They felt that it would be extremely detrimental to allow the Soviet Union to win the propaganda war on Korea. As a result, the number of participants in the Korean War coalition had to be increased at all costs. On August 11, 1950, Dean Acheson thus sent the following cable to U.S. embassies in the United Kingdom, France, Canada, the Netherlands, and New Zealand:

> [Ambassador] Malik's statement in UN and present [Soviet] propaganda make it clear that one of the main [Soviet] objectives is to obscure UN character of Korean action by placing emphasis on fact that burden of fighting is being undertaken by US forces virtually alone. Imme[diate] and decisive action is called for to place UN decision in true light . . . we consider it essential that all those nations whose mil[itary] capabilities are adequate for the purpose increase their contribution by sending of ground troops as a matter of urgency.[37]

Acheson also contacted President Truman and asked him to send a presidential directive to the Pentagon communicating "clearly and unmistakably the policy that we are to do everything possible to encourage offers of actual military forces from other countries."[38] Acheson thus requested a direct repeal of how the recruitment process had been handled by the Pentagon. "Diplomatic considerations must from now on trump military expediency," Acheson insisted. "Adequate" forces were all that was necessary to be a fit candidate for the Korean War. The president concurred. By early August 1950, the State Department thus took over political control of the coalition-building process for the Korean War. The Joint Chiefs of Staff criteria of military convenience would only serve as a general guideline in discussing offers; they would no longer determine recruitment choices.

Once the State Department had taken over control of the recruitment process for the Korean War, it launched a global PR campaign to sway countries to join the coalition by issuing public calls for participation. These calls specified that the United States no longer required countries to contribute any specific military assets. All they had to do was show up. Despite these PR efforts, however, the large majority of countries remained unmoved. Many of the countries contacted by the U.S. government to join the Korean War thought that the Korean conflict was none of their business. Many states in Latin America, for instance, reckoned that their countries had nothing to gain and everything to lose by sending their blood and money to Korea.[39] Communist parties in these states rallied public opinion against attempts to send Latin American boys to serve as "cannon fodder" or "colonials" for the North American colossus.[40] Moreover, some countries believed that it was simply impossible for them to bear the costs of training, arming, transporting, and provisioning forces for a deployment to Korea.[41] President Getúlio Vargas of Brazil, for instance, argued that while he was not necessarily opposed to the intervention, his top policy priority at the time was "feeding his people, not putting chains on Communists around the world."[42] These attitudes thus clearly show that very little "preference convergence" existed among the international community with regard to the Korean War.

Searching for Coalition Contributions

The lack of enthusiasm left some U.S. government officials "immensely concerned."[43] They realized that they had to change their strategy to receive greater troop contributions. Most importantly, they had to find out what preferences states held with regard to the intervention and what external incentives the U.S. government could provide to change their stances. How could that be done? How could such information be accessed? To overcome this dilemma, U.S. officials began instrumentalizing U.S. diplomatic networks. On August 5, 1950, Livingston

Merchant, a high-ranking official in the State Department, instructed all heads of regional bureaus in the State Department to actively seek troop contributions in their respective geographical areas of responsibility:[44] each bureau had to purposefully collect information on the variables of interest using all sources it had at its disposition. Early August 1950 thus constituted an important transition period. The Truman government switched from merely having diplomatic networks to exploiting them as a strategic asset, a power capability to organize collective action and construct the Korean War coalition.

The Latin America bureau soon reported that several Latin American countries might constitute promising recruitment targets: via diplomatic channels, U.S. diplomats had learned that if the right external incentives were offered, some of them might be relatively easy targets to be swayed to join the coalition. With regard to Uruguay, for example, U.S. diplomats stationed in Montevideo reported back to Washington that Uruguayan president Luis Batlle Berres would consider a deployment of 2,000 troops to Korea if the U.S. government would revisit its longstanding refusal to sell arms to Uruguay.[45] Similarly, U.S. diplomats based in Santiago reported that Chile was willing to consider a ground deployment to Korea but the Chilean government thought that the equipment of the Chilean Army, Navy, and Air Force was too limited and antiquated for a major deployment and that public opinion was not yet prepared to support the war efforts.[46] If, however, the United States was willing to provide new equipment, it might reconsider its position. Finally, U.S. diplomats also learned that Colombia was potentially interested in a deployment to Korea but it also had difficulties arming, provisioning, and transporting the troops.[47] In short, if the United States could provide these countries with the necessary military aid, a force deployment to Korea was likely to be forthcoming.

To be able to offer such military aid, the State Department required approval from the Pentagon.[48] General Matthew Ridgway, the Army's deputy chief of staff for administration, however, told State Department officials that "there was no legal way in which . . . equipment and services could be made available [to these potential coalition participants] . . . without full reimbursement."[49] In other words, the U.S. government could only provide such equipment to coalition participants if they paid for it. Nevertheless, the State Department insisted that a more "cordial" solution had to found, and at a meeting on August 24, 1950, a compromise was hammered out. A committee of State and Pentagon officials produced a document titled "Interim Guidance Paper" that outlined how to deal with countries whose participation in the Korean War coalition was politically desired but required financial and material deployment support. The compromise foresaw that if a country was discouraged to deploy to Korea by the prospect of having to reimburse U.S. deployment support, a simple agreement to "negotiate the terms of settlement" at a later date would suffice.[50] On August 29, 1950, the interim proposal was sent to President Truman, and on September 1, 1950, a paper titled "Utilization of Offers of Foreign Assistance in Korea" was officially distributed to the service secretaries by Secretary of Defense Louis Johnson. Nevertheless, it was not until Secretary Johnson's resignation on September 12, 1950, and the installation of George Marshall as secretary of defense that the directive was fully implemented.[51] By fall 1950, the offer to provide "deployment subsidies" to Korean War participants became official U.S. government policy.

The new policy directive coincided with an intensification of the Korean War. In mid-October 1950, China entered the war. By late November 1950, coalition forces were clashing almost daily with vastly superior numbers of Chinese troops. By Christmas, the Chinese had pushed the coalition forces all the way back to the 38th parallel, recapturing Seoul on January 4, 1951. American casualties reached approximately forty thousand dead, wounded, or missing by the end of 1950 and grew at a rate of a thousand per week in the first months of 1951.[52] This military catastrophe led the U.S. government to an enhanced push for new recruits. Interestingly, this time around the Pentagon was as keen as the State Department to expand the Korean War coalition.[53] Secretary Marshall personally sent a list of potential recruits to the State Department and was eager to receive "strategic" input on how to convince them to join the coalition. He was willing to follow the political lead of the State Department, with one exception: Great Britain and NATO countries on the European continent should not be pressed to furnish additional troops, as their resources would be better used for the protection of Europe.[54] Marshall's letter led to an intense back and forth between State and Defense on how best to proceed. State then suggested that the two agencies should join their forces. How about if they both used their respective diplomatic channels—civilian and military—to collect information on suitable recruits? Once such information was available, officials from State and Defense could meet and produce a "prospect list"—a list of countries that U.S. diplomats and military officials would target to conduct more elaborate coalition negotiations.[55] The Pentagon agreed. On February 13, 1951, State and Defense officials met to create that list.[56]

The first countries that were discussed at this joint meeting were again those located in Latin America. State and Defense officials exchanged notes on what information they had received from their respective sources. Both departments then pledged that they would make an extra effort to expedite coalition negotiations—notably with Uruguay, Chile, and Colombia, as already stated. Next, the interagency team discussed Canada, Australia, New Zealand, South Africa, and Sweden. State department officials mentioned that they had worked very hard to cajole the U.K., Canada, Australia, and New Zealand to deploy a "Commonwealth Unit" to Korea. This Commonwealth Unit was now underway, and the interagency team concluded that some of the countries participating in this unit could be pushed a little harder to further increase their troop contribution to Korea. Diplomatic sources had, in particular, revealed that Australia was a suitable candidate to "be asked to furnish a replacement battalion in Japan for the battalion that had originally been transferred from Japan to Korea."[57] Australia was eager to negotiate a defense pact with the United States and therefore a good prospect state for such a troop increase.[58] With regard to Sweden and South Africa, the group, however, concluded that no new démarches should be undertaken "because of political considerations."[59] Next, the viability of troop contributions from other world regions was assessed. The deputy assistant secretary of state for near eastern affairs, Burton Y. Berry, stated that there was practically no chance of securing any voluntary contributions of military forces to the Korean campaign from Middle Eastern states. Only serious "pump priming" (that is, side payments) would bring further contributions.[60] He mentioned, for instance, that U.S. diplomatic channels had reported that Turkey "was requesting a direct security commitment from the United States and 100 million dollars to balance its budget" in exchange for troops contributions.[61] The Turkish prime minister had handed an *aide-mémoire* to U.S. assistant secretary for near eastern, south Asian, and African affairs George C. McGhee already in August 1950 that included an urgent plea to include Turkey in NATO.[62] Again in September 1950, the Turkish ambassador to the United States raised the same issue with Berry, and even the Turkish president himself mentioned to the U.S. ambassador to Turkey that Turkey wished to join the Atlantic Pact.[63] The possibility of contributions from Ethiopia, Iran, Iraq, Israel, India, and Pakistan was considered last. Quickly, however, the panel concluded again that "political considerations" made it highly improbable that any further assistance would be offered by these countries.[64] The session concluded with the agreement that "the appropriate bureaus of the Department of State should, as soon as possible, take action in accordance with the consensus of view of the meeting in hope that some additional forces could be provided in early spring."[65]

On February 16, 1950, three days after the interagency meeting, Acheson followed up with Marshall, summarizing the results of the latter meeting and adding his own personal assessment. In particular, he suggested to Marshall to refrain from pressing Turkey for further troop contributions. Acheson was indeed very skeptical of a Turkish accession to NATO, and he did not want such a quid pro quo to happen. He concluded his note rather dimly, suggesting that "there are no worthwhile prospects [for troop contributions] except those discussed above."[66]

Similar discussions between State and Defense on which countries to approach for troop contributions and how to structure the negotiations continued throughout 1951. Each one of them was based on information both State and Defense systematically collected via their respective diplomatic channels around the world. In April of that year, Dean Acheson, for instance, provided the Pentagon with an update on the "extensive bilateral negotiations the [State] Department has been conducting in recent weeks" to obtain troop contributions for Korea. With regard to Latin America, he mentioned that "advantage was taken recently of the presence [in Washington, D.C.] of the Foreign Ministers of the Latin American Republics to bring the pressing need for additional ground forces in Korea directly to the attention of those Latin American states most likely to be able to contribute." With regard to Turkey, Acheson remarked that the State Department was "making arrangements to assist in financing and expansion of the Turkish military establishment, in order to augment the size of the country's forces and to strengthen their fighting capabilities." Nevertheless, he again cautioned the Pentagon against pushing Turkey too hard. "The Turkish insistent demand for a full-fledged United States security commitment," he advised, made it "inadvisable at this time to solicit additional Turkish troops for Korea." He also recommended that Greece not be further approached for troop contributions given the exceedingly lofty Greek demands for financial aid. He also warned that Iran could not "divert any armed strength from its own needs." Lastly, he concluded that "Israel and the Arab States are [also] unlikely sources, in view of the modest military establishments maintained and the existing tension in the area. Pakistan would not favor withdrawal of any of its forces from the country until the Kashmir issue is settled and relations with India enter a more cordial phase."[67]

By the summer of 1951, the situation had grown so desperate in Korea, that the Pentagon reversed its initial stance on NATO countries. As a result, Acheson used the NATO Ottawa talks and the post-Ottawa talks in Washington to ask NATO allies for troop contributions.[68] Both summits were converted into coalition negotiation venues. Although NATO was not involved in the Korean War, Acheson used these international gatherings to approach his foreign counterparts and make face-to-face appeals for troop contributions. Diplomatic embeddedness thus provided another critical resource in addition to information: interpersonal interactions of leaders at the sidelines of regularly scheduled multilateral meetings. By then both State and Defense had agreed that Turkey should be further courted for troop contributions and that the U.S. should seriously consider including Turkey in NATO in exchange for its solid commitment in Korea.[69] Moreover, State Department officials again started consulting each other as to what role the UN could have in searching for coalition participants. The key question raised was whether it would make sense to ask the UN secretary-general to make another official appeal in his name for troop contributions to the Korean War coalition. The acting U.S. ambassador to the United Nations, Ernest Gross, opined in this regard on June 6, 1951, that an

> appeal by [the secretary-general] would not generally be regarded . . . as a step promising much result. Not much fruit dropped when he shook the tree last time. . . . However, an appeal by the [secretary-general], might be excellent *prelude* . . . we might then confidentially explore with selected members . . . only if they seemed to hold promise in light of diplomatic exploration. . . . Diplomatic groundwork could be laid bilaterally with . . . members and this in itself would constitute a continuing pressure point.[70]

Gross's memo indeed illustrates in detail U.S. techniques to deliberately exploit diplomatic embeddedness for recruitment purposes. It also illustrates how such techniques had turned into a systematic practice over the course of 1950 and 1951: "to confidentially explore [troop contributions] with selected members" instead of making wide, impersonal appeals as U.S. diplomats had initially done when the war erupted; and to do "diplomatic groundwork" (that is, deliberately collect information) to assess whether states "hold promise" for detailed coalition negotiations rather than approach states randomly.

Acheson responded on June 19, 1951, to the memo recommending that the secretary-general should be asked to make a public request. He was hoping that "such public request will act as [a] catalyst in bringing to fruition [a] number of bilateral negotiations."[71] Gross confirmed on June 22, 1951, that the appeal had gone forward alongside the initiation of bilateral consultations with thirty-nine countries.[72] Acheson approved: "Continuation [of the] bilateral approach greatly preferable to full discussion . . . US [should] stress informally. . . [the] need for additional troops. [The State Department] is indicating . . . details [for] various bilateral [negotiations] and selected [UN delegations] which [we should] approach informally."[73] Acheson thus further confirmed the key dynamics at play: the coalition-building process for the Korean War was deeply structured: (1) via diplomatic channels, U.S. officials accessed information on deployment preferences (as in "state department is indicating details for negotiations") of potential participants; (2) IO officials, such as UN secretary-general Lie were perceived as useful cooperation brokers—transmitting information from UN members to the U.S. and acting as a "catalyst" or "prelude" for bilateral coalition negotiations; and (3) coalition negotiations benefited from informality (that is, negotiations take place on the sidelines of official events often exploiting personal sympathies and affection).

Individual Countries' Bargaining Outcomes

This section looks at five individual instances of coalition negotiations. It assesses the negotiations of the three largest coalition contributors after the United States and South Korea (the U.K., Canada, and Turkey) as well as two cases that diverge in terms of diplomatic embeddedness with the United States: the Philippines (deeply embedded with the United States) and South Africa (weakly embedded with the United States). Overall, the objective of this section is to assess whether diplomatic embeddedness influenced the negotiation process in these five instances and if so, how? Moreover, in what ways did preference convergence and power asymmetries affect the negotiation outcomes?

The United Kingdom

The United Kingdom contributed over 14,000 ground troops to the Korean War coalition. The British deployment can, however, hardly be considered a self-motivated act. Rather, it resulted from intense U.S. prodding. Great Britain ranked second in terms of U.S. diplomatic embeddedness in 1950 (only topped by Canada, as we shall see), and it was these networks that the U.S. exploited to cajole Great Britain to participate in the Korean War in the size and shape the U.S. desired.

British intrinsic preferences with regard to the Korean War can be roughly summarized as follows: Great Britain supported the general notion of resisting communist aggression. The British government considered it plausible that the Soviet Union had a hand in the North Korean aggression.[74] Thus, the invasion could not be ignored. Nevertheless, the government of British prime minister Clement Attlee doubted that the Soviets were willing to embark on a general war.[75] It was more likely that the Soviets plotted to bog down the Western powers in Asia to distract them from Europe.[76] A British Foreign Office memorandum drafted on June 25, 1950, the day of the North Korean invasion, summarized this position as follows: Great Britain shares "to a slight extent the American interest in the retention of a non-Communist foothold in the N.E. Asian mainland opposite to Japan, now that China had fallen to the Communists"—nevertheless, such action was not a British government priority.[77] Because of these intrinsic preferences, Attlee welcomed U.S. initiatives in the United Nations on June 25 and June 27.[78] Moreover, Great Britain put the British Pacific fleet under American command within forty-eight hours[79]—a move that British officials called "symbolic support."[80] Yet, the U.S. government quickly signaled to Attlee that such support was not enough.[81] Instead, the U.S. expected Great Britain to contribute ground troops.[82]

It took the Attlee government until July 25, 1950 (roughly one month) to heed this request. The final decision was the result of exhaustive U.S. diplomatic maneuvering. The key diplomatic relationship that was eventually able to tip the balance in favor of a British ground deployment to Korea was the very close relationship U.S. secretary of state Dean Acheson had established with Sir Oliver Franks, the British ambassador in Washington. Acheson's appointment books attest to this. Acheson held more meetings with Franks than with all other foreign ambassadors in Washington, D.C., combined.[83] Acheson recalls in his memoirs:

> Franks [was] one of the most able—and also most delightful—men it has ever been my good fortune to know and work with. I [first] met him [during World War II, when he was] planning supplies for UNRRA's relief work.... [Once he had become British ambassador in Washington D.C.], I made him an unorthodox proposal.... I suggested that we talk regularly, and in complete personal confidence, about any international problem we saw arising. Neither would report or quote the other unless, thinking that it would be useful in promoting action, he got the other's consent and agreement.... We discussed situations already emerging or likely to do so, the attitudes that various people in both countries would be likely to take, what courses of action were possible and their merits, the chief problems that could arise.[84]

Did diplomatic embeddedness play a role in establishing such tight friendship? Maybe a little bit: Acheson met Franks at the United Nations Relief and Rehabilitation Administration (UNRRA), an international organization both the U.S. and the U.K. were members of.[85]

Initially, the bond between Acheson and Franks could not move the Attlee government in favor of a ground deployment to Korea. Especially the British military was staunchly opposed to such a deployment, arguing that the British government had no troops and no money for such an endeavor.[86] British forces were involved in a counterinsurgency struggle in Malaya and had to protect Hong Kong from a newly communist China.[87] The British Defense Committee thus officially rejected on July 5, 1950, a possible ground deployment to Korea—a motion that was fully supported by the Attlee Cabinet.

Given such overwhelming opposition, the Attlee government looked for a different way to solve the Korean crisis—a way that would not involve a British ground deployment to Korea. On July 6, 1950, Sir David Kelly, the British ambassador to Moscow, approached the Soviet deputy foreign minister, Andrei Gromyko, in Moscow with the intention to learn under what conditions the Soviet Union might be willing to influence the North Korean leadership to stop the fighting. What Kelly gathered was that the Soviet Union was inclined to engage in a potential peace deal if in exchange the Western powers were willing to discuss the entry of communist China into the UN and the future of Formosa (Taiwan).[88] Attlee and his foreign secretary, Ernest Bevin, considered this Soviet proposal a viable option to bring peace to the Korean peninsula and immediately informed Dean Acheson. Acheson, however, profoundly disliked the British initiative and firmly rejected the proposal.[89] To make his position crystal clear, Acheson even went as far as to send the U.S. ambassador in London, Lewis Douglas, to visit Bevin in a London hospital (where he was recovering from surgery) on July 11, 1950, to tell him that any types of "peace initiatives" had to stop immediately. Douglas also threatened Bevin that if U.S. wishes were not heeded, the "possible consequences on the relationship between [the U.K. and the U.S.] might be very serious indeed."[90] Bevin was deeply shocked by this brutal rebuttal.[91] Bevin thus ordered that the "peace talks" with the Soviets be stopped. Moreover, he tasked Ambassador Franks in Washington, D.C., with mending the situation and sent a remorseful telegram to Acheson.[92]

Ambassador Franks was deeply in favor of a British ground deployment to Korea. It is unclear whether this conviction stemmed from his own reading of the situation or whether he wanted to please the United States, thereby reinforcing his status with the Truman administration and especially with Acheson. Either way, Ambassador Franks sensed that Bevin's desire to seek "U.S. forgiveness" represented an opening to revisit the question of a British ground deployment to Korea. Franks thus sent a handwritten note to Attlee on July 15, 1950. In this note, he highlighted that a ground deployment to Korea was intimately tied to the future of the U.K.-U.S. relationship. He argued that the United States was testing "the quality of the [U.K.-U.S.] partnership by our attitude to the notion of a token ground force."[93] Five days later, he sent another note. In it, he summarized high-level U.K.-U.S. talks that he had chaired in Washington over the previous days.[94] He mentioned that U.S. officials had used these talks to urge their British counterparts once more to send ground forces to Korea.[95] It had been the principal interest of the Americans in meeting the British.[96] To emphasize the urgency of the call, he reiterated that "there was no doubt . . . that what was said to us [about Korea] had been carefully thought out beforehand and had the highest authority."[97]

In response to the second message, the British Foreign Office asked Franks to assess in precise detail the reaction of the U.S. government and the U.S. public if Britain did opt to provide troops. Would Great Britain substantially benefit from such a move? Could it strengthen its hand with the U.S. administration?[98] Franks's response was one of the most trenchant messages he sent as British Ambassador in Washington, D.C.[99] He pointed out that the United States saw in a British deployment a catalyst for other countries to join, most notably other Commonwealth nations. Countries such as Canada and Australia had signaled to the United States that they would be willing to deploy to Korea but only as a Commonwealth Division under British leadership.[100] That is why the U.S. administration was so insistent on a British deployment because it would trigger the commitment of other nations. Moreover, he argued that

> the reaction of the United States administration to a negative decision by us [would be] deep and prolonged. I am not thinking primarily of the effects which it would have on relatively short term matters however important, such as additional appropriations for European defence and the third appropriation of the ERP [European Recovery Programme]. The important consideration is the effect our decision will have on the basic relationship of the two countries. I believe that because of the rational and irrational elements in the American mind about this for them unparalleled undertaking to act as a policeman in the world, a negative decision would seriously impair the long term relationship.[101]

Franks's cables impacted Attlee's thinking. Attlee knew of Franks's exceptionally close relationship with Acheson. Therefore, Attlee recognized that Franks was not just speculating but rather describing accurately a topic he understood well. This was a serious matter: the U.K. could not expect special collaboration with the United States to continue if the British would not deliver on ground troops.[102] Attlee thus arranged for another British Defense Committee meeting on July 23, 1950—this time under his own chairmanship. At the meeting, Sir William Slim, chief of the Imperial General Staff, spoke by pre-arrangement on behalf of his colleagues: "Although in their view it was still militarily unsound, they recognized that strong political arguments" to deploy ground forces to Korea existed.[103] The Committee then agreed to send a brigade to Korea. The decision was confirmed by the Cabinet on July 25, 1950.[104] The U.S. government thus had exploited diplomatic embeddedness with Great Britain to get ground troops: most importantly, the threat that the bilateral relationship would suffer gained greatly in credibility because of the depth of the relationship between Franks and Acheson. Would the same threat have worked without the existing personal networks in place? The Vietnam War, which Great Britain refused to join, represents an ideal case in point. Scholars have argued that British domestic opposition required the government of Prime Minister Harold Wilson to reject U.S. president Lyndon B. Johnson's repeated requests for ground troops.[105] Similar opposition, however, also existed to the Korean War (and, more recently, to the Iraq War). In both instances, U.K. prime ministers were able to devise political strategies to overcome such opposition (or at least abate it) in the name of "the special relationship." Why did this not happen in the Vietnam War? While a detailed analysis of the question exceeds the scope of this chapter, the absence of a comparable relationship to the one between Acheson and Franks certainly mattered. Relations between the Prime Minister Wilson and Johnson were fraught. Johnson profoundly distrusted Wilson and vice versa. Information did not flow freely between two leaders.[106] In July and August 1965, the Johnson administration discussed the possibility of coercing Great Britain to join the Vietnam War by linking U.S. financial help to a British troop commitment in Vietnam[107]—a threat similar to the threat made during the Korean War. In the end, however, Johnson vetoed such action. Johnson was terrified that Wilson might leak the coercive attempt to the media, thus further exposing America's precarious situation in Vietnam.[108] During the Korean War, Acheson had at no point feared such a scenario. The close relationship between Acheson and Franks had assured the Americans that Great Britain would keep quiet. The comparison thus illustrates that even negative linkage attempts require the exploitation of diplomatic embeddedness as a lubricant to assure effectiveness.

Canada

Canada's decision to send over 6,000 ground troops to Korea can also not be fully understood without U.S. diplomatic maneuvering. Canada ranked first in terms of U.S. diplomatic embeddedness in 1950. The U.S. government used this multitude of ties to influence Canada's deployment decision. Canada first got introduced to the Korean conflict in the fall of 1947 when the United States asked Canada to serve on the United Nations Temporary Commission on Korea (UNTCOK)—a UN commission created to supervise elections on the Korean peninsula. Prior to that request, "for most of the [Canadian] cabinet, Korea was an obscure place on the western side of the Pacific . . . best known because the people were known to wear strange hats."[109] The U.S. request to serve in UNTCOK triggered a startling Canadian cabinet crisis that fell just short of shattering the government of Canadian prime minister Mackenzie King.[110] King himself was UNTCOK's staunchest opponent. He feared that the mission would entangle Canada in dangerous foreign situations.[111] Canada would be blamed for future events in Korea and for any Soviet responses.[112] However, after complex U.S.-Canadian negotiations, Canada did serve in UNTCOK.[113] When the North Korean aggression occurred on June 25, 1950, Canada thus did not look at Korea as a complete novice. Rather, it lauded the U.S. dispatch of troops and supported all three UN resolutions on Korea. Nevertheless, with regard to another active military involvement in Korea, the Canadian government was again very cautious. Indeed, its intrinsic preferences with regard to a ground deployment to Korea can be summarized as follows: First, Canada deeply cared about the UN.[114] It was worried that the UN could suffer the same fate as the League of Nations if the Korean invasion was ignored by the international community (that is, if the principle of collective security was not upheld).[115] Second, Canada shared some of the Cold War concerns of the U.S. government, though not to the same degree. Most importantly, most senior officials in the Canadian government were convinced that the main strategic front in the Cold War was Europe. Korea merely "comprised a peripheral engagement which must not be allowed to drain Canada's strength from more important theaters."[116] Third, Canada cared about U.S.-Canadian relations. Canada's initial refusal to serve in UNTCOK in 1947 had illustrated to Canadian officials what it meant to be perceived by Washington as a disloyal friend.[117] Based on these preferences, Canada decided to volunteer three destroyers to join the United States in its Korean expedition.

The U.S. government quickly signaled to Canada that these three destroyers were, however, not enough.[118] From a U.S. point of view, they constituted a mere token force. When Canada refused to change its mind, the U.S. government started a relentless campaign to pressure Canada to send ground troops. Escott Reid, the deputy under-secretary for external affairs, recalls that in July 1950, U.S. pressure was "intolerable—the worst arm-twisting I ever saw."[119] Foreign Minister Lester B. Pearson also felt the heat. He tersely informed Dean Acheson that "we [are] giving earnest consideration in Ottawa to these matters [of ground troops] but . . . we [do not] like to be needled about them from Washington."[120]

The U.S. "needling" campaign had various components, all of which made use of diplomatic embeddedness. The first component of the campaign focused on Canada's sensibilities with regard to the UN. Many U.S. diplomats had witnessed Canadian foreign minister Pearson's active engagement at the UN conference in San Francisco and even in the preparatory phase prior to the conference.[121] They were therefore fully aware of his personal attachment to the institution.[122] They knew that he did not want to let the UN down. As a result, the U.S. government used UN secretary-general Lie to plead with Canada to provide ground forces. The incident unfolded in the following way: On the evening of July 13, 1950, U.S. ambassador to the UN Warren Austin read to Lie an oral communication from the U.S. government requesting him to communicate an urgent request to Canada to provide ground troops for Korea.[123] Ambassador Austin specifically asked that the appeal had to come from Lie alone (that is, Lie was not allowed to mention U.S. involvement).[124] U.S. government officials felt that an appeal from Lie could be less easily refused by Pearson, who deeply cared about the UN. What made Lie's appeal all the more potent was its publicity.[125] A request from Lie required a public reply from the Canadian government to the United Nations, which would—if negative—openly contradict Pearson's prior enthusiastic support for the UN and its staunch support for the principle of collective security.[126] U.S. action can therefore be seen as carefully crafted to entrap Pearson in his own pro-UN rhetoric.[127]

The second component of the U.S. cajoling strategy focused on Canadian fears of being the only isolated international actor that did not contribute to Korea. On that account, the United States deliberately fed Canada information that other countries were sending forces in great numbers. The U.S. government even used false information to do so, such as telling the Canadians that Pakistan intended to send ground forces to Korea knowing full well that this was untruthful.[128]

Finally, and arguably most importantly, the U.S. government worked tirelessly to construct a Commonwealth Division, as stated previously.[129] Why did this matter for Canada? Well, when U.S. pressure mounted, the Canadian government found itself in a bind. Deep political frictions emerged.[130] The matter of sending ground troops to Korea was discussed in five Canadian cabinet meetings between July 19 and August 7.[131] At the request of the Cabinet, Canada's military leadership developed possible ground force deployment options. The military's baseline was that Canada could not easily spare any ground troops.[132] Nevertheless, if a ground deployment was an absolute necessity, the Canadian government had to decide between two scenarios: first, sending an independent brigade, which, however, "would take almost every trained infantry solider in the Army"[133] to Korea or, second, sending Canadian forces within the context of a Commonwealth Division. The second option would allow Canada to make use of British supply lines, allowing for a minimal logistical tail.[134] The military leadership made it abundantly clear that it was overwhelmingly in favor of the second option.[135] Thus, the existence of a Commonwealth Division became Canada's implicit political condition (and justificatory narrative) on whether it would send ground troops to Korea; unless there was a Commonwealth Division, Canada could not deploy any ground forces.

Via diplomatic channels, U.S. government officials quickly learned about this new Canadian attitude. They then tried to move heaven and earth to make such a Commonwealth force a reality.[136] Their efforts were marked with success on July 25, when Great Britain officially decided to lead such a division (see above). The British announcement was quickly followed by Australia and New Zealand. Once the Commonwealth Division was a reality, Canada felt that it had to follow up on its promise. It had to act unless it was willing to risk ridicule and severe damage to the U.S.-Canadian relationship. Interestingly, by then Great Britain was also intensively lobbying Canada to participate.[137]

On July 29, Foreign Minister Pearson flew to Washington to declare Canada's willingness to deploy to Korea.[138] Canada's stance on a ground deployment to Korea, however, remained unenthusiastic. In late October 1950, the Canadian cabinet was again discussing the possibility of canceling the deployment and sending most of Canada's force to Western Europe instead of Korea.[139]

What mechanism then best explains Canada's ground troop commitment to Korea? U.S. pressure no doubt played the key role. Nevertheless, in contrast to the U.K. above, the pressure was subtler: there were no threats to the "complete demise" of the relationship. Rather, U.S. diplomats used bilateral and multilateral networks to exploit Pearson's ideological weak spots, notably his desire to support the UN. They also entrapped Canada in its promise to deploy to Korea if a Commonwealth Division was to be created. Given the multitude of ties, the United States was also able to multiply pressure points: it was able to "needle" many important figures in Canadian politics (even using false information) to gain its way.

Similar to the U.K., Canada also avoided entering the Vietnam War. What went differently in the Canadian case roughly fifteen years later? In contrast to the Truman government, the Johnson government never made an effort to woo Canada to serve in the coalition.[140] Johnson himself had determined that Pearson, who was then prime minister, was unlikely to ever oblige—especially after Pearson's public rebuke of U.S. Vietnam policy at Temple University in April 1965.[141] For the Vietnam War, U.S.-Canadian embeddedness was thus never instrumentalized: there was no needling and no deliberate entrapment.

Turkey

Turkey sent over 5,000 troops to Korea. Turkey ranked forty-third in terms of diplomatic embeddedness with the United States in 1950. According to the theory presented in chapter 2, Turkey was thus an unlikely candidate to deploy to Korea. What explains this discrepancy? In contrast to the U.K. and Canada, Turkey actually volunteered to join the Korean War coalition. It was a "self-starter." By offering to serve in the Korean War, Turkey wanted to gain membership in NATO.[142] NATO had come into being in April 1949 as an alliance exclusively restricted to Western European states. Turkey, especially in the eyes of the Truman administration, was a Middle Eastern country, and U.S. interests in that region of the world were minimal.[143] The United States thus denied the Turkish request when it first applied for admission in May 1950.[144] Turkey then started a relentless diplomatic campaign to reverse the rejection, culminating in its decision to join the Korean War coalition with full force. The head of Turkey's Nation Party, Hikmet Bayur, expressed this strategy as follows: "if sending troops will result in [acceptance into NATO], the sacrifice that is being made is justified."[145]

The Turkish wager received immediate public support from U.S. Senator Harry P. Cain, who replied to a question asked at a news conference in Ankara on July 25, 1950, as follows: "I can say we are going to be much more sympathetic in helping those who helped most in Korea."[146] Nevertheless, all other key U.S.

actors were initially only willing to offer Turkey associate membership of the alliance in exchange for the Korean War contribution.[147] The Joint Chiefs of Staff, in particular, favored such an outcome, believing that "the inclusion of Turkey . . . as full members in the North Atlantic Treaty Organization might adversely affect the progress which is now evident in North Atlantic Treaty arrangements."[148] Nevertheless, by mid-1951 many Truman administration officials had changed their mind. One of the reasons was certainly Turkey's remarkable performance in the Korean War. Turkey fought tooth and nail in Korea. Between November 26 and December 1, 1950, the Turkish brigade had lost almost 20 percent of its force. This enormous sacrifice did not go unnoticed; European and U.S. media were full of praise. *The Chicago Tribune* proclaimed, "The Turks are our best allies!" And even the Soviet TASS Agency remarked: "This time, it was the Turks who saved" the United States.[149] Turkey was no longer considered a burden but rather a potential asset for the NATO alliance.[150] In September 1951, the NATO Council of Ministers unanimously agreed that Turkey (along with Greece) should become full members of NATO.[151]

The Philippines

In 1950, the Philippines were deeply diplomatically embedded with the United States, ranking sixteenth globally—and among the highest non-Western states. The Philippines also agreed to send almost 1,500 troops to Korea. Can these two facts be linked? It is safe to say that Philippine intrinsic interests in the Korean War were minimal. Other political subjects kept the Philippine government awake at night, most notably the fact that the Philippines were at the brink of national bankruptcy. Throughout 1950, the Philippine government had appealed to the United States—its colonial ruler until 1946—to come to its rescue. Nevertheless, the Truman government had been reluctant to grant such aid, particularly because it viewed the Philippine government led by Elpidio Quirino as inefficient and corrupt. After the outbreak of the Korean War and the lack of coalition contributions, the Truman administration revisited this attitude. The U.S. government had trained the Philippine military for decades. It trusted that the Philippines could make a valuable contribution to the Korean War. For this contribution it was willing to reward the Philippine government. Under the leadership of Daniel Bell, the U.S. government thus sent an economic mission to Manila to assess the degree of the economic crisis. The Bell survey became intimately intertwined with negotiations over a Philippine deployment to Korea. Most importantly, the Philippine agreement to send troops to Korea was used in Washington to help silence critics in the American press and in U.S. Congress of a possible American aid package for the Philippines.[152] An argument was spun that if the United States did not provide the Philippines with massive budget support, it could not finance its deployment to Korea.[153] In the end, the U.S. government offered the Philippines a financial bailout package of roughly $250 million[154] in addition to bankrolling the entire Philippine deployment to Korea. The latter amounted to an additional $48 million in U.S. support.[155] Without diplomatic embeddedness between the United States and the Philippines, such a deal would not have occurred. The Philippines would not have volunteered to serve in Korea (certainly not under the dire economic circumstances it was in), and the United States would not have agreed to provide a massive financial bailout. Rather, decades of close cooperation during U.S. occupation from 1898 to 1946 had led to a social-diplomatic environment (including feelings of responsibility and affection) that made this deal a possibility.

South Africa

In 1950, South Africa ranked forty-second in terms of diplomatic embeddedness with the United States—a low score. Expectations would thus predict that other factors besides diplomatic networks motivated South Africa to join the Korea War. And this is indeed the case: similar to Turkey, South Africa was a "self-starter." What makes the South African case distinct is the degree to which the South African government was able to push its own agenda: despite its "subordinate" power position to the United States, it was able to control coalition negotiations.

The South African government first heard of the U.S. call for contributions to the Korea War in July 1950. South African prime minister D. F. Malan initially did not pay much attention: Korea was far away, certainly outside of South Africa's sphere of security interests.[156] Moreover, Malan, a right-wing Nationalist Afrikaner, considered the growing discontent of the disenfranchised black majority in South Africa the principal security threat faced by his country—and not communists in Korea. He had just embarked on implementing a set of racial policies, which would soon to become known as apartheid.[157] Nevertheless, a few members in Malan's cabinet viewed the issue differently. Many of them were still deeply scarred by the Anglo-Boer War. Consequently, they were eager to exit the British sphere of influence and become closer to the United States.[158] Moreover, many of them believed that the United States would best be able to protect South Africa from the rapidly rising tide of anti–South African sentiment and the slowly forming communist movements sweeping across the African continent. A South African deployment to Korea could hence be used to further South African interests: South Africa could gain a valuable quid pro quo from the United States. What they wanted from the United States, in concrete terms, was free (or heavily subsidized) U.S. military hardware (especially military aircraft), U.S. military training, and, if possible, a regional security pact similar to NATO.[159] Thus far, the Truman government had refused to agree to these requests.[160] On his first trip to Washington, D.C., in August 1949, the South African defense minister, F. C. Erasmus, was, for instance, told by U.S. secretary of defense Louis Johnson that South Africa was not a strategic priority for the United States.[161]

With this recent setback still on his mind, Erasmus now took the lead in constructing a possible deal: what if South Africa traded its participation in Korea for new U.S. military aircraft? To get U.S. approval, it would probably be best to send an air squadron to Korea. Only 20 percent of South Africa's aircraft were serviceable at the time.[162] Thus, if the United States wanted South Africa to join the coalition, it had to provide South Africa with aircraft, which, ideally, South Africa could then keep after the war—or buy cheaply. In addition, a South African deployment to Korea would create goodwill in the United States and thus lead to further U.S. military goodies. Erasmus managed to convince his fellow cabinet members of the viability of this plan, and South Africa officially announced its contribution to the Korean War effort on August 4, 1950.[163]

In early October 1950, Erasmus made a return visit to Washington, D.C., in an attempt to collect the benefits he anticipated gaining in exchange for South African participation in the Korean War. He met with Dean Acheson and George Marshall.[164] Nevertheless, Erasmus was rebuffed once again. Acheson remained noncommittal. Marshall, in turn, told Erasmus that if South Africa wanted any U.S. military equipment, including aircraft, it had to pay the regular price for it.[165] Erasmus was furious. He ordered the South African ambassador in Washington, Gerhardus Petrus Jooste, to draft a letter requesting that the Americans extend "the least onerous financial terms" for the equipment.[166] Moreover, he informed Prime Minister Malan of the U.S. refusal to help South Africa.[167]

In mid-October 1950, China crossed the Yalu river and entered the Korean War, and by early January 1951 the Chinese had pushed the coalition forces all the way back to Seoul. The Korean military catastrophe led to an enhanced U.S. push for contributions to the war effort.[168] By mid-1951, the recruitment situation was so desperate that the United States began to implore states to join the war effort; very little substitutability of troop contingents existed.[169] South African defense minister Erasmus quickly realized that U.S. recruitment needs represented a strategic opportunity for South Africa to finally get the planes he desired—and this time around, he would not beg and beseech the Americans. Rather, he would threaten them. In September 1951, he thus instructed Ambassador Jooste to send a warning to Washington: if the United States would not provide new military aircraft to South Africa by the first quarter of 1952, South Africa would withdraw its troops from Korea—and thus further weaken the U.S. position on the peninsula.[170] In response to the threat, the U.S. government agreed to conclude a sale of military equipment, for internal use, with South Africa.[171] Still, the issue of U.S. military aircraft was left outstanding. Thus, in early 1952 Erasmus took further action. On February 11, 1952, he once more instructed Ambassador Jooste to write an explicit letter to Acheson announcing that South Africa would ground its air squadron in Korea for three months.[172] A letter from Prime Minister Malan followed quickly thereafter, stating that South Africa would reconsider the decision of withdrawing its Korean contingent only if it was given "definite assurance of receiving jets within six months."[173]

These drastic actions had an effect on the Truman administration, especially on Acheson and his colleagues at the State Department. Acheson saw no alternative to the South African air squadron. Moreover, he feared that the grounding of the South African squadron was likely to have important spillover effects. In particular, it might very well start a "chain reaction [in the] reduction [of] forces [of] other countries [in] Korea with attendant weakening of UN position and encouragement [of the] enemy."[174] As a result, the State Department used its influence to sway the Pentagon to provide South Africa with the aircraft it so desired. On February 18, the day the Malan letter was received, the assistant secretary of state for international organization affairs, John D. Hickerson, wrote to the secretary of defense, Robert A. Lovett, that "the [State] Department is concerned over the possible repercussions of the South African action on the United Nations diplomatic and military position in Korea. . . . In this connection, the [State] Department requests the Department of Defense again to review the problem of equipping the South African squadron with jet aircraft."[175] The Pentagon's response was a promise to review the South African request in three months.[176] In September 1952, Dean Acheson officially confirmed that the aircraft would arrive soon.[177] The sale was finalized in October 1952.[178] The aircraft acquisition terms were extremely favorable; aircraft that usually retailed at $58,000 each were acquired by South Africa for a mere $5,447 each.[179] Acheson is on record as having been very relieved when he was able to persuade the South Africans to keep their squadron flying.[180]

Once the deal over military hardware was settled, the Malan government made an additional request of the Americans in October 1952. It sought U.S. influence to avoid acrimonious UN debates on apartheid and to defeat any UN resolution condemning South Africa. Once more, the Nationalist Afrikaner government emphasized in its démarche that South Africa strongly supported the UN-sanctioned American military effort in Korea and therefore deserved praise at the UN rather than abuse.[181] Prior to the Korean War, the U.S. government had been openly critical of the problems of racial discrimination in South Africa. Nevertheless, in October 1952, Dean Acheson agreed with the South African demand, arguing that "in the present case there is very little that the UN can and should do vis-à-vis the policies of South Africa in terms of actual results."[182] The United States thus started to effectively protect the South African regime from international condemnation, in particular, in the United Nations.[183]

Summary of Findings

The key objective of this chapter was to illustrate how the process of multilateral military coalition building unfolded for the Korean War. My intention was to open the "black box" of diplomatic embeddedness and provide evidence for some of the benefits that diplomatic embeddedness can provide to pivotal states that want to construct military cooperation. I also tried to assess whether the diplomatic embeddedness framework presented in chapter 8 fits the empirical evidence of the Korean War coalition.

With regard to preferences, an easy conclusion can be drawn: very few countries shared the same preference intensity to intervene in Korea as the U.S. government. Rather, preferences with regard to Korea were widely diverse. Most countries around the world saw little value in containing Soviet aggression in Korea. In their eyes, the Korea War was not "their war." As a result, the United States had to actively recruit coalition participants. In this process, it served as the pivotal state. It sought out and bargained states into the coalition. The U.S. motivation to go to such great lengths in building a multilateral coalition was arguably based mostly on legitimacy concerns: the idea of "buying allies" gained steam when Soviet propaganda was able to depict the U.S. military venture as lacking international support.

Since the Korean War represented the first instance in which the UN umbrella was used to build a multilateral coalition, no formal protocols existed on how the U.S. government would cooperate with the world organization during the coalition-building process. Thus, an interesting back and forth between U.S. and UN officials ensued concluding in an official document that intended to codify how UN force generation processes would unfold from then on. The document foresaw that the

TABLE 4.1 Results of case study: Korean War

	DEEPLY EMBEDDED WITH THE UNITED STATES	WEAKLY EMBEDDED WITH THE UNITED STATES
Bandwagoneer	–	–
Self-starter	–	Turkey
		South Africa
Coalition recruit	United Kingdom	–
	Canada	
	Philippines	

UN would serve as a "post office": its main task would be to transmit information on deployment preferences of UN member states to the United States. The United States would then be in charge of all other recruitment tasks. This document offers an interesting glimpse into how the search process for coalition contributions was theoretically conceived by the United States from the beginning. From the U.S. perspective, information on deployment preferences was a key factor in determining potential coalition participants, and U.S. officials quickly realized that the UN could come in handy in this regard: people such as UN secretary-general Lie were well placed to sound out countries' interests in the Korean War. Lie thus served as a cooperation broker. His idea was to provide information and serve as a prelude to or catalyst for bilateral U.S.-UN deployment negotiations. For all other aspects of the recruitment process, the United States preferred to be fully in charge, considerably limiting the role of the UN. A prelude to or catalyst for bilateral U.S.-led deployment negotiations.

Overall, there can be no doubt that the U.S.-led search process for coalition contributions made deliberate use of diplomatic embeddedness. Initial attempts to recruit military forces were based on military-strategic calculations. Nevertheless, meager initial results forced the Truman administration to reconsider its recruitment strategy. By August 1950, U.S. officials had instrumentalized U.S. diplomatic networks for recruitment purposes. By January 1951, the Defense Department was also part of the process. Together, State and Defense established very specific lists of countries to be approached for force contributions—"prospect lists." Countries were pre-selected based on what they could bring to the table—though that ultimately mattered the least. Rather, officials focused on intrinsic motivations and possible external incentives. To determine both, U.S. officials made a purposeful attempt to gather information from their local embassies and other networks on deployment preferences. In other words, prospect lists were the result of exploiting diplomatic embeddedness: via diplomatic ties, U.S. officials were able to access private information, which they then used to assess the probability of a country deploying to Korea. Did the United States select countries for its prospect list that it found particularly vulnerable to its pressure? On certain occasions this was certainly also true. U.S. knowledge of the desolate financial situation the Philippines was experiencing made it an "easy" target for coalition appeals. Even in the case of Great Britain, the U.S. government used its superior power position to intimidate the Attlee government.

With regard to the individual coalition negotiations, the U.K., Canada, and the Philippines can be considered "coalition recruits"—they were approached by the United States to join the war. Turkey and South Africa, on the other hand, were "self-starters"—they self-initiated negotiations with the Truman government.

In the British case, the U.S. government engaged in a relentless campaign to cajole Great Britain into contributing ground troops to Korea. The themes used to convince the Attlee government to join the Korean enterprise were exquisitely adapted to British concerns, notably the British desire to maintain a close U.K.-U.S. "special relationship." Via British Ambassador Franks, Dean Acheson was able to credibly communicate that U.K.-U.S. relations were in real jeopardy if no ground deployment was forthcoming. This was a coercive threat. It exploited British asymmetrical dependencies on the United States. Still, without exploiting the close relationship between Acheson and Franks, such a threat would arguably have been less effective. Why? The close relationship assured the Americans that the coercion attempt would not be leaked to the media by the British, thus exposing the difficulties the United States was facing in recruiting forces for Korea. Similar assurances did not exist during the Vietnam War mostly due to the lack of a trusting relationship between President Johnson and U.K. prime minister Wilson.

In the Canadian context, the U.S. government gathered information via diplomatic networks on Canadian sensitivities with regard to (1) the survival of the UN; (2) Canada's potential political isolation if it did not contribute troops; and (3) Canada's promise to contribute forces if a Commonwealth Division was to deploy. Canada was thus not "bought" to participate in the Korean War. Rather, U.S. diplomats were able to entrap Canada in its own discourse, preferences, and sensibilities. Moreover, the United States "needled" Canada persistently, targeting the Canadian elite across the political spectrum. Without extensive preexisting networks, such a widespread campaign would have been unthinkable, and without using such techniques, it is highly unlikely that Canada would have committed such a large number of ground troops to Korea. Diplomatic embeddedness thus undoubtedly played a critical role in the Canadian deployment decision. In the Philippine case, diplomatic embeddedness made the quid pro quo possible: the United States targeted the Philippines, its former colony, as a coalition participant because it had extensive contacts in the country. The United States had over decades trained the Philippine army. The preexisting ties provided trust and opportunities to construct and justify an issue linkage (e.g., the financial bailout).

The deployment decisions of Turkey and South Africa tell, of course, a different story. Both were only weakly diplomatically embedded with the United States and—as expected—diplomatic embeddedness played a minimal role in both instances. Rather, both volunteered to join the Korean War coalition in exchange for a specific quid pro quo with the United States. Both countries pursued very different strategies to achieve their objectives: The Turks committed fully to the war in an attempt to impress the U.S. leadership of their worthiness to become an

American ally. South Africa, instead, coerced the United States into compliance. It threatened to withdraw its forces in a critical moment to get what it thought it deserved. The South African example thus potently illustrates how much bargaining power "weaker" coalition participants can hold in coalition negotiations. South Africa knew how much the U.S. government feared its withdrawal from Korea—knowledge that considerably increased its negotiating leverage.

The accumulated evidence presented in this chapter largely rejects the "preference convergence model." So what about the "coercion model"? Did cooperation in the Korean War result from voluntary bargaining or rather from coercive threats? Table 4.1 summarizes the findings. There can be no doubt that the United States exploited its hegemonic position during the coalition-building process: Because of this position, the U.S. government was able to dominate discussions in the UN and to offer issue linkages and side payments. It was also able to use unexploited bargaining power in existing bilateral relationships (for instance, with the U.K., the Philippines, and Australia) to bring third parties on board. And yet, the U.S. government also showed an unequivocal willingness to "subsidize" coalition contributions; moreover, U.S. diplomats spoke of pump-priming rather than coercing countries into joining the war. Thus, it appears that the Truman administration understood the limits of coercion: cajoling, coaxing, and bribing states was considered more efficient than the manipulation of asymmetrical dependencies. Moreover, the case study also shows how relatively weak states (for instance, South Africa) were able to hold considerable bargaining power and thus forced the hegemon's hand and not vice versa.

SAVING DARFUR

UNAMID (2007–)

Sudan, the largest country in Africa, has been almost incessantly afflicted by civil war since its independence from the British Empire in 1956. Most of the blood was shed in a violent struggle pitting the Sudanese South against the North. Nevertheless, in February 2003, Darfur, Sudan's western region, also caught fire. Many inhabitants of Darfur felt that their region was being ignored.[1] Over the years, Darfur had suffered appalling neglect. The government in Khartoum awarded most local government posts to Arabs, although they constituted the ethnic minority in the region. Moreover, it had rarely paid for roads, schools, hospitals, civil servants, or communication facilities.[2] Many Darfuris thus concluded that, if they ever wanted to see their needs met, they would have to take up arms against the Khartoum regime and endeavor to get the world's attention.[3] The first attack against Sudanese government forces was staged by the Sudan Liberation Army (SLA) in the town of Golo on February 26, 2003. Shortly after the SLA's attack, another rebel group announced its formation: The Justice and Equality Movement (JEM). On the morning of April 25, 2003, the SLA and the JEM mounted a joint attack on the government airbase in El Fasher, destroying seven planes and killing more than seventy government soldiers.[4] The El Fasher incident shocked the Khartoum regime and prompted Sudanese president Omar Al-Bashir to orchestrate a ruthless military campaign to defeat the Darfuri insurgency[5]—indeed, one of the most brutal ethnically motivated repression campaigns witnessed in the twenty-first century. Over three hundred thousand Darfuris are estimated to have died; almost three million were displaced because of the violence.[6]

To stop the bloodshed in Darfur, the United Nations, in cooperation with the African Union, formed one of the largest and most expensive peacekeeping operations ever deployed. The operation took the name United Nations-African Union Mission in Darfur (UNAMID). The adoption of UN Security Council Resolution 1769 formally established the operation on July 31, 2007. Its maximum strength stood at 17,764 troops, 5,318 police, 313 military observers, and 1,097 international civilian personnel[7] provided by the following countries: Nigeria (3,700 military and police forces), Rwanda (3,430 forces), Egypt (2,650 forces), Ethiopia (2,400 forces), Senegal (1,330 forces), Bangladesh (1,080 forces), Tanzania (1,030 forces), Burkina Faso (970 forces), South Africa (850 forces), Thailand (832 forces), Pakistan (796 forces), Jordan (700 forces), Nepal (640 forces), Sierra Leone (400 forces), Gambia (343 forces), China (323 forces), Ghana (310 forces), Zambia (200 forces), Yemen (190 forces), Togo (150 forces), Indonesia (150 forces), Kenya (90 forces), Mongolia (70 forces), the Philippines (70 forces), Namibia (40 forces), Cameroon (35 forces), Malaysia (35 forces), Burundi (25 forces), Niger (20 forces), Jamaica (15 forces), and Fiji (12 forces) as well as token forces from the United States, Tajikistan, Mali, Germany, Malawi, Côte d'Ivoire, Madagascar, Zimbabwe, Kyrgyzstan, Guatemala, Iran, South Korea, Ecuador, Italy, Uganda, Palau, the Netherlands, and Canada.[8]

The United States initiated and orchestrated the most important political aspects that made the deployment of UNAMID possible. The United States was the key financial sponsor and broker of the successive Darfur peace agreements.[9] At the United Nations, the United States was intimately involved in the drafting and negotiation of UN resolutions pertaining to the Darfur issue and prodded various UN Security Council members to support the respective resolutions.[10] When Sudanese President Al-Bashir first rejected the deployment of a UN force to Darfur, U.S. diplomats worked tirelessly to change his mind. Most importantly, however, once UNAMID was approved by the UN Security Council, the United States was deeply involved in recruiting UNAMID participants. Some countries, such as Egypt, China, Canada, and Ethiopia had a political stake in the Darfur conflict and thus volunteered forces to deploy to Darfur. Nevertheless, the large majority of countries did not join UNAMID on their own initiative. Rather, they were wooed into the coalition by the United States. U.S. officials thereby followed specific practices to recruit these troops. Many of these practices exploited diplomatic embeddedness: U.S. officials used preexisting ties to ascertain the deployment preferences of potential recruits and constructed issue linkages and side payments. The United States was assisted in the UNAMID coalition-building process by UN staff, most notably from the UN Department of Peacekeeping Operations (UNDPKO). UNDPKO took on an important planning and brokerage role. It transmitted information on deployment preferences from UN member states to the United States, and once the United States had gained political promises from states to deploy to Darfur, UNDPKO took charge of most of the technical details of the deployment.

This chapter focuses on the deployment decisions of Nigeria, Rwanda, and Egypt, the three largest UNAMID troop-contributing countries; Germany, a deeply embedded state with the United States in 2007; and Thailand, a weakly embedded state with the United States in 2007. The deployment decision of the largest UNAMID contributor (Nigeria), in the form and shape it took, was greatly influenced by the United States. The George W. Bush government used its extensive diplomatic networks with Nigeria to lure the Olusegun Obasanjo government into the coalition. Rwanda, the second-largest UNAMID contributor, was a "self-starter." It offered its service in exchange for military aid from the United States. Egypt, the third-largest UNAMID contingent, can be considered a "bandwagoneer"—it had an intrinsic motivation to the join the mission. For Germany, which was deeply embedded with the United States, the U.S. government instrumentalized its diplomatic ties to woo Angela Merkel's government into the coalition. Finally, Thailand (which was weakly diplomatically embedded with the United States) used UNAMID to negotiate a quid pro quo: UNAMID troops for the removal of economic sanctions. It thus has to be considered another "self-starter."

Origins of U.S. Involvement in Darfur

To the surprise of many, the Darfur conflict became one of the Bush administration's top foreign policy priorities. On the campaign trail, candidate George W. Bush had shown very little interest in Sudan in particular, or even Africa more generally. In fact, he was once quoted as saying: "Africa does not fit into the national strategic interests" of the United States.[11] As a result, the Africa dossier was quickly handed over to the business wing of the Bush team. Walter H. Kansteiner III, a canny businessman who had made a fortune advising African governments on privatizations, was appointed assistant secretary of state for African affairs.[12] His nomination set the tone for the Bush administration's priorities for Africa: business opportunities and oil—the latter really being "the only American interest in Africa," as Kansteiner confided to *The Economist* in October 2002.[13] "What is going to stand between me and my strategy for Africa?" Kansteiner allegedly asked at one of the very first staff meetings of the U.S. State Department's Africa Bureau. The answer: "Sudan" and "Zimbabwe." "Any legislation concerning Africa that had to pass through Congress will be an uphill battle if Sudan is not resolved," Charles Snyder, the acting assistant secretary at the Bureau of

African Affairs at the State Department, recalls having told Kansteiner, "it might cost you a considerable amount of political capital."[14] Snyder was referring to a group of congressmen, chief among them representatives Frank Wolf, Donald Payne, and Tom Tancredo and senators Bill Frist and Sam Brownback, who were determined to do something about Sudan. Wolf, Tancredo, Frist, and Brownback represented conservative Christian evangelical constituencies, who had long been deeply troubled by the apparent persecution and enslavement of Southern Sudanese Christians by Northern Sudanese Muslims.

To please these evangelical constituencies (who were able to multiply their political leverage by collaborating with Jewish organizations,[15] African American organizations,[16] and the U.S. oil lobby),[17] the incoming George W. Bush administration decided to revive the stalled peace talks between North and South Sudan.[18] The negotiations initially made impressive progress, as Khartoum appeared willing to compromise. It was suffering under U.S. sanction policy, and in the wake of the U.S. invasion in Afghanistan in 2001, it wished to avoid being added to the Bush administration's target list.[19] One Northern Sudanese politician stated that after 9/11, "the United States looked like a wounded lion. It was very difficult for us to predict what kind of action they would take tomorrow. We had to wait and see, and watch what we said and what we did—and engage."[20]

The negotiations were indeed going so well that when the first information on the growing repression in Darfur emerged, the U.S. special envoy to Sudan, John Danforth, told the UN head of humanitarian operations, Jan Egeland, "Don't rock the boat; we're trying to finish this [the North-South peace agreement]."[21] It was indeed not until the spring of 2004 that this U.S. attitude started to change. A significant increase in violence in Darfur, compounded by the ten-year anniversary of the Rwandan genocide, arguably triggered the reversal. Within a single week, in late March/early April 2004, six articles comparing Darfur to Rwanda appeared on the editorial pages of major U.S. newspapers. As a result of this media focus, President Bush issued his first public statement condemning the atrocities in Darfur.[22] The U.S. government then began to conceive of a political solution to the crisis. It suggested that Darfur mediation efforts shift from a bilateral approach led by Chadian president Idriss Déby to one with a more prominent role for the African Union[23] and that a small "observer mission" should be deployed to Darfur, also known as the African Union Mission in Sudan (AMIS).[24] By October 2004, as U.S. congressional elections were underway, AMIS comprised 465 personnel from ten African countries.[25]

The tale of U.S. involvement in the Darfur crisis could have stopped here. The key reason that it did not was the creation of a U.S. advocacy movement of impressive proportions: the Save Darfur Coalition. The meeting that laid the foundation for this movement took place on July 14, 2004, at the City

University of New York.[26] Over time, the coalition grew into an alliance of more than 180 faith-based, advocacy, and humanitarian organizations and disposed of an annual budget of approximately $14 million.[27] People wore "Save Darfur" bracelets, played "Save Darfur" video games, and wore "Save Darfur" T-shirts.[28] By mid-2005, the key objective of the Save Darfur Coalition had become the replacement of AMIS with a full-blown United Nations peacekeeping force.[29] In early 2006 the Save Darfur Coalition launched the "Million Voices Campaign," a postcard campaign urging President Bush to support "a stronger multinational force to protect the civilians in Darfur."[30] The movement also organized nationwide rallies on April 30, 2006, which attracted over thirty-five thousand participants.[31]

As the Save Darfur Coalition swelled to unprecedented proportions, the White House considered various options of how to appease "the masses" with respect to Darfur. It even considered the possibility of a unilateral U.S. intervention. Yet the White House faced fierce opposition to this prospect from the U.S. Department of Defense, which vociferously refused to seriously engage with the Darfur issue. From 2004 to 2007, the key preoccupations of the Department of Defense were Iraq and Afghanistan, and Darfur was considered a conflict in which U.S. national interests were remote, to say the least.[32] The assistant secretary of state for African affairs, Jendayi Frazer, recalls the Pentagon's lack of enthusiasm on the matter: "Officials at [DOD] weren't keen, so they would come up with these ridiculous estimates like 'you need 120,000 troops to succeed.' Then of course they would say, 'Well, we don't have that because of Iraq.'"[33] Since the Bush administration was unwilling to clash with top U.S. defense officials in its efforts to engage in Darfur, troops had to be found elsewhere. The U.S. government briefly considered turning to NATO, but other heads of NATO members quickly signaled that they had no interest in deploying to Darfur.[34] "Only when it became clear that NATO was not a live option did we realize we were left with the UN," recalls President Bush's senior policy adviser, Michael Gerson.[35]

Planning for Coalition Intervention

UN Resolution 1769 (2007) foresaw the deployment "of up to 19,555 military personnel, including 360 military observers and liaison officers, and an appropriate civilian component including up to 3,772 police personnel and 19 formed police units comprising up to 140 personnel each."[36] Nevertheless, it also stated that the mission should have a "predominantly African character and the troops should, as far as possible, be sourced from African countries." The latter provision was inserted by Sudan. The regime in Khartoum was vehemently opposed to a UN operation in Darfur. It did not want other countries or international organizations interfering on its territory.[37] Nevertheless, by November 2006 the United States, in cooperation with the UN and other international actors, had put Sudan under such political pressure that it agreed to accept a UN force—with the condition that mostly African forces would be serving in UNAMID. Only if African countries were unable to meet force requirements would it accept troops from other contributing countries.[38] As a result of this condition, UNAMID turned into a UN-AU "hybrid operation." Moreover, the focus of UNAMID recruits had to be on Africa. It was a political planning condition that the U.S. government had to meet. In addition to this political criterion, all forces had to conform with basic UN deployment standards, for instance they all had to arrive with serviceable equipment that reflected UN minimum requirements spelled out in a UN Memorandum of Understanding (MOU).[39]

Searching for Coalition Contributions

The U.S. government first started exploring potential troop contributions for UNAMID in February 2006, when U.S. Ambassador John Bolton publicly invited possible troop contributors to indicate their interest to the UN Secretariat.[40] Once UNAMID was officially approved, the U.S. mission to the UN sent an official letter to all relevant UN missions in New York asking once more for UNAMID troop contributions. These bilateral initiatives occurred in parallel to public calls from the UN to contribute forces to UNAMID. Some countries immediately volunteered forces. These included Egypt, Ethiopia, China, and Canada.[41] However, together these countries were too small to launch a viable operation. Moreover, several of these countries were riddled by accusation of bias in the Darfur conflict. The head of UNDPKO, Jean-Marie Guéhenno, recalls: "We could not have too many troops from Ethiopia, because of its enmity with Eritrea, which was close to some of the [Darfuri] rebels, or from Egypt, because of its closeness with Khartoum."[42] Thus, additional contingents had to be found. Overall, despite the humanitarian character of the operation, very few countries were willing to put the lives of their own soldiers at risk in Darfur;[43] in other words, very few bandwagoneers existed.

U.S. government officials, especially at the State Department, were not surprised by the reluctance of states to contribute troops to UN peacekeeping operations. Over the years, they had become used to this scenario and had developed specific practices of how to actively recruit peacekeeping forces.[44] These practices relied on the deliberate exploitation of diplomatic networks. Given the operational planning constraints of UNAMID (that is, that it had to consist of predominantly African forces), such instrumentalization of diplomatic ties had to focus on Africa: U.S. officials had to repurpose existing networks in Africa to fill UNAMID recruitment needs. The State Department thus put its Africa Bureau in charge of the process—in cooperation with the State Department's Political-Military (POL-MIL) Bureau, an office that was in charge of peacekeeping policy more generally.[45]

As a first step, U.S. officials began gathering information on deployment preferences of suitable African UNAMID participants in an attempt to draft a "prospect list" for troop contributions. This process was described by one of my interviewees in the following way: "[Officials] would sit around and they figure 'All right, which countries are likely to be favorably inclined [to deploy]' . . . and then there are a whole host of factors that can go into why they might be favorably declined."[46]

To collect relevant information, both the POL-MIL and Africa bureaus would intentionally get in touch with their respective contacts across Africa (and later in the process also other regions). The POL-MIL Bureau's contacts would thereby mostly be U.S. military attachés or other U.S. civilian or military officers in charge of U.S.-African military cooperation programs such as the African Contingency Operations Training and Assistance Program (ACOTA) and its successor program, the Global Peace Operations Initiative (GPOI).[47] ACOTA and GPOI were set up to provide training to African and other military forces to improve their ability to conduct peacekeeping operations.[48] By 2007, the United States expected to train almost thirty thousand peacekeepers from fifteen African states.[49] For these reasons, ACOTA and GPOI provided the U.S. government with extensive knowledge of the military capabilities of African states as well as personal contacts among elite African soldiers who had participated in the program. This information and these contacts proved to be incredibly helpful in assessing the military readiness as well as political attitudes toward a potential deployment to Darfur. Sue Ann Sandusky, who served as U.S. defense attaché in various African countries, recalls: "[U.S.-trained soldiers] were plugged into their hierarchy and their politics and wouldn't want to be identified as American lapdogs. . . [yet] what I could always count on was that they would at least talk to me . . . and give [me] messages."[50] These messages proved to be critical in ascertaining preferences across African states for a UNAMID deployment.

The Africa Bureau, in turn, relied mostly on U.S. diplomats based in Africa to collect information on the deployment preferences of political elites in African nations. Such data focused on how intrinsically individual African governments were interested in the Darfur conflict and what other concerns these African countries had which could then be used to motivate a deployment to Darfur. The breadth of information available per country thereby varied greatly depending on the degree of diplomatic embeddedness: the more bilateral and multilateral ties the United States entertained with a country, the greater the number of local contact persons. This greater number of local access points, in turn, increased the range of issue areas in which information could be collected. Charles Snyder recalled that, based on this knowledge, the Africa Bureau would often look at the draft "prospect list" produced by POL-MIL and say, "No way, those countries will never sign up." Still, the POL-MIL Bureau's input was appreciated. In the end, "military capabilities [and military contacts] did matter quite a bit."[51]

On occasion, the State Department would also consult the Department of Defense, the intelligence community, and the National Security Council (NSC) and ask them for recommendations for suitable recruits.[52] The information provided by these institutions differed from the data gathered by the State Department, as one of my interviewees describes:

> [The difference is] mostly context. A DOD report will tend to be quite technical in other words [military] caliber [of potential troop-contributing states]. . . . An intelligence community report will tend to be very much looking at the trees rather than the forest . . . a lot of details on a specific incident or person without assessing what it means for U.S. interests. A diplomat's report will pay a lot of attention to background and context . . . and what it means for U.S. interests.[53]

Once the State Department had settled on a preliminary prospect list of potential UNAMID contributing states, it sent out cables to the U.S. embassies in the identified countries, requesting the local ambassadors to undertake "démarches"— visits to the local authorities to ask whether the government would be willing to send troops to Darfur.[54] These démarche requests included precise pitches and talking points based on the deployment preferences of the individual states. John Campbell, who served as U.S. ambassador in Nigeria, explains how these démarches normally unfolded:

> You would go in at the highest level possible. . . . You would go make the pitch and the response would be noncommittal. The pitch comes directly from Washington with the talking points, which I would then print out on a plain white piece of paper and hand it over because, in that meeting, there might be no note takers and therefore there was always the concern that what you were saying would simply be disappearing into a black hole.[55]

Once these démarches were completed, the ambassadors reported back to the State Department regarding their host government's responses and whether the host state voiced any additional conditions they wished to see fulfilled before they could agree to join UNAMID. The conditions ranged from very basic requests (such as an airlift to the conflict theater) to various equipment needs or complex political bargains. High-ranking officials in the State Department and the White House (including the secretary of state and the president) then handled the follow-up either by discussing the requests at a bilateral or multilateral meeting (so-called "corridor discussions") or by making a phone call to the leadership of the country in question (so-called "7th floor and NSC calls").[56]

Once U.S. government officials gained a "political pledge" to contribute forces to UNAMID, they would ask their recruits to bring their deployment intention to the attention of UNDPKO in New York and to "engage UNDPKO in direct discussions of its precise requirements."[57] In other words, the U.S. government perceived its recruitment work to be over once a political promise had been made. It ceded almost all technical negotiations to the UN. Nevertheless, if the U.S. government learned from the UN that these political pledges were not being fulfilled, the State Department would again instruct its ambassadors to remind their host governments of what they had promised in earlier discussions. For instance, Indonesia, Bangladesh, and Pakistan had all made political pledges to the United States to contribute to UNAMID. Indonesia pledged a 140-person Formed Police Unit (FPU) to North Darfur, Bangladesh a 327-person multi-role logistic unit to South Darfur, and Pakistan a 329-person engineer company to West Darfur and a 156-person hospital to South Darfur. All three countries were, however, slow in fulfilling their commitments. Therefore, in early October 2008, the U.S. secretary of state requested that U.S. embassies in Jakarta, Dhaka, and Islamabad "contact high-level host government counterparts to assess the readiness of the host government to make good on this pledge to UNAMID. Post should urge counterparts to press forward with key steps in the deployment process."[58]

In the early stages of the UNAMID recruitment process, the U.S. government was especially eager to find an African country that could take on a leadership role in UNAMID.[59] Such a role entailed a large troop commitment in addition to providing the UNAMID force commander. The U.S. government's top prospect to fulfill this role was Nigeria. Nigeria possessed one of Africa's largest, best-trained, and best-equipped military forces. Moreover, the United States and Nigeria were deeply diplomatically embedded; Nigeria ranked third among all countries in Africa after Ethiopia and Liberia. Nigeria, for instance, was an active participant in the ACOTA program. The U.S. had trained 202 Nigerian soldiers in 2005, 920 in 2006, and planned to train 670 in 2007.[60] From these sources, U.S. officials had learned that Nigeria was at least minimally intrinsically interested in Darfur. Nigerian president Obasanjo wanted to boost the prestige of his country by solving the Darfur conflict. Moreover, Sudan hosted an important Nigerian diaspora estimated to number between six and seven million with close ties to Nigeria.[61] Obasanjo had an interest in appealing to these people.[62] The United

States thus urged Nigeria to deploy troops to Darfur under the umbrella of the African Union.[63] When Obasanjo agreed to such deployment, the U.S. government provided Nigeria with the necessary military equipment[64] and lifted 150 Nigerian peacekeepers to Darfur in October 2004.[65] Nevertheless, with regard to UNAMID, a range of political factors threatened to derail U.S-Nigerian cooperation on Darfur. First, there was Charles Taylor, the Liberian dictator, who was living in exile in Nigeria. The U.S. government wanted him to be extradited to The Hague—a move that the Nigerian government refused to heed. There was also the issue of the Benue massacre. In October 2001, U.S. Congress had imposed sanctions on all U.S. military cooperation programs with Nigeria after a massacre in which Nigerian soldiers allegedly killed more than one hundred civilians in a revenge attack.[66] In order for the U.S. government to further support and finance Nigerian peacekeepers to be sent to Darfur, these sanctions had to be lifted, which involved approval by U.S. Congress. The United States thus could not be assured of Nigerian support and had to consider other candidates. Most of these other candidates were ACOTA/GPOI alums: during the 2005–2007 period, the United States had indeed trained large numbers of peacekeepers from Rwanda (8,000), Senegal (6,570), Ghana (3,343), Benin (1,756), and Mali (1,391).[67] All of these states were now considered key recruitment targets.[68]

In their quest for UNAMID troop contributions, the U.S. government received help from UNDPKO and other UN agencies. Staff working in these agencies served as important cooperation brokers. For example, on November 5, 2007, U.S. deputy secretary of state John Negroponte met with UN under-secretary-general for peacekeeping Jean-Marie Guéhenno. At that time, UNAMID was desperately looking for specific aviation assets. When Negroponte asked about possible candidates to fill these gaps, Guéhenno mentioned South Africa, Nigeria, Poland, the Czech Republic, Ukraine, and Brazil. Guéhenno, however, also stated that "only South Africa and Nigeria have a direct interest in the conflict."[69] Earlier in the UNAMID force generation process, UN special representative for Sudan Jan Pronk consulted with high-ranking Indian government official Sanjiv Arora about a possible Indian deployment to UNAMID. Assistant Secretary-General for Peacekeeping Operations Hédi Annabi raised the same topic with Arora a bit later in the process. Both officials later relayed what they had learned to their U.S. counterparts.[70] Possibly, many more of these cooperation brokerage activities occurred between UN and U.S. officials.

In summary, the U.S.-led search process for UNAMID provides evidence that the U.S. government instrumentalized diplomatic embeddedness for recruitment purposes. First, U.S. officials activated their networks, especially in Africa, to purposefully collect information on deployment preferences. This information was then used to establish a "prospect list" for UNAMID troop contributions. The information also informed the bilateral démarches that U.S. officials undertook in pre-selected countries: the information was used to phrase tailored talking points. They made it possible to assess "which countries [were] likely to be favorably inclined"[71] to deploy and why. Second, UN officials took on important planning and brokerage roles. They relayed information about deployment preferences of UN member states to U.S. government officials thus fulfilling once again a "post office" role, as discussed in the preceding chapter of this book. Interestingly, in contrast to the Korean War coalition-building process, no explicit switch from "having" diplomatic networks to "using" them for recruitment purposes occurred. Rather, it seems that over the years, U.S. officials had developed a routine to use these networks to engage third parties in collective action—the strategy had become tacit, inarticulate, and automatic.[72]

Individual Countries' Bargaining Outcomes

This section looks at five individual instances of UNAMID coalition negotiations. It assesses the negotiations of the three largest coalition contributors (Nigeria, Rwanda, and Egypt) as well as two cases that diverge in terms of diplomatic embeddedness with the United States: Germany (high on diplomatic embeddedness) and Thailand (low on diplomatic embeddedness).

Nigeria

Prior to UNAMID, Nigeria had gradually contributed approximately 2,000 troops to AMIS, the African Union force in Darfur. Still, this early commitment to the Darfur conflict cannot fully explain the fact that Nigeria agreed to increase its troop contribution to Darfur to roughly 3,700 forces under the umbrella of UNAMID. Instead, this large commitment to the operation should be seen as the result of coalition negotiations between the United States and Nigeria in which diplomatic embeddedness played a critical role.

Nigerian president Obasanjo had for a long while opposed a large-scale UN intervention in Darfur.[73] In August 2004, while on a visit to Khartoum, Obasanjo went so far as to publicly play down any possible military intervention in Darfur.[74] He continued to boast of this stance in October 17, 2004, when he attended a meeting that included the leaders of Libya, Egypt, Sudan, Chad, and Nigeria in which he publicly concluded that no UN intervention should ever occur in Darfur.[75] This anti-intervention attitude resounded well with the Nigerian public, which, by the early 2000s had developed a strong anti-peacekeeping attitude. Nigeria's peacekeeping adventures in Liberia and Sierra Leone had cost the

Nigerian government over $8 billion and thousands of Nigerian lives,[76] leading many Nigerians to believe that their government should focus on the socioeconomic problems at home instead of engaging in military escapades abroad.[77] With regard to Darfur specifically, a GlobeScan poll in June 2005 revealed that only 8 percent of Nigerians cared greatly about the Darfur conflict, 16 percent cared a moderate amount, and 60 percent had heard little or nothing at all about the conflict.[78] Moreover, from the military front, the Nigerian armed forces were completely overstretched. General Martin Luther Agwai, then serving as chief of staff of the Nigerian Army, indeed suggested in our interview that another Nigerian deployment was technically impossible: "There were no troops, there was no equipment."[79] Overall, the Nigerian military numbered 80,000 troops. In October 2004, 4,000 of those troops were deployed to the UN operations in Sierra Leone (UNAMSIL) and Liberia (UNMIL); another 4,000 were training to replace the battalions in UNAMSIL and UNMIL; two units were designated to the ECOWAS Standby Brigade; a company of military police was deployed in Burundi; a company of mechanized infantry and a company of engineers were deployed in Benin; and another company was deployed to Monrovia. In addition, Nigeria had military observers stationed in the southwest Sahara, Cote d'Ivoire, and the Democratic Republic of Congo. At the same time, twelve battalions (approximately 25,000 troops) were committed internally, including on the Bakassi Peninsula, the Plateau State, and the Niger Delta. All three areas were major domestic hot spots with a serious potential to flare up at any moment.[80]

So, which factors changed Nigeria's deployment equation? First, the Bush White House succeeded in convincing U.S. Congress to remove the sanctions it had imposed on Nigeria due to the Benue massacre.[81] This allowed the U.S. government to provide Nigeria with additional military aid and equipment for its deployment to Darfur.[82] Indeed, by early 2009, the U.S. government had trained and equipped over 10,000 Nigerian troops.[83] Second, and arguably more important, Nigeria and the United States reached a political agreement. Obasanjo's top foreign policy priority of his presidency was debt relief. Most of Nigeria's $33 billion debt was held by the Paris Club, an informal group of creditor countries, among them the United States, the United Kingdom, France, and Germany. The debt had been accumulated by military governments preceding Obasanjo's presidency. This debt, Obasanjo concluded, was a major cause of Nigeria's developmental failures. Disposing of it would represent a fresh start, a second chance for a new Nigeria.[84] By September 2004, Obasanjo was growing increasingly nervous that his plan of debt reduction would not be achieved. Previous successful examples of debt reductions (Cote d'Ivoire, Congo, and Cameroon, for instance) had shown that debt reduction was granted not only because of economic factors but also due to political rationales. In all three cases, France had been instrumental in pushing the deals to fruition.[85] As a result, Obasanjo reckoned that he needed a "great power" to champion his cause.[86] U.S. diplomats had learned about these fears from their local contacts in Nigeria (i.e., via diplomatic embeddedness).[87] The Bush White House thus adopted a strategy to exploit this information and signal to Obasanjo that the United States was willing to become Nigeria's "debt relief sponsor." In exchange, however, Nigeria had to agree to expand its involvement in the Darfur crisis. Nigeria took the bait. On December 2, 2004, President Bush met Obasanjo at the White House. As a follow-up to that meeting, Obasanjo wrote a letter to President Bush including the following extract:[88]

> As you are aware, we are actively working on the crisis in Darfur. . . . I have invested my personal time and effort in this and committed Nigerian troops and resources to resolving these conflicts. . . . With regard to Nigeria, the one main issue where I would request your support is that of our quest for Debt Relief. You have recently shown remarkable leadership on this front as regards Iraq and I would like to congratulate you and the Iraqis on your success.

On May 5, 2005, Obasanjo again met with President Bush. The meeting once more focused on debt relief and Darfur. Scott McClellan, White House spokesman at the time, summarized the conversation as follows: "The President thanked [Obasanjo] for his strong leadership in Darfur and talked about the importance of resolving the situation in Sudan." In addition, Obasanjo raised the question of debt relief for Nigeria, asking Bush to "use his good offices" to press the issue with his European counterparts.[89] Finally, on June 30, 2005, the debt deal was approved. The Paris Club agreed to a 60 percent reduction of Nigeria's debt. The official agreement was signed in Paris on October 26, 2005. A bilateral U.S.-Nigerian agreement followed on December 17, 2005. The United States government and the Bush White House, in particular, played critical roles in the final negotiations. U.S. Ambassador to Nigeria John Campbell recalls: "Nigeria did not meet the requirements for debt relief. The [U.S.] Treasury's concern was that if you grant debt relief to Nigeria, the whole principle—the whole structure—of debt relief would be undermined."[90] Nevertheless, "despite rancorous disagreements among the involved agencies, the White House imposed an interagency policy in support of debt relief for Nigeria."[91]

In return for the debt relief deal, Nigeria increased its troop deployment to Darfur to roughly three infantry battalions.[92] To cope with the required deployment numbers, Nigeria had to change its military rotation policy. Nigerian troops normally rotated every six months, with six months in the field and six months off to rest and train. The new rotation policy entailed that troops serving in the

UN missions in Liberia and Sierra Leone would stay for one year instead. This change freed a substantive number of troops for deployment to Darfur.[93] Nevertheless, Agwai recalls that the demands on Nigerian troops were still immense: "Some soldiers came back from Sierra Leone or Liberia and were sent straight to the Plateau State or the Niger Delta with no rest in between."[94]

Once the debt deal was concluded in late 2005, another topic took center stage in Obasanjo's agenda: his desire to continue as Nigeria's president beyond 2007. This required a revision of the Nigerian constitution, which allowed for only two, and not three, electoral terms. When U.S. diplomats were informed of Obasanjo's desire to revise the constitution, they profoundly disliked the plan.[95] "Presidents for life" should not be tolerated in Africa. It was one of the reasons, they felt, that Africa had experienced such great political and economic difficulty. The U.S. embassy in Abuja thus issued a statement affirming that "executive term limits should be respected."[96] The U.S. statement contributed to the motion failing to achieve the necessary majority in the Nigerian parliament, despite Obasanjo's intense lobbying efforts.[97] Obasanjo then reverted to a different strategy to manipulate the Nigerian political system. To salvage his political power, he orchestrated to get *himself* elected as chairman of the governing party's Board of Trustees, a lifetime position that would enable him to retain much of the substance of presidential power.[98] Moreover, in April 2007, he imposed his choice for presidential candidate, Umaru Yar'Adua, an obscure governor from northern Nigeria who was in ill health.[99] Given the obvious election shenanigans, Washington refused to receive the newly elected Yar'Adua, and only low-level representatives were sent to the presidential inauguration.[100]

In response to this U.S. snub, Nigeria announced in mid-2007 that it would conduct an official review of its peacekeeping efforts in Darfur, with the possibility that this could lead to a full withdrawal.[101] The announcement was intended as a threat to the United States, and it worked. The Nigerian review sent chills down the spine of key decision-makers in Washington. Nigeria was slated to be one of backbone nations of the UNAMID force; U.S. government officials could think of few other states to replace the Nigerian contingent. As a result, the U.S. government reversed its stance on the Nigerian election fraud. In June 2007, the assistant secretary of state for African affairs, Jendayi Frazer, emphasized Nigeria's continuing importance to the United States in her testimony to Congress: "The stakes are too great to walk away from Nigeria. . . . Its government remains one of our most dependable allies on the continent on a wide array of diplomatic initiatives such as Darfur, peacekeeping, counter-terrorism, and HIV/AIDS."[102] On December 12, 2007, Yar'Adua was invited to the White House. To the surprise of no one, the lingering Darfur crisis again dominated the bilateral talks. In the end, Nigeria agreed to deploy a fourth battalion to Darfur.[103] U.S. Ambassador to Nigeria John Campbell suggested in our interview that, at the time, the U.S. government was frantic to find troops for Darfur. For this reason, Campbell recalled, Nigeria held significant bargaining leverage over the United States.[104] Nigeria would get whatever it wanted.

In summary, although the Nigerian government cared about Darfur, it also faced domestic constraints that limited its involvement. As a result, the size of the Nigerian deployment to Darfur cannot be fully understood without taking U.S.-Nigerian coalition negotiations into account. Diplomatic embeddedness mattered in these negotiations. Most importantly, the U.S. government learned via diplomatic ties that Obasanjo was panicking about debt relief. This was private information that U.S. diplomats were only able to access because of their local contacts in Nigeria. Moreover, the U.S. government could manipulate a diplomatic tie (a debt agreement via the Paris Club in which the United States was the key stakeholder) to induce Nigeria to join the UNAMID coalition. U.S. asymmetrical power capabilities thus clearly affected the Nigerian decision-making process. Still, diplomatic embeddedness created payment flexibility: it was arguably easier for the U.S. government to negotiate debt relief than mobilize the equivalent amount in fresh money. As a result, the availability of such an issue linkage increased the likelihood of negotiation success. Nigeria's willingness to increase its troop deployment to Darfur was arguably not the only factor that made the international debt relief deal happen.[105] Nevertheless, it was a critical factor: it secured the White House's goodwill toward Nigeria and thus toward the debt relief agreement as a whole. The aftermath of the "debt relief for deployment" deal also illustrates, however, how U.S. bargaining power waned once Nigeria deployed to Darfur. U.S. diplomats shivered when Nigeria threatened to withdraw its troops and agreed to fully recognize Yar'Adua. Hegemonic power can thus partly but not fully explain the negotiation outcome that occurred.

Rwanda

Rwanda served as the second largest UNAMID troop contributor after Nigeria. It contributed roughly 3,430 forces to UNAMID. In contrast to Nigeria, U.S.-Rwandan diplomatic embeddedness was very low in the runup to UNAMID. Rwanda ranked thirty-fifth in terms of U.S. diplomatic embeddedness in Africa. As a result, we would expect that other mechanisms explain Rwanda's UNAMID participation. And this is indeed the case. Rwanda was a "self-starter." Given the genocidal atrocities it had experienced in the past, Rwanda shared the security and humanitarian objectives of UNAMID. Nevertheless, it did not possess the necessary military, financial, and logistical resources to be an effective UNAMID participant.[106] Therefore, it asked the United States to subsidize its deployment.

Given the dire recruitment situation, the United States agreed. On September 3, 2008, the United States offered Rwanda approximately $20 million in equipment and transportation support items intended for use by Rwanda's UNAMID contingent in Darfur.[107] Moreover, it agreed to provide pre-deployment training to Rwandan battalions, which were slated to be deployed to Darfur.[108] The decision to bankroll the Rwanda's deployment was arguably made easier by Rwanda's active ACOTA participation. Indeed, in FY 2005 and FY 2006, the United States had trained over 6,000 Rwandan peacekeepers.[109]

Egypt

Egypt provided the third-largest contingent to UNAMID, amounting to roughly 2,650 troops. Egypt was deeply diplomatically embedded with the United States, ranking seventh globally. Nevertheless, these ties did not matter much in the UNAMID recruitment process. Egypt volunteered to serve in UNAMID. It was a bandwagoneer. UNDPKO even had to reject Egyptian troop offers (that is, only one of the three proposed Egyptian infantry battalions ended up participating in UNAMID) because Darfuri rebels had put pressure on UNDPKO to not allow Egyptian troops into Darfur. They thought that Egypt was partisan to the Al-Bashir government in Khartoum.[110] Indeed, Egypt had an intense intrinsic interest in the Darfur crisis: it relied heavily on Nile water resources and thus was keen on keeping a good relationship with Al-Bashir. In addition, Egypt wanted to show leadership in Africa. Egyptian president Hosni Mubarak personally addressed Egyptian troops on January 2, 2008, prior to their UNAMID deployment. In a public statement regarding the address, presidential spokesman Soliman Awaad highlighted that this peacekeeping contribution was part of extensive efforts by Egypt, Libya, Chad, and Eritrea as well as some non-African countries to "put an end to the bloodshed in Darfur."[111] Prior to the Egyptian UNAMID deployment, Egypt had already hosted a conference with Sudan's neighboring countries to find a solution to the crisis.

Germany

Germany contributed a transport aircraft to UNAMID. Moreover, it ranked very high in terms of diplomatic embeddedness with the United States (10th from the U.S. perspective). Is there a connection between these two facts? The Save Darfur Movement had much less of a following in Germany than in the United States, and there is very little evidence that Germany was intrinsically motivated to participate in UNAMID for any other reasons. As a result, it is highly probable that Germany would not have deployed to Darfur of its own accord. Nevertheless, in

September 2007, the Bush administration tasked Andrew Natsios, the U.S. special envoy to Darfur, to travel to Germany to urge the German government to contribute forces to UNAMID. During the trip, Natsios met with the chief foreign policy advisor to German Chancellor Angela Merkel and the foreign policy head of the Christian Democratic Party (CDU). Natsios tried to make the case that if the Darfur problem was not resolved, the whole region would collapse. Natsios did not, however, think that the Germans were entirely convinced by this argument. Instead, what the Germans wanted was to improve bilateral relations with the United States after Iraq.[112] After Germany's "no" to the Iraq War, the German government had largely lost its status as one of the principal foreign interlocutors of the U.S. administration—a loss that hurt U.S.-German diplomatic relations in multiple ways. Thus, Germany now tried very hard to regain favorability with the U.S. government, and UNAMID constituted such an opportunity. Without U.S. diplomats exploiting diplomatic embeddedness, Germany's deployment to Darfur would thus have been much less likely.

Thailand

Thailand sent approximately 800 troops to Darfur. U.S.-Thai diplomatic embeddedness was weak—forty-fourth from the U.S. perspective. As expected, Thailand was thus not recruited by exploiting bilateral diplomatic networks. Rather, Thailand was another "self-starter." Thailand had little to no interest in the Darfur conflict. Nevertheless, following the September 19, 2006, coup d'état in Thailand, the United States had suspended all U.S.-Thai military cooperation programs, totaling over $29 million.[113] As a result, one of my interviewees suggested that Thailand seized upon the opportunity presented to them—that the United States was struggling in 2007 to find UNAMID force contributions—to ask for a suspension of U.S. sanctions in exchange for a Thai troop deployment to UNAMID.[114] If this was indeed the case, the strategy appears to have been successful. In February 2008, the United States resumed funding for all Thai military cooperation programs.[115]

TABLE 5.1 Results of case study: UNAMID

	DEEPLY EMBEDDED WITH THE UNITED STATES	WEAKLY EMBEDDED WITH THE UNITED STATES
Bandwagoneer	Egypt	–
Self-starter	–	Rwanda
		Thailand
Coalition recruit	Nigeria	–
	Germany	

Summary of Findings

What conclusions can we draw from the UNAMID recruitment process? Does the coalition-building process match the mechanisms identified in chapter 2? Does it vary in significant ways from the Korean War?

Similarly to the Korean War, the United States used its entire power arsenal—military, economic, and diplomatic power capabilities—to build UNAMID. This might come as a surprise. UN operations are often considered coalitions of self-motivated actors.[116] And yet, in UNAMID, this was only partially true. Some states certainly joined UNAMID on their own initiative (for instance, Egypt). Others saw in UNAMID a valuable opportunity to negotiate a quid pro quo (Rwanda and Thailand). Most members of the international community, however, were passive. They did not share the same urgency to intervene in Darfur as the United States did. The preference convergence model thus cannot fully explain how the coalition came about.

To fill the gaps in the coalition lineup, the United States purposefully instrumentalized diplomatic embeddedness. In exchange for its consent to UNAMID, Sudan requested that mostly African forces would serve in the operation. The United States thus activated, in particular, its diplomatic networks in Africa to search for UNAMID troop contributions. The State Department leadership instructed U.S. diplomats and military officers to collect information on where African states stood with regard to a possible deployment to Darfur. The UN assisted the United States in this search process, serving as a cooperation broker. At the same time, UN officials also took charge of the technical details of the UNAMID deployment. Did the United States at any point use vulnerability considerations in its process to search for coalition contributions? A range of variables appears to have been used to determine suitable recruits, or as one of my interviewees stated: "There are a whole host of factors that can go into" why the United States would believe that countries "might be favorably declined."[117] Nevertheless, the available evidence does not suggest that U.S. officials deliberately and systematically tried to exploit asymmetrical dependencies in potential coalition participants.

With regard to coalition negotiations, diplomatic embeddedness certainly impacted coalition negotiations with Nigeria. Deep diplomatic ties provided access to private information. For example, it was via such diplomatic ties that the U.S. government learned that Obasanjo was panicking that his top foreign policy priority, a debt deal, might falter. Moreover, diplomatic embeddedness offered payment flexibility. It allowed the United States to use an already-established institutional tie (the Paris Club) to channel a side payment. Creating a budget line of the equivalent amount of money ($600 million) or shifting pre-assigned budget lines to fund a Nigerian deployment to Darfur would have certainly caused more domestic opposition in the U.S. Congress, USAID, the State Department, or the Department of Defense. In the German case, diplomatic embeddedness was also important. Germany participated in UNAMID only after Natsios's visit to Berlin to ask for a German contribution to UNAMID. Germany viewed such deployment as a gesture of reconciliation with the United States after Iraq.

Were any of these countries at any point coerced into cooperation? The influence of the hegemonic position of the United States in the UNAMID case is undeniable. Rwanda and Thailand, both only weakly embedded with the United States, self-initiated negotiations because of the American power position in global politics. Rwanda was eager to receive U.S. military training and equipment, while Thailand appears to have joined UNAMID to receive U.S. sanction relief. Moreover, without U.S. financial power, Nigeria, for instance, would never have been in debt to the United States via the Paris Club.

And yet, is coercion the best way to describe what happened? When I asked some of my Nigerian interviewees this question, many of them stated that the debt relief negotiations were a win for Nigeria. They considered the Nigerian deployment to Darfur as a bargaining chip they held in the debt relief negotiations: a deployment to Darfur was the one thing that the United States really cared about and that Nigeria could provide. Many of them thought that Nigeria had played it well. As a result, Nigeria's deployment to Darfur was largely seen as a self-serving and deliberate move, not a coerced action. The U.S. ambassador to Nigeria at the time, John Campbell, concurred. He suggested that the U.S. government was desperate to find troops for Darfur. The debt deal was complicated. Both domestic actors (mainly the U.S. Treasury) as well as international actors had to be brought on board. Nevertheless, the Bush White House was willing to move heaven and earth to make this deal happen. For this reason, Campbell suggests, Nigeria actually held significant leverage over the United States.[118] This becomes even clearer after the Nigerian deployment, when the U.S. government agreed to fully recognize Yar'Adua despite the fraudulent elections.

The UNAMID coalition-building process thus illustrates that power capabilities matter greatly to organize collective action—even in the UN context. Nevertheless, pivotal states rarely use "brute" coercion, nor do subordinate states volunteer forces to UN operations out of submissiveness to authority. Rather, UN coalition building results from complex bargaining in which financial wealth and military power act alongside information and the facility to construct issue linkages and side payments—resources that arise if pivotal states instrumentalize diplomatic networks.

FIGHTING FOR INDEPENDENCE IN EAST TIMOR

INTERFET (1999–2000)

On September 4, 1999, Dili, the capital of East Timor, was in chaos. After a large majority of East Timorese had voted in favor of independence from Indonesia in a UN-organized ballot, anti-independence militias unleashed a systemic campaign of terror on the small island. Extreme violence swept across the island, as houses were set on fire and gunfire unleashed, leaving thousands of East Timorese seeking protection. After only a few days, most of the buildings, utilities, and agricultural facilities throughout the island were destroyed; almost the entire population was displaced, with over 250,000 transported by the Indonesian Army (TNI) or anti-independence militias to West Timor, the part of Timor that was still under Indonesian control. It is estimated that roughly 1,400 civilians died during these first days of violence.[1]

It was in this context that Australia decided to launch a multilateral military intervention to stop the bloodshed in East Timor. The force Australia assembled was called the International Force East Timor (INTERFET). The UN Security Council authorized INTERFET via UN Resolution 1264 on September 15, 1999. Operations, which drew on approximately 11,000 troops, were launched on September 20, 1999, and lasted until February 28, 2000, when a UN follow-on force (UNTAET) took over. The following countries participated in the operation: Australia (5,500 forces), Thailand (1,580 forces), Jordan (700 forces), the Philippines (600 forces), Italy (600 forces), Canada (600 forces), France (500 forces), New Zealand (500 forces), South Korea (400 forces), the United Kingdom (270 forces), Singapore (medical detachment of 254 personnel), the United States

(200 forces and logistic support), Fiji (191 forces), Germany (medical unit of 100 personnel), Kenya (100 forces), Argentina (50 forces), and Brazil (50 forces), with token contributions from Denmark, Norway, Egypt, Malaysia, Mozambique, Singapore, and Sweden.[2]

Despite the humanitarian character of the intervention (and its UN mandate), few of these participants joined INTERFET on their own initiative. Rather, Australia had to conduct an explicit recruitment process that involved cajoling countries to join the operation. Australia's diplomatic networks played an indispensable role in this process: Australian officials exploited these networks to retrieve information on deployment preferences of potential coalition participants. Australia also used the APEC summit in Auckland and the UN General Assembly (UNGA) in New York as opportunities to make bilateral appeals for troop contributions. Nevertheless, Australia's diplomatic cloud had its limitations. Especially when it came to recruiting countries from outside of the Asia-Pacific region, Australian networks were insufficient. Australia thus turned to the United States and the United Kingdom for assistance in drawing multilateral support for its coalition, thereby leaving these states to function as cooperation brokers. This assistance proved to be critical; as one senior Australian official recalled, "The fact that the Americans were committed to [INTERFET] meant that a whole lot of people put in forces which might not otherwise [have]."[3]

This chapter focuses on the deployment decisions of the three largest troop-contributing countries: Thailand, Jordan, and the Philippines; Canada, a deeply embedded state with Australia; and Brazil, a weakly embedded state with Australia. The deployment decisions of the top three INTERFET contributors (Thailand, the Philippines, and Jordan) were all influenced by a mixture of personal appeals, financial incentives, and asymmetrical dependence considerations vis-à-vis Australia (or, in the case of Jordan, vis-à-vis the United States). Canada, a deeply diplomatically embedded country with Australia, was wooed to join INTERFET by Australian prime minister John Howard, who used his personal friendship with Canadian prime minister Jean Chrétien to bring the country on board. Finally, Brazil, a marginally embedded state with Australia, was a bandwagoneer. It sent troops to East Timor due to religious, colonial, and linguistic links with the island and after some delicate prodding by Portugal.

Origins of Australian Involvement in East Timor

Australia's relationship with East Timor dates to the independence of the island from Portugal in 1974 and its subsequent annexation by Indonesia the following year. Most countries in the world refused to recognize Indonesian sovereignty over East Timor.[4] Australia was one of the exceptions. In fact, Australia's support for Indonesia's occupation of East Timor was arguably the most steadfast of all nations in the world.[5] Nevertheless, domestic criticism of Australian policy toward Indonesia never abated. Especially with the fall of Indonesia's long-term dictator Suharto in 1998, the topic remerged as a preeminent issue in Australian society. Suharto's successor, B. J. Habibie, soon indicated that Indonesia would be open to reconsidering the status of East Timor. He envisaged a "special status" for the territory, which would entail autonomy in all areas of government except defense, foreign affairs, and monetary policy.[6]

Australia's foreign minister, Alexander Downer, received Habibie's announcement with particular interest. In it he saw a chance to redeem Australia's wrongful support for Indonesia's annexation of the country as well as a means to win the political support of sections of the Australian population that had been advocating a more critical stance toward Indonesia.[7] It also represented an opportunity to improve Australian-Indonesian relations, which had been severely strained in the recent past.[8] Downer therefore convinced Howard to draft a letter to Habibie urging him to include in his proposal "a future act of self-determination" for East Timor.[9] Habibie took the bait and agreed to hold a UN-monitored referendum in six months' time that would offer the East Timorese the choice between autonomy within Indonesia or independence.[10]

When the violence in East Timor after the UN-monitored referendum erupted, Australia thus felt guilty. The "Howard letter" had, at least partially, prompted Habibie to hold the referendum. Australian officials from the highest levels downwards felt they had a responsibility to contain the bloodshed.[11] Australia's initial response was to mount Operation Spitfire and evacuate Australian citizens, UN staff, and almost 1,900 East Timorese from the island.[12] However, it soon became apparent that this would not be enough. An intervention force in some respect would be needed to stop the terror campaign.[13] The thought of mounting a forceful operation, however, disturbed Howard. Intervening in East Timor meant going to war with Indonesia, the most powerful player in Southeast Asia: a country of over 200 million people with an army of over 200,000 men, 25,000 of whom were stationed in East Timor.[14] Australia's military commanders felt utterly ill-prepared to confront such a massive military force, leading Canberra to turn toward the United States for assistance.[15] During the preparation process of the UN ballot, the U.S. military's Pacific Command had approached Australia regarding the possibility of a U.S. peace enforcement operation if the situation went badly in East Timor.[16] Thus, Canberra assumed that the United States would be willing to take the lead on East Timor. Yet that did not happen. When Howard first requested U.S. assistance in East Timor, Bill Cohen, the U.S. secretary of defense, allegedly brushed this plea to the side, responding "It's your baby."[17] Cohen represented the dominant view in Washington, D.C., in the fall of 1999: Indonesia was of great strategic importance to the United States, while East Timor was not important at all.[18] On his second attempt, U.S. president Bill Clinton rebuffed Howard personally. "We're much stretched," Clinton said, "there's a lot of resistance to us committing ourselves any further. We've got many thousands [of troops] in Kosovo."[19]

Australia then made a bold move. Speaking on CNN on September 7, 1999, Australia's foreign minister, Alexander Downer, publicly criticized the Clinton administration for its inaction in East Timor.[20] Australia felt that "this was a violation of the ANZUS alliance. Australia was being dumped."[21] Australia also coordinated with Portugal, which felt equally strongly that the violence in its former colony had to be stopped. Portuguese prime minister António Guterres called Clinton the same day that Downer went on CNN and threatened to pull Portuguese troops out of the Kosovo war, which was ranging in parallel, if no peacekeeping forces were deployed to East Timor. To make his point even clearer, Guterres also prevented sixteen U.S. military flights from departing from the Portuguese airbase in the Azores islands, an important stopover for U.S. military planes on their way to Europe (and Kosovo).[22] The Clinton administration finally came around. A senior U.S. official described the U.S. reversal with regard to East Timor in the following way: "We don't have a dog running in the East Timor race, but we have a very big dog running down there called Australia and we have to support it."[23] Australia (and Portugal) had also been aided by a burst of NGO activity.[24] In a flurry lasting a few days, U.S. agencies had received tens of thousands of email messages from religious and human rights organizations.[25] As a result, several senators and members of the U.S. House of Representatives began to look at the issue a bit more favorably.[26]

As a first concrete step of U.S. support, President Clinton rang Howard to inform him that the United States would help Australia with strategic airlift, intelligence support, and logistics. Clinton also promised that he would throw all of America's diplomatic clout behind Australia to make INTERFET happen, or what Howard called "an all-out diplomatic effort in support of what Australia wanted."[27] At the time, Australia's greatest but most difficult goal was for Indonesia to acquiesce to the deployment of INTERFET.[28] The United States thus pulled all the diplomatic levers on Indonesia it had, notably pressure from the World Bank and the IMF.[29] The United States also made it clear to Indonesia that any attempt to oppose INTERFET would be met with an overwhelming U.S. military response.[30] The immense pressure on Indonesia eventually produced results. On September 13, 1999, Habibie informed UN secretary-general Kofi Annan that he would "invite" a peacekeeping force of "friendly nations" to East Timor.[31]

Planning for Coalition Intervention

Military planning for INTERFET was in the hands of General Peter Cosgrove, who would also command the intervention force. Cosgrove and his team projected that it would require at least three battalions to successfully bring peace to East Timor. Australia was willing to take the military lead in these operations and supply the bulk of the personnel and equipment needed. Nevertheless, for political reasons, Australian officials considered it imperative to construct a multilateral intervention force. Most importantly, Australia wanted to deter Indonesia from opposing the operation, both politically and militarily.[32] Mike Keating, the head of military planning for Australia's East Timor intervention, remembers: "If Australia would have gone in by herself, the Indonesians might have reacted differently but with twenty odd countries and a UN resolution, it would have been really difficult for them to oppose the intervention."[33] Interestingly, in contrast to other operations covered in this book, the Australian government did not worry about domestic or international legitimacy concerns. Indeed, the Australian public favored intervention even more adamantly than its government.[34] Howard remembers: "I was basically being attacked by everybody for not invading the place."[35]

What type of force would make it particularly difficult for Indonesia to oppose it? Many Indonesians believed that Australia was seeking to humiliate their country and stage a Christian crusade against the world's largest Muslim-majority nation.[36] As a result, Australia considered it vital to bring Asian, non-Western, and non-Christian states on board of INTERFET. In particular, Australia wanted to recruit members of the Association of Southeast Asian Nations (ASEAN), the regional organization that included Indonesia.[37] Moreover, ideally one or two Muslim countries would join the operation to signal to the Indonesian population that this was not an anti-Muslim endeavor.

Searching for Coalition Contributions

The official search process for INTERFET began on September 6, 1999, when UN secretary-general Kofi Annan formally asked John Howard if Australia would be willing to lead an intervention in East Timor. Although Annan's request was a mere formality, it nevertheless jump-started Australia's recruitment efforts to secure participants for INTERFET.

Australia had very little experience in multilateral military coalition building. Thus, its initial approach to constructing a coalition was rather naive. Many officials thought that merely informing countries of the possibility of joining

INTERFET was enough for them to sign up: "Because we're having a coalition, we can pick and choose who comes."[38] Australia soon learned better. Most of Australia's calls for participation rang hollow, and as a result, very few countries volunteered to join INTERFET. Especially in Asia, many countries did not enthusiastically support the idea of an Australian-led intervention in East Timor. They feared Indonesia's wrath. Moreover, they believed that the separation of East Timor from Indonesia could potentially lead to a "balkanization" of the region. It could worsen domestic political instability in Indonesia and might even lead to a complete disintegration of the archipelagic state, which could then spread throughout the entire region, thereby jeopardizing political stability and economic growth for decades to come.[39] These fears largely trumped their humanitarian concerns.

Australian officials thus had to revert to a different recruitment technique: "countries needed to be wooed into the coalition" and "you had to be clever how you did it," as Steve Ayling put it. Ayling, who served as director of strategic planning of INTERFET, also observed that Australia "had to double-think why people would not come and encourage them to come."[40] In short, Australia had to instrumentalize diplomatic embeddedness. Starting from a position of merely having diplomatic networks, Australia had to switch to exploiting them as a strategic asset to construct allied cooperation.

To do so, Australian officials started to purposefully collect information on the specific preferences states held with regard to INTERFET. Moreover, they tried to assess what external incentives Australia could offer to sway these countries to join the coalition. Officials working at the Australian Department of Foreign Affairs and Trade (DFAT) used the Australian embassy network to collect such data.[41] They instructed Australian embassy employees and defense attachés to feel out their local counterparts with respect to INTERFET. They also approached resident foreign embassies in Canberra with informal inquiries about a potential INTERFET participation. In addition, Australian military officials were tasked to consult with their foreign military counterparts in Asia and around the world. They also tapped into the alumni networks of Australia's military academies, which have a long tradition of training foreign military elites.[42] Overall, Steve Ayling recalls the extent to which "personal influence counted."[43] The better the local contacts and the larger their number, the more precise information Australia could retrieve. In short, diplomatic embeddedness determined the breadth and quality of information.

Australia's top priority in the early days of the INTERFET coalition-building process was to find a country that would take on the position of deputy commander of INTERFET. Given Indonesian sensitivities (especially its criticism of Australia hedging a "neocolonial Western invasion into

South-East Asian territory"[44]), Australia considered it imperative to recruit a Southeast Asian country to assume this role, ideally a country that was a member of the Association of Southeast Asian Nations (ASEAN). Diplomatic embeddedness between Australia and ASEAN countries looked as follows: Indonesia and the Philippines topped the list (65 ties each), followed by Thailand and Malaysia (59 ties) and Singapore (47 ties). All other ASEAN countries significantly lagged behind. This ranking roughly mirrored the states Australian officials considered as chief prospects to serve as second-in-command of INTERFET.

Initially, officials considered Malaysia to be the top contender for the position. Malaysia was deeply diplomatically embedded with Australia,[45] was a member of ASEAN, had extensive UN peacekeeping experience, and was a Muslim-majority country, and its population understood Indonesia's native language, Bahassa. These features combined made it an ideal INTERFET deputy commander.[46] Nevertheless, when Australian officials approached their contacts in Kuala Lumpur, they received mixed messages. Malay military officers signaled to Australia that they would be eager to join INTERFET.[47] Nevertheless, Australian diplomats reported that Malaysian prime minister Mahathir Bin Mohamad disliked Howard as a result of Howard throwing his support behind the U.S.-led air campaign against Iraq in 1998 (Operation Desert Fox)—an operation that Mahathir considered to be "white people . . . bombing Muslims."[48] Moreover, Mahathir was annoyed that Howard had condemned his handling of Malay opposition candidate Anwar Ibrahim, who was, from the Australian perspective, unfairly arrested for corruption and sodomy.[49] For these reasons, Australian diplomats warned that coalition negotiations with Malaysia might run into trouble.

The country that Australian diplomats were arguably more enthusiastic about was Thailand. While Thailand had less peacekeeping experience than Malaysia, coalition negotiations were more likely to succeed with the Thai government, given that the country was politically indebted to Australia. Approximately a year prior to INTERFET, in the wake of the Asian financial crisis, Australia had provided a one-billion-dollar loan to Thailand.[50] In addition, just months prior to INTERFET, Australia had maintained staunch support for Thailand's candidate, Supachai Panitchpakdi, as the new head of the World Trade Organization (WTO).[51] Australian diplomats argued that the bilateral loan and the support for Supachai had generated considerable goodwill toward Australia in Thailand and that this goodwill could play a critical role in coalition negotiations. On top of this, military-to-military relations between Thailand and Australia were very good. Many high-ranking Thai military officers had received training in Australia, including the Thai crown prince at the time, a graduate of the Australian Royal Military College, Duntroon, in Canberra. Through these alumni networks,

Australian officials also picked up signals that indicated that the Thai military was eager to serve in INTERFET.[52]

In addition to Malaysia and Thailand, Australia considered a range of other countries to take on "smaller" roles in INTERFET. Most importantly, Australia expected that it could sway the U.K., New Zealand, and Canada to send a contribution to INTERFET. Diplomatic relations between the U.K. and Australia were deep and extensive. The U.K. was Australia's close military ally, Commonwealth partner, and former colonizer. New Zealand, in turn, was Australia's neighbor and closest regional ally. And, finally, Howard was convinced that he could count on his friend, Canadian prime minister Jean Chrétien, to help him out in the East Timor crisis. The two leaders maintained a very close personal relationship in addition to being connected via the Five Eyes agreement and the Commonwealth.[53] For political reasons, Australian officials also expected South Korea, the Philippines, and Brunei to be good candidates for coalition contributions in addition to other countries, notably from the Asia-Pacific Economic Community (APEC) and the British Commonwealth.[54] Among the Commonwealth nations, Pakistan in particular stood out. DFAT had received information coming out of Islamabad that Pakistan was interested in joining the intervention if the right incentives were provided.[55]

The initial strategy to bring these identified countries into INTERFET was to sell them on the benefits of the intervention. Leading the way on this front was Steve Ayling, who sought to carry out this policy by inviting the defense attachés of the identified countries to attend briefings on the situation in INTERFET. His objective was "to make them feel to be part of a big team." The tone Ayling was trying to convey was "What? You're not coming?" With regard to the potential benefits of participating in INTERFET, Ayling presented the following four motivations: First, this was a legitimate operation with full UN support. Second, this was a good cause; East Timor and its people needed help. Third, Australia needed assistance, and it would grant great leeway to its coalition partners. Australia would not treat its partners "like the Yanks did" (that is, in a "submissive" capacity). And fourth, Australia was really trying to run a good show. It put all its effort into making this a successful operation. Ayling also took his briefings on the road. Whenever an Australia embassy picked up signals that their local governments would be interested in an INTERFET deployment, Ayling or one of his assistants would travel abroad and do their spiel. Ayling recalls that selling a Timor operation was relatively easy. No major dangers were looming on the island, so in that respect, "selling Afghanistan must have been much harder," he reckoned.[56] Nevertheless, only in very few cases did the briefings lead to an immediate commitment to participate in INTERFET. Most briefings merely served as a prelude to coalition negotiations.

Australia's search process does bear some resemblance to the U.S.-led search processes analyzed in previous chapters. After a brief period in which Australia assumed that parties would volunteer forces for INTERFET, Australia reverted to instrumentalizing its diplomatic networks to construct cooperation. For political reasons, Australia prioritized Asian, non-Christian countries to participate in INTERFET. Australia thus trained its networks on countries that fit these characteristics: first, Australian officials used diplomatic networks (both civilian and military) to investigate what preferences these states held with regard to INTERFET and how they could be swayed to participate in the operation. Second, using this information, Australia produced a prospect list of states that were most suitable for bilateral démarches.

Negotiation Process

Prime Minister Howard himself took the political lead in negotiating countries into joining INTERFET.[57] He recalls the period between September 6 and the start of the operation as one of practically living on the phone "in pursuit of both diplomatic and potential military assistance."[58] Roughly one week after Kofi Annan's official request to Howard to lead a multilateral intervention force, APEC heads of state were scheduled to meet in Auckland for their yearly summit. APEC, an economic institution, had never served as a forum to discuss security issues before. Nevertheless, it became the decisive venue for Australia's coalition negotiations. As Australian foreign minister Downer recalled: "I don't know what would have happened without this APEC meeting."[59] It was at the margins of this summit where Howard was able to schedule bilateral meetings with APEC leaders to make direct personal approaches regarding troop contributions. Howard conferred, in particular, with those countries that had earlier been identified by DFAT as key "prospect states" to join INTERFET, as explained above.[60] At the summit, Howard gained numerous "in principle" promises of support. Howard stated that in convincing his conversation partners to support INTERFET, "the angle of how I approached each country would very much depend on the individual country."[61] This suggests that political incentives tailored to the preferences of individual states were front and center in these negotiations. Overall, Howard recalled the APEC meeting as "another example of how the occasion of international meetings provides the opportunity for leaders to resolve issues in separate 'corridor' discussions, often quite unrelated to the formal agenda of the meeting."[62] In other words, the APEC summit provided an extremely useful coalition negotiation venue.

On September 14, just one day after the APEC summit concluded in Auckland, the annual UN General Assembly (UNGA) opened in New York. Howard was unable to go to New York. Nevertheless, Foreign Minister Downer attended in his place. He was able to continue what Howard had started in Auckland: he met with prospective coalition contributors on the sidelines of the UNGA and lobbied them to join INTERFET.[63] Downer received help in this process from the U.S. government. Both U.S. president Bill Clinton and U.S. secretary of state Madeleine Albright served as important cooperation brokers. They were able to bridge structural holes and connect Australia with third parties it did not know. They also used their own resources to bargain countries into the coalition. This support was invaluable, as one senior Australian official recalled: "Whenever the coalition started to look a bit shaky, somehow somebody talked to them and . . . people stopped wavering."[64]

Immediately after the UNGA concluded, the vice chief of the Australian Defence Force, Air Marshal Doug Riding, was tasked to go on a rapid tour of Southeast Asia and follow up on the "in-principle" agreements to participate in the INTERFET coalition reached by Prime Minister Howard and Foreign Minister Downer in Auckland and New York. Riding and a team of three staff officers were mandated to conduct detailed coalition negotiations in Malaysia, Singapore, Thailand, the Philippines, and Brunei. The visits began poorly, however, when the Malaysian government changed its mind about contributing to INTERFET. Singapore also offered a much smaller group than anticipated.[65] Nevertheless, Thailand and the Philippines followed through on their commitments (see below for details).

Back in Canberra, two new institutions were created to further continue the coalition negotiations initiated by Howard, Downer, and Riding. These institutions were the East Timor Policy Unit and the INTERFET Branch, both located in the Australian Department of Defence. Their mandate included negotiating the technical details (for instance, the exact size and timing) of the deployments and acting as "strategic coalition managers."[66] Most Australian officials working in both units were surprised by the range of practical demands these countries were making once their political leadership had agreed to deploy to East Timor. Military representatives of many of the developing countries arrived with laundry lists of equipment and other services that they required from the Australians before any deployment would be conceivable. The requests included items such as military kits (weapons, ammunition, vehicles, clothing, sunglasses, and so on) and other random equipment such as generators, refrigerators, and health services, which ran the gamut from health checkups to health and disability insurance coverage.[67] Many of these countries also asked for strategic air- and sealift. Indeed, many states, if not most, arrived in Australia with "pretty much . . . nothing."[68] To satisfy their requests, Australia set up a UN Trust Fund to reimburse INTERFET coalition forces as well as pay for other operation- and reconstruction-related expenses. Australia managed to collect donations for the Trust Fund amounting to $147 million.[69] Many INTERFET participants (for instance, Thailand, Jordan, and Kenya) received reimbursement payments for their troop deployments from this fund.[70]

In sum, the INTERFET coalition negotiation process was influenced by the following factors: First, diplomatic embeddedness provided for important negotiation venues, or as Downer recalled: "I don't know what would have happened without this APEC meeting."[71] Downer and Howard used these negotiation venues to get political promises from heads of state to deploy to East Timor. Second, high-level U.S. officials, notably Bill Clinton and Madeline Albright, served, at Australia's request, as crucial cooperation brokers: Using America's widespread diplomatic networks, they helped Australia woo countries into the INTERFET coalition. Third, most of the coalition negotiations that Downer and Howard conducted focused on political considerations, such as what type of help Australia could provide to ease (and sweeten) individual countries' potential deployments to East Timor. Information on these variables was gathered exploiting diplomatic networks. Once these political negotiations were concluded, the East Timor Policy Unit and the INTERFET Branch took over organizing the technical aspects of the deployment, which involved further negotiations of more practical matters (such as deployment timetables and equipment needs).

Individual Countries' Bargaining Outcomes

This section looks at five individual instances of INTERFET coalition negotiations. It assesses the negotiations of the three largest coalition contributors (Thailand, the Philippines, and Jordan) as well as two cases that diverge in terms of diplomatic embeddedness with Australia: Canada (high on diplomatic embeddedness) and Brazil (low on diplomatic embeddedness). Overall, the objective of this section is to assess how diplomatic embeddedness impacted the negotiation process in these instances. It also explores the question of the ways that preference convergence and power asymmetries affected the negotiation outcomes.

Thailand

Thailand, which served as the deputy force commander to INTERFET, provided the second-largest contingent to the coalition after Australia. Operational planning foresaw that Australia focused its recruitment effort on Southeast Asia and in particular ASEAN. Among Southeast Asian nations, Thailand was one of the most diplomatically embedded with Australia, ranking second among all ASEAN nations (tied with Malaysia). How can these facts be connected?

Thailand did not volunteer any forces to INTERFET. Its domestic political landscape was too divided for such a decision to take place. The two groups that opposed each other were as follows: In staunch opposition to the intervention were Prime Minister Chuan Leekpai and most of the members of his cabinet. Many of them feared that an independent East Timor could lead to the ethnic breakup of Indonesia[72]—a move with potentially grave repercussions for Thailand.[73] In addition, many cabinet officials disliked the idea of Western interference in the domestic affairs of an ASEAN nation.[74] The Thai deputy foreign minister, M. R. Sukhumbhand Paribatra, summarized this attitude in the following way: "We have always said that we don't want other countries, especially the superpowers, to interfere in the region. . . . The time has come to show that we can solve the region's problems ourselves."[75] Moreover, many of them feared that Thailand's relationship with Indonesia would suffer. Thailand had important economic ties with Indonesia, and Indonesia was likely to perceive a Thai deployment to East Timor as a major betrayal. Finally and most importantly, in September 1999 Thailand was still recovering from the Asian financial crisis, which had shattered its entire economic system. In fact, Chuan's premiership had been completely absorbed with containing the aftershocks of the Asian financial crisis.[76] As a result, for Chuan and many of his collaborators, an intervention in East Timor was simply not a political priority.

In staunch support of participating in INTERFET was the Thai military. It saw in the East Timor intervention an opportunity to enhance its collaboration with Australia, broaden its range of activities, strengthen its domestic legitimacy, and gain international exposure and financial resources.[77] These officers found support in Thailand's foreign minister, Surin Pitsuwan, who also fully embraced the idea of Thailand's participation in INTERFET. Pitsuwan held a PhD from Harvard and had spent many years in the United States working in international relations and human rights issues with (among others) the Asia Foundation and American University in Washington, D.C. Pitsuwan was thus very well connected in the West, and INTERFET reflected his progressive foreign policy stance on collective international intervention.[78]

So what tilted the balance in favor of INTERFET participation? First, as mentioned earlier, Prime Minister Chuan felt indebted to Australia. Australia was the sole Western nation that had lent money to Thailand during the Asian financial crisis just months prior to INTERFET.[79] In addition, Australia's support for Thailand's candidate, Supachai Panitchpakdi, as the new head of the WTO, had been a morale boost for the battered Thai government. Second, Thailand was hoping that Australia would further help with its economic recovery.[80] Thailand wished that Australia would negotiate a free trade agreement with Thailand and extend further credit to the struggling nation. Third, close personal contacts between Australian and Thai military officers and diplomats mattered. Steve Ayling, who organized the INTERFET coalition-building process, was a classmate of the Thai crown prince at Duntroon.[81] These contacts now positively influenced the Thai government's attitude toward INTERFET.

The exact coalition negotiations unfold in the following way. Thailand's official decision to make a substantial troop commitment to INTERFET took place at the APEC summit in Auckland.[82] Both Thai prime minister Chuan and Thai foreign minister Surin Pitsuwan attended the summit. Prime Minister Howard and U.S. president Clinton, at Howard's request, met Prime Minister Chuan in bilateral meetings organized on the sideline of the summit. The conversation between Howard and Chuan was primarily focused on financial issues. Chuan said that Thailand would consider deploying to East Timor, but due to the dire economic situation in Thailand it could not shoulder the costs of such a deployment; Thailand's deployment expenses had to be defrayed.[83] Howard then assured him that there would be available resources, either directly from Australia or from the United Nations Trust Fund.[84] At Downer's request, U.S. secretary of state Madeleine Albright also met with Thai foreign minister Surin Pitsuwan during the UN General Assembly in New York. Albright offered further assurances to Pitsuwan that Thailand's INTERFET deployment expenses would be covered.[85] The Howard government then sent Doug Riding, the vice chief of the Australian Armed Forces, to Thailand to follow up on Chuan's "in principle" promise made in Auckland. Riding arrived in Bangkok on September 16, 1999, and was cordially welcomed by about forty military and civilian officials in a banquet hall in Bangkok. At the meeting, Prime Minister Chuan solemnly declared that "Thailand has the honor to contribute 1,500 troops to INTERFET."[86] The large number of troops surprised Riding and his delegation. It appeared that the Thai military had been influential in determining the precise size of Thailand's contribution. Because of its enthusiasm and its tight connections with the Australian military, it was able to lobby Chuan for a larger force than anyone had expected.[87]

Once Riding had returned from Canberra, the INTERFET Branch started negotiating with Thailand over the technical details of the Thai deployment, including financial allowances to Thai soldiers and medical and disability insurance for Thai troops.[88] Further political negotiations ensued once INTERFET was underway. In November 1999, Foreign Minister Downer himself traveled to Bangkok to devise an agenda that would help Thailand's economic recovery. Included on Downer's agenda were treaties to expand the Australian-Thai trade and investment relationship.[89] What followed was, according to Downer, a complete overhaul of the Thai-Australian relations: "When I first visited Bang-kok in 1996, the relationship bordered indifference. Now it was almost love." Aus-tralia and Thailand soon started negotiations for a free trade agreement (FTA), a development that, according to Downer, followed from Thailand's engagement in East Timor.[90] It was Australia's third FTA ever negotiated.

Jordan

Jordan contributed 700 troops to INTERFET, following Thailand as the second-largest troop contributor to INTERFET (excluding Australia). In contrast to Thailand, Jordan was only minimally diplomatically embedded with Australia. It ranked eighty-third from the Australian perspective. Indeed, it was not diplo-matic embeddedness with Australia that influenced the Jordanian deployment to East Timor. Rather, the United States acted as a cooperation broker. As men-tioned before, Australia wanted at least a small number of Muslim countries to serve in INTERFET so that the operation would not look like an "anti-Muslim" crusade. Australia, however, lacked an extensive network of diplomatic ties in the Muslim world. As a result, it asked the United States for help. In the late 1990s, Jordan was one of the Muslim countries with which the United States was most diplomatically embedded. In particular, the U.S. government was aware that the newly crowned King of Jordan, Abdullah II, was eager to get closer to the United States.[91] So, at the UN General Assembly in New York, the United States approached Jordan and suggested that it contribute to INTERFET. The Jorda-nian government then instructed its military to contact Australia and inquire about the details of a potential deployment. Steve Ayling remembers the Jorda-nian phone call in the following way: "It came in the middle of the night. It was a major general from Jordan. [I mentioned that] I was just back from the U.S. Army War College. I had met [Jordanian] Brigadier General Abdul Halim there. *He is a good friend of mine.*"[92] The caller then replied: "Abdul Halim, he is like a brother to me. We went to the academy at the same time." Ayling reckons that their common connection (via the U.S. Army War College) with Abdul Halim broke the ice between them. It created a sense of familiarity and trust. It imme-diately eased the negotiation process. When the two officers later met in person in Canberra, the Jordanian major general gave Ayling—to the surprise of his colleague—a big hug, saying, "Abdul Halim sends his best wishes." It was during his visit to Canberra when the Jordanian major general also declared that Jordan was willing to participate in INTERFET. He suggested that the best way to pro-ceed was that "we descend our men and you provide the [military] equipment." Steven Ayling, however, could not make such a promise. Australia was unable to shoulder the burden of financing Jordan's military needs. The United States thus once more stepped in and provided Jordan with all the military and financial resources it required. The U.S. government also arranged for the Jordanian contingent to be transported to East Timor.[93]

The Philippines

The Philippines contributed 600 troops to INTERFET, the third-largest military contingent (excluding Australia). Similar to Thailand (and in contrast to Jordan), the Philippines were deeply diplomatically embedded with Australia ranking first (tied with Indonesia) among ASEAN nations. The Philippine government had mixed feelings with regard to East Timor. On the one hand, the highly influential Philippine Catholic Church was deeply worried about its fellow Catholics in neighboring East Timor and thus supported intervention. Nevertheless, its voice was largely drowned out by political concerns that a Philippine deployment to East Timor could severely hurt the Philippine-Indonesian relationship. Indonesia was important to the Philippines not only because of its economic power but also because it had provided the Philippine government with substantial support in negotiations with Philippine Muslim rebels in Mindanao—a secessionist conflict that constituted a major political and security challenge to the Philippine government.[94] Even worse, the East Timor referendum had inspired these rebels to propose a similar type of independence vote to be held in the Philippines—an idea that was fiercely opposed by the Philippine government, which was unwilling to cede any ground to the secessionist movement.[95] A Philippine deployment to East Timor in defense of the island's independence would only lend further credence to Mindanao's independence claims.[96] For these reasons, it is highly unlikely that the Philippine government would have contributed to INTERFET on its own initiative. Instead, it relied heavily on Australia's influence in basing its decision to join the coalition.

The Australian government had provided the Philippines with much-needed military and economic support over the years. In the wake of the U.S. closing its military bases in the early 1990s, Australia had considerably increased its defense cooperation with the Philippines.[97] As a result, John Howard, Steve Ayling, and Douglas Riding, all of whom negotiated with the Philippines, could rely on Philippine goodwill with regard to INTERFET as well as asymmetrical dependence on continued Australian aid. Still, the Philippines attached two conditions to its deployment to East Timor: first, in an attempt to downplay the military nature of the deployment (which could potentially offend Indonesia), it insisted that its contribution to INTERFET be called a "humanitarian task force."[98] Second, it asked Australia to fully finance the Philippine deployment. The Australian government agreed to both conditions and fully covered the deployment expenses of the Philippine contingent.[99]

Canada

Canada contributed about 600 troops to INTERFET. Moreover, it ranked very high in terms of diplomatic embeddedness with Australia (tenth from the Australian perspective). Undoubtedly, these diplomatic ties influenced the Canadian decision-making process. Through numerous shared international organization memberships, especially the Commonwealth, Howard and Canadian prime minister Jean Chrétien had grown very close. With regard to this relationship, Howard writes in his biography: "I was in office for almost twelve years and thus had the opportunity of many associations with fellow leaders. Most of them did not progress beyond the stage of professional cordiality, either through infrequency of meetings or departure from office or, in some instances, not finding much to talk about except the business at hand. [Some friendships, though] became closer. . . . Into that category I would place . . . Jean Chrétien."[100] The Chrétien Cabinet was indeed split in its support for a Canadian participation in INTERFET. Canada's foreign minister, Lloyd Axworthy, a staunch and public promoter of the concept of "human security" at the United Nations, was firmly in favor of a Canadian deployment to East Timor.[101] However, most other cabinet members were significantly less enthusiastic about the plan.[102] The dominant opinion was that assisting East Timor was not worth the risk of straining relations with Indonesia.[103] Moreover, at the time Canada was also busy in the NATO deployment to Kosovo, to which it was contributing about 1,500 troops. As a result, when initial rumors emerged that Canada would be participating in INTERFET, Chrétien quickly declared: "We are not at that stage. Canada is always considering any difficult situation, but we are not there yet."[104] Nevertheless, Howard personally appealed to Chrétien at the APEC summit in Auckland and insisted that Canadian help would be essential. Chrétien thus relented. Howard himself explained the Canada reversal the following way: "it certainly had a lot to do with Jean Chrétien and me getting along. . . ."[105]

Brazil

Brazil sent a detachment of 50 military personnel to participate in INTERFET. Brazilian diplomatic embeddedness with Australia was low, ranking thirty-third from the Australian perspective. So why did Brazil participate? Brazilian motivations were multifaceted. Its connection to East Timor was cultural. Both countries had been Portuguese colonies, and in both countries, Portuguese was the official language. Moreover, while Portugal was barred from participating in INTERFET because of its colonial connection, Brazil was encouraged to deploy by multiple actors, notably Portugal.[106] Brazil can thus be considered a bandwagoneer. It had intrinsic motivation to help its fellow lusophone country East Timor in its struggle for independence.

Summary of Findings

The key objective of this chapter was to investigate whether Australia's coalition-building techniques significantly differ from those employed by the United States. Do less hegemonic powers build coalitions differently? Moreover, the chapter also sought to uncover how the specific characteristics of the INTERFET operation (its humanitarian character, the UN mandate, and so on) affected the coalition-building process.

Overall, the INTERFET coalition-building process matches the mechanisms identified in chapter 2 quite well—despite INTERFET being set up by Australia and not the United States.

The preferences held by individual states in the international community with regard to East Timor were very diverse. While many countries were appalled by the situation in East Timor, very few were willing to volunteer military forces to stop the bloodshed. This is certainly true for United States, which had to be pressured by Australia and Portugal to actively support the intervention, and other Western countries. For them, East Timor did not constitute a top foreign policy priority, despite the humanitarian urgency and the UN mandate. East Timor was far away and most of them were absorbed with the Kosovo crisis. While they were willing to help Australia politically (speak favorably of a potential intervention at the UN and the like), they still refused to deploy troops to East Timor. The situation among Asian countries was even more dire. Many of these states did not particularly like the idea of an Australian-led (Western, Christian) intervention in East Timor. They either feared for their relationship with Indonesia or were worried about a "balkanization" of the region. As such, preference convergence cannot be offered to explain the coalition we observed. INTERFET did not form "organically."

TABLE 6.1   Results of case study: INTERFET

	DEEPLY EMBEDDED WITH AUSTRALIA	WEAKLY EMBEDDED WITH AUSTRALIA
Bandwagoneer	–	Brazil
Self-starter	–	–
Coalition recruit	Thailand The Philippines Canada	Jordan (recruited via the United States)

Australia had to actively recruit INTERFET participants. To do so it instrumentalized diplomatic embeddedness. It searched for and bargained countries into INTERFET. What explains Australia's motivation to take on this role? Guilt for the "Howard letter" and a domestic groundswell in favor of intervention propelled the Australian government to intervene in East Timor. Yet Australia feared that Indonesia would antagonize a coalition containing only white Australian forces. It thus considered it essential to build a multilateral coalition composed of as many Asian, nonwhite, non-Christian forces as possible. Given these operational constraints, Australia exploited especially the diplomatic networks it had with Southeast Asia. Australian officials obtained information on deployment preferences of potential coalition participants through Australian embassy networks, military-to-military contacts, and alumni networks of foreign Australian military academy graduates. Using this information, DFAT produced a "prospect list" of countries fit for bilateral démarches. Howard and Downer then approached these countries during the APEC summit in Auckland and the UN General Assembly in New York to discuss a possible deployment.

Interestingly, Australia thought it necessary to seek help from the United States in identifying and negotiating with potential INTERFET participants. Both at the APEC summit and the UN General Assembly, U.S. officials, most notably Bill Clinton and Madeline Albright, helped Australia in their coalition-building quest. This feature of "great power cooperation brokerage" was absent in the previous instances of coalition building analyzed in this book. It suggests that although Australia's diplomatic network is powerful, especially in the Asia-Pacific region, when it came to recruiting countries from other geographical regions (for instance, the Middle East), it fell short. The United States had to help to bridge structural holes (that is, connect Australia with third parties it was not embedded with).

When choosing suitable INTERFET recruits, did Australia pick countries that it found particularly vulnerable to its coercive pressure? During the INTERFET search process, Australia certainly did not ignore the fact that countries such as Thailand and the Philippines were dependent on Australian aid. Similarly, the United States was aware of Jordan's desire to get closer to the United States when it suggested to the Jordanian government that it should join INTERFET. Asymmetrical vulnerabilities in this respect mattered in the search process for INTERFET contributions. Nevertheless, during the negotiation process, explicit threats (cuts of bilateral aid and the like) do not appear to have been used. Instead, a healthy bargaining spirit, deeply steeped in diplomatic embeddedness, prevailed. Steve Ayling, in particular, made this attitude apparent when he mentioned that "you had to negotiate people into a coalition and you had to be clever how you did it."[107]

With regard to Thailand, it is safe to say that the Thai government did not volunteer any forces to INTERFET. Rather, Australia wooed Thailand to join the coalition. Thailand is deeply diplomatically embedded with Australia, and these connections proved beneficial during the coalition-building process. First, diplomatic embeddedness allowed Australia to assess Thailand's deployment preferences. Most importantly, Australian officials exploited the fact that Thailand owed Australia a favor because Australia had extended loans to Thailand during the Asian financial crisis (a bilateral diplomatic tie) and had helped the Thai WTO candidate to win the nomination process amid fierce competition (a multilateral diplomatic relationship). Moreover, Australia could rely on close personal connections, especially in the Thai military, which had been established via common training exercises and Australia's military academies. These connections played an important role in swaying the Thai government not only to join INTERFET but also to send a substantive force and provide the deputy force commander. Moreover, Australian officials used summits of APEC and the UN— international organizations that they shared with Thailand—to negotiate in person over a coalition contribution. Both Howard and Downer confirmed that these personal encounters with the Thai leadership mattered greatly. The Thai example thus illustrates three of the key benefits of diplomatic embeddedness: (1) access to private information; (2) payment flexibility (via goodwill accounts); and (3) the utility of negotiating venues (APEC and the UN). What was the role of power in these negotiations? There is no doubt that Australia used its superior economic capabilities to cajole Thailand. Nevertheless, the bargaining outcome was still a quid pro quo exchange: Australia guaranteed that Thailand's deployment expenses would be fully covered. Moreover, Australia negotiated a trade agreement with Thailand in the aftermath of INTERFET—a development which would not have happened without Thai participation in INTERFET. Thailand thus got pretty much everything it wanted.

With regard to Jordan, U.S. brokerage stands out as a critical determinant for the Jordanian decision to deploy to East Timor. In this context, the United States certainly used (at least implicitly) the existing power asymmetries between the United States and Jordan and built upon Jordan's eagerness to get closer to the United States to raise the country's interest in INTERFET. Moreover, U.S. willingness to pick up the Jordanian deployment bill and provide it with military equipment also certainly affected its INTERFET deployment decision.

The Philippine case, in turn, again highlights the impact of Australia's diplomatic networks and the influence of Australian aid and security relationships in the Asian Pacific. Overall, the Philippine deployment to East Timor can only be understood when considering Philippine dependence on Australian aid and Australia's willingness to bankroll the Philippine deployment.

In summary, the three cases of the largest troop contributions (selected on the dependent variables) thus all confirm that deployment decisions were not self-motivated. Rather, all three countries required external incentives to motivate their force contribution. Nevertheless, power asymmetries clearly mattered in all three instances.

Finally, what do we learn from Brazil (low diplomatic embeddedness) and Canada (high diplomatic embeddedness)? As expected in the Brazilian case, diplomatic embeddedness mattered little. Brazil was self-motivated to join the operation. In contrast, in the Canadian case, social connections and friendship built up via diplomatic embeddedness made all the difference. Canadian prime minister Chrétien had grown close with Howard. Via extensive common international organization membership they had interacted with each other on a frequent basis. The resulting friendship impacted Canada's decision to deploy to East Timor.

In sum, the INTERFET case firmly rejects the preference convergence model. The coercion model, however, cannot be dismissed. Indeed, the Thai and Philippine cases illustrate the importance of asymmetric power capabilities—even in the case of Australia, a much less powerful state than the United States. With regard to diplomatic embeddedness, INTERFET illustrates that it matters in ways big and small. In comparison to the previous chapters, the following advantages (and novel findings) stand out: First, diplomatic embeddedness provided important negotiation venues. Australia made substantial use of multilateral summits such as the APEC summit and the UNGA in New York. These events indeed became the epicenters for Australian recruitment activity mainly insofar as they presented Australia with opportunities for corridor discussions unrelated to the actual agenda of the summits. Second, diplomatic embeddedness changed the bargaining atmosphere by making a "personal" difference in coalition negotiations (for instance, with the Thai military). A classified report later drafted by the Australian Department of Defence titled "Coalition Building—INTERFET Lessons Learned" presents this as follows: "The value of military personal relationships developed through previous training and operational activities with other nations cannot be emphasized enough [. . .]. The management of military professional and personal relationships is of primary importance."[108] Third, the case of Thailand nicely illustrates how diplomatic embeddedness can create goodwill in partner countries that can then be retrieved on the occasion of a coalition-building exercise.

RESISTING REBELS IN CHAD AND THE CENTRAL AFRICAN REPUBLIC

EUFOR Chad-CAR (2008–2009)

The key to understanding the conflict in Chad and the Central African Republic (CAR) lies in the outbreak of the Darfur crisis in early 2003 (for details, see also chapter 5). Darfur borders Chad and the CAR in the west. At the beginning of the Darfur conflict, key members of the Darfur rebel factions organizing the insurgency against Khartoum were of Chadian origin. They were using the Chadian and Central African sides of the border region as support bases for their fight against Sudanese president Al-Bashir.[1] Traditionally, Al-Bashir had kept a good relationship with the Chadian president Idriss Déby. So when the Darfur crisis erupted, Al-Bashir asked Déby to assist him in suppressing the rebellion from his side of the border. Initially, Déby agreed to support Al-Bashir in exchange for money and military equipment from Sudan. However, Déby was forced to renege on his agreement shortly thereafter due to mounting disapproval among his domestic ethnic support base.[2] Displeased by Déby's reversal, Al-Bashir responded by throwing his support behind disgruntled Chadians eager to see their president overthrown.[3] By mid-2005, over 275,000 refugees were trapped in the middle of this Sudanese-Chadian proxy war. Most of them were forced to live in crowded, unsanitary refugee camps on the Chadian and Central African sides of the border,[4] wherein banditry and violent attacks as well as human rights abuses such as sexual violence were prevalent.[5]

In an effort to address this complex situation, the EU deployed EUFOR Chad-CAR. The key objective of the force was to protect civilians living in the refugee camps, facilitate the delivery of humanitarian aid, and ensure the safety of humanitarian personnel operating in the conflict area.[6] The operation was authorized by UN Resolution 1778, which passed on September 25, 2007. The EU Council approved the force on October 15, 2007, and the first EU military troops deployed to Chad-CAR in early February 2008. Operations lasted until March 2009, when a UN follow-up force (MINURCAT) took the relay from EUFOR Chad-CAR. The operation involved approximately 3,700 troops provided by the following countries: France (2,000 forces), Ireland (450 forces), Poland (400 forces), Sweden (280 forces), Austria (170 forces), Russia (100 forces), Italy (90 forces), Netherlands (90 forces), Spain (80 forces), Belgium (70 forces), Finland (60 forces), Albania (60 forces), Croatia (15 forces), and Slovenia (15 forces).

France initiated and politically orchestrated the deployment of EUFOR Chad-CAR. France worked relentlessly at the UN to pass a UN resolution that would authorize the EU mission and plan for the EU-UN transition.[7] France introduced the issue at the EU Council and lobbied EU member states to support the proposal.[8] Most EU members did not share France's urgency to deploy an EU operation to Chad-CAR. So it was up to France to cajole these countries to contribute forces to the coalition. In this process, France instrumentalized diplomatic embeddedness. It exploited its EU connections and other diplomatic ties to assess deployment preferences of potential troop contributors and to construct issue linkages and side payments.

This chapter focuses on the deployment decisions of the three largest troop-contributing countries: Ireland, Poland, and Sweden; Austria, a deeply embedded state with France; and Russia, a less embedded state with France. The deployment decisions of Ireland and Poland resulted from side payments directly linked to the EU context, while Sweden was largely self-motivated to join the operation. It was a bandwagoneer. Austria, on the other hand, which is deeply embedded with France, joined EUFOR Chad-CAR because it was eager to link the EUFOR deployment with its bid for a nonpermanent seat on the UN Security Council. Russia (which is less diplomatically embedded with France), in turn, was a self-starter. Its announcement to join EUFOR Chad-CAR occurred on the same day that the EU met in Brussels to decide on an EU observer mission to monitor the Russian withdrawal from Georgia in the aftermath of the Russia-Georgia War in 2008. There can be no doubt that Russia wanted to garner EU goodwill in this tense situation.

Origins of French Involvement in Chad and the CAR

In March 2006, Sudanese president Al-Bashir almost succeeded with his plan of overthrowing Chadian president Idriss Déby. Sudanese-financed Chadian rebels were able to stage a surprise attack on N'Djamena, the capital of Chad—a coup attempt that likely would have been successful had the French military not intervened to protect the Déby regime. What were French motives to launch this unilateral protection effort? Geostrategic reasons were arguably predominant. Chad had been a French colony until 1960. Upon achieving independence, France negotiated a military assistance agreement with the country, which provided France with the use of a major military base outside of N'Djamena.[9] Located almost perfectly in the middle of the African continent, halfway between the French West African base in Gabon and its East African base in Djibouti,[10] this base eventually turned into one of France's key military installations in Africa.[11] For France to maintain the base, it required that the Chadian government remain amenable to French interests.[12] By 2006, the French government had realized that Idriss Déby was not an "ideal" president to support. Nevertheless, France could not think of another suitable Francophile candidate who could take over from Déby.[13] Thus, the French kept Déby in power—even using French military forces to do so.

After the attempted coup against Déby in 2006, France put the Chadian conflict on the agenda of the UN Security Council. French officials suggested that a UN peacekeeping force be deployed to Chad to stabilize the situation.[14] French diplomats maintained that such a force could serve as a buffer between Sudan and Chad, preventing Sudanese-sponsored rebel groups from overrunning N'Djamena as they had done in March 2006.[15] They further argued that such a policy would also prevent a larger regional destabilization (that is, regional chaos expanding to Niger or even the African Great Lakes region). One French diplomat noted that in this situation, France was seeking "stability" in Chad, adding: "The rebels aren't any better than Déby, we simply wish to avoid a situation of continuous warfare affecting the broader region."[16] Following the French peacekeeping request, the UN Peacekeeping Department (UNDPKO) sent a fact-finding mission to Chad in February 2007.[17] Many UN officials were highly skeptical of the French plan and tried to stall a UN peacekeeping deployment to the best of their abilities.[18] These officials reckoned that the operation had a taste of France using the UN to advance its own political agenda in Chad.[19]

In May 2007, the French people elected Nicolas Sarkozy to replace Jacques Chirac as their president. Sarkozy thus inherited the Chad dossier. Although Sarkozy himself did not care much about the issue,[20] his foreign minister, Bernard Kouchner, quickly picked up the topic.[21] Prior to becoming the French foreign minister, Kouchner had founded the international humanitarian organization Médecins Sans Frontières (Doctors Without Borders). He had also been a key architect of the "responsibility to protect" (R2P) doctrine. For Kouchner, Chad represented a humanitarian catastrophe linked tightly to the Darfur conflict: hundreds of thousands of civilians were trapped in refugee camps, where they were exposed to violent attacks. Kouchner thus suggested establishing "humanitarian corridors" in Chad—a concept that had been used during the Balkan wars to provide food and assistance to UN safe havens in Bosnia.[22] Nevertheless, the policy had produced mixed results at the time, and the idea quickly lost momentum. To fill the vacuum, Kouchner's advisers resurrected the idea of deploying a military operation to Chad. They argued that such an operation could kill two birds with one stone: it could provide protection to the refugees and could also be used to deter rebels from crossing the border into Chad and overthrowing Déby.[23] Since the refugee camps were also on the northeastern CAR side of the border, France included CAR in the operational plans.

After some consultations, Nicolas Sarkozy agreed to the proposal. On the one hand, Sarkozy saw the geostrategic benefits of the intervention. On the other hand, and maybe more importantly, Sarkozy wanted to accommodate Kouchner, who was lobbying hard for the deployment. To soften his reputation as a fierce right-wing conservative, Sarkozy had put together a cabinet of ministers representing not only his own conservative right-wing party but also the French socialist and center parties.[24] Kouchner was the most prominent addition to this cabinet. Thus, he held considerable bargaining power. Without Kouchner, Sarkozy's "gouvernement d'ouverture" would fall apart.[25]

Planning for Coalition Intervention

Kouchner suggested that France launch the operation via the European Union. A unilateral intervention in Chad was out of the question due to fears that domestic and international audiences would accuse the French government of neocolonialism.[26] Moreover, Kouchner wanted a fast deployment, which was difficult to achieve in the UN context. An EU operation, on the other hand, would deploy quickly, and the "Europeanization" of the intervention would provide an elevated level of authority and legitimacy.[27] It also would enable France to split some of the costs of the mission with other EU members.[28] Indeed, the final plan that the French government developed looked as follows: The EU would stay in Chad-CAR for about a year, after which the UN would take over from the EU. The EU was thus supposed to act in a "bridging" function: it would stabilize the situation in the region before the UN would move in. French military planners anticipated that the EU component of the force should consist of ten companies (some 3,500 troops) with a significant air component for enhanced mobility.[29]

This operational plan put constraints on the force recruitment effort. First, France had to focus on EU member states. While non-EU member states can serve in EU operations, a minimum number of EU forces had to be found.

Otherwise, criticism of the operation would spike. In addition, among the available EU forces, France was eager to recruit "neutral" countries, that is, states that had little history of interference in African wars such as Ireland, Sweden, Austria, and Finland. France thereby intended to further dampen claims of political bias toward Idriss Déby. If these countries joined the coalition, how could it be a prejudiced operation? Second, France needed some force contributors that could provide aviation assets, especially helicopters.

Searching for Coalition Contributions

The first critical recruitment task French officials hoped to accomplish was to fill the position of EUFOR Operation Commander, the highest-ranking position in the EU force. Traditionally, this position was given to the country that also provided the largest national contingent to the operation. Nevertheless, France intended to break this rule. France would provide the largest contingent, but EUFOR Chad-CAR needed a non-French citizen to serve as Operation Commander to highlight the European character of the operation and to mitigate the claims of French bias toward the Chadian government.

France's initial key contender for the position of EUFOR Operation Commander was Sweden. Sweden was, of course, a member of the European Union. Additionally, even among EU member states, Sweden ranked among the nations most diplomatically embedded with France. It ranked eighth globally—sixth in the EU context. Via their extensive connections, French government officials were in almost constant contact with their Swedish counterparts. These links revealed that Swedish government officials, notably Swedish foreign minister Carl Bildt, were intrigued by the prospect of deploying to Chad.[30] Bildt was a staunch defender of European defense integration. Moreover, he strongly believed that Europe and the Nordic states, in particular, should get more involved in Africa, no matter the country or conflict. At numerous EU meetings, he had passionately defended the point of view that Africa was where future conflicts loomed. During the first half of 2008, Sweden was also the lead nation of the EU Battlegroup on standby.[31] The EU Battlegroup concept had been developed for exactly this purpose—a quick EU deployment to address critical security or humanitarian emergencies.[32] Bildt had been highly supportive of the Battlegroup idea as well as the creation of a Nordic Battlegroup composed of Sweden, Finland, Norway, Estonia, and Ireland. Since the development of such a military entity led to significant changes in the character of the Swedish armed forces and force structure, French officials reckoned that Bildt would be eager to show off the results of the reforms to the Swedish and European publics.[33]

In case the Swedish option fell through, French officials also looked to Ireland as a backup option. Ireland was one of France's co-members in the EU, but it scored somewhat lower than Sweden in terms of diplomatic embeddedness with France (it ranked sixteenth among EU member states in 2005). Still, via common diplomatic connections, France learned that Irish troops were available (and eager) for a new deployment. The UN operations in which Irish troops had been serving, most notably in Liberia and Lebanon, were dwindling, which relieved available Irish troops.[34] France also knew that the Irish Department of Defense had been actively looking for a new deployment because "you can't let the boys hang out in the barracks for too long."[35] Irish defense officials had signaled to France that EUFOR Chad-CAR was "an interesting operation" for them.[36] It promised to be more demanding than anything the Irish military had ever done before—an appealing factor given the Irish military's desire to step up its peace-keeping experience and reputation, both in Europe and around the world.[37] Still, some French officials were not entirely convinced that Ireland would actually deploy under an EU (instead of a UN) umbrella. Important sections in the Irish population strongly opposed the EU's common defense policy. They feared that such a policy would drag "neutral" Ireland into continental European military adventures.[38]

EU administrative procedures foresaw that the Operation Commander would lead the recruitment process of EU forces by means of a series of "force gen-eration conferences" in which participating member states pledged assets and capabilities for the operation in a dynamic of supply and demand.[39] As a result, French officials initially counted on that legal mechanism to recruit troops for EUFOR Chad-CAR:[40] once the UN mandate for EUFOR Chad-CAR was success-fully secured on September 25, 2007, France prompted EU officials to start hold-ing these conferences at the EU headquarters in Brussels. The first such meeting took place in Brussels on September 24, 2007. Counter to French expectations, the event was a "disaster" in that "practically no meaningful contributions (apart from the French) were made."[41] "The process resembled a game of poker," one participant recalled, "everybody knew how important this operation was to the French. They thus knew that holding out could only be to their advantage. Even-tually, the French would chip in."[42]

The French government thus realized that it had to dramatically change its recruitment strategy. It had to instrumentalize its diplomatic networks; it had to exploit them as a strategic asset and as a power capability in order to construct the EUFOR coalition. At the Quai D'Orsay, the French Foreign Office, a cell was formed with the specific task of managing the recruitment process for EUFOR Chad-CAR. One of Bernard Kouchner's closest advisers, Éric Chevallier, was named Special Representative for EUFOR Chad-CAR and tasked to head the cell.

Chevallier then instructed French diplomats to purposefully collect information on EUFOR deployment preferences of EU member states but also states outside of the EU, using all sources they had at their disposal. French embassy employees and military attachés were told to feel out their local counterparts with respect to EUFOR Chad-CAR. They also approached resident foreign embassies in Paris with informal inquiries about a potential EUFOR participation. Chevallier's staff would then combine this information with the specific EUFOR capability needs and the gaps in the coalition lineup to produce a "prospect list" of countries to be approached for detailed bilateral negotiations. Chevallier would then visit the political leadership at the highest possible level in the identified countries.[43] Each visit was carefully orchestrated by the Quai d'Orsay: based on the information it had collected via diplomatic embeddedness, it was able to provide detailed talking points on how the topic of Chad-CAR should be approached, which local actors might support a deployment, which actors might oppose it, what side payments might be offered to tilt the political balance in favor of a deployment, and so forth. For example, with regard to Albania's contribution to EUFOR, the French military attaché in Tirana reported that the Albanian leadership would be inclined to join the force if France subsidized the deployment; Albania wanted France to cover food rations, uniforms, vehicles and other types of military equipment. Chevallier then used this information to pin down the exact Albanian needs.[44] In November 2007, Alexis Morel, Chevallier's collaborator, summarized the process the following way: "obtaining commitments from EU partners [is] not automatic and [entails] some wrangling . . . we are in the nuts-and-bolts phase of putting this thing together and we will push our way through."[45]

Chevallier and his team at the Quai d'Orsay were assisted in their work by the French foreign minister, Bernard Kouchner; the French defense minister, Hervé Morin; and even President Sarkozy. All three used every bilateral and multilateral meeting they attended during fall and winter 2007 to approach suitable force contributors. Often, they had also been briefed by the Quai d'Orsay on how best to bring up the topic of Chad-CAR to the identified countries. Many of these face-to-face conversations were informal, as in: "By the way, have you decided upon your contribution to EUFOR? Is there anything we can do to help to make your decision easier?"[46] Prominent EU officials, most importantly EU High Representative for Foreign Affairs Javier Solana and the chairman of the EU Military Committee, Henri Bentégeat, also assisted in these efforts, repeating the message and explaining the operation to potential troop-contributing nations.[47] Bernard Kouchner even asked the U.S. special envoy to Sudan, Andrew Natsios, and the U.S. assistant secretary of state for African affairs, Jendayi Frazer, for help in influencing other EU members to support the EU intervention.[48] Both were asked to explain to hesitant EU member states the importance of the mission with respect to stabilizing the broader Sahel region.[49] These individuals thus served as cooperation brokers.

Subsequent force generation conferences in Brussels were also heavily influenced by France. In particular, when it came to whom to invite from outside of the EU and NATO, French diplomats consistently had their fingers in the pie.[50] They suggested, more specifically, Brazil, Switzerland, Morocco, South Africa, Argentina, and Turkey.[51] France maintained close diplomatic relationships especially with Switzerland (ranking eighth), Brazil (twelfth), Morocco (twenty-first) and Argentina (twenty-eighth). France thought that these ties would help to lure these states into EUFOR. Moreover, some of these countries had previously served in EU operations—which provided for another important persuasion point. Turkey, for instance, had deployed with EU operations in Bosnia-Herzegovina (EUFOR Althea, EUPM BiH), Kosovo (EULEX Kosovo), Macedonia (EUPOL Proxima, Concordia), and the Democratic Republic of Congo (EUFOR RD Congo, EUPOL Kinshasa). Brazil and South Africa both participated in the EU operation Artemis in the DRC in 2003, and Argentina had served in EUFOR Althea in Bosnia.[52]

In summary, France instrumentalized its diplomatic networks to search for EUFOR participants. Similarly to the United States during the Korean War and Australia during INTERFET, such instrumentalization did not occur automatically. Rather, the calamitous first force generation conference in Brussels triggered the strategy reversal. In this moment, French officials realized that states would not join EUFOR on their own accord. Rather, they had to be bargained into joining the coalition. In this process, diplomatic networks constituted an invaluable asset, a strategic capability to organize collective action. To determine which states might be most suitable for bilateral démarches, France relied on information collected via diplomatic embeddedness. Moreover, high-ranking French officials, including President Sarkozy, used multilateral and bilateral summits to ask countries for troop contributions. These summits thus served as coalition negotiation venues. Finally, France solicited help from EU officials such as EUFOR Force Commander Pat Nash, EU High Representative for Foreign Affairs Javier Solana, and Chairman of the EU Military Committee Henri Bentégeat—and even U.S. officials Andrew Natsios and Jendayi Frazer. These actors were used as cooperation brokers.

Individual Countries' Bargaining Outcomes

This section looks at five instances of coalition negotiations. It assesses the negotiations of the three largest EUFOR Chad-CAR contributors (excluding France):

Ireland, Poland, and Sweden. Moreover, it also looks at two cases that diverge in terms of diplomatic embeddedness with France: Austria (high on diplomatic embeddedness) and Russia (lower on diplomatic embeddedness).

Ireland

Ireland's participation in EUFOR Chad-CAR was highly contested domestically. Overall, Ireland was split into two camps. On the one hand, Irish aid organizations were largely supportive of the mission. Irish human rights NGOs and the Irish Catholic Church were active in mobilizing domestic constituencies to stop the genocide in Darfur.[53] An EU operation that would address the plight of the Darfuri refugees was thus something they could get behind. In addition to these humanitarian and religious groups, the Irish military also liked the idea of deploying to Chad-CAR. Since its first peacekeeping deployment to the Congo in the 1960s, the Irish army had prided itself on being one of the most engaged Western peacekeeping nations in the world.

On the other hand, however, Irish diplomats and important actors in the Irish cabinet were staunchly opposed to such deployment. From their point of view, Irish participation in an EU military operation was an immensely risky undertaking.[54] In mid-2007, Ireland had yet to vote on the EU constitutional treaty known as the Lisbon Treaty. A referendum on Irish accession to the Lisbon Treaty was planned for early 2008. The treaty included further provisions on EU cooperation in military and defense affairs. Irish opponents to the treaty were particularly critical of European defense policy, and EUFOR Chad-CAR exemplified their worries. An op-ed published in the *Irish Times* neatly summarized this viewpoint:

> The Chad operation highlights the fears that many Irish people have about the direction of Irish and EU military developments, even before the Lisbon Treaty takes us further down the same road. Might Ireland's honourable record of impartial participation in UN peacekeeping be compromised by participation in EU operations that could serve as fig-leaves for the promotion of the interests of the French state, or of other EU states? It is precisely because of such concerns that opponents of the Lisbon Treaty are alarmed at the proposals to extend the types of tasks EU forces may engage in.[55]

For these reasons, the Irish Foreign Office was strongly critical of Irish EUFOR participation. It feared that any problems in Chad could be exploited by the Irish anti-EU camp, thereby jeopardizing the "yes" vote in the scheduled referendum.[56] A rejection of the Lisbon Treaty by Irish voters was, however, a nightmare scenario. In 2001, the Irish had rejected the Nice Treaty, an EU treaty preceding the Lisbon Treaty. This action had very negative repercussions for Irish diplomacy and for Ireland's reputation in the European Union. Irish diplomats felt ostracized by other EU member states until 2004, when the Irish EU presidency managed to turn things around.

So what tipped the balance in favor of an Irish EUFOR participation? It was Bertie Ahern, the Irish Taoiseach. Ahern was not interested in EUFOR Chad-CAR for humanitarian or geopolitical reasons.[57] Ahern was a "local guy."[58] He had risen through the ranks of the Fianna Fáil party because of his economic credentials. Instead, Ahern's interest in sending Irish troops to Chad originated from his desire to win French support for his candidacy as EU president.[59] In mid-2007, Ahern's chances to land the job looked rather good. At that time, Ahern was one of the longest-serving and most popular European heads of state. His masterful management of the Irish EU presidency in 2004 had made him the chief contender for the presidency of the EU Commission three years earlier.[60] Twenty-one EU leaders preferred Ahern over João Barroso for president of the EU Commission. However, Ahern declined the opportunity. Regarding this matter, Ahern wrote in his memoirs:

> There is no doubt I gave it serious thought [to become president of the EU Commission in 2004]. I was confident I had the numbers. I didn't seem to have many enemies and had shown that I was capable of doing the job. The big three powers, Britain, Germany, and France, all wanted me to run. . . . In the end, I decided no.[61]

But Ahern admitted:

> Partly it was because I thought there was still a job to be done at home. There was the question of living in Brussels, which didn't appeal much. And then there was the thought that while president of the commission was a good job, it was also a thankless one. Perhaps if the constitution came into effect in 2006 and they were looking for a permanent EU president of the council, maybe then I might let my name go forward. But that question hadn't come up yet.[62]

In mid-2007, Ahern's key contenders for the EU presidency were former British prime minister Tony Blair and the prime minister of Luxembourg, Jean-Claude Juncker.[63] France had initially supported Tony Blair as its preferred candidate for EU president, even though Blair was a difficult candidate to back.[64] Blair had little support in most other EU member states, chiefly because of his steadfast support for the U.S. invasion of Iraq in 2003. Recognizing this, France was willing to reconsider its position. Nevertheless, it would not do so without any political payoff. With this in mind, on September 21, 2007, Sarkozy invited Ahern to attend a rugby match between Ireland and France in Paris. Ahern's invitation to Paris constituted the first Franco-Irish bilateral meeting since Sarkozy's election in May 2007. Preceding the rugby match, both heads of state attended a working lunch. Several of my interviewees (as well as media sources) confirmed that France appears to have made an offer to Ireland that day: if Ireland was willing to contribute troops to EUFOR Chad-CAR, France would consider backing Ahern's candidacy to become EU president. While the details of the offer are not clear, Irish participation in EUFOR was definitely decided at that particular lunch.[65] Michael Howard, the secretary-general of the Irish Department of Defense, recalls, for instance, the following regarding the Paris lunch:

> I was in charge of telling the [Irish] treasury department how much the Chad operation would cost. We had made our calculations. Since this was probably the most challenging operation Ireland had ever participated in, we didn't want to send our boys out with bad equipment. So we came up with an estimate of €50 million—which is a lot of money. I knew that the Treasury wouldn't be happy about it. So when I went to meet the secretary-general of the Treasury. I was kind of worried. However, when I walked into the room, the Secretary General [of the Treasury Department] said, "Well, this has better been an effing nice lunch, because it will cost me €50 million dollars." In this moment I knew that Bertie Ahern had already done the whole work and the operation would go forward.[66]

On September 26, 2007, only five days after the Franco-Irish meeting in Paris, the Irish cabinet approved the deployment of 350 Irish soldiers to Chad and the CAR.[67] A week later, on October 2, the Irish government announced that Irish General Pat Nash had been appointed Operation Commander of EUFOR Chad-CAR.[68] In early November, the Irish foreign minister, Dermot Ahern, traveled to Chad to further discuss the mission with government officials in Chad and Sudan.[69] Concurrently, the government augmented Irish participation from 350 to 450 troops. Interestingly, once Ireland had committed troops to EUFOR Chad-CAR, the Irish Foreign Office worked very hard to forestall any potentially catastrophic repercussions of the Irish deployment to Chad on the scheduled Irish EU referendum. Most importantly, the Irish government insisted on special assurances from France to evacuate the operation in case of an emergency.[70] Ireland also pushed for the inclusion of a "neutrality clause" in the EUFOR operational plan to appease its domestic constituency, which had begun questioning the real motivations behind the Irish Chad deployment.[71] Upon securing these safeguards, Ireland finally deployed to Chad in February 2008. Diplomatic embeddedness was thus critical in constructing the issue linkage between Bertie

Ahern's candidacy to become EU president and the Irish deployment to Chad-CAR. Without common EU membership, such issue linkage could not have occurred.

Poland

Poland sent approximately 400 troops to Chad-CAR, the third-largest national contingent of EUFOR. Poland did not initially consider a military deployment to Chad-CAR whatsoever. Poland had no political or economic relationships with neither Chad nor CAR. Moreover, in contrast to Ireland, there were no domestic constituencies that were actively following the Darfur conflict and pushing for intervention. Also in contrast to Ireland, the Polish military was not keen on deploying to Chad. In mid-2007, approximately 5,000 Polish troops were still serving in the U.S.-led Iraq operation and NATO's Afghanistan operation, quite a substantial deployment by Polish standards. Therefore, to fully understand the Polish deployment to Chad we again need to take into account French lobbying efforts and diplomatic embeddedness. According to my interviews, Polish participation in the EUFOR coalition was decided shortly before the Lisbon Informal EU Summit on October 18, 2007.[72] France used the Lisbon Treaty negotiations—negotiations that would affect the future institutional makeup of the EU—to construct a side payment that would include Polish participation in EUFOR Chad-CAR. By then, French diplomats were fully aware that Poland was adamantly opposed to the introduction of a new EU council voting mechanism (that is, a voting mechanism that would be based on the double majority of EU citizens and EU countries). Poland had threatened several times to veto the Lisbon Treaty, first at the Brussels EU Council Summit in June 2007 and then at the Lisbon meeting in October 2007.[73] What Poland wanted in return for its support of the Lisbon Treaty was the inclusion of the Ioannina mechanism—a mechanism that would require the EU Council to freeze decisions for two years if (a) at least three quarters of the population or (b) at least three quarters of the number of EU member states necessary to constitute a blocking minority indicate their opposition to the council adopting an act by qualified majority. From the Polish perspective, such a mechanism would prevent the "big" EU countries, especially Germany, from dictating EU policy.[74] The inclusion of this mechanism was, however, opposed by almost all other EU members. Yet, to recruit Poland for EUFOR Chad-CAR, France declared its support for the measure (and thus the inclusion of the mechanism discussed above in the treaty) in October 2007.[75] After the Polish elections in November 2007, the new Polish defense minister, Bogdan Klich, confirmed Poland's promise to send soldiers to Chad.[76] However, new conditions were added to the Polish participation, such as logistical support for the Polish deployment as well as military equipment. A French report estimates that France provided €2.43 million in such supplies to the Polish contingent for its military involvement in Chad-CAR overall.[77] Thus, similar to Ireland, diplomatic embeddedness between France and Poland was a necessary precondition for this issue linkage to become a reality.

Sweden

As mentioned earlier, Sweden was the key French contender to serve as Operation Commander of EUFOR. Sweden is highly diplomatically embedded with France, as already demonstrated. Several high-ranking French government officials had expansive relationships with Swedish officials, particularly Sweden's foreign minister, Carl Bildt. They anticipated that he would be instrumental in deciding on a Swedish deployment to Chad-CAR. When approached by France, Bildt seriously considered deploying a substantive Swedish contingent to Chad. However, Bildt's enthusiasm for EUFOR diminished somewhat during a fact-finding mission to Chad in August 2007. During that trip, he saw the extreme lack of infrastructure in Chad and was concerned about the immense logistical costs Sweden would have to shoulder if it participated in the operation.[78] In addition, during the fact-finding mission, a scandal broke in Sweden causing the resignation of Swedish defense minister Mikael Odenberg.[79] Following that, Bildt had to downgrade Sweden's participation in EUFOR Chad-CAR from commanding the whole group to contributing only 200 Special Forces. The Swedish deployment can thus be considered self-motivated. Sweden was a bandwagoneer.

Austria

Austria served as the fourth-largest EUFOR troop contributor. Similar to Sweden, Austria is also deeply embedded with France. It ranked eleventh among all EU member states from the French perspective. Nevertheless, in contrast to Sweden, Austria had very little interest in a deployment to Chad-CAR. The most widely read newspaper in Austria, the *Kronen Zeitung*, publicly opposed any involvement in Chad-CAR, and an opinion poll published in January 2008 showed that 73 percent of Austrians were against sending soldiers to Chad.[80] So when rumors of a potential operation first appeared in Austria, Austrian defense minister Norbert Darabos explicitly declared that Austria would not participate in EUFOR.[81] Still, in October 2007, the Austrian government changed its mind. It first announced that it would send about 100 troops to Chad-CAR and then further increased this number to 240 in early November 2007.[82] What had happened? The Austrian deployment decision was related to French lobbying efforts.

In the fall of 2007, Austria was preparing its bid for a nonpermanent UN Security Council seat for the 2009–2011 period. France was fully aware of this campaign. It was also aware that Austria would have a hard time winning the elections in the UN General Assembly in the fall of 2008. The competition in the Western European and Other Group (WEOG), the UN group to which Austria belonged, was fierce. Moreover, Austria had a tainted political reputation because of extreme right-wing political figures such as Jörg Haider that had been part of the Austrian governing coalition. Austria had been running an extensive campaign using mainly its foreign aid funds to win votes.[83] Still, the tally looked bad. To remedy the situation, France offered its support; as a P5 member, France had prestige in the UN Security Council. Moreover, it disposed of dense political networks, especially in Africa, which could assist in rallying votes. How could such "positive synergies" between EUFOR Chad-CAR and Austria's UN bid be rejected?[84] They couldn't—although publicly, such justification was not acceptable for the Austrian people and parliament.[85] Once deployed, the Austrian media, particularly conservative news outlets, thus still viewed Austrian participation in EUFOR Chad-CAR extremely critically, and the Austrian foreign minister insisted on very stringent engagement conditions (caveats) to minimize any potential fatalities in Africa.[86] In the Austrian case, diplomatic embeddedness thus also proved to be critical: UN and EU connections were tied together.

Russia

Russia contributed roughly 100 troops and some helicopters to EUFOR Chad-CAR. Russia is not a member of the European Union. Moreover, its diplomatic embeddedness score with France is at the lower end, ranking fifty-sixth globally from the French perspective. Why did Russia deploy to Chad-CAR? Russia was a self-starter. EUFOR desperately needed helicopters.[87] For months, France had been begging countries to contribute these critical assets to EUFOR. It even rented helicopters from a commercial provider, the Ukrainian company ADB. During a visit to Paris on March 11, 2008, Russian foreign minister Sergey Lavrov then made a political pledge to join EUFOR. On the same occasion, Lavrov and Kouchner also discussed a possible EU-Russia strategic partnership agreement, which France promised to push through at the EU during the French EU presidency starting in July 2008. The agreement focused, in particular, on EU-Russian cooperation in Afghanistan and Chad.[88] Nevertheless, despite this political pledge, Russia did not actually undertake any concrete steps to deploy to Chad until September 1, 2008. That day, EU heads of state were meeting in Brussels to discuss the deployment of an EU military observer mission to oversee Russian withdrawal from Georgia.[89] Russian troops had invaded Georgia roughly one month earlier. While no official statement exists proving that Russia wanted to influence European or (at least) French attitudes on Russian actions in Georgia, the timing of the Russia announcement speaks volumes. It is highly unlikely that Russian president Dimitri Medvedev chose the day randomly. Rather, it is likely that he wanted to gain political goodwill in Europe—and particularly with the French, who were leading the Georgian response effort. Despite U.S. warnings, France (and the EU) accepted the Russian offer. Force Commander Pat Nash recalls: "Anybody who might have got in my way as regards those helicopters was answered very clearly: Be consistent in your own policy. You [the United States] are using corridors to support Afghanistan. I need helicopters for Chad."[90] Once deployed, France provided Russia with housing in Chad at a cost of €200,000.[91]

Summary of Findings

The key objective of this chapter was to assess the patterns of multilateral coalition building conducted not through the United Nation or ad hoc, as previous chapters have shown, but under the umbrella of a regional organization: the European Union. In addition, this chapter examined the coalition-building techniques of another pivotal nation: France. Do the causal mechanisms stipulated in chapter 2 hold under these different circumstances of multilateral coalition building?

With regard to preference convergence, EUFOR Chad-CAR supports the social-institutional framework laid out in chapter 2: even European Union member states do not coalesce naturally to address a common security problem. Sweden appears to have been the only self-motivated country to join EUFOR Chad-CAR. All other countries analyzed in this chapter did not volunteer any forces. Rather, they had to be cajoled into joining the operation. France was willing to offer external incentives to countries in exchange for joining EUFOR Chad-CAR. It appears that France constructed a multilateral coalition to intervene in Chad-CAR to maximize the political legitimacy of the operation. France feared a domestic backlash if it intervened unilaterally in its former colony. To a

TABLE 7.1   Results of case study: EUFOR Chad-CAR

	DEEPLY EMBEDDED WITH FRANCE	WEAKLY EMBEDDED WITH FRANCE
Bandwagoneer	Sweden	–
Self-starter	–	Russia
Coalition recruit	Ireland	–
	Poland	
	Austria	

lesser degree, France also sought to reduce the costs of the intervention by split-ting some of the expenses with fellow EU member states.

France's initial search strategy for EUFOR contributions relied on the EU machinery in Brussels. France assumed that EU officials, notably EU Operation Commander Pat Nash, had enough leverage to recruit EUFOR forces. France however, soon realized that it had erred: Pat Nash did not possess such lever-age, and no force pledges were forthcoming. Many EU member states indeed intentionally held back their troop pledges because they knew how important the operation was to France. They smelled a good opportunity to trade favors with France, and playing hard to get would only increase their bargaining power. Thus, France almost completely reverted to a different recruitment technique. It instrumentalized diplomatic embeddedness to construct the EUFOR coalition. It bilaterally approached countries it deemed willing and capable to participate in EUFOR Chad-CAR. To determine potential targets, France produced a "pros-pect list" of potential EUFOR recruits. EU member states as well as countries outside of the EU (Turkey, Switzerland, Brazil, South Africa, Russia, and Ukraine, for example) were included on that list. French officials gathered data on the deployment preferences of these states via their diplomatic networks. For Swe-den, Poland, and Ireland, EU networks played a critical role. For Austria, UN networks came in handy. French high-level officials also used bilateral and multi-lateral summits to approach potential participants with regard to EUFOR. In this process, EU officials played an important brokerage role. Interestingly, France even asked U.S. officials for assistance in the recruitment process (Special Envoy to Sudan Andrew Natsios and Assistant Secretary of State for African Affairs Jen-dayi Frazer). Both were tasked with explaining to hesitant EU member states the importance of the mission with respect to stabilizing the broader Sahel region.[92]

Did France use vulnerability metrics to guide the recruitment process? Some cases fit into this category. Austria, for example, sought French support for its UN Security Council candidacy. Without France's P5 status, Austria would have been less eager to gain French help. Similarly, France is a powerful player in the EU and could influence EU negotiations to the benefit of Poland and Ireland. Still, overall it appears that a quid pro quo attitude rather than coercion per se dominated the recruitment process. Each trade described above enabled both parties—France and the EUFOR contributing state—to maximize their own specific preference priorities. Therefore, it is fair to say that these exchanges were self-serving and discretionary rather than coerced.

The Irish EUFOR Chad-CAR contribution was closely tied to Bertie Ahern's desire to win French support for his candidacy as EU president. It thus was directly linked to diplomatic embeddedness—especially via the EU. Interest-ingly, Ahern's strategy to become EU president did not come to fruition. Because of delays in the ratification process, the Lisbon Treaty only came into effect in December 2009. By then, Ahern had lost his job in Dublin due to his involvement in a financial scandal. In addition, his international reputation took a hit when the Irish economy crumbled in the aftermath of the global financial crisis in 2008.

A similar story about the centrality of EU connections can also be told about the Polish deployment. Poland had very little intrinsic interest in Chad-CAR. Its deployment decision therefore cannot be fully understood without examining the link France constructed between the Lisbon Treaty negotiations and EUFOR Chad-CAR. Diplomatic embeddedness between France and Poland opened information channels between the two countries and made a successful issue linkage possible. Without diplomatic embeddedness, the Polish deployment to Chad-CAR would have been highly unlikely. The Austrian deployment, in turn, was connected to the UN context. Austria was eager to gain "positive synergies" from France for its bid of a nonpermanent UN Security Council seat. France could exploit its multilateral connections with Austria to make the Austrian deployment a reality. In the case of Russia, diplomatic embeddedness arguably played no role. Russia was a self-starter. It saw in France's desperate search for helicopters an opportunity to gain from France an EU-Russia strategic cooperation agreement and also (later on) to influence French attitudes toward Russian actions in Georgia. Finally, Sweden was a bandwagoneer. It held intrinsic motivations to join EUFOR Chad-CAR.

Overall, EUFOR Chad-CAR provides limited support for the preference convergence model. Nevertheless, this lack of preference convergence among EU member states did not stop France from constructing a coalition. Rather, France bargained states into joining EUFOR Chad-CAR. To do so, France exploited its EU connections to assess deployment preferences and construct issue linkages. French officials also made use of multilateral summits (especially in the context of the EU) to make bilateral approaches for EUFOR contributions. Similarly to Australia during the INTERFET coalition-building process, France also asked for help from the United States to serve as cooperation broker in order to cajole EU states to commit troops to Chad, but U.S. influence appears to have been minimal. EU officials also played brokerage roles helping France match coalition demand and supply.

Could France have fulfilled this coalition-building role without relying on its asymmetrical power capabilities? The answer is no. Both in the EU and the UN contexts, France's institutional power resources mattered greatly. Nevertheless, France largely refrained from using coercive language in its coalition-building effort. Rather, France cajoled these states by offering interesting quid pro quo possibilities. The value of diplomatic connections can thus not be reduced to its coercive capabilities.

POWER, DIPLOMACY, AND DIPLOMATIC NETWORKS

Most multilateral military coalitions—including those operating under the umbrella of an international organization—are purposefully constructed by states that are most interested in the deployment of a particular operation. These pivotal states thereby instrumentalize diplomatic embeddedness; they use their diplomatic networks as a resource, as a strategic capability to construct allied cooperation. Diplomatic embeddedness grants pivotal states trust, information, and a facility to construct issue linkages and side payments. Moreover, common institutional contacts often serve as cooperation brokers, and institutional venues are repurposed to function as face-to-face coalition negotiation fora. Most pivotal states are politically powerful and wealthy. Yet asymmetrical power capabilities alone often cannot account for the coalition negotiation outcomes we observe. Relatively weak states in fact are often able to drive a hard bargain. They are aware of the pivotal states' desire for their coalition contribution and thus hold considerable power in coalition negotiations or, as Moravcsik put it: "the power of each government [at the negotiating table] is inversely proportional to the relative value it places on an agreement."[1]

The social-institutional theory of multilateral military coalition building that I develop in this book explains the theoretical underpinnings of these dynamics in detail. It also expounds which countries are most likely to join a given coalition, why some coalitions form while others fail to assemble, and why some coalitions are strong while others are weak. I have shown the validity of this framework through an integrative mixed-method research design using both quantitative and qualitative research methodologies. The large-N regression analysis illustrated that diplomatic embeddedness impacts coalition contributions; it substantively increases the likelihood of joining a multilateral intervention. The case study chapters, in turn, depicted the causal mechanisms that undergird the concept of diplomatic embeddedness. Moreover, they tested key assumptions about the causal interactions between convergent preferences, coercion, and diplomatic ties. Detailed process-tracing also allowed examining whether there was a backdoor causal path that better explains coalition commitments than the diplomatic embeddedness framework. The four cases studies on the Korean War, Darfur, East Timor, and Chad-CAR were chosen for their extreme factorial variation. This variation was able to depict the consistency of the stipulated mechanisms across a wide range of coalitions (U.S.-led and non-U.S.-led operations; operations conducted under the umbrella of the UN and other regional organizations such as the European Union; and between alliance and non-alliance operations), thereby confirming the key hypothesis of this book: coalition-building processes follow a systematic pattern. Most states do not join military coalitions at their own initiative but are bargained into these coalitions by pivotal states. In this process, pivotal states exploit diplomatic embeddedness as outlined in chapter 2. Yet my research also uncovered cases that challenge my argument and provide new insights about how coalition building works. This last chapter brings all these findings together, outlines key theoretical implications, proposes avenues for future research, and discusses lessons for policy.

Implications for Scholarship

This book, both in its successes and failures, identifies several important research frontiers for scholars of multilateral military coalition building, burden-sharing, collective action, and international cooperation. Helen Milner theorized that cooperation can be achieved in three different ways. It can be tacit; it can be imposed; and it can be negotiated in an explicit bargaining process.[2] I want to make the case that especially the last category of "negotiated cooperation" requires refinement. Most importantly, the following questions need answers: Who initiates these negotiations? Who sits at the bargaining table? Do "history," diplomacy, and social-institutional structures matter in these negotiations? If so, how? And who holds power in these negotiations?

Goddard and Nexon suggest that security studies and the study of global politics more generally "should be concerned not with the production of universal and invariant laws or with the creation of a 'grand theory' of world politics, but rather with the identification of recurrent processes, the mechanisms through which they operate, and how they configure to produce specific outcomes."[3] I share their objectives and advocate for a more dynamic, precise, and wide-ranging approach to analyzing the processes and mechanisms of how security cooperation comes about. I argue that such an approach needs to take the preferences of cooperation partners seriously. It also needs to better understand leadership and power dynamics in multilateral cooperation endeavors. Relatedly, searching for cooperation partners requires greater attention. Finally, I argue that diplomatic embeddedness serves as a potent cooperation multiplier. Being "networked" matters in international politics; diplomatic ties constitute a strategic resource to construct cooperation.

Taking Preferences Seriously. . . .

Most of the existing literature suggests that multilateral military coalition building happens quasi-automatically with only minimal diplomatic organization: states coalesce instinctively, balancing common threats or sharing other types of common interests, institutions, political ideologies, or norms and values.[4] Ward and Dorussen, for instance, observe that most military deployments constitute "a collective response of a coalition of countries that perceive a common interest to intervene in a particular situation."[5] Auerswald and Saideman make a similar case: "Countries often join military coalitions or an alliance effort because they share common interests."[6]

The argument and evidence of this book challenge this assumption. They show that states in the international system rarely hold similar intrinsic preferences and preference intensities with regard to the launch of a multilateral intervention. This finding is true for operations that are conducted for primarily humanitarian purposes (Darfur, Chad, and East Timor) as well as operations that pursue geostrategic aims (Korea). It also holds true regardless of the organizational structure of the coalition (UN, regional, or ad hoc), the intensity of the operation, the type of state targeted, and what country spearheads the coalition.

Indeed, across the twenty mini–case studies that I examined in detail in this book (see table 8.1), I only came across three bandwagoneers. In the UNAMID case, Egypt had national security interests in Sudan and joined UNAMID at its own initiative resultantly; in the INTERFET case, Brazil joined the operation due to cultural and ethno-linguistic ties with East Timor; and Sweden shared a security interest with France with regard to EUFOR Chad-CAR. A larger number of states fell into the "self-starter" category: they self-initiated negotiations with the pivotal state. Thailand, for instance, approached the U.S. government and offered to join UNAMID in exchange for sanction relief, and Turkey offered to join the Korean War to get admitted to NATO. Overall, however, most states get actively

TABLE 8.1 Summary results of micro-cases (1)

	BANDWAGONEERS	SELF-STARTERS	COALITION RECRUITS
Korean War		Turkey	U.K.
		South Africa	Canada
			The Philippines
UNAMID	Egypt	Thailand	Nigeria
		Rwanda	Germany
INTERFET	Brazil		Thailand
			The Philippines
			Jordan
			Canada
EUFOR Chad-CAR	Sweden	Russia	Ireland
			Poland
			Austria

TABLE 8.2 Summary results of micro-cases (2)

	DEEPLY EMBEDDED WITH PIVOTAL STATE	WEAKLY EMBEDDED WITH PIVOTAL STATE
Bandwagoneers	Sweden	Brazil
	Egypt	
Self-starters		Thailand
		Rwanda
		Russia
		South Africa
		Turkey
Coalition recruits	U.K.	Jordan
	Canada (Korean War)	
	Canada (INTERFET)	
	The Philippines (Korean War)	
	The Philippines (INTERFET)	
	Nigeria	
	Germany	
	Thailand	
	Ireland	
	Poland	
	Austria	

recruited by pivotal states. Especially, those countries that are deeply embedded with pivotal states overwhelmingly join multilateral coalitions because of deliberate recruitment attempts (see table 8.2).

Taking these preferences seriously matters for two key reasons. First, the existing literature on coalition building often assumes that countries attempt to free ride if they are unwilling to join a multilateral military coalition—a view fiercely propagated, among others, by the Trump administration.[7] The approach presented here instead suggests some countries just care less about specific security crises than others, and it is because of this lack of interest that no coalition participation is forthcoming. Only by looking closely at these precise preferences can we determine what explanation better fits reality. In the cases examined in this book, I found indeed very few explicit attempts of free riding. Rather, states varied in their assessment of the necessity for intervention. With regard to the Korean War, many counties simply felt that this was not "their war," or as a State Department official summarized it, "the main reason we do not have more foreign troops in Korea is that other peoples are not sure that we are fighting for goals of equal importance to them."[8] Other issues simply had higher priority. A somewhat similar story can also be told for INTERFET. Despite the obvious humanitarian atrocities occurring in East Timor, only Australia and Portugal demonstrated an unequivocal interest in intervening on the island. All other countries were hesitant to intervene. Overall, these findings should make us rethink whether collective action theory is a useful tool to analyze multilateral military coalition building. To what degree are multilateral deployments collective goods? Who benefits from these interventions and why? Do only UN deployments constitute public goods? If so, what explains the equally diverse set of intrinsic preferences with regard to UN operations? If Europeans are reluctant to participate in NATO interventions, does this really constitute free riding? Or do they simply care less about the coalition objective? Future research should study this question in greater detail, especially the precise causal mechanisms that lead to free riding. How can we empirically distinguish between free riding and diversity in preference intensities toward the public good to be created?

Second, these preferences matter because they directly affect coalition negotiations. Pivotal states require information on these preferences to persuade potential coalition participants to join a given coalition—either via "truth-seeking" or side payments.[9] Without access to such information, both of these processes are likely to fail.[10] Thus far, of course, we are still largely tapping in the dark when it comes to how exactly these intervention preferences get formed. No general theory exists. Rather, an array of factors has been identified that impact state interests with regard to military deployments: alliance commitments, threat perceptions, normative motivations, public opinion, and so forth. Ideally, future research could bring some greater clarity into these preference formation processes. Which countries are particularly prone to hold what type of preferences and what kind of behavior can we expect from these states in coalition negotiations? Future research should also further address the "self-starters." It appears that a distinct group of states views coalition deployments as a unique opportunity for an exchange: a quid pro quo. These exchanges are discretionary political actions. They represent opportunities to transmit power resources from an area of relative strength (for instance, a troop deployment) to an area of relative weakness (indebtedness to international donors). So what distinguishes these "self-starters" from other members of the international community? Is it greed? Or rather domestic pressure combined with political desperation? And what political strategies do these states employ to achieve their aims?

Taking Leadership Seriously. . . .

Much of the existing literature on multilateral coalition building suggests that military alliances or international organizations such as NATO, the UN, and the AU organize the coalition-building process. Weitsman, for instance, states that "institutions of interstate violence [such as NATO] serve as ready mechanisms for employing force."[11] Similarly, Coleman suggests that "once the UN Security Council has mandated a UN peacekeeping operation, the task of force generation [. . .] falls largely to the UN Peacekeeping Department."[12] This book, of course, makes a different claim. It suggests that pivotal states organize the coalition-building process. These states initiate and orchestrate much of the political work that is required to launch a multinational operation. They put the topic of a potential intervention on the agenda of the international community. Often, they sponsor peace or ceasefire negotiations that precede the multilateral intervention. At the UN, they draft UN resolutions and prod UN Security Council members to support the motions. They scan possible coalition participants and attract and push them into coalitions through persuasion and other forms of incentive. Thus, pivotal states play a critical role in fielding a multilateral intervention. The evidence presented in this book of the work done by pivotal states is overwhelming. There can be no doubt that the operations that deployed to Korea, Darfur, East Timor, and Chad-CAR were the constructions of the United States, Australia, and France. Each country worked tirelessly to bring these operations to fruition.

Yet one of the key limits of this book is its underdeveloped understanding of how states become pivotal states. This book merely highlights that a combination of domestic and material factors allows states to take on this role. But what are the exact domestic and international processes that lead states to decide to serve as pivotal state? What is the exact ratio of material power and institutional connections that allows states to succeed in building a multilateral coalition? Moreover, this book develops the notion of a small "coalition" of pivotal states. Notably, in the quantitative analysis, these small groupings of pivotal states are quite numerous. Nevertheless, the qualitative chapters only look at cases in which one state took on the task of building a coalition. Future works should analyze how the division of labor between these pivotal states is organized. Moreover, how do pivotal states and IOs share the work of constructing cooperation? Where do the practical and political responsibilities of each one begin, and where do they end?[13]

Searching for Cooperation Partners

Thus far, IR theory has paid very little attention to the phenomenon of searching for cooperation partners. Most cooperation frameworks assume a two-stage process: a bargaining phase followed by an enforcement phase.[14] But who are the chosen few who get to bargain? In the security context, Fang and Ramsay and Wolford and Ritter are among those who have looked at this question systematically. Fang and Ramsay conclude that systemic factors such as bipolarity and multipolarity influence the search process,[15] while Wolford and Ritter focus on the characteristics of the coalition organizers.[16]

This book focuses on the informational challenges of such a search process. The evidence in this book suggests that in their search for coalition participants, pivotal states are chiefly constrained by political criteria (although military criteria do play a role sometimes). For UNAMID, the U.S. government wanted African forces. Australia was eager to recruit Asian forces and forces from the Muslim world for INTERFET, and France preferred troops from "neutral" European countries to join EUFOR Chad-CAR. Nevertheless, these criteria (in most cases) still left plenty of room to maneuver. As a result, questions such as the following turned into the principal search criteria: (1) how much does a state want to serve in this coalition, and (2) what payment could entice that state to join the effort. I theorized in this book that pivotal states rely on diplomatic embeddedness to access such information. For example, via diplomatic embeddedness, U.S. diplomats learned that Nigerian president Olusegun Obasanjo was panicking that his debt relief objective would fail. Also via diplomatic embeddedness, French officials became privy of the Irish Taoiseach's desire to become EU president. Both diplomatic scoops constituted private information that was not publicly available at the time. Moreover, this book also illustrated that pivotal states use IO officials and friendly powers as additional information sources. For instance, U.S. officials during the Korean War perceived the UN as a "post office" that would transmit messages and information on deployment preferences of UN member states to the United States. The INTERFET and EUFOR Chad-CAR case studies, in turn, illustrate how Australia and France used the United States respectively as a cooperation broker to bridge structural holes. Especially in the INTERFET case, the United States was able to help Australia connect to the Muslim world and especially Jordan—a country that Australia was not embedded with.

These findings make it imperative that we change our conception of how cooperation comes about and think of cooperation endeavors as a three-step (instead of a two-step) process including (1) a search phase, (2) a bargaining phase, and (3) an enforcement phase. The key task for future work is to fully understand how these three phases interact.

Moreover, these findings highlight the cooperation brokerage function of IO and state officials, who help link cooperation demand and supply. Such function has thus far not been analyzed in international politics. With regard to IO officials, in particular, the literature has focused mainly on the rational-legal authority and legitimacy they embody[17] and their control over technical expertise and information.[18] Interesting questions arise: Does this brokerage function constitute another key power source of IOs? Are there ways that IOs could become even more efficient in this process? Can IOs create formal mechanisms matching cooperation supply and demand? Future work should address these questions.

Diplomatic Embeddedness as an Enabler of Collective Action

This book introduces into the IR discourse the term *diplomatic embeddedness*. As explained earlier, diplomatic embeddedness refers to the cumulative number of institutional connections. If instrumentalized, these ties create structural opportunities. They provide pivotal states with resources that can be exploited to pursue collective action; they constitute a fundamental capability to engage other states in collective mobilization.

Thus far, IR research has mainly focused on the effects *individual* international regimes and institutions have on state behavior.[19] IR scholars interested in social network analysis are one exception to this trend.[20] These scholars have developed two principal approaches to analyzing cumulative institutional effects. The first approach is often called the "networks-as-structures" approach. Its key focus of analysis is the position actors hold in a given social network.[21] Scholars working in this field argue that these positions can constrain actors but also provide them with unique resources.[22] The second approach is labeled "networks-as-actors."[23] It conceives networks as a special institutional form and thus an actor unto itself (for instance, the advocacy networks described in Keck and Sikkink).[24]

The notion of diplomatic embeddedness as developed in this book adds predominantly to the concept of networks-as-structures. Similar to the latter approach, I argue that diplomatic embeddedness is a power tool.[25] Nevertheless, in contrast to the existing literature on networks-as-structures, I am less interested in the network position individual actors hold. Instead, I argue that irrespective of network position, states can derive benefits from being bilaterally and multilaterally connected. Nevertheless, for this to happen, states need to use diplomatic embeddedness instrumentally. They need to perceive institutional connections as a fungible asset. In this sense, I make a distinction between being connected and deliberately using these connections as a tool.[26] With regard to the latter issue, I particularly focus on the individual. I ask: how do individual government officials activate the resources that diplomatic embeddedness provides in accomplishing their goal of building a multilateral military coalition?[27]

This distinction between having diplomatic ties and instrumentalizing them is indeed a critical feature of this book. Existing research on networks-as-structures has a tendency to assume that individuals benefit from network connections quasi-automatically. Hafner-Burton and Montgomery, for instance, argue that states gain "social power" merely by being connected.[28] The theory this book proposes differs from this assessment. It suggests instead that states need to purposefully exploit diplomatic connections to unlock their true power potential. For social-institutional networks to act as concrete state capabilities, these networks need to be activated, they need to be instrumentalized. To turn structural assets into power requires constant work. It does not happen automatically.

Nexon began a journey examining how institutional networks affect collective mobilization. He argues that in situations of low interest homogeneity but high network density, collective mobilization is possible.[29] This book builds on Nexon's insights and develops his ideas by looking closely at the exact processes and mechanisms that undergird such collective mobilization processes in the military arena (that is, the five benefits of diplomatic embeddedness)

Nevertheless, there are certain aspects of diplomatic embeddedness that I do not address in this work. First, I do not address the negative aspects of diplomatic embeddedness.[30] Scholars have argued that embeddedness has a tendency to lead to clientalization.[31] When groups become too tightly knit and information passes only among a select few, institutional networks can become competency traps.[32] Carruthers called this tendency "the business equivalent of incest."[33] This aspect of diplomatic embeddedness and its risks to multinational cooperation efforts certainly warrant future research. Second, I bracket from my analysis the effects of nongovernmental ties, that is, ties between journalists, traders, and clergymen, as well as personal relationships between friends. Since military coalitions are almost exclusively constructed by states, government-affiliated actors are likely to exert the greatest influence in multilateral military coalition-building processes—although, of course, not exclusively. Third, my research only brushes over the question of whether diplomatic embeddedness is used purposefully in coalition-building efforts or has become an internalized practice. Do agents deliberately reflect on their actions or rather follow internalized routines?[34] And if they follow the latter, how did these practices diffuse? How did they institutionalize? And, most importantly, what are their consequences? What's their effect on social structures, ideas, taboos, laws, rites, and the like? Future work ought to analyze these questions.[35]

Finally, this book does not address the question of where diplomatic embeddedness comes from. Instead, I take the existence of these ties as a given at the moment the coalition-building processes begin. This certainly constitutes one of the key limitations of this book.

Rethinking Hegemony and Power Politics

The tension between hegemonic order, power asymmetries, and diplomatic embeddedness is at the center of this book. Much of the research on multilateral coalition building thus far highlights the role of traditional power resources: economic wealth and military capabilities. Imbalances of power—often in the form of "hierarchies"—lead to coalition contributions either via the usage of "brute coercion" or via means of political authority which leads to "submissiveness" or obeisance to hierarchical orders.[36] From this point of view, coalition building resembles the imposed cooperation variety proposed by Milner rather than the negotiated form (see above). But even if negotiations ensue, much of the literature assumes that traditional power asymmetries determine bargaining outcomes, with the overall stronger actors (normally the pivotal states) obtaining the more favorable terms.[37]

In this book, I have tried to add nuance to these assumptions. The evidence in this book suggests that states do not volunteer forces out of "submissiveness" to the hegemon. Rather, in almost all cases, coalition negotiation ensued. Moreover, during the coalition negotiation processes two types of "power" matter. The first is material power; the second is power that states derive from having a good BATNA.[38] Potential coalition participants—even quite weak ones—often hold considerable amounts of this second source of power: they are less interested in the coalition deployment than pivotal states. South Africa in the Korean War was an extreme case in this regard. It "coerced" the United States to supply new jet aircraft by exploiting U.S. desperation to prevent a South African withdrawal from the Korean peninsula. Nigeria was also able to exploit similar preference asymmetries in its UNAMID negotiations with the United States. The United States agreed to actions and polices that it might not have done otherwise, becoming beholden to a corrupt government and condoning political practices that contradict its values. Even Poland was able to pressure France into supporting the Ioannina mechanism in exchange for a Polish troop contribution to EUFOR Chad-CAR.

A key implication of this book is thus that traditional power capabilities, of course, matter in multilateral military coalition-building efforts. Most pivotal states analyzed in this book (and included in the dataset) are wealthy and powerful. Their superior material power resources allow them to provide issue linkages and side payments to reluctant coalition participants. Similarly, diplomatic embeddedness cannot be delinked from such resources. Only wealthy and powerful states have the means to entertain embassies around the world and finance international institutions.[39]

And yet, these material power asymmetries do not automatically translate into coalition contributions, nor do they guarantee that pivotal states always come out on top in coalition negotiations. Why not? First, potential troop contributors often know how much pivotal states want their troop commitment. By making direct coalition participation appeals, pivotal states reveal their preferences, which lowers their bargaining power. Second, powerful states often refrain from blatantly coercing countries into cooperation. Pivotal states have understood that side payments and issue linkages are often more effective politically than coercion. Indeed, there are costs to coercion.[40] Coercion leaves scars; it triggers resistance, escape, avoidance, and counter control.[41] Coerced coalition partners do not constitute a good fighting force. Their morale decreases, and their eagerness to take operational risks is minimal. Moreover, coercive coalition-building risks tarnishing the legitimacy of the operation—and bolstering legitimacy is often the key reason to construct a coalition in the first place. On the contrary, compensation packages produce positive results.[42] They enhance the potential for future cooperation and boost fighting effectiveness.[43]

Indeed, it is precisely for these latter two reasons that diplomatic embeddedness takes on such an important role in coalition negotiations: diplomatic networks increase pivotal states' power to construct cooperation. By exploiting diplomatic embeddedness, pivotal states can reduce information asymmetries, build trust, and offer side payments and issue linkages. If instrumentalized, diplomatic embeddedness thus constitutes a critical power resource alongside guns, money, and ideas.

In short, the argument and evidence in this book compel us to move beyond simple carrots-and-sticks models associated with some hegemonic-order theories. Coalition negotiations are indeed one of the few instances when the most powerful states find themselves quite weak and relatively weak states can dominate negotiations, thus reversing traditional hierarchies in international affairs. Effective hegemony is a complex endeavor, and diplomatic embeddedness might be a critical capability to engage other states in collective mobilization.[44]

What Is Diplomacy Good For?

Finally, this book contributes to our understanding of diplomacy. Diplomacy is generally defined as the conduct of international relations by communication and negotiation.[45] With regard to its purpose, however, great confusion still reigns.[46] Jönsson, for instance, argues that the study of diplomacy has been "long on typologies" but "short on theory,"[47] while Sharp complains that "what diplomacy is remains a mystery."[48] Realist accounts often treat diplomacy as "automatic, unproblematic, and ultimately unimportant."[49] Constructivists, in turn, emphasize the socialization aspects of diplomacy. Sustained interactions make actors switch from a "logic of consequences" to a "logic of appropriateness": their interests and preferences adapt and become open for redefinition.[50]

The embeddedness approach laid out in this book proposes a middle ground between the "undersocialized" realist perspective and the "oversocialized" constructivist perspective.[51] It suggests that diplomatic interactions matter. In the aggregate, diplomacy and diplomatic networks constitute a strategic reservoir to construct collective action. The seemingly endless bilateral and multilateral meetings, summits, champagne receptions, courtesy calls, officer exchanges, and military training exercises—all of these diplomatic activities contribute meaningfully to this reservoir. Each single interaction opens information channels and related opportunities to construct issue linkages and side payments. Such encounters create the possibility of personal relationships, which naturally may lead to trust, friendship, and affection. In the aggregate these interactions do not necessarily change identity and preferences. However, they enable states to better understand these identities and preferences, manipulate them, and thus organize collective mobilization.

Implications for Policy

This book has implications for how governments, international organizations, scholars, and informed citizens analyze multilateral military coalition building and make policies to deal with it. I focus on three areas that appear particularly relevant: how to initiate multilateral military coalition building, how to minimize the potential negative effects of "constructed" coalitions, and the political benefits of diplomatic connections in world politics.

A Manual for Coalition Building

This book can function as a manual for how to construct a multilateral military coalition. It can be of use to governments seeking to serve as pivotal states, to IO officials wondering what influence states have in recruiting troop contributors, and to citizens and NGOs interested in advocating for or opposing military interventions.

Overall, this book shows that constructing cooperation is feasible. For an international intervention to occur, convergent intrinsic preferences among a large swath of countries is not a necessity. Instead, all that is required is a highly motivated pivotal state. A key policy implication of this book is thus that mass publics are less important in understanding international intervention endeavors than specific state actions. Several policy implications emerge from viewing coalition building through this lens.

First, states interested in launching a multilateral military intervention should focus less on finding "like-minded" states and instead use their diplomatic connections to bargain third parties into joining a multilateral coalition. As this book has amply shown, irrespective of the coalition aim, like-minded coalition partners hardly exist. That is a reality pivotal states need to reckon with.

Second, civil advocates of multilateral military interventions (for instance, for humanitarian purposes) should focus their energy on mobilizing a specific state (or a small group of states) rather than mobilizing an international organization or a vague "international community." Relatedly, opponents of military interventions need to pay attention to which states lead the fray in organizing an intervention proposal rather than addressing an international organization or an unspecified international public.

Third, the evidence presented in this book suggests that when recruiting coalition participants, pivotal states often subordinate military proficiency of their recruits to political considerations—a policy that is likely to affect the operational success on the ground. Indeed, a number of studies have shown that intervention effectiveness, in particular in the peacekeeping realm, requires adequate resources especially in terms of personnel numbers and equipment.[52] Thus, pivotal states also hold at least some responsibility if operations are too fragile to have an impact on the ground or if the deployed troops are unfit to fulfill the tasks at hand. After all, coalition strategy can rarely make up for weak or inexperienced coalition members. Relatedly, when coalition members violate mandates or engage in criminal activity, pivotal states hold sway over these perpetrators—at least over their governments—which often receive subsidies and side payments from pivotal states in exchange for their troop commitment. Therefore, practitioners, scholars, advocates, and observers of peacekeeping and other types of multilateral military operations can and should hold pivotal states accountable. Until now, IOs have most often been blamed if operations go awry or fall short of recruitment targets—at least in the context of peacekeeping operations.[53]

The Promises and Perils of Constructed Coalitions

How efficient are "constructed" coalitions? Military interventions and peacebuilding, after all, are very difficult tasks. Michael Doyle, for instance, argues that "effective peacebuilding . . . creates a unified polity, one army, a return to civilian participatory rule, an economy geared to civilian consumption, and the first steps toward reconciliation" and if successful, "peacebuilding changes not merely behavior, but, more importantly, [. . .] transforms identities and institutional contexts."[54] Can strategic, incentive-based cooperation really achieve these tasks? Or rather, is the "artificial" construction of cooperation one of the reasons that recent coalition operations have often failed?

Optimists suggest that constructed coalitions operate no differently from other types of coalitions. Once deployed, states that were previously not intrinsically motivated to join a coalition (that is, did not care about a security crisis) adopt new values. They learn to care during their deployment and thereafter. Why? By joining a coalition, government officials are required to publicly justify their actions. In this process, a cognitive dissonance arises between what is publicly justified and argued for and what is secretly or privately believed.[55] Laboratory and experimental work suggests that human beings in these situations have a tendency to resolve such dissonance by adapting their preferences to their behavior; that is, they internalize the justification.[56] They start believing in the "true" necessity of the military operation. Furthermore, coalitions socialize participating actors. In this process, strategic, incentive-based cooperation often turns into intrinsic motivation: if your coalition partners care, you will start caring too.[57] Lastly, a growing number of countries view multilateral deployments as valuable, self-serving opportunities for exchange. These states benefit from multilateral military deployments in ways that other international areas do not permit them to do. They do not want to lose these opportunities, so they try to do a good job when deployed to the operational theater.[58] Uruguay, for instance, is said to have earned $129 million from UN peacekeeping from 1992 to 2003—making UN peacekeeping Uruguay's most profitable export industry.[59]

Pessimists are more skeptical. They point to NATO's operation in Afghanistan (ISAF) and argue that enduring differences in intrinsic motivations (at least partially) translated into different behavior on the ground. For example, coalition participants with minimal intrinsic interests implemented "caveats" and other operational restrictions that impacted the overall effectiveness of the operation. On this point, Ricks writes: "The Dutch did good patrols, on foot. The Italians only patrolled by vehicle. . . . The Japanese didn't patrol at all. . . . [U]nder their rules of engagement which provided only for self-defense, the Japanese weren't permitted to secure their own perimeter and had to rely on the Dutch to do it. . . . The Thai battalion's rules didn't even allow them to leave their camp near Karbala."[60] Relatedly, these pessimists argue that because so many countries see in coalition deployments an opportunity to benefit financially (or otherwise), a deleterious propensity toward profit has infiltrated multilateral coalition-building efforts. Many coalition participants limit their coalition commitment to ensure a "profit margin." In other words, they restrict their involvement to a degree that is minimally necessary not to jeopardize the deal made with the pivotal state.[61] The examples in this book also show coalition participants at times acting opportunistically (by threatening to withdraw their forces if their demands are not met, for instance). Why is such "profit-maximizing" behavior feasible? First, there are monitoring challenges. It is very hard for pivotal states to observe what is going on in the deployment theater at all times and places. As a result, coalition participants are tempted to look for shortcuts to protect their assets: Why undertake undue risks? Why engage with difficult targets if easier activities can be undertaken? Second, pivotal states face punishment challenges, especially in environments in which coalition participants are scarce. Pivotal states then have little leverage to discipline deviant coalition participants if they desperately rely on them. Lastly, some pessimists would even go so far as to suggest that "constructed" coalitions can create negative externalities in troop-contributing countries. Financial side payments and issue linkage can generate jealousy and social tensions[62] and open the potential for corruption, favoritism, and nepotism.[63] The money, material, and training provided by pivotal states also risk increasing domestic political repression and even the probability of coups.[64]

The policy implication of this discussion is that policymaking needs to pay attention to these eventual perils (and opportunities) when constructing coalitions. A thorough analysis of whether mission failure can be attributed to potential moral hazard dilemmas would have great value. In other circumstances, moral hazard concerns have been overcome by crafting cooperation agreements that try to forestall exploitation.[65] A UN report suggests in this regard that what is expected from troops in the field ought to be better codified in what they term a deployment "compact."[66] Moreover, the UN has also started to provide bonus payments if contingents show exceptional bravery in situations of risk. Pivotal states could implement similar practices; for instance, side payments could be paid over time and conditioned on performance in the field. Moreover, pivotal states could purposefully use diplomatic embeddedness as a commitment device if the performance of contingents in the field leaves the pivotal states wanting. Still, of course, these techniques cannot address the power discrepancies that arise when coalition contributors are scarce and pivotal states have little leverage over the few that agreed to serve.

Get Connected!

This book is a manifestation of the power of diplomatic connections. In our day-to-day life, being well connected is generally considered a good thing. Many elite colleges and universities in the United States and around the world flaunt the advantages of their alumni networks in finding jobs and having successful careers. Many sociologists and economists confirm that social connections affect job searches and promotions,[67] the cost of capital,[68] and consumer purchasing decisions[69]—to name just a few of the recent discoveries. International relations practitioners also appear to have understood the advantages of personal connections—even at the highest levels of government. George H. W. Bush, for instance, wrote in his biography that "there are actually commonsense reasons for an American president to build relationships with his opposites. If a foreign leader knows the character and the heartbeat of the president (and vice versa), there is apt to be far less miscalculation on either side.... This knowledge helps a president formulate and adjust policies that can bring other leaders along to his own point of view."[70] Also, when asked what made him the ideal U.S. secretary of state, James Baker answered: "I knew a lot of the players."[71] However, as the U.S. administration promotes an "America First" policy and undertakes actions to withdraw from international agreements, the value of "being connected" appears to have become less recognized. This makes the findings of this book and their policy implications more important than ever.

Overall, this book unabashedly shows that diplomatic connections matter. Diplomatic embeddedness, if used purposefully, constitutes an invaluable state asset. States can reap benefits from institutional connections that go way past the specific purposes for which the individual institutions were created. Bilateral and multilateral relationships can be profitable. By using them as a resource, states can achieve things in an easier and less costly way.[72]

What are these benefits? This book lists five. First, each diplomatic interaction, whether bilateral or multilateral, represents an opportunity to learn about personalities, policy preferences, cultural currencies, and working methods[73]—information that is not readily available from public accounts.[74] Possessing such detailed private information increases bargaining power in the context of international negotiations. Second, diplomatic interactions shape a country's credibility and trustworthiness.[75] Viewed through a social-psychological lens, diplomatic embeddedness creates sympathy, affection, and reputational concerns.[76] Members of networks care about each other.[77] Consequently, they can be expected to behave in prescribed ways so not to hurt their "friend," or as Granovetter put it: "I may deal fairly with you not only because it is in my interest, ... but because we have been close for so long that we expect this of one another, and I would be mortified and distressed to have cheated you even if you did not find out (though all the more so if you did)."[78] Third, diplomatic embeddedness provides for payment flexibility. Already existing bilateral or multilateral networks can be used to channel side payments, and transactions can be divvied up. This greatly facilitates the construction of external incentives. Fourth, diplomatic embeddedness allows the employment of cooperation brokers who can bridge structural holes and thus help match cooperation supply and demand. Lastly, diplomatic embeddedness provides for negotiation venues. Social psychologists have found that solidarity and cooperation are often intensified by these types of face-to-face interaction.[79]

Coercion and material power cannot be disassociated from diplomatic embeddedness. That said, it is an illusion to think that coercive tools alone can substitute for the benefits of diplomatic embeddedness. Coercion leaves scars, whereas diplomatic embeddedness serves as a cooperation multiplier.

This book, of course, focuses on military coalition building. Nevertheless, many of the mechanisms and techniques exposed here are likely to also apply to other areas of international cooperation, such as human rights, the environment, economics sanctions, and arms control. After all, almost all international cooperation initiatives involve negotiation and coalition building. Or, as Riker argued, "the process of reaching a decision in a group is a process of forming a subgroup. This subgroup is a coalition."[80] Many such coalitions need to be planned and built; they do not emerge naturally.[81]

The policy implication that emerges from viewing international politics through this lens is that diplomatic ties need to be honed, cultivated, and appreciated. Diplomatic embeddedness can even be consciously pursued. Diplomatic networks are not a natural given but are constructed through explicit investment strategies.[82] Moreover, once the network is in place, diplomatic ties need to be deliberately instrumentalized.[83] In short, diplomats and diplomatic work constitute an invaluable tool in a state's power infrastructure. What's more, these ties affect not only "low" politics but also security cooperation: most multilateral intervention coalitions are constructed using these networks. Diplomatic embeddedness, if used purposefully, thus represents the lubricant that makes international cooperation possible—"being networked" constitutes a fundamental asset in world politics.

Notes

1. THE PUZZLE OF ORGANIZING COLLECTIVE ACTION

1. UN Resolution 83 (1950) S/1511. Available at http://daccess-ods.un.org/access. nsf/Get?Open&DS=S/RES/83%20(1950)&Lang=E&Area=RESOLUTION (last accessed December 25, 2016).

2. Brazilian President Vargas on the Korean War, as quoted in Bohlin, "United States–Latin American Relations and the Cold War, 1949–1953," PhD dissertation, University of Notre Dame, 1985, 204.

3. As quoted in ibid., 156, emphasis added.

4. George Marshall to Dean Acheson, September 30, 1950, Selected Records Relating to the Korean War, Department of State: Topical File Subseries, Staff Member Office Files (SMOF), President's Personal Files (PPF), 6. Contributions to the UN effort [2 of 3: August 1950–December 1951], Harry S Truman Papers, Harry S Truman Library, Independence, Missouri.

5. Goddard and Nexon, "The Dynamics of Global Power Politics: A Framework for Analysis," *Journal of Global Security Studies* 9, no. 1 (2016): 7.

6. See for instance Jervis, "Security Regimes," *International Organization* 36, no. 2 (1982); Lipson, "International Cooperation in Economic and Security Affairs," *World Politics* 37, no. 1 (1984); Betts, "Should Strategic Studies Survive?" *World Politics* 50, no. 1 (1997); Snidal, "Relative Gains and the Pattern of International Cooperation," *American Political Science Review* 85, no. 3 (1991).

7. Morey, "Military Coalitions and the Outcome of Interstate Wars," *Foreign Policy Analysis* 12, no. 4 (2016). Scholars have found, however, that multilateral wars are longer, bloodier, and more destructive than bilateral wars. See for instance Sarkees and Wayman, *Resort to War: 1816–2007. Correlates of War* (Washington, DC: CQ Press, 2010). Multilateral coalitions are also said to increase the likelihood of crisis escalation and the expansion of conflicts and can reduce fighting effectiveness. On the former premise, see Wolford, *The Politics of Military Coalitions* (Cambridge: Cambridge University Press, 2015); on the latter, see Weitsman, *Waging War: Alliances, Coalitions, and Institutions of Interstate Violence* (Stanford, CA: Stanford University Pres, 2014), 37.

8. See for instance Singer, *Corporate Warriors: The Rise of the Privatized Military Industry* (Ithaca, NY: Cornell University Press, 2003), 159–60.

9. See for instance Kiszely, "Coalition Command in Contemporary Operations," *Whitehall Report* (London: Rusi, 2008); Weisiger, "When Do States Abandon Coalition Partners During War?" *International Studies Quarterly* 60, no. 4 (2016); Weitsman, *Waging War*, 25; Schmitt, *Allies That Count: Junior Partners in Coalition Warfare* (Washington, DC: Georgetown University Press, 2018); Byman and Waxman, *The Dynamics of Coercion: American Foreign Policy and the Limits of Military Might* (Cambridge: Cambridge University Press, 2002).

10. See for instance Levin, MacKay, and Nasirzadeh, "Selectorate Theory and the Democratic Peacekeeping Hypothesis: Evidence from Fiji and Bangladesh," *International Peacekeeping* 23, no. 1 (2016); Savage and Caverley, "When Human Capital Threatens the Capitol: Foreign Aid in the Form of Military Training and Coups," *Journal of Peace Research* 54, no. 4 (2017); Dwyer, "Peacekeeping Abroad, Trouble Making at Home: Mutinies in West Africa," *African Affairs* 114, no. 455 (2015): 217.

11. See for instance Bratt, "Explaining Peacekeeping Performance: The UN in Internal Conflicts," *International Peacekeeping* 4, no. 3 (1997); Findlay, *The Use of Force in UN Peace Operations* (Oxford: Oxford University Press, 2002); Hultman, Kathman, and Shannon, "United Nations Peacekeeping and Civilian Protection in Civil War," *American Journal of Political Science* 57, no. 4 (2013); Jett, *Why Peacekeeping Fails* (New York: Palgrave 1999); Jones, *Peacekeeping in Rwanda: The Dynamics of Failure* (Boulder, CO: Lynne Rienner, 2001); Kreps, "Why Does Peacekeeping Succeed or Fail? Peacekeeping in the Democratic Republic of Congo and Sierra Leone," in *Modern War and the Utility of Force: Challenges, Methods, and Stratgy,* ed. Angstrom and Duyvesteyn (London: Routledge, 2010); Skogmo, *UNIFIL: International Peacekeeping in Lebanon, 1978–1988* (Boulder, CO: Lynne Rienner, 1989).

12. Weitsman, *Waging War*, 2; Snyder, "The Security Dilemma in Alliance Politics," *World Politics* 36, no. 4 (1984).

13. Cox and O'Connor, "Australia, the US, and the Vietnam and Iraq Wars: 'Hound Dog, Not Lapdog,'" *Australian Journal of Political Science* 47, no. 2 (2012): 12; Davidson, *America's Allies and War: Kosovo, Afghanistan, and Iraq* (New York: Palgrave Macmillan, 2011).

14. Weitsman, *Waging War*, 2.

15. Wolford, *Politics of Military Coalitions*, 13.

16. See for instance Schelling, *The Strategy of Conflict* (Cambridge, MA: Harvard University Press, 1960), 2; Lake, "Authority, Coercion, and Power in International Relations," working paper, 2010. Available at www.princeton.edu/~pcglobal/conferences/basics/papers/lake_paper.pdf (last accessed August 8, 2018).

17. Newnham, "Coalition of the Bribed and Bullied? US Economic Linkage and the Iraq War Coalition," *International Studies Perspectives* 9, no. 2 (2008): 86.

18. Lake, "Authority, Coercion, and Power in International Relations."

19. Lake, *Hierarchy in International Relations* (Ithaca, NY: Cornell University Press, 2009), 173. See also Tago, "Is There an Aid-for-Participation Deal? US Economic and Military Aid Policy to Coalition Forces (Non)Participants," *International Relations of the Asia-Pacific* 8, no. 3 (2008).

20. Ward and Dorussen, "Standing Alongside Your Friends: Network Centrality and Providing Troops to UN Peacekeeping Operations," *Journal of Peace Research* 53, no. 3 (2016): 406. Ward and Dorussen focus on peacekeeping operations.

21. For a similar argument, see Zyla, "NATO Burden Sharing: A New Research Agenda," *Journal of International Organization Studies* 7, no. 2 (2016); Goddard and Nexon, "The Dynamics of Global Power Politics"; Wight et al., "The Mother of All Isms: Causal Mechanisms and Structured Pluralism in International Relations Theory," *European Journal of International Relations* 19, no. 3 (2013); Pouliot, *International Pecking Orders* (Cambridge: Cambridge University Press, 2016); Adler-Nissen and Pouliot, "Power in Practice: Negotiating the International Intervention in Libya," *European Journal of International Relations* 20, no. 4 (2014).

22. Wolford's *The Politics of Military Coalitions* is a notable exception. Some case studies on individual ad hoc operations have also looked at these questions. Examples include Bennett et al., *Friends in Need: Burden Sharing in the Persian Gulf War* (New York: St. Martin's Press, 1997); Baltrusaitis, *Coalition Politics and the Iraq War* (Boulder, CO: First Forum Press, 2009); Davidson, *America's Allies and War*; and Von Hlatky, *American Allies in Times of War: The Great Asymmetry* (Oxford: Oxford University Press, 2013). Each one of these studies finds that a mixture of material power, alliance concerns, domestic politics, and economic dependence influences the coalition negotiation process. Nevertheless, none of these studies engages in a comparative analysis across operations or across coalition organizers.

23. I borrow the term *embeddedness* from the literature in economic sociology. The term was developed by economic sociologists trying to explain how markets that suffer under information asymmetries function. See for instance Granovetter, *Getting a Job: A Study of Contacts and Careers* (Chicago: University of Chicago Press, 1995); Uzzi, "Social Structure and Competition in Interfirm Networks: The Paradox of Embeddedness," *Administrative Science Quarterly* (1997); DiMaggio and Louch, "Socially Embedded Consumer Transactions: For What Kinds of Purchases Do People Most Often Use Networks?" *American Sociological Review* (1998).

24. Hafner-Burton and Montgomery, "Power Positions: International Organizations, Social Networks, and Conflict," *Journal of Conflict Resolution* 50, no. 1 (2006): 2. My focus in this book is on government officials, a group that includes government bureaucrats, elected officials, and military officers. I bracket from my analysis ties between nongovernment related actors and institutions (school, church, or NGO exchanges, business relationships, and so on).

25. Blackburn, *Mercenaries and Lyndon Johnson's "More Flags": The Hiring of Korean, Filipino, and Thai Soldiers in the Vietnam War* (Jefferson, NC: McFarland, 1994), 41.

26. Burt, *Brokerage and Closure: An Introduction to Social Capital* (Oxford: Oxford University Press, 2005), 16.

27. Martin, *Coercive Cooperation* (Princeton, NJ: Princeton University Press 1992), 39–40.

28. Critics might ask what the difference is between "normal" diplomacy and diplomatic embeddedness. I address this concern at length in the following chapters.

29. For a similar view, see Pouliot, *International Pecking Orders*; and Adler-Nissen and Pouliot, "Power in Practice."

30. For a similar definition, see Weitsman, *Waging War*, 26.

31. Purists might reject a concurrent analysis of multilateral coalitions constructed ad hoc and under the umbrella of the UN or regional organizations. In particular, they might single out UN coalitions as an entirely different animal because (1) they focus predominantly on "peacekeeping" instead of peace enforcement or regime change; (2) they are perceived as more "legitimate"; and (3) the UN disposes of a unique financing mechanism that subsidizes UN peacekeeping contributions. These distinctions—while valid—do not preclude a simultaneous analysis. Most importantly, the lines that once clearly delineated UN operations from other types of multilateral interventions are today very fuzzy indeed. Most importantly, the operational principles that in the past guided UN coalitions (including target state consent, impartiality, and limited use of force) and distinguished UN operations from other military operations no longer hold up. UN operations today have been deployed in circumstances in which target state consent was wholly absent (Kosovo) as well as in failed states in which consent was impossible (Somalia). UN operations have also supported government forces over rebel groups (Afghanistan, Democratic Republic of Congo) or democratic forces against the de facto government using heavy weaponry, offensive tactics, and considerable firepower (Haiti, Cote d'Ivoire). A similar change can be witnessed in the perceived legitimacy of the United Nations. Today only a minority of citizens around the world believe that UN approval is necessary to conduct a military intervention. Finally, with regard to the financing of UN operations, this book will illustrate that the UN troop and equipment reimbursement system has not led to an "automated" coalition-building process. Instead, similar to ad hoc and regional operations, UN operations also require states to initiate and orchestrate the coalition building process.

32. Morey, "Military Coalitions and the Outcome of Interstate Wars," 535.

33. Seawright, *Multi-Method Social Science: Combining Qualitative and Quantitative Tools* (Cambridge: Cambridge University Press, 2016), 9.

34. Gerring, "Is There a (Viable) Crucial-Case Method?" *Comparative Political Studies* 40, no. 3 (2007): 42; George and Bennett, *Case Studies and Theory Development in the Social Sciences* (Cambridge, MA: MIT Press, 2005), 20; Seawright, *Multi-Method Social Science*, 64.

35. Seawright, *Multi-Method Social Science*, 68.

2. CONSTRUCTING MULTILATERAL MILITARY COALITIONS

1. See Bellamy and Williams, *Understanding Peacekeeping* (Cambridge: Polity, 2010), 43–45.

2. Other scholars have made similar observations regarding coalition building outside of the military sphere. Dupont calls these actors "drivers," Wolford refers to "principal belligerents," while Lax and Sebenius speak of "entrepreneurship." The idea is always the same: collective action requires organization. It does not happen automatically. States that are particularly interested in a collective outcome coordinate, motivate, and control participation. See Dupont, "Negotiation as Coalition Building," *International Negotiation* 1, no. 1 (1996); Wolford, *The Politics of Military Coalitions*; Lax and Sebenius, *The Manager as Negotiator: Bargaining for Cooperation and Competitive Gain* (New York: Macmillan, 1986).

3. Dupont, "Negotiation as Coalition Building," 56.

4. On the weakness of IO officials in this regard, see Henke, "Great Powers and UN Force Generation: A Case Study of UNAMID," *International Peacekeeping* 23, no. 3 (2016).

5. See Pouliot, *International Pecking Orders.*

6. See the *Multilateral Military Coalitions Dataset Codebook,* available on the author's website. For a theory on how pivotal states arise, see Henke, "Why Did France Intervene in Mali in 2013? Examining the Role of Intervention Entrepreneurs," *Canadian Foreign Policy Journal* 23, no. 3 (2017).

7. See Wolford, *Politics of Military Coalitions*, 8.

8. For a similar way of graphing preferences, see, for instance, Ferejohn and Shipan, "Congressional Influence on Bureaucracy," *Journal of Law, Economics, and Organization* 6 (1990); Milner, *Interests, Institutions, and Information: Domestic Politics and International Relations* (Princeton, NJ: Princeton University Press, 1997).

9. The graph above depicts three pivotal states (A–C). This number can, of course, vary depending on the specific coalition to be formed.

10. See for instance Passmore, Shannon, and Hart, "Rallying the Troops: Collective Action and Self-Interest in UN Peacekeeping Contributions," *Journal of Peace Research* 55, no. 3 (2018); Olson and Zeckhauser, "An Economic Theory of Alliances," *Review of Economics and Statistics* 48, no. 3 (1966); Bobrow and Boyer, "Maintaining System Stability Contributions to Peacekeeping Operations," *Journal of Conflict Resolution* 41, no. 6 (1997); Khanna, Sandler, and Shimizu, "Sharing the Financial Burden for UN and NATO Peacekeeping, 1976–1996," *Journal of Conflict Resolution* 42, no. 2 (1998); Shimizu and Sandler, "Peacekeeping and Burden-Sharing, 1994–2000," *Journal of Peace Research* 39, no. 6 (2002); Bennett, Lepgold, and Unger, *Friends in Need: Burden Sharing in the Persian Gulf War* (New York: St. Martin's Press, 1997), 5.

11. Olson suggested that this applies especially to poor individuals. As a result, individuals (or states) with more resources will have to carry a higher burden in the provision of the public good. See Olson, *The Logic of Collective Action* (Cambridge, MA: Harvard University Press, 1965).

12. See for instance Khanna, Sandler, and Shimizu, "Sharing the Financial Burden"; Passmore, Shannon, and Hart, "Rallying the Troops."

13. See for instance Perkins and Neumayer, "Extra-Territorial Interventions in Conflict Spaces: Explaining the Geographies of Post-Cold War Peacekeeping," *Political Geography* 27, no. 8 (2008): 900; Siverson and Starr, *The Diffusion of War: A Study of Opportunity and Willingness* (Ann Arbor: University of Michigan Press, 1991); Regan, *Civil Wars and Foreign Powers: Outside Intervention in Intrastate Conflict* (Ann Arbor: University of Michigan Press, 2002); Wolford, *Politics of Military Coalitions*, 8.

14. See for instance Brysk, *Global Good Samaritans: Human Rights as Foreign Policy* (Oxford: Oxford University Press, 2009).

15. See for instance Velazquez, "Why Some States Participate in UN Peace Missions While Others Do Not: An Analysis of Civil-Military Relations and Its Effects on Latin America's Contributions to Peacekeeping Operations," *Security Studies* 19, no. 1 (2010); Sotomayor, *The Myth of the Democratic Peacekeeper: Civil-Military Relations and the United Nations* (Baltimore, MD: Johns Hopkins University Press, 2014); Kathman and Melin, "Who Keeps the Peace? Understanding State Contributions to UN Peacekeeping Operations," *International Studies Quarterly* 61, no. 1 (2016).

16. See for instance Cunliffe, *Legions of Peace: UN Peacekeepers from the Global South* (London: C. H. Hurst & Co., 2013).

17. Most of the literature on multilateral military coalition building has indeed focused on teasing out the different reasons for why states join military interventions. For an overview, see, for instance, Bellamy and Williams, *Providing Peacekeepers: The Politics, Challenges, and Future of United Nations Peacekeeping Contributions* (Oxford: Oxford University Press, 2013).

18. Does the spectrum vary between peacekeeping and counterinsurgency operations? Possibly. Since peacekeeping operations are generally less controversial and less risky, more states might be positively inclined to support it (that is, stay in the D–S range in Figure 2.1 above). On the contrary, I would expect most states to be in the W–Z range with regard to controversial and risky counterinsurgency operations.

19. As quoted in Bohlin, "United States–Latin American Relations and the Cold War, 1949–1953," 204.

20. See for instance Engberg, *The EU and Military Operations: A Comparative Analysis* (London: Routledge, 2013), 139; Pouliot, *International Pecking Orders*, 62, 77.

21. Quinlivan, "Force Requirements in Stability Operations," *Parameters* 25, no. 4 (1995). The force strength of a mission is usually determined by the size of the population in the mission theater, although wide variety exists on the force-to-population ratio that gets applied.

22. See for instance Thompson, *Channels of Power: The UN Security Council and US Statecraft in Iraq* (Ithaca, NY: Cornell University Press, 2009); Coleman, *International Organizations and Peace Enforcement: The Politics of International Legitimacy* (Cambridge: Cambridge University Press, 2007); Hurd, *After Anarchy: Legitimacy and Power in the United Nations Security Council* (Princeton, NJ: Princeton University Press, 2007); Eichenberg, "Victory Has Many Friends: US Public Opinion and the Use of Military Force, 1981–2005," *International Security* 30, no. 1 (2005); Jentleson, "The Pretty Prudent Public: Post Post-Vietnam American Opinion on the Use of Military Force," *International Studies Quarterly* (1992); Jentleson and Britton, "Still Pretty Prudent: Post-Cold War American Public Opinion on the Use of Military Force," *Journal of Conflict Resolution* 42, no. 4 (1998); Feaver and Gelpi, *Choosing Your Battles: American Civil-Military Relations and the Use of Force* (Princeton, NJ: Princeton University Press, 2004); Welsh, "Authorizing Humanitarian Intervention," in *The United Nations and Global Security*, ed. Price and Zacher (London: Palgrave Macmillan, 2004).

23. Various scholars have analyzed U.S. motives to intervene in Korea. See for example Stueck, *The Road to Confrontation: American Policy toward China and Korea, 1947–1950* (Chapel Hill: University of North Carolina Press, 1981); Cumings, *The Korean War: A History* (New York: Modern Library, 2011); Fordham, *Building the Cold War Consensus: The Political Economy of US National Security Policy, 1949–51* (Ann Arbor: University of Michigan Press, 1998); Acheson, *The Korean War* (New York: Norton, 1971).

24. Dean Acheson to UN mission of the United States, July 12, 1950, Selected Records Relating to the Korean War, Department of State: Topical File Subseries, Staff Member Office Files (SMOF), President's Personal Files (PPF), 6. Contributions to the UN effort [1 of 3: June–July 1950], Harry S Truman Papers, Harry S Truman Library, Independence, Missouri.

25. See for instance Dean Acheson to US embassy London, August 11, 1950, Selected Records Relating to the Korean War, Department of State: Topical File Subseries, SMOF, PPF, 6. Contributions to the UN effort [2 of 3: August–December 1950], Truman Papers, Truman Library.

26. As cited by Stueck, *The Korean War: An International History* (Princeton, NJ: Princeton University Press, 2005), 56.

27. Cooper, *The Lost Crusade: America in Vietnam* (New York: Dodd Mead, 1970), 267.

28. Memorandum by the Government of Australia, April 11, 1965, Document 12, *FRUS* 1964–1968, XXVII.

29. James A. Baker Private Papers, box 172, folder JAB III, Transcript, August 25, 1993, p. 12, Seeley G. Mudd Manuscript Library, Princeton University, Princeton, New Jersey.

30. Secretary of State to Embassies Dhaka, Islamabad, New Delhi, Pretoria, Luanda, New York, Darfur Collective, "Démarche Request: Transport and Logistics Units for the UN-AU-Hybrid Operation in Darfur (UNAMID)," March 7, 2008. Document in possession of the author.

31. Secretary of State to Embassies in Amman, Colombo, Dhaka, Islamabad, "Urgent Darfur Demarche for Aviation Support and Enabling Assets," May 9, 2008. Document in possession of the author.

32. Dijkstra, "The Military Operation of the EU in Chad and the Central African Republic: Good Policy, Bad Politics," *International Peacekeeping* 17, no. 3 (2010): 6.

33. See for instance Recchia, *Reassuring the Reluctant Warriors: US Civil-Military Relations and Multilateral Intervention* (Ithaca, NY: Cornell University Press, 2015); Tierney, "Multilateralism: America's Insurance Policy against Loss," *European Journal of International Relations* 17, no. 4 (2011): 655–78; Rumsfeld, *Known and Unknown: A Memoir* (London: Penguin, 2011), 445; Baker, *Days of Fire: Bush and Cheney in the White House* (New York: Anchor, 2013), 208.

34. Kiszely, "Coalition Command in Contemporary Operations," 8.

35. See for instance Snyder, "The Security Dilemma in Alliance Politics," Morrow, "Alliances: Why Write Them Down?" *Annual Review of Political Science* 3, no. 1 (2000): 69–70; Pilster, "Are Democracies the Better Allies? The Impact of Regime Type on Military Coalition Operations," *International Interactions* 37, no. 1 (2011).

36. *Bandwagoning* generally refers to relatively weak states aligning with a stronger, adversarial power judging that the costs of opposing the stronger power exceed its benefits. See for instance Mearsheimer, *The Tragedy of Great Power Politics* (New York: Norton, 2001), 162–63.

37. Non-lethal equipment most often includes vehicles, vehicle spare parts, generators, tentage and other accommodation equipment, medical equipment, mine detectors, water purifiers, night-vision goggles, communication equipment, uniforms, and boots and foot rations. Lethal equipment can include rifles, light machine guns, semi-automatic self-loading rifles (SLRs), mortars, and rocket-propelled grenades. Pivotal states

negotiate different arrangements with third parties. Some contingents are allowed to keep the equipment once the mission is over; others are required to return it. See for instance Berman, "The Provision of Lethal Military Equipment: French, UK, and US Peacekeeping Policies Towards Africa," *Security Dialogue* 34, no. 2 (2003): 202.

38. The United States and the European Union have both set up peacekeeping training programs: ACOTA/GPOI and EURORECAMP, respectively. Once countries have participated in these training programs, they are not legally required to deploy. Nevertheless, a deployment is "encouraged."

39. Passmore, Shannon, and Hart, "Rallying the Troops," 2; Bellamy and Williams, *Providing Peacekeepers*, 1. Henke, "Buying Allies: Payment Practices in Multilateral Military Coalition-Building," *International Security* 43, no. 4 (2019): 128–62.

40. Colman and Widen, "The Johnson Administration and the Recruitment of Allies in Vietnam, 1964–1968," *History* 94, no. 316 (2009): 10.

41. Minutes, Meeting of the NSC Deputies Small Group, December 3, 1992, folder "NSC/DC 403A," OA/ID 90024, H-Files NSC/DC Meetings Files, Bush Presidential Records, George Bush Presidential Library.

42. Engberg, *The EU and Military Operations*, 78.

43. Theoretical work in IR has also suggested that pivotal states seek coalition participants that are reliable, loyal, and credible and that democracies are more likely to meet these criteria than autocracies. See Maoz, *Networks of Nations: The Evolution, Structures, and Impact of International Networks, 1816–2001* (New York: Cambridge University Press, 2011), 9.

44. See also Wolford, *Politics of Military Coalitions*, 56–57.

45. Rathbun, *Diplomacy's Value: Creating Security in 1920s Europe and the Contemporary Middle East* (Ithaca, NY: Cornell University Press, 2014), 27.

46. As research on negotiations has shown, favorable distributions of interests are not sufficient for generating win-win outcomes in bargaining situations. See for instance Tomz, *Reputation and International Cooperation: Sovereign Debt across Three Centuries* (Princeton, NJ: Princeton University Press, 2007), 16; Moravcsik, *The Choice for Europe: Social Purpose and State Power from Messina to Maastricht* (Ithaca, NY: Cornell University Press, 1998); Krasner, "Global Communications and National Power: Life on the Pareto Frontier," *World Politics* 43, no. 3 (1991); Bernauer and Ruloff, *The Politics of Positive Incentives in Arms Control* (Columbia: University of South Carolina Press, 1999); Lax and Sebenius, *Manager as Negotiator*; De Dreu, Koole, and Steinel, "Unfixing the Fixed Pie: A Motivated Information-Processing Approach to Integrative Negotiation," *Journal of Personality and Social Psychology* 79, no. 6 (2000); O'Connor and Carnevale, "A Nasty but Effective Negotiation Strategy: Misrepresentation of a Common-Value Issue," *Personality and Social Psychology Bulletin* 23, no. 5 (1997); Olekalns and Smith, "Mutually Dependent: Power, Trust, Affect and the Use of Deception in Negotiation," *Journal of Business Ethics* 85, no. 3 (2009): 347–48; Risse, "'Let's Argue!': Communicative Action in World Politics," *International Organization* 54, no. 1 (2000): 21.

47. Vatahov, "U.S. Recognises 'Functioning' Economy," *Sofia Echo*, March 6, 2003.

48. For a similar argument, see Wolford, *Politics of Military Coalitions*.

49. Memo, John T. McNaughton to McGeorge Bundy, December 4, 1965, Files of McGeorge Bundy, Box 17, NSF, Lyndon Baines Johnson Presidential Library, Austin, Texas.

50. I borrow the term "embeddedness" from economic sociologists who have studied the impact of social networks at the individual level on the pursuit of economic and social goals, e.g., Granovetter, "Economic Action and Social Structure: The Problem of Embeddedness," *American Journal of Sociology* 91, no. 3 (1985); *Society and Economy: Framework and Principles* (Cambridge, MA: Harvard University Press, 2017).

51. Hafner-Burton and Montgomery, "Power Positions," 2.

52. Loosely following Adler and Pouliot, I define *practices* as patterned actions that "reproduce similar behaviors with regular meanings." See Adler and Pouliot, "International Practices: Introduction and Framework," in *International Practices*, ed. Adler and Pouliot (Cambridge: Cambridge University Press, 2011), 7.

53. Pouliot, *International Pecking Orders*, 29.

54. Granovetter, "The Strength of Weak Ties," *American Journal of Sociology* (1973). Slaughter writes of the effect of these ties: "[strong] ties create trust and easy collaboration, but they are less successful at bringing new flows of ideas and information into the innovation process. [Weak] ties cast a broad net to capture the new, but they are harder to activate for purposes of cocreation. Formal ties can be directed; informal ties are unexpected but bring the value of serendipity." See Slaughter, *The Chessboard and the Web: Strategies of Connection in a Networked World* (New Haven, CT: Yale University Press, 2017), 188.

55. Bull, *The Anarchical Society: A Study of Order in World Politics* (London: Palgrave Macmillan, 1977), 158; Rathbun, *Diplomacy's Value*, 11; Jönsson and Hall, "Communication: An Essential Aspect of Diplomacy," *International Studies Perspectives* 4, no. 2 (2003): 197.

56. Sending, Pouliot, and Neumann, *Diplomacy and the Making of World Politics* (Cambridge: Cambridge University Press, 2015), 223; Neumann, *At Home with the Diplomats: Inside a European Foreign Ministry* (Ithaca, NY: Cornell University Press, 2012), 19.

57. Neumann, *At Home with the Diplomats*, 7; Bull, *Anarchical Society*, 181.

58. Rozental and Buenrosto, "Bilateral Diplomacy," in *The Oxford Handbook of Modern Diplomacy*, ed. Cooper, Heine, and Thakur (Oxford: Oxford University Press, 2013), 232–33; Rana, "Embassies, Permanent Missions, and Special Missions," in *The Sage Handbook of Diplomacy*, ed. Constantinou, Kerr, and Sharp (London: Sage, 2016), 151.

59. De Neuilly, "Devenir Diplomate Multilatéral," *Cultures and Conflicts*, no. 3 (2009): 89–90; Cooley and Nexon, "Interpersonal Networks and International Security: US-Georgia Relations During the Bush Administration," in *The New Power Politics: Networks and Transnational Security Governance*, ed. Avant and Westerwinter (Oxford: Oxford University Press, 2016), 79.

60. Lazarsfeld and Katz, *Personal Influence* (Glencoe, IL: Free Press, 1955).

61. As cited in Krieger, Souma, and Nexon, "US Military Diplomacy in Practice," in *Diplomacy and the Making of World Politics*, ed. Sending, Pouliot, and Neumann (Cambridge: Cambridge University Press, 2015), 237.

62. Pouliot, *International Pecking Orders*, 63; Bosco, "Assessing the UN Security Council: A Concert Perspective," *Global Governance* 20, no. 4 (2014): 551–52; Juncos and Reynolds, "Political and Security Committee: Governing in the Shadow" *European Foreign Affairs Review* 12 (2007): 144.

63. Holmes, "The Force of Face-to-Face Diplomacy: Mirror Neurons and the Problem of Intentions," *International Organization* 67, no. 4 (2013); Hall and Yarhi-Milo, "The Personal Touch: Leaders' Impressions, Costly Signaling, and Assessments of Sincerity in International Affairs," *International Studies Quarterly* 56, no. 3 (2012).

64. Neumann, *At Home with the Diplomats*, 32; Rana, "Embassies, Permanent Missions, and Special Missions," 151.

65. Rathbun, *Diplomacy's Value*, 12; Yarhi-Milo, *Knowing the Adversary: Leaders, Intelligence, and Assessment of Intentions in International Relations* (Princeton, NJ; Princeton University Press, 2014), 1.

66. Risse, "'Let's Argue!': Communicative Action in World Politics," 10–11.

67. The informational benefits of diplomatic embeddedness can be reaped at all levels of hierarchy and across issue areas. Nevertheless, its effective usage hinges on the existence of domestic institutions that optimize the information flow. Indeed, information gathered via diplomatic embeddedness needs to be efficiently aggregated, transmitted, and redistributed among all government actors involved in the multilateral military coalition-building process.

Officers working with the same country but on different topics need to transmit their information to a central institution that can then aggregate and transfer the information to the people that need it the most. In the U.S. context, two types of centralizing institutions exist. First, inside the State Department and the Department of Defense (DOD), country desks serve as information gathering places with regard to specific states. These desks are in charge of collecting all information (on security, economic, or other topics) relevant to the bilateral relationship. Regional bureaus, in turn, aggregate all of the information of individual country desks operating in a particular geographical region. In addition, during the process of multilateral military coalition building, regular interagency meetings are held, bringing together, in particular, the country specialists of the State Department and the DOD.

68. U.S. Ambassador to NATO (Ivo Daalder) to U.S. Secretary of State, Cable "Dutch say U.S. Afghanistan Message must be a 'strong one,'" November 4, 2009. Document in possession of the author.

69. Author's interview.

70. Baker, *The Politics of Diplomacy*, 283–85.

71. Singer, *Corporate Warriors*, 159–60.

72. Keohane, *After Hegemony: Cooperation and Discord in the World Political Economy* (Princeton, NJ: Princeton University Press, 1984); Martin, *Coercive Cooperation* (Princeton, NJ: Princeton University Press, 1992).

73. Axelrod, *The Evolution of Cooperation* (New York: Basic Books, 1984); Cooley and Spruyt, *Contracting States: Sovereign Transfers in International Relations* (Princeton, NJ: Princeton University Press, 2009).

74. Granovetter, *Society and Economy*, 59.

75. Das and Teng, "Between Trust and Control: Developing Confidence in Partner Cooperation in Alliances," *Academy of Management Review* 23, no. 3 (1998): 494; Leach and Sabatier, "To Trust an Adversary: Integrating Rational and Psychological Models of Collaborative Policymaking," *American Political Science Review* 99, no. 4 (2005): 92; Hardt, *Time to React: The Efficiency of International Organizations in Crisis Response* (Oxford: Oxford University Press, 2014), 101; Rathbun, "Before Hegemony: Generalized Trust and the Creation and Design of International Security Organizations," *International Organization* 65, no. 2 (2011); Burt, *Brokerage and Closure: An Introduction to Social Capital*, 93–101; Cooley and Nexon, "Interpersonal Networks and International Security," 79.

76. Granovetter, "Problems of Explanation in Economic Sociology," in *Networks and Organization*, ed. Nohria and Eccles (Boston, MA: Harvard Business School Press, 1992), 44.

77. March and Olsen, "The Logic of Appropriateness," in *Oxford Handbook of Political Science*, ed. Goodin (Oxford: Oxford University Press, 2011).

78. Minutes, Meeting of the NSC Deputies Small Group, December 3, 1992, folder "NSC/DC 403A," OA/ID 90024, H-Files NSC/DC Meetings Files, Bush Presidential Records, George Bush Presidential Library.

79. Memorandum of Conversation "Korea" by John C. Ross, June 28, 1950, Selected Records Relating to the Korean War, Department of State: Topical File Subseries, SMOF, PPF, 6. Contributions to the UN effort [1 of 3: June–July 1950], Truman Papers; Truman Library.

80. Dean Acheson to Ernest A. Gross, June 19, 1951, Selected Records Relating to the Korean War, Department of State: Topical File Subseries, SMOF, PPF, 6. Contributions to the UN effort [3 of 3: February–September 1952], Truman Papers, Truman Library.

81. Burt, *Brokerage and Closure*, 16; Estrada and Arrigo, "Predicting Triadic Closure in Networks Using Communicability Distance Functions," *SIAM Journal on Applied Mathematics* 75, no. 4 (2015): 1725–44.

82. James A. Baker III Personal Papers, box 172, folder 5, Series 12: The Politics of Diplomacy, Transcripts Baker 1993–1994, Tab 13 (JAB III—August 30, 1993, Boulder Wyoming am only), pp. 1–2, Mudd Library.

83. Friman, "Side-Payments Versus Security Cards: Domestic Bargaining Tactics in International Economic Negotiations," *International Organization* 47, no. 3 (1993): 390; Huber and Shipan, *Deliberate Discretion? The Institutional Foundations of Bureaucratic Autonomy* (Cambridge: Cambridge University Press, 2002), 2.

84. See Henke, "The Rotten Carrot: US-Turkish Bargaining Failure over Iraq in 2003 and the Pitfalls of Social Embeddedness," *Security Studies* 27, no. 1 (2018).

85. Morgan, "Issue Linkages in International Crisis Bargaining," *American Journal of Political Science* (1990): 320; Drezner, "The Trouble with Carrots: Transaction Costs, Conflict Expectations, and Economic Inducements," *Security Studies* 9, no. 1–2 (1999).

86. Drezner, "The Trouble with Carrots," 190.

87. See for instance Putnam, "Diplomacy and Domestic Politics: The Logic of Two-Level Games," *International Organization* 42, no. 3 (1988); Tollison and Willett, "An Economic Theory of Mutually Advantageous Issue Linkages in International Negotiations," *International Organization* 33, no. 4 (1979): 445; Mayer, "Managing Domestic Differences in International Negotiations: The Strategic Use of Internal Side-Payments," *International Organization* 46, no. 4 (1992): 804; Morgan, "Issue Linkages in International Crisis Bargaining," 320; Iida, "Involuntary Defection in Two-Level Games," *Public Choice* 89, no. 3–4 (1996); Mo, "Domestic Institutions and International Bargaining: The Role of Agent Veto in Two-Level Games," *American Political Science Review* 89, no. 4 (1995); Davis, "International Institutions and Issue Linkage: Building Support for Agricultural Trade Liberalization," *American Political Science Review* 98, no. 1 (2004); "Linkage Diplomacy: Economic and Security Bargaining in the Anglo-Japanese Alliance, 1902–23," *International Security* 33, no. 3 (2008/9).

88. See for instance Hoekman, "Determining the Need for Issue Linkages in Multilateral Trade Negotiations," *International Organization* 43, no. 4 (1989): 697; Keohane and Nye, *Power and Interdependence: World Politics in Transition* (Boston, MA: Little and Brown, 1977), 30; Moravcsik, *The Choice for Europe*, 65.

89. See for instance Dreher, Sturm, and Vreeland, "Development Aid and International Politics: Does Membership on the UN Security Council Influence World Bank Decisions?" *Journal of Development Economics* 88, no. 1 (2009).

90. Coleman calls this phenomenon "credit slip." He argues that if A does something for B and trusts B to reciprocate in the future, this establishes an expectation in A and an obligation on the part of B to keep the trust. This obligation can be conceived of as a "credit slip" held by A to be redeemed by some performance of B. If A holds a large number of these credit slips from a number of persons with whom he has relations, then the analogy to financial capital is direct: the credit slip constitutes a large body of credit on which A can draw if necessary—unless, of course, the placement of trust has been unwise and the slips represent bad debts that will not be repaid. Such "goodwill accounts" can certainly exist with or without diplomatic embeddedness. Nevertheless, more common bilateral and multilateral ties automatically trigger a priori a higher volume of interactions. As a result, the more diplomatically embedded a country pair, the more opportunities there are to both add funds to the goodwill account and to make use of accumulated goodwill in those partner countries. See Coleman, *Foundations of Social Theory* (Cambridge, MA: Belknap Press, 1990), 306.

91. Blackburn, *Mercenaries and Lyndon Johnson's "More Flags,"* 41.

92. Edwards and Goldsworthy, "Facing North: A Century of Australian Engagement with Asia," (Melbourne: Melbourne University Press, 2001), 251.

93. Author's interview with Richard Hecklinger, former U.S. ambassador to Thailand, Washington, D.C., March 2012. Supachai had been up against the New Zealander, Mike Moore. Australia had gone to great lengths to broker a deal under which Supachai and Moore would divide the WTO directorship, consequently angering not only its closest

neighbor, New Zealand, but also the United States, which much preferred Moore over Supachai.

94. Dee, "'Coalitions of the Willing' and Humanitarian Intervention: Australia's Involvement with Interfet," *International Peacekeeping* 8, no. 3 (2001): 10.

95. Cooper, "The Changing Nature of Diplomacy," in *The Oxford Handbook of Modern Diplomacy*, ed. Cooper, Heine, and Thakur (Oxford: Oxford University Press, 2013), 36.

96. Festinger, Back, and Schachter, *Social Pressures in Informal Groups: A Study of Human Factors in Housing*, vol. 3 (Palo Alto, CA: Stanford University Press, 1950).

97. Yarhi-Milo, *Knowing the Adversary*, 18.

98. Devin, "Paroles de diplomates: Comment les négociations multilatérales changent la diplomatie," in *Négociations Internationales*, ed. Petiteville and Placidi-Frot (Paris: Presses de Sciences Po, 2013), 92–93; Pouliot, *International Pecking Orders*, 63.

99. Krieger, Souma, and Nexon, "US Military Diplomacy in Practice," 238; Cooper, "Changing Nature of Diplomacy," 37.

100. Kelly, *The March of Patriots: The Struggle for Modern Australia* (Melbourne: Melbourne University Publishing, 2009), 509.

101. Howard, *Lazarus Rising* (Pymble, Australia: HarperCollins, 2010), 347.

102. Funabashi, *The Peninsula Question: A Chronicle of the Second Korean Nuclear Crisis* (Washington, DC: Brookings Institutions Press, 2007), 231.

103. Kesgin and Kaarbo, "When and How Parliaments Influence Foreign Policy: The Case of Turkey's Iraq Decision," *International Studies Perspectives* 11, no. 1 (2010): 26.

104. See for instance Checkel, "International Institutions and Socialization in Europe: Introduction and Framework," *International Organization* 59, no. 4 (2005); Bearce and Bondanella, "Intergovernmental Organizations, Socialization, and Member-State Interest Convergence," *International Organization* 61, no. 4 (2007).

105. Pouliot, *International Pecking Orders*.

106. Bourdieu and Wacquant, *An Introduction to Reflexive Sociology* (Chicago: University of Chicago Press, 1992), 119.

107. On this point, see for instance Kwon and Adler, "Social Capital: Maturation of a Field of Research," *Academy of Management Review* 39, no. 4 (2014); Obukhova and Lan, "Do Job Seekers Benefit from Contacts? A Direct Test with Contemporaneous Searches," *Management Science* 59, no. 10 (2013); Dika and Singh, "Applications of Social Capital in Educational Literature: A Critical Synthesis," *Review of Educational Research* 72, no. 1 (2002).

108. For a similar analysis, see Adler-Nissen and Pouliot, "Power in Practice: Negotiating the International Intervention in Libya."

109. McKibben, *State Strategies in International Bargaining: Play by the Rules or Change Them?* (Cambridge: Cambridge University Press, 2015), 17–18; Odell, *Negotiating the World Economy* (Ithaca, NY: Cornell University Press, 2000); Voeten, "Outside Options and the Logic of Security Council Action," *American Political Science Review* 95, no. 4 (2001).

110. The cost of the coercive threat to the pivotal state is small, especially if it disposes of unexploited bargaining power in the existing relationship. See Wagner, "Economic Interdependence, Bargaining Power, and Political Influence," *International Organization* 42, no. 3 (1988).

111. Passmore, Shannon, and Hart, "Rallying the Troops."

112. Slantchev, "Feigning Weakness," *International Organization* 64, no. 3 (2010).

113. For a similar account of how weak states can sometimes dominate negotiations, see Keohane, "The Big Influence of Small Allies," *Foreign Policy* 2 (Spring 1971). Cooley and Nexon, "Interpersonal Networks and International Security"; Schelling, *The Strategy of Conflict*, 20; Henke, "The Politics of Diplomacy: How the United States Builds Multilateral Military Coalitions," *International Studies Quarterly* 61, no. 2 (2017).

114. James Webb to Embassy Cape Town, February 13, 1952, Selected Records Relating to the Korean War, Department of State: Topical File Subseries, SMOF, PPF, 6. Contributions to the UN effort [3 of 3: February–September 1952], Truman Papers, Truman Library.

115. Colman and Widen, "The Johnson Administration and the Recruitment of Allies in Vietnam, 1964–1968," 498.

116. Wright to Rostow, September 19, 1967, Document 359, FRUS 1964–1968 XXVII.

117. Funabashi, *The Peninsula Question*, 231.

118. Ibid., 232.

119. Ibid., 234.

120. Thompson, *Channels of Power*, 19; Thomas, *Ethics of Destruction* (Ithaca, NY: Cornell University Press, 2001), 36.

121. Colman and Widen, "The Johnson Administration and the Recruitment of Allies in Vietnam, 1964–1968," 496–97; Dumbrell, "The Johnson Administration and the British Labour Government: Vietnam, the Pound and East of Suez," *Journal of American Studies* 30, no. 2 (1996).

122. See for instance Record, *Wanting War: Why the Bush Administration Invaded Iraq* (Lincoln, NE: Potomac Books, 2010); Harvey, *Explaining the Iraq War: Counterfactual Theory, Logic, and Evidence* (Cambridge: Cambridge University Press, 2012); Packer, *The Assassins' Gate: America in Iraq* (New York: Farrar, Straus and Giroux, 2005).

123. Saunders, *Leaders at War: How Presidents Shape Military Interventions* (Ithaca, NY: Cornell University Press, 2011); Logevall, *Choosing War* (Berkeley: University of California Press, 1999).

124. Seawright, *Multi-Method Social Science*, 68.

125. Hurd, "Legitimacy, Power, and the Symbolic Life of the UN Security Council," *Global Governance* 8 (2002): 37; Gaibulloev et al., "Personnel Contributions to UN and Non-UN Peacekeeping Missions: A Public Goods Approach," *Journal of Peace Research* 52, no. 6 (2015).

126. Seawright, *Multi-Method Social Science*, 90.

127. Henke, "Rotten Carrot."

128. I develop such a theory elsewhere. See Henke, "Why Did France Intervene in Mali in 2013?"

129. Coleman, "The Legitimacy Audience Shapes the Coalition: Lessons from Afghanistan, 2001," *Journal of Intervention and Statebuilding* 11, no. 3 (2017).

130. Collier, Brady, and Seawright, "Outdated Views of Qualitative Methods: Time to Move On," *Political Analysis* 18, no. 4 (2010): 506.

131. Pouliot, *International Security in Practice: The Politics of Nato-Russia Diplomacy*, vol. 38 (Cambridge: Cambridge University Press, 2010), 28.

132. See for instance Davidson, *America's Allies and War*; Weitsman, *Waging War*; Mousseau, "Democracy and Militarized Interstate Collaboration," *Journal of Peace Research* 34, no. 1 (1997); Von Hlatky, *American Allies in Times of War*; Cunliffe, *Legions of Peace*; Bove and Elia, "Supplying Peace: Participation in and Troop Contribution to Peacekeeping Missions," *Journal of Peace Research* 48, no. 6 (2011); Sotomayor, *Myth of the Democratic Peacekeeper*.

133. See for instance Davidson, *America's Allies and War*; Kreps, *Coalitions of Convenience: United States Military Interventions after the Cold War* (Oxford: Oxford University Press, 2011); Baltrusaitis, *Coalition Politics and the Iraq War*; Bennett, Lepgold, and Unger, *Friends in Need: Burden Sharing in the Persian Gulf War*.

134. Checkel, "Norms, Institutions, and National Identity in Contemporary Europe," *International Studies Quarterly* 43, no. 1 (1999); Bearce and Bondanella, "Intergovernmental Organizations, Socialization, and Member-State Interest Convergence."

135. Martin, *Coercive Cooperation*, 18.

136. Ibid.

137. Krasner, "Global Communications and National Power," 339–40.

138. Martin, *Coercive Cooperation*, 775.

139. Among the scholars making this argument are Bennett, Lepgold, and Unger, *Friends in Need*; Baltrusaitis, *Coalition Politics and the Iraq War*; Lake, *Hierarchy in International Relations*; Tago, "Is There an Aid-for-Participation Deal?"; Newnham, "Coalition of the Bribed and Bullied?" Hegemonic power theory suggests that hegemonic powers invest capital to bring their "subordinate" states into their ideological fold. For example, in the military realm, they might use military education and training programs to socialize foreign interlocutors into American military norms, procedures, and practices. In the civilian realm, they can shape ideas, norms, and values through international organizations and bilateral treaties.

140. Following Thompson, I define *coercion* as "efforts to convince a target to take a certain course of action—to initiate a new action or to halt an existing one—by imposing or threatening to impose costs." See Thompson, *Channels of Power*, 16.

141. See for instance Schelling, *The Strategy of Conflict*, 2. Baltrusaitis, for instance, finds ample evidence that the United States made use of coercive threats in its endeavor to assemble a "coalition of the willing" for the invasion of Iraq in 2003. See Baltrusaitis, *Coalition Politics and the Iraq War*.

142. Lake, "Authority, Coercion, and Power in International Relations," working paper, 2010. Both pathways are intimately related in the use of violence to enforce commands and thus hard to distinguish in practice. As a result, I combine them in this analysis.

143. As quoted in Rathbun, *Diplomacy's Value*, 13.

144. Keohane and Nye, *Power and Interdependence*.

145. See for instance Gilpin, *War and Change in World Politics* (Cambridge: Cambridge University Press, 1981), 9–10; Grieco, "Anarchy and the Limits of Cooperation: A Realist Critique of the Newest Liberal Institutionalism," *International Organization* 42, no. 3 (1988). (Neo)realism posits that hegemons often run "security rackets," linking protection to economic issues. Analyzing the effects of asymmetric power relations has been the most successful application of realist theory to the current modes of security cooperation.

146. Zartman and Rubin, "The Study of Power and the Practice of Negotiations" in *Power and Negotiations,* ed. Zartman and Rubin (Ann Arbor: University of Michigan Press, 2002).

147. Lake, *Hierarchy in International Relations*, 173.

148. Baldwin argues that an agent's immediate reaction to sticks usually differs from his or her immediate reaction to carrots. Whereas fear, anxiety, and resistance are typical responses to threats, the typical responses to promises are hope, reassurance, and attraction. See Baldwin, "Thinking about Threats," *Journal of Conflict Resolution* 15, no. 1 (1971): 31.

149. Ellis, "The Hobbesian Problem of Order: A Critical Appraisal of the Normative Solution," *American Sociological Review* 36, no. 4 (1971).

150. Minutes, Meeting of the NSC deputies Small Group, December 3, 1992, folder "NSC/DC 403A," OA/ID 90024, H-Files NSC/DC Meetings Files, Bush Presidential Records, George Bush Presidential Library.

3. A QUANTITATIVE TEST

1. As explained in the preceding chapter, I argue that operational plans constitute a first filter in coalition-building processes. If a pivotal state intends to recruit a large force, it uses diplomatic embeddedness to assess which state among those that could contribute such force is most likely to oblige. The same is true of token contributions.

2. See for instance Bennett, Lepgold, and Unger, *Friends in Need*, 846; Dibb, "The Future of International Coalitions: How Useful? How Manageable?" *The Washington Quarterly* 25, no. 2 (2002): 132; Morrow, "A Spatial Model of International Conflict," *American Political Science Review* 80, no. 4 (1986); Snyder, *Alliance Politics* (Ithaca, NY: Cornell University Press, 1997), 12; Weitsman, "Alliance Cohesion and Coalition Warfare: The Central Powers and Triple Entente," *Security Studies* 12, no. 3 (2003): 20; Smith, "Alliance Formation and War," *International Studies Quarterly* 39, no. 4 (1995): 410.

3. See for instance Walt, "The Origins of Alliances" (Ithaca, NY: Cornell University Press, 1987); Sandler, "The Economic Theory of Alliances: A Survey," *Journal of Conflict Resolution* 37, no. 3 (1993); Snyder, *Alliance Politics*; Davidson, *America's Allies and War*; Weitsman, "Alliance Cohesion and Coalition Warfare"; Gibler and Sarkees, "Measuring Alliances: The Correlates of War Formal Interstate Alliance Dataset, 1816–2000," *Journal of Peace Research* 41, no. 2 (2004); Leeds et al., "Alliance Treaty Obligations and Provisions, 1815–1944," *International Interactions* 28, no. 3 (2002).

4. See for instance Finnemore, *The Purpose of Intervention: Changing Beliefs about the Use of Force* (Ithaca, NY: Cornell University Press, 2003); Wheeler, *Saving Strangers: Humanitarian Intervention in International Society* (Oxford: Oxford University Press, 2000); Lebovic, "Uniting for Peace? Democracies and United Nations Peace Operations after the Cold War," *Journal of Conflict Resolution* 48, no. 6 (2004); Andersson, "Democracies and UN Peacekeeping Operations, 1990–1996," *International Peacekeeping* 7, no. 2 (2000); Risse-Kappen, *Bringing Transnational Relations Back In: Non-State Actors, Domestic Structures, and International Institutions* (Cambridge: Cambridge University Press, 1995); Auerswald, "Explaining Wars of Choice: An Integrated Decision Model of NATO Policy in Kosovo," *International Studies Quarterly* 48, no. 3 (2004).

5. Bellamy and Williams, *Providing Peacekeepers*; Cunliffe, *Legions of Peace*.

6. See for instance Brysk, *Global Good Samaritans*, 77–80; Ingebritsen, "Norm Entrepreneurs: Scandinavia's Role in World Politics," *Cooperation and Conflict* 37, no. 1 (2002).

7. See for instance Stähle, "China's Shifting Attitude towards United Nations Peacekeeping Operations," *China Quarterly* 195 (2008); Dodds, *Global Geopolitics: A Critical Introduction* (Upper Saddle River, NJ: Prentice Hall, 2005); Jakobsen, "The Transformation of United Nations Peace Operations in the 1990s: Adding Globalization to the Conventional 'End of the Cold War Explanation,'" *Cooperation and Conflict* 37, no. 3 (2002); Rathbun, *Partisan Interventions: European Party Politics and Peace Enforcement in the Balkans* (Ithaca, NY: Cornell University Press, 2004), 197; Vucetic, "The Anglosphere and US-Led Coalitions of the Willing, 1950–2001," *European Journal of International Relations* 17, no. 1 (2011); Lebovic, "Uniting for Peace?"

8. See for instance Velazquez, "Why Some States Participate in UN Peace Missions While Others Do Not"; Kathman and Melin, "Who Keeps the Peace?"

9. See for instance Perkins and Neumayer, "Extra-Territorial Interventions in Conflict Spaces," 900; Siverson and Starr, *The Diffusion of War*.

10. See for instance Klare, *Blood and Oil: The Dangers and Consequences of America's Growing Dependency on Imported Petroleum* (New York: Owl Books, 2005); Gilligan and Stedman, "Where Do the Peacekeepers Go?" *International Studies Review* 5, no. 4 (2003); Fortna, *Does Peacekeeping Work? Shaping Belligerents' Choices after Civil War* (Princeton, NJ: Princeton University Press, 2008).

11. Thompson, *Channels of Power*, 16.

12. Newnham, "Coalition of the Bribed and Bullied?" 86. For a similar argument, see also Tago, "Is There an Aid-for-Participation Deal?"; Sarantakes, "In the Service of Pharaoh? The United States and the Deployment of Korean Troops in Vietnam, 1965–1968," *Pacific Historical Review* 68, no. 3 (1999).

13. Lake, *Hierarchy in International Relations*, 165–67.

14. U.S.-led coalitions have the following characteristics: (1) the United States provides the largest portion of the coalition forces; (2) a U.S. military officer serves as commander of the multilateral forces, or the U.S. military command designates what friendly forces do in the theater through coordination; and (3) at least one state deploys its armed forces to a war zone by accepting a request from the United States. See Tago, "Why Do States Join US-Led Military Coalitions?: The Compulsion of the Coalition's Missions and Legitimacy," *International Relations of the Asia-Pacific* 7, no. 2 (2007): 188–90.

15. This indicator is used to measure foreign policy autonomy from the United States. The more the potential participant has "independent alliances," the less hierarchical the security relationship between the potential participant and the United States. See Lake, *Hierarchy in International Relations*, 69–70.

16. For the sources of all variables, see Lake, *Hierarchy in International Relations*.

17. Pevehouse, Nordstrom, and Warnke, "The Correlates of War 2 International Governmental Organizations Data Version 2.0," *Conflict Management and Peace Science* 21, no. 2 (2004).

18. I counted all bilateral treaties concluded since 1945 toward the overall number of bilateral ties. This includes all types of bilateral agreements, such as security, socioeconomic and immigration treaties. If a specific state did not exist in 1945, bilateral treaties are counted from the date of its creation.

19. Lake, *Hierarchy in International Relations*, 169.

20. The unclassified version of the directive is available at https://fas.org/irp/offdocs/pdd/pdd-25.pdf (last accessed February 9, 2017).

21. I list these operations (and explain their inclusion) in the online appendix.

22. The aid data come from the OECD DAC database. Available at www.oecd.org/dac/stats/idsonline.htm. Trade data come from the COW Trade Dataset (Version 2.01). Available at www.correlatesofwar.org/data-sets/bilateral-trade. See Barbieri and Keshk, "Correlates of War Project Trade Data Set Codebook (Version 2.01)," (2012); Barbieri, Keshk, and Pollins, "Trading Data: Evaluating Our Assumptions and Coding Rules," *Conflict Management and Peace Science* 26, no. 5 (2009). Aid and trade data are log transformed.

23. This variable, which is based on the *Affinity of Nation Index,* tries to control for the overall similarity of a dyad's revealed preferences. See Gartzke, "The Affinity of Nations Index, 1946–2002" (2006); Voeten, Strezhnev, and Bailey, "United Nations General Assembly Voting Data" (Harvard Dataverse, 2009).

24. Trade interests influence the calculus of potential interveners. See for instance Aydin, *Foreign Powers and Intervention in Armed Conflicts* (Palo Alto, CA: Stanford University Press, 2012); Stojek and Chacha, "Adding Trade to the Equation: Multilevel Modeling of Biased Civil War Interventions," *Journal of Peace Research* 52, no. 2 (2015). Embassies or consulates are usually only opened in places in which a country has something at stake. This is especially the case for developing countries for which the maintenance of an embassy/consulate constitutes a substantive financial burden. Diplomatic representation data has been retrieved from the COW Diplomatic Exchange Dataset (Version 2006.1). See Bayer, "Diplomatic Exchange Data Set, V2006.1," Online: http://correlatesofwar. org (2006). To measure the relative importance of each particular economic tie from a potential participant to a target country, I divide the overall bilateral aid and trade flows again by the GDP of the participant.

25. I use the POLITY-2 score from the POLITY IV project. See Marshall, Jaggers, and Gurr, "Polity IV Data Series Version 2010," University of Maryland, College Park, Maryland. Retrieved from www. systemicpeace. org/polity/polity4. htm (2010).

26. Data come from the World Bank. I use the log of GPD per capita.

27. Data come from Singer, Bremer, and Stuckey, "Capability Distribution, Uncertainty, and Major Power War, 1820–1965," in *Peace, War, and Numbers*, ed. Russett (Beverly Hills, CA: Sage, 1972).

28. More precisely, the variable captures the cumulative number of separate alliances in a particular year in which both states are members (overlapping for at least one day). The data on common alliance memberships were retrieved from the Correlates of War (COW) *Formal Alliance Dataset* (Version 3.03). See Gibler, "The Costs of Reneging Reputation and Alliance Formation," *Journal of Conflict Resolution* 52, no. 3 (2008). Data on conflict involvement comes from the COW MID Dataset (4.1). See Palmer et al., "The Mid4 Dataset, 2002–2010: Procedures, Coding Rules and Description," *Conflict Management and Peace Science* 32, no. 2 (2015).

29. Model 2 thus attempts to exclude symbolic or token contributions.

30. For a very similar model choice, see Wolford, *The Politics of Military Coalitions*, 77.

31. I also run robustness checks controlling for intra-class correlation among coalitions and participants. The substantive results do not change.

32. See for instance Mouw, "Social Capital and Finding a Job: Do Contacts Matter?" *American Sociological Review* (2003); Shalizi and Thomas, "Homophily and Contagion Are Generically Confounded in Observational Social Network Studies," *Sociological Methods and Research* 40, no. 2 (2011).

33. See for instance Halaby, "Panel Models in Sociological Research: Theory into Practice," *Annual Review of Sociology* 30 (2004).

34. For a similar finding, see Wolford, *Politics of Military Coalitions*.

35. For a similar finding, see Tago, "Why Do States Join Us-Led Military Coalitions?."

36. Models 1 and 2 from Table 3.2 were used to perform the analysis. The estimation shows a confidence interval of 95 percent.

37. See online appendix for all robustness checks.

38. At the 0.01 level for all contributions and at the 0.05 level for contributions equal to or larger than 100 troops.

39. Because of the immense difficulty of gathering accurate data on coalition contributions, I excluded from the dataset the following types of coalitions: (1) coalitions deployed in response to a natural disaster; (2) coalitions with the sole purpose of evacuating foreign nationals; (3) multilateral naval forces enforcing a trade embargo; and (4) multilateral air deployments enforcing a no-fly zone. Operations involving fewer than 100 military and/or police forces have also been left out to avoid operations with a merely "political" objective (that is, to show the flag). See the *Multilateral Coalitions Dataset Codebook* for details, which is available in the online appendix.

40. United Nations Bibliographic Information System. Available at http://unbisnet.un.org.

41. Any UN member state, whether permanent or nonpermanent or a nonmember of the UN Security Council at the time of deliberations, can request to address the UN Security Council during its public sessions on a particular security topic. I assume that states having intense preferences with regard to a specific operation are particularly likely to request permission to address the UN Security Council on that subject matter.

42. See *Multilateral Coalitions Dataset Codebook* for details. In case of a major discrepancy between the speech record analysis and the "action" analysis, I put more weight on the action analysis.

43. For a similar approach see Tago, "Too Many Problems at Home to Help You: Domestic Disincentives for Military Coalition Participation," *International Area Studies Review* 17, no. 3 (2014), as well as "Is There an Aid-for-Participation Deal? US Economic and Military Aid Policy to Coalition Forces (Non)Participants" and "Why Do

States Join US-Led Military Coalitions? The Compulsion of the Coalition's Missions and Legitimacy."

44. Data for coalition participation/troop contributions again come from the International Institute for Strategic Studies (IISS) Military Balance (years 1990–2006), the United Nations Peacekeeping Department (UNDPKO), the Réseau Francophone de Recherche sur les Opérations de Paix (ROP), the Stockholm International Peace Research Institute (SIPRI), as well as other secondary sources. See *Multilateral Coalitions Dataset Codebook* for specific data sources.

45. The aid data have been retrieved from the OECD DAC database. Trade data come from the Correlates of War Trade Dataset (Version 2.01).

46. See for instance Walt, "Origins of Alliances," 43; Snyder, *Alliance Politics*. The variable captures the cumulative number of separate alliances in a particular year in which both states are members (overlapping for at least one day). Data on common alliance memberships have been retrieved from the Correlates of War *Formal Alliance Dataset* (Version 3.03) by Gibler and Sarkees, "Measuring Alliances."

47. Data on contiguity come from the Correlates of War Direct Contiguity Dataset (Version 3.1). See Douglas et al., "The Correlates of War Project Direct Contiguity Data," *Conflict Management and Peace Science* 19, no. 2 (2002).

48. The literature on conflict management suggests that countries are more likely to intervene in conflicts closer to home. See for instance Perkins and Neumayer, "Extra-Territorial Interventions in Conflict Spaces," 900; Siverson and Starr, *The Diffusion of War*; Regan, *Civil Wars and Foreign Powers*.

49. Trade interests influence the calculus of potential interveners. See for instance Aydin, *Foreign Powers and Intervention in Armed Conflicts*; Stojek and Chacha, "Adding Trade to the Equation." Embassies or consulates are usually only opened in places in which a country has something at stake. Diplomatic representation data have been retrieved from the COW Diplomatic Exchange Dataset (Version 2006.1) by Bayer, "Diplomatic Exchange Data Set, V2006. 1." Aid data come from the OECD DAC database (see above), and trade data from the Correlates of War Trade Dataset (Version 2.01). See Barbieri, Keshk, and Pollins, "Trading Data." To measure the relative importance of each particular economic tie from a potential participant to a target country, I divide the overall bilateral aid and trade flows again by the GDP of the participant.

50. I use the POLITY-2 score from the POLITY IV project. See Marshall, Jaggers, and Gurr, "Polity IV Data Series Version 2010."

51. Data come from the World Bank. I use the log of GPD per capita.

52. Singer, Bremer, and Stuckey, "Capability Distribution, Uncertainty, and Major Power War, 1820–1965."

53. As explained above, the variable captures the cumulative number of separate alliances in a particular year in which both states are members (overlapping for at least one day). Data on common alliance memberships have been retrieved from the Correlates of War (COW) *Formal Alliance Dataset* (Version 3.03) by Gibler and Sarkees, "Measuring Alliances." Data on conflict involvement come from the COW MID Dataset (4.1) by Palmer et al., "The Mid4 Dataset, 2002–2010."

54. All models were run with a dummy variable controlling for missing data coded zero. The coefficient estimates of the dummy did not achieve statistical significance in any of the models.

55. In my analysis, the risk exists that observations of the dependent variable might not be completely independent from one another: coalition participation by one state might be conditional upon whether another country signs up for that same coalition. Furthermore, these decisions might also depend on previous deployments of that same state or on

the target state of the deployment (that is, a country with experience in a specific conflict theater might be more likely to sign up for a new operation targeting that same state). See for instance Poast, "Dyads Are Dead, Long Live Dyads! The Limits of Dyadic Designs in International Relations Research," *International Studies Quarterly* 60, no. 2 (2016); Erikson, Pinto, and Rader, "Dyadic Analysis in International Relations: A Cautionary Tale," *Political Analysis* 22, no. 4 (2014); Cranmer, Desmarais, and Menninga, "Complex Dependencies in the Alliance Network," *Conflict Management and Peace Science* 29, no. 3 (2012); Aronow, Samii, and Assenova, "Cluster–Robust Variance Estimation for Dyadic Data," *Political Analysis* 23, no. 4 (2015).

56. As mentioned above, I assume that one state might make its participation conditional on whether another state participates.

57. See online appendix for all robustness checks.

4. CHAINING COMMUNISTS

1. Stueck, *Rethinking the Korean War: A New Diplomatic and Strategic History* (Princeton, NJ: Princeton University Press, 2002), 61.

2. Acheson, *The Korean War*, 2.

3. Numbers refer to peak strength on July 27, 1953—the day the Armistice Agreement was signed. USFK Public Affairs Office, "United Nations Command." Available at www.usfk.mil/About/UnitedNationsCommand.aspx (last accessed on December 18, 2015).

4. John Dreier to Miller, January 25, 1951, FRUS, 1951, Volume 2, 938.

5. For case selection criteria, see chapter 2.

6. "Korean War." Available at https://en.wikipedia.org/wiki/Korean_War (last accessed February 1, 2016).

7. Cumings, *The Korean War*, 11.

8. Acheson, *Korean War*, 20.

9. Stueck, *The Road to Confrontation,* 186.

10. Acheson, *Korean War*, 13.

11. Stueck, *Rethinking the Korean War*, 15.

12. Truman, *Memoirs: Volume 2: Years of Trial and Hope, 1946–1952* (New York: Doubleday, 1956), 351.

13. Paige, *The Korean Decision, June 24–30, 1950* (New York: Free Press, 1968), 36.

14. Ibid., 38.

15. On the importance of NSC68, see also Fordham, *Building the Cold War Consensus.*

16. Dean Acheson to UN mission of the United States, July 12, 1950, Selected Records Relating to the Korean War, Department of State: Topical File Subseries, Staff Member Office Files (SMOF), President's Personal Files (PPF), 6. Contributions to the UN effort [1 of 3: June--July 1950], Harry S Truman Papers, Harry S Truman Library, Independence, Missouri.

17. Dean Acheson to US embassy London, August 11, 1950, Selected Records Relating to the Korean War, Department of State: Topical File Subseries, SMOF, PPF, 6. Contributions to the UN effort [2 of 3: August–December 1950], Truman Papers, Truman Library. See also George Marshall to Dean Acheson, January 30, 1951, Selected Records Relating to the Korean War, Department of State: Topical File Subseries, SMOF, PPF, 6. Contributions to the UN effort [2 of 3: August 1950–December 1951], Truman Papers, Truman Library.

18. As cited by Stueck, *The Korean War*, 56.

19. Dean Acheson to Foster Dulles, July 11, 1950, Selected Records Relating to the Korean War, Department of State: Topical File Subseries, SMOF, PPF, 6. Contributions to the UN effort [1 of 3: June–July 1950], Truman Papers, Truman Library.

20. George Marshall to Dean Acheson, January 30, 1951, Selected Records Relating to the Korean War, Department of State: Topical File Subseries, SMOF, PPF, 6. Contributions to the UN effort [2 of 3: August 1950–December 1951], Truman Papers, Truman Library.

21. George W. Perkins to Francis T. Williamson, July 14, 1950, Selected Records Relating to the Korean War, Department of State: Topical File Subseries, SMOF, PPF, 5. Role of the UN in the Korean Conflict [2 of 2: September–December 1950], Truman Papers, Truman Library.

22. Memorandum by John C. Dreier, August 7, 1950, Selected Records Relating to the Korean War, Department of State: Topical File Subseries, SMOF, PPF, 6. Contributions to the UN effort [1 of 3: June–July 1950], Truman Papers, Truman Library, 3.

23. Stueck, *Korean War*, 56.

24. W. Stuart Symington, "Recommended Policies and Actions in Light of the Grave World Situation," NSC 100, January 11, 1951, FRUS, 1951, Volume 1, 7. See also George Marshall to Dean Acheson, January 30, 1951, Selected Records Relating to the Korean War, Department of State: Topical File Subseries, SMOF, PPF, 6. Contributions to the UN effort [2 of 3: August 1950–December 1951], Truman Papers, Truman Library.

25. As cited in Bohlin, "United States–Latin American Relations and the Cold War, 1949–1953," 151.

26. Memorandum of Conversation "Korea" by C. P. Noyes, June 30, 1950, SMOF, PPF, Selected Records Relating to the Korean War, Department of State: Topical File Subseries, SMOF, PPF, 1. North Korean aggression: Immediate evaluation and reaction [1 of 2: June 1950], Truman Papers, Truman Library.

27. Ibid.

28. Memorandum of Conversation "Korea" by John C. Ross, June 28, 1950, Selected Records Relating to the Korean War, Department of State: Topical File Subseries, SMOF, PPF, 6. Contributions to the UN effort [1 of 3: June–July 1950], Truman Papers, Truman Library.

29. Dean Acheson to UN mission of the United States, July 12, 1950, Selected Records Relating to the Korean War, Department of State: Topical File Subseries, SMOF, PPF, 6. Contributions to the UN effort [1 of 3: June–July 1950], Truman Papers, Truman Library.

30. The idea of a mixed UN legion was also another nonstarter for the U.S. government. U.S. officials instead insisted that all UN units must come from nations that remain responsible for their own nationals. See John MacVane, "Emphasizing UN Aspect of Korean Operation," Memorandum of Conversation, July 25, 1950, Selected Records Relating to the Korean War, Department of State: Topical File Subseries, SMOF, PPF, 1. North Korean aggression: Immediate evaluation and reaction [1 of 2: June 1950], Truman Papers, Truman Library.

31. Warren Austin to Dean Acheson, September 1, 1950, Selected Records Relating to the Korean War, Department of State: Topical File Subseries, SMOF, PPF, 5. Role of the UN in the Korean Conflict [2 of 2: September–December 1950], Truman Papers, Truman Library.

32. Bohlin, "United States–Latin American Relations and the Cold War, 1949–1953," 153.

33. George Marshall to Dean Acheson, September 25, 1950, Selected Records Relating to the Korean War, Department of State: Topical File Subseries, SMOF, PPF, 6. Contributions to the UN effort [2 of 3: August–December 1950], Truman Papers, Truman Library.

34. As quoted in Bohlin, "United States–Latin American Relations and the Cold War, 1949–1953," 154.

35. As quoted in ibid., 156.

36. Stueck, *Korean War*, 57.

37. Dean Acheson to U.S. embassy London, August 11, 1950, Selected Records Relating to the Korean War, Department of State: Topical File Subseries, SMOF, PPF, 6. Contributions to the UN effort [2 of 3: August–December 1950], Truman Papers, Truman Library.

38. As quoted in Bohlin, "United States–Latin American Relations and the Cold War, 1949–1953," 155–56.

39. Ibid., 159.

40. Ibid.

41. Ibid., 161.

42. Ibid., 204.

43. As quoted in ibid., 164.

44. Ibid., 157.

45. Ibid., 177–80.

46. Ibid., 180.

47. Ibid., 183.

48. H. Freeman Matthews to General James H. Burns, August 9, 1950, FRUS, 1950, Volume 1, 648.

49. As quoted in Bohlin, "United States–Latin American Relations and the Cold War, 1949–1953," 169.

50. The State Department had pushed for language that would have watered down the necessity of reimbursement even further. Nevertheless, the Pentagon continued to stand by the latter principle, that countries that received aid to deploy to Korea would have to reimburse the United State in some form or another. See ibid., 170–71.

51. Johnson had been deeply opposed to the measure and thus had stalled its implementation. See ibid., 171.

52. Ibid., 190.

53. George Marshall to Dean Acheson, January 30, 1951, Selected Records Relating to the Korean War, Department of State: Topical File Subseries, SMOF, PPF, 6. Contributions to the UN effort [2 of 3: August 1950–December 1951], Truman Papers, Truman Library.

54. Ibid.

55. Livingston Merchant to Harry Shooshan, February 2, 1951, Selected Records Relating to the Korean War, Department of State: Topical File Subseries, SMOF, PPF, 6. Contributions to the UN effort [2 of 3: August 1950–December 1951], Truman Papers, Truman Library.

56. Minutes of Meeting on Military Assistance for Korea, February 13, 1951, Selected Records Relating to the Korean War, Department of State: Topical File Subseries, SMOF, PPF, 6. Contributions to the UN effort [3 of 3: February–September 1952], Truman Papers, Truman Library.

57. Ibid.

58. Stueck, *Korean War*, 73–74.

59. Ibid.

60. Ibid.

61. Ibid.

62. Memorandum by Assistant Secretary of State for Near Eastern, South Asian, and African Affairs (McGhee) to the Deputy Under Secretary of State (Matthews), August 14, 1950, FRUS 1950, Volume 5, 1289.

63. Telegram, Ambassador to Turkey (Wadsworth) to the Secretary of State, September 12, 1950, FRUS 1950, Volume 5, 1312.

64. Minutes of Meeting on Military Assistance for Korea, February 13, 1951, Selected Records Relating to the Korean War, Department of State: Topical File Subseries, SMOF, PPF, 6. Contributions to the UN effort [3 of 3: February–September 1952], Truman Papers, Truman Library.

65. Ibid.

66. Dean Acheson to George Marshall, February 16, 1951, Selected Records Relating to the Korean War, Department of State: Topical File Subseries, SMOF, PPF, 6. Contributions to the UN effort [2 of 3: August 1950–December 1951], Truman Papers, Truman Library.

67. Dean Acheson to George Marshall, April 2, 1951, Selected Records Relating to the Korean War, Department of State: Topical File Subseries, SMOF, PPF, 6. Contributions to the UN effort [3 of 3: February–September 1952], Truman Papers, Truman Library.

68. John D. Hickerson to Weinhouse, September 21, 1951, Selected Records Relating to the Korean War, Department of State: Topical File Subseries, SMOF, PPF, 6. Contributions to the UN effort [2 of 3: August 1950–December 1951], Truman Papers, Truman Library.

69. Robert A. Lovett to Dean Acheson, August 16, 1951, Selected Records Relating to the Korean War, Department of State: Topical File Subseries, SMOF, PPF, 6. Contributions to the UN effort [2 of 3: August 1950–December 1951], Truman Papers, Truman Library.

70. Ernest A. Gross to Dean Acheson, June 6, 1951, Selected Records Relating to the Korean War, Department of State: Topical File Subseries, SMOF, PPF, 6. Contributions to the UN effort [3 of 3: February–September 1952], Truman Papers, Truman Library. Emphasis added.

71. Dean Acheson to Ernest A. Gross, June 19, 1951, Selected Records Relating to the Korean War, Department of State: Topical File Subseries, SMOF, PPF, 6. Contributions to the UN effort [3 of 3: February–September 1952], Truman Papers, Truman Library.

72. Gross to Dean Acheson, June 22, 1951, Selected Records Relating to the Korean War, Department of State: Topical File Subseries, SMOF, PPF, 6. Contributions to the UN effort [3 of 3: February–September 1952], Truman Papers, Truman Library.

73. CADEL to Embassy Paris, December 5, 1951, Selected Records Relating to the Korean War, Department of State: Topical File Subseries, SMOF, PPF, 6. Contributions to the UN effort [2 of 3: August 1950–December 1951], Truman Papers, Truman Library.

74. Dockrill, "The Foreign Office, Anglo-American Relations, and the Korean War, June 1950–June 1951," *International Affairs (Royal Institute of International Affairs 1944–)* 62, no. 3 (1986): 459.

75. Both diplomats and the military leadership agreed on this point, see Greenwood, "'A War We Don't Want': Another Look at the British Labour Government's Commitment in Korea, 1950–51," *Contemporary British History* 17, no. 4 (2003): 4.

76. Ibid., 14.

77. Dockrill, "The Foreign Office, Anglo-American Relations, and the Korean War, June 1950–June 1951," 459.

78. Ibid., 460.

79. Greenwood, "'A War We Don't Want,'" 1.

80. Ibid., 4.

81. Ibid., 8.

82. Hopkins, "The Price of Cold War Partnership: Sir Oliver Franks and the British Military Commitment in the Korean War," *Cold War History* 1, no. 2 (2001): 36.

83. Ibid., 32.

84. Acheson, *Present at the Creation: My Years in the State Department* (New York: Norton, 1969), 323.

85. The United Nations Relief and Rehabilitation Administration (UNRRA) was an international relief agency. It was founded in 1943 and became part of the United Nations in 1945. It shut down operations in 1947.

86. Greenwood, "'A War We Don't Want,'" 8.

87. Hopkins, "Price of Cold War Partnership," 35.

88. Dockrill, "The Foreign Office, Anglo-American Relations, and the Korean War, June 1950–June 1951," 461.

89. The UK and the U.S. held dissimilar attitudes toward communist China. Britain had indeed recognized communist China in January 1950. Such action was, however, totally anathema to Acheson. See ibid., 459.

90. Public Record Office, Foreign Office 371/84084, Foreign Office to Franks, Washington D.C., Tel. No. 3159, July 12, 1950.

91. Hopkins, "Price of Cold War Partnership," 38.

92. Ibid.

93. Public Record Office, Prime Minister's Papers 8/1405 Part I, Franks to Attlee, July 15, 1950.

94. Hopkins, "Price of Cold War Partnership," 37.

95. Ibid., 39.

96. Farrar-Hockley, "Official History: The British Part in the Korean War. Volume I: A Distant Obligation" (London: HMSO, 1990), 99.

97. Public Record Office, Foreign Office 371/84091, FK 1022/222G, Franks to Foreign Office, Tel. No. 2022, July 21, 1950.

98. Public Record Office, Foreign Office 371/84091, FK 1022/222G, Foreign Office to Franks, Tel. No. 3225, July 22, 1950.

99. Hopkins, "Price of Cold War Partnership," 41.

100. Grey, *The Commonwealth Armies and the Korean War: An Alliance Study* (Manchester: Manchester University Press, 1990), 35.

101. Public Record Office, Foreign Office 371/84091, FK 1022/222G, Franks to Foreign Office, Tel. No. 2036 (later corrected to 2037), July 23, 1950.

102. Farrar-Hockley, "Official History," 103.

103. As quoted in ibid.

104. Hopkins, "Price of Cold War Partnership," 42.

105. See for instance Vickers, "Harold Wilson, the British Labour Party, and the War in Vietnam," *Journal of Cold War Studies* 10, no. 2 (2008); Wilson, *A Personal Record: The Labour Government, 1964–1970* (Boston: Little, Brown, 1971), 341.

106. See for instance Ellis, *Britain, America, and the Vietnam War* (Westport, CT: Greenwood Publishing Group, 2004), XVII; Colman, *A "Special Relationship"?: Harold Wilson, Lyndon B Johnson and Anglo-American Relations "at the Summit," 1964–8* (Manchester: Manchester University Press, 2004), 1.

107. Ellis, *Britain, America, and the Vietnam War*, 116; Dumbrell, "The Johnson Administration and the British Labour Government," 211.

108. Colman, *A "Special Relationship"?* 84–85; Dumbrell, "The Johnson Administration and the British Labour Government," 211.

109. Brook Claxton, then serving as Canada's Defense Minister, quoted in Prince, "The Limits of Constraint: Canadian-American Relations and the Korean War, 1950–51," *Journal of Canadian Studies* 27, no. 4 (1993): 133.

110. Pearson, *Mike: The Memoirs of the Rt. Hon. Lester B. Pearson, Volume Two: 1948–1957* (Toronto: University of Toronto Press, 1973), 137; Stairs, *The Diplomacy of Constraint: Canada, the Korean War, and the United States* (Toronto: University of Toronto Press, 1974), 3–28; Prince, "Limits of Constraint," 133.

111. "Limits of Constraint," 133.

112. Stairs, *Diplomacy of Constraint*, 14.

113. Prince, "Limits of Constraint," 133.

114. Stairs, *Diplomacy of Constraint*; Egerton, "Lester B. Pearson and the Korean War: Dilemmas of Collective Security and International Enforcement in Canadian Foreign Policy, 1950–53," *International Peacekeeping* 4, no. 1 (1997).

115. Stairs, *Diplomacy of Constraint*, 39–43.

116. In this regard, Canada mirrored British attitudes with regards to Korea. See Stairs ibid., 76.

117. Pearson, *Mike*, 2:139–41.

118. Stairs, *Diplomacy of Constraint*, 73.

119. As quoted in ibid.

120. Pearson, *Mike*, 2:135.

121. Ibid., 274.

122. Ibid., 264–78.

123. Ibid., 155.

124. Ibid.

125. Stairs, *Diplomacy of Constraint*, 71.

126. Prince, "Limits of Constraint," 139.

127. Cf. Schimmelfennig, "The Community Trap: Liberal Norms, Rhetorical Action, and the Eastern Enlargement of the European Union," *International Organization* 55, no. 01 (2003).

128. Fraser, "Backstage in Ottawa," September 15, 1950, 66; Prince (1992–3), fnt 60. All the U.S. government really knew at the time about a Pakistani deployment was that the Pakistani Army had asked the Pakistani government to send troops.

129. Grey, *Commonwealth Armies and the Korean War*, 35.

130. Prince, "Limits of Constraint," 140.

131. Ibid., fnt 69.

132. Ibid., 139.

133. Wood, *Strange Battleground: The Operations in Korea and Their Effects on the Defence Policy of Canada* (Ottawa: R. Duhamel, Queen's printer, 1966), 20.

134. Stairs, *Diplomacy of Constraint*, 76.

135. Ibid., 75.

136. Grey, *Commonwealth Armies and the Korean War*, 31.

137. Stairs, *Diplomacy of Constraint*, 85.

138. Ibid.

139. Prince, "Limits of Constraint," fnt 72.

140. Levant, *Quiet Complicity, Canadian Involvement in the Vietnam War* (Toronto: Between the Lines, 1986), 2, 3, 5.

141. Preston, "Balancing War and Peace: Canadian Foreign Policy and the Vietnam War, 1961–1965," *Diplomatic History* 27, no. 1 (2003). Some scholars suggest, however, that Canada helped the United States via economic means. See for instance Taylor, *Snow Job: Canada, the United States, and Vietnam (1954 to 1973)* (Concord: House of Anansi Press, 1974); Eayrs, *In Defence of Canada: Indochina: Roots of Complicity*, vol. 5 (Toronto: University of Toronto Press, 1983).

142. Turkmen, "Turkey and the Korean War," *Turkish Studies* 3, no. 2 (2002): 167. In March 1945, the Soviet Union had refused to renew its 1925 Treaty of Friendship and Non-aggression with Turkey. Pressure further mounted throughout the late 1940s, including the mobilization of Soviet troops along the Turkish border in 1947. Turkey perceived NATO as the ideal way to balance these actions.

143. Hale, *Turkish Foreign Policy since 1774* (London: Routledge, 2013), 84.

144. Lippe, "Forgotten Brigade of the Forgotten War: Turkey's Participation in the Korean War," *Middle Eastern Studies* 36, no. 1 (2000): 95.

145. As quoted in Brown, "The One Coalition They Craved to Join: Turkey in the Korean War," *Review of International Studies* 34, no. 01 (2008): 103.

146. Telegram, US Embassy Ankara to Department of State, July 25, 1950, FRUS, 1950, Volume 5, 1286.

147. Hale, *Turkish Foreign Policy since 1774*, 85.

148. Memo by the Joint Chiefs of Staff to the Secretary of Defense (Johnson), September 9, 1950, FRUS, 1950, Volume 5, 1307.

149. As quoted in Turkmen, "Turkey and the Korean War," 174. See also Lippe, "Forgotten Brigade of the Forgotten War," 97.

150. Brown, "One Coalition They Craved to Join," 105.

151. Turkmen, "Turkey and the Korean War," 177. In addition to securing NATO membership, Turkey also requested financial assistance from the U.S. government to defray Turkish deployment expenses.

152. Memorandum of Conversation by the Chief of Mission of United States Economic Survey Mission to the Philippines (Bell) and the deputy Chief of Mission, Manila, August 21, 1950, FRUS, 1950, Volume VI, 1479.

153. Telegram, The Chief of Mission, United States Economic Survey Mission to the Philippines (Bell) to the Secretary of State, Manila, August 25, 1950, FRUS, 1950, Volume 6, 1480–81.

154. Eggan, "The Philippines and the Bell Report," *Human Organization* 10, no. 1 (1951): 1.

155. Congress, Senate, Committee on Foreign Relations. Republic of the Philippines: Hearings before the Subcommittee on United States Security Agreements and Commitments Abroad, Part 1, 91st Congress, 1st session, 1969, 36.

156. Boulter, "FC Erasmus and the Politics of South African Defense, 1948–1959" (Grahamstown: Rhodes University 1997), 184.

157. Van der Waag-Cowling, "South Africa and the Korean War, the Politics of Involvement," *Scientia Militaria: South African Journal of Military Studies* 44, no. 1 (2016): 224. South Africa was also suffering financially. It had made massive financial sacrifices during World War II, from which it had not yet recovered.

158. Worrall, *South Africa: Government and Politics* (Pretoria: Van Schaik (JL), 1980), 288; Ovendale, "The South African Policy of the British Labour Government, 1947–51," *International Affairs (Royal Institute of International Affairs 1944-)* 59, no. 1 (1982): 44; Van der Waag-Cowling, "South Africa and the Korean War, the Politics of Involvement," 226. One of the first actions of the newly elected Afrikaner government was to terminate the military exchange program with Great Britain (see Borstelmann, *Apartheid's Reluctant Uncle: The United States and Southern Africa in the Early Cold War* (Oxford: Oxford University Press, 1993), 90.

159. See for instance Winship to Secretary of State, June 14, 1949; US State Department–Central Files, 848A.00/0458; Military Attaché to Defense Department, July 2, 1949; US State Department–Central Files, 848A.00/0476; Minutes of Meeting with Mr F.C. Erasmus, August 17, 1949; US State Department–Central Files, 848A.00/0507.

160. See for instance Barber and Barratt, "South Africa's Foreign Policy 1948–88: The Search for Status and Security" (Cambridge: Cambridge University Press, 1990), 49.

161. Minutes of Meeting with MR F.C. Erasmus, August 17, 1949; US State Department–Central Files, 848A.00/0507.

162. Van der Waag-Cowling, "South Africa and the Korean War, the Politics of Involvement," 229.

163. Boulter, "FC Erasmus and the Politics of South African Defense, 1948–1959," 184.

164. Memorandum of Conversation of the Secretary of State and the South African Defense Minister, October 5, 1950, FRUS, 1950, Volume 5, 1837–1839. Available at http://digicoll.library.wisc.edu/cgi-bin/FRUS/FRUS-idx?type=turn&entity=FRUS.FRUS1950v05.p1861&id=FRUS.FRUS1950v05&isize=M (last accessed November 17, 2017).

165. Boulter, "FC Erasmus and the Politics of South African Defense, 1948–1959," 186.

166. As cited in ibid.

167. Ibid.

168. George Marshall to Dean Acheson, January 30, 1951, Selected Records Relating to the Korean War. Department of State: Topical File Subseries, SMOF, PPF, 6. Contributions to the UN effort [2 of 3: August 1950–December 1951], Truman Papers, Truman Library.

169. See for instance George Marshall to Dean Acheson, January 30, 1951, Selected Records Relating to the Korean War, Department of State: Topical File Subseries, SMOF, PPF, 6. Contributions to the UN effort [2 of 3: August 1950–December 1951], Truman

Papers, Truman Library; Livingston Merchant to Harry Shooshan, February 2, 1951, Selected Records Relating to the Korean War, Department of State: Topical File Subseries, SMOF, PPF, 6. Contributions to the UN effort [2 of 3: August 1950–December 1951], Truman Papers, Truman Library; Minutes of Meeting on Military Assistance for Korea, February 13, 1951, Selected Records Relating to the Korean War, Department of State: Topical File Subseries, SMOF, PPF, 6. Contributions to the UN effort [3 of 3: February–September 1952], Truman Papers, Truman Library.

170. Boulter, "FC Erasmus and the Politics of South African Defense,`` 1948–1959," 189.

171. Borstelmann, *Apartheid's Reluctant Uncle*, 185.

172. Embassy of the Union of South Africa to Dean Acheson, February 11, 1952, Selected Records Relating to the Korean War, Department of State: Topical File Subseries, SMOF, PPF, 6. Contributions to the UN effort [2 of 3: August 1950–December 1951], Truman Papers, Truman Library.

173. John D. Hickerson to Robert A. Lovett, February 18, 1952, Selected Records Relating to the Korean War, Department of State: Topical File Subseries, SMOF, PPF, 6. Contributions to the UN effort [3 of 3: February–September 1952], Truman Papers, Truman Library.

174. James Webb to Embassy Cape Town, February 13, 1952, Selected Records Relating to the Korean War, Department of State: Topical File Subseries, SMOF, PPF, 6. Contributions to the UN effort [3 of 3: February–September 1952], Truman Papers, Truman Library.

175. John D. Hickerson to Robert A. Lovett, February 18, 1952, Selected Records Relating to the Korean War, Department of State: Topical File Subseries, SMOF, PPF, 6. Contributions to the UN effort [3 of 3: February–September 1952], Truman Papers, Truman Library.

176. Memorandum of Conversation "Maintenance of South African Air Squadron in Korea," March 31, 1952, Selected Records Relating to the Korean War, Department of State: Topical File Subseries, SMOF, PPF, 6. Contributions to the UN effort [3 of 3: February–September 1952], Truman Papers, Truman Library.

177. Memorandum of Conversation "Courtesy Call of Deputy Prime Minister Havenga," September 16, 1952; RG 59, Records of the Executive Secretariat (Dean Acheson), Memos of Conversation Oct 1950–Dec 1952, box 14, lot 53D444, National Archives Washington D.C.

178. Borstelmann, *Apartheid's Reluctant Uncle*, 185.

179. Van der Waag-Cowling, "South Africa and the Korean War, the Politics of Involvement," 233.

180. Dean Acheson to U.S. Embassy in Capetown, February 13, 1952, 745A.5622/2-1352, Record Group 59, National Archives; Acheson to U.S. Embassy in Capetown, April 1, 1952, 745A.5622/3-2652, Record Group 59, National Archives; Department of State memorandum, June 20, 1952, 745A.5622/6-2052, Record Group 59, National Archives; Acheson to U.S. Embassy in Capetown, September 12, 1952, FRUS, 1952–54, 11:927.

181. Borstelmann, *Apartheid's Reluctant Uncle*, 188.

182. Memorandum of Conversation with G. P. Jooste, October 14, 1952, Acheson Papers, Truman Library. Available at http://www.trumanlibrary.org/whistlestop/study_collections/achesonmemos/pdf.php?documentid=71-2_20&documentYear=1952#zoom=300 (last accessed February 17, 2017).

183. Curtis S. Strong, "The Dilemma for the United States Presented by the South Western Africa Question," August 26, 1952, FRUS, 1952–1954, 3: 1146–47. Available at https://history.state.gov/historicaldocuments/frus1952-54v03/d799 (last accessed February 9, 2016); Borstelmann, *Apartheid's Reluctant Uncle*, 187–88.

5. SAVING DARFUR

1. Williams, "Military Responses to Mass Killing: The African Union Mission in Sudan," *International Peacekeeping* 13, no. 2 (2006): 174.

2. Power, "Dying in Darfur: Can Ethnic Cleansing in Sudan Be Stopped?" *The New Yorker* 2004.

3. Ibid.

4. Hamilton, *Fighting for Darfur: Public Action and the Struggle to Stop Genocide* (New York: Macmillan, 2011), 22.

5. The regime in Khartoum feared that showing weakness in Darfur would reduce its bargaining power in the North-South negotiations. Many of the foot soldiers in the Sudanese army were drawn from Darfur. Khartoum did not trust them. They thus recruited militias—the Janjaweed—to do the job. See Stedjan and Thomas-Jensen, "The United States," in *The International Politics of Mass Atrocities: The Case of Darfur*, ed. Black and Williams (London: Routledge, 2010), 166.

6. Q&A: Sudan's Darfur Conflict, BBC. Available at http://news.bbc.co.uk/2/hi/africa/3496731.stm (last accessed February 9, 2016).

7. United Nations Peacekeeping Department, "UNAMID Fact Sheet." Available at www.un.org/en/peacekeeping/missions/unamid/facts.shtml (last accessed June 7, 2012).

8. Réseau Francophone de Recherche sur les Opérations de Paix, "MINUAD." Available at www.operationspaix.net/78-operation-minuad.html (last accessed August 2, 2012).

9. The United States was at the heart of shifting the Darfur peace process first initiated by the Chadian President Déby to the African Union (AU). Once this change had been established, the United States defrayed most of the expenses related to the peace talks. Deputy Secretary of State Robert Zoellick and Assistant Secretary of State for African Affairs Jendayi Frazer personally participated in the final round of the negotiations concluding in the Darfur Peace Agreement (DPA) in May 2006.

10. See for instance Embassy Manila to Secretary of State, "The Philippines to support UNSCR Resolution on Darfur," July 27, 2004, Darfur Collection, box 2, The National Security Archive and Rebecca Hamilton, Washington, D.C.

11. Huliaras, "Evangelists, Oil Companies, and Terrorists: The Bush Administration's Policy towards Sudan," *Orbis* 50, no. 4 (2006): 711.

12. Walter Kansteiner, Assistant Secretary of State for Africa, *Foreign Policy in Focus*, April 1, 2001.

13. "Black Gold: America Is Increasingly Interested in Africa's Oil Reserves," *The Economist*, October 24, 2002.

14. Author's interview with Charles Snyder, U.S. acting assistant secretary at the Bureau of African Affairs, March 2012.

15. Huliaras, "The Evangelical Roots of US Africa Policy," *Survival* 50, no. 6 (2008): 168. Michael Horowitz, a former Reagan administration official and a senior fellow at the Hudson Institute, was a significant figure in bringing about this alliance. "Christians are the Jews of the 21st century," he prominently claimed in the *Wall Street Journal* on July 5, 1995, referring to the persecution of Christians in Sudan.

16. Ibid., 170.

17. Woodward, *US Foreign Policy and the Horn of Africa* (Burlington, VT: Ashgate 2006), 113; Power, "Dying in Darfur."

18. As a framework for peace negotiations, the United States opted for a troika approach, bringing in Great Britain and Norway as junior partners. Franklin Graham, one of America's most famous evangelicals and a friend of George W. Bush, is said to have personally urged the president to turn his sights on Sudan. See Huliaras, "Evangelical Roots of US Africa Policy," 170.

19. Power, "Dying in Darfur."

20. As quoted in Johnson, *Waging Peace in Sudan: The Inside Story of the Negotiations That Ended Africa's Longest Civil War* (Long Island City, NY: Apollo Books, 2011), 19.

21. As quoted in Hamilton, *Fighting for Darfur*, 24.

22. Ibid., 32.

23. Secretary of State to American Embassy Maputo, "Sudan: Chissano willing to consider AU or UN request to send Mozambican troops to Darfur," September 28, 2004, Darfur Collection, box 1, The National Security Archive and Rebecca Hamilton, Washington D.C.

24. Ibid.

25. Author's interview with Sue-Ann Sandusky, U.S. Military defense attaché, March 2017.

26. Mamdani, *Saviors and Survivors: Dafur, Politics, and the War on Terror* (New York: Doubleday, 2009), 22.

27. Ibid., 23.

28. Author's interview with Ann-Louise Colgan, official at Africa Action, March 2012.

29. Lanz, "Save Darfur: A Movement and Its Discontents," *African Affairs* 108, no. 433 (2009): 673; Mamdani, *Saviors and Survivors*, 41.

30. Hamilton, *Fighting for Darfur*, 80–81.

31. Darfur by the Numbers, Save Darfur Coalition. Available at www.savedarfur.org/pages/darfur_by_the_numbers//print/ (last accessed June 14, 2012).

32. Bolton, *Surrender Is Not an Option: Defending America at the United Nations* (New York: Simon and Schuster, 2007), 351.

33. Hamilton, *Fighting for Darfur*, 75.

34. Secretary of State to EU Member States Collective, "Approaching the EU in Advance of April 25 Foreign Ministers Meeting (GAERC), April 19, 2005, Darfur Collection, box 2, The National Security Archive and Rebecca Hamilton, Washington, D.C.

35. As quoted in Hamilton, *Fighting for Darfur*, 79.

36. UN Resolution 1769 (2007). Available at https://www.securitycouncilreport.org/atf/cf/%7b65BFCF9B-6D27-4E9C-8CD3-CF6E4FF96FF9%7d/CAC%20SRES%201769.pdf (last accessed August 6, 2018).

37. Author's interview with Andrew Natsios, U.S. special envoy to Darfur, March 2012. Sudan could tolerate the African Union peacekeepers because it knew they were militarily weak and also because it maintained a certain degree of political leverage over many African Union governments deploying troops.

38. UNAMID Deployment on the Brink, December 2007, joint NGO report. Available at www.fidh.org/IMG/pdf/unamid1207web.pdf (last accessed April 11, 2012).

39. Troops and police serving in UN operations are compensated for their service. Staff officers, military observers, and individual civilian police officers receive a mission subsistence allowance ranging from $56/day to $208/day depending on location. Troop and police personnel is reimbursed at a current base rate of $1410 per contingent member per month. In addition, the UN pays a specialist rate of $303/month for a set proportion of the deployed troops (25% of logistics units, 10% of all other units). All troop and police personnel also receive $68/month per contingent member as a "personal clothing, gear and equipment allowance" and $5/month per contingent member for "personnel weaponry and training ammunition." In addition to personnel compensation rates, all UN contingents are also reimbursed for major military and other equipment items they use in the field. The UN's *Contingent-Owned-Equipment (COE) Manual* provides detailed reimbursement rates for either "wet" or "dry" lease arrangements. Wet leases entail that the contributing state assumes responsibility for the equipment's maintenance. These are by far the most common agreements. Specified monthly wet lease rates range from $7 for a pair of loudspeakers to $33,532 for a level-three hospital. For some "special case equipment" items (for instance, radars), the reimbursement rate is determined on a case-by-case

basis. If a country contributes air assets or naval ships, it receives reimbursements based on the hours of usage. See Coleman, "The Political Economy of UN Peacekeeping: Incentivizing Effective Participation," (New York: International Peace Institute, 2014).

40. "Sudan: Security Council Explores Transition from African Union to UN," *Africa News*, February 3, 2006.

41. On Canada, see Embassy Ottawa to Secretary of State, "The Politics of Canada's Darfur Involvement," May 16, 2005. Document in possession of the author.

42. Guéhenno, *The Fog of Peace: A Memoir of International Peacekeeping in the 21st Century* (Washington, DC: Brookings Institution Press, 2015), 206.

43. Ibid., 205.

44. Author's interview with Bill Martin, deputy director of peace operations, U.S. State Department, February 2012.

45. Author's interview with John Campbell, U.S. ambassador to Nigeria, March 2017.

46. Ibid.

47. ACOTA originated as an Africa Bureau program in 1997 under the name of Africa Crisis Response Initiative (ACRI). President Bill Clinton established ACRI as the first of a whole array of new military programs aimed at expanding U.S. military activities on the African continent. In 2004, ACRI was expanded and renamed ACOTA. Today the Africa Bureau maintains the policy lead and regional political expertise for ACOTA input, while the POL-MIL bureau oversees the budget process and contractors implementing ACOTA training. GPOI extended the ACOTA programs to countries outside of Africa. GPOI is funded through the Peacekeeping Operations (PKO) account, which is managed by the POL-MIL Bureau. It had a budget of $660 million (FY2005–FY2008) to fund potential TCCs' training and deployment needs. Countries which were beneficiaries of ACOTA or GPOI are not legally required to deploy to peacekeeping operations. Nevertheless, it "is a process the US encourages."

48. Volman, "US to Create New Regional Military Command for Africa: Africom," *Review of African Political Economy* 34, no. 114 (2007).

49. Serafino, "The Global Peace Operations Initiative: Background and Issue for Congress" (Washington DC: Congressional Research Service, 2007).

50. Author's interview with Coronel Sue Ann Sandusky, U.S. military attaché, March 2017.

51. Author's interview with Charles Snyder, U.S. acting assistant secretary at the Bureau of African Affairs, March 2012.

52. Author's interview with John Campbell, U.S. ambassador to Nigeria, March 2017.

53. Ibid.

54. Such a list was, of course, periodically updated. States were removed and others added. It was a continuous process.

55. Ibid.

56. See for instance Secretary of State to Embassies Berlin, Cairo, Copenhagen, Moscow, New Delhi, Pretoria, Kyiv, The Hague, Seoul, "Urgent Darfur Demarche for Aviation Support and Transportation Assets," October 23, 2007. Document in possession of the author.

57. Ibid.

58. Secretary of State to Embassies Dhaka, Islamabad, Jakarta, Addis Ababa, Cairo, Khartoum, New York "Sudan—Confirmation of Force Contributions to UNAMID," October 9, 2008. Document in possession of the author.

59. Secretary of State to all African diplomatic posts, "All African embassies démarche on Sudan," September 27, 2004, Darfur Collection, The National Security Archive and Rebecca Hamilton, Washington, D.C.

60. Serafino, "Global Peace Operations Initiative," 21.

61. "We Are building a Nigerian Community in Sudan—Ambassador Dahiru," *Africa News*, August 1, 2006.

62. Author's interview with John Campbell, U.S. ambassador to Nigeria, March 2017.

63. Embassy Abuja to Secretary of State, "Sudan: Nigeria Agrees to Deployment of Vmt Monitors to Darfur," April 15, 2004. Document in possession of the author.

64. Embassy Abuja to Department of State (AF/RSA) and (AF/W), "Nigeria requests Assistance for Darfur Deployment," July 19, 2004. Document in possession of the author.

65. Secretary of State to all African diplomatic posts, "Africa Press Guidance October 28, 2004," October 18, 2004, Darfur Collection, The National Security Archive and Rebecca Hamilton, Washington, D.C.

66. Nigeria: Soldiers Massacre Civilians in Revenge Attack in Benue State. Available at www.hrw.org/news/2001/10/25/nigeria-soldiers-massacre-civilians-revenge-attack-benue-state (last accessed January 8, 2016). Prior to the Benue Massacre, U.S.-Nigerian military relations had been continuously on the rise. President Obasanjo was anxious to train and professionalize the Nigerian army. For this he enlisted the U.S. military, which eagerly agreed to assist, with the rationale that it could further strengthen military ties with an important military ally in Africa. The U.S. military thus ran Operation Focus Relief—a military training program worth $66 million.

67. Serafino, "Global Peace Operations Initiative," 21.

68. The ACOTA agreement asked beneficiary states to deploy to UN missions if the United States so requested—though no deployment was mandatory.

69. Secretary of State to Darfur Collective, UNSC Collective, Embassies Abuja, Brasilia, Buenos Aires, Kiev, Prague, Pretoria, Warsaw, New York, "Deputy Secretary Negroponte's Meetings with U/SYF Guehenno," November 9, 2007. Document in possession of the author.

70. Embassy Delhi to Secretary of State, "India Pondering a possible expanded role in Sudan Peacekeeping," March 14, 2006. Document in possession of the author.

71. Author's interview with John Campbell, U.S. ambassador to Nigeria, March 2017.

72. See Pouliot, *International Security in Practice*, 28.

73. Iliffe, *Obasanjo, Nigeria, and the World* (Woodbridge, England: Boydell & Brewer, 2011), 283.

74. Ibid.

75. "African Leaders Reject Foreign Intervention in Darfur," *Taipei Times*, October 19, 2004.

76. Iliffe, *Obasanjo, Nigeria, and the World*, 218.

77. Ajayi, "Why Did Nigeria Go to Liberia? Nigeria and Sub-Regional Security: The Case of Ecowas Monitoring Group—Ecomog," master's thesis, University of Ibadan, 2000, 399.

78. Adebajo, "Nigeria," in *Providing Peacekeepers: The Politics, Challenges, and Future of United Nations Peacekeeping Contributions,* ed. Bellamy and Williams (Oxford: Oxford University Press, 2013), 266.

79. Author's interview with Martin Luther Agwai, UNAMID commander, May 2012.

80. Campbell, *Nigeria: Dancing on the Brink* (Lanham, MD: Rowman & Littlefield, 2011).

81. Author's interview with John Campbell, U.S. ambassador to Nigeria, March 2017.

82. U.S. diplomats knew that the U.S. Congress would only move on the sanction issue if Obasanjo delivered a speech recognizing the Nigerian military's accountability for the massacre. After significant U.S. pressure, Obasanjo complied and delivered an acceptable speech. Even so, however, it took U.S. Congress a year to lift all sanctions. In the meantime, funding to Nigeria was provided by sources other than those controlled by Congress.

83. Serafino, "Global Peace Operations Initiative," 18.

84. Campbell, *Nigeria*, 17–18.

85. Moss, Standley, and Birdsall, "Double-Standards, Debt Treatment, and World Bank Country Classification: The Case of Nigeria," *Center for Global Development Working Paper*, no. 45 (2004): 22.

86. Embassy Abuja to Assistant Secretary of State for African Affairs Newman, "U.S./ Nigeria Bilateral Relationship: Obasanjo Lays Down Marker," September 17, 2004. Document in possession of the author.

87. Author's interview with John Campbell, U.S. ambassador to Nigeria, March 2017. See also Embassy Abuja to Assistant Secretary of State for African Affairs Newman, "U.S./ Nigeria Bilateral Relationship," September 17, 2004. Document in possession of the author.

88. Embassy Abuja to Department for African Affairs (Dan Epstein), OECD Paris, "Letter from President Obasanjo to President Bush Re Follow-up on December 2, 2004 Meeting at White House," December 23, 2004. Document in possession of the author.

89. Ibid.

90. Author's interview with John Campbell, U.S. ambassador to Nigeria, March 2017.

91. Campbell, *Nigeria*, 19.

92. Eric Wong (AF/SPG) to Brian Schmitt (AF/SPG) and Kendra Gaither (AF/S), "Follow up HIRC briefing materials [AMIS TCC info for A/S Frazer testimony]," May 18, 2006, Darfur Collection, box 1, The National Security Archive and Rebecca Hamilton, Washington D.C.

93. Author's interview with General Pennap, head of peace operation planning, Nigerian Army, May 2012. There are also rumors that Obasanjo resolved the controversial dispute with Cameroon over the Bakassi Peninsula in an attempt to get troops out of Bakassi and into Darfur.

94. Author's interview with Martin Luther Agwai, UNAMID commander, May 2012.

95. Campbell, *Nigeria*, 88–89.

96. "Nigeria: US Warns against 3rd Term," *Africa News*, May 1, 2006.

97. "The Right Thing in Nigeria," *The International Herald Tribune*, May 19, 2006.

98. Campbell, *Nigeria*, 95.

99. Ibid., 105. Yar'Adua had won the elections with 24 million votes—a ridiculous number of votes in an election in which international and domestic observers estimated total turnout of no more than 14 million.

100. Ibid., 110.

101. Author's interview with John Campbell, U.S. ambassador to Nigeria, March 2017. "Nigeria Reportedly Reviews Darfur Peacekeeping Role over Troop Safety Concerns," *BBC Monitoring Africa*, October 30, 2007. Moreover, Nigeria flatly rejected another U.S. request to send troops, this time not to Darfur but to the African Union mission in Somalia.

102. State Department Archive Press Release. Available at http://2001-2009.state.gov/p/af/rls/rm/86195.htm (last accessed November 17, 2017).

103. Author's interview with U.S. diplomat, March 2012. All four battalions were funded by the United States.

104. Author's interview with John Campbell, U.S. ambassador to Nigeria, March 2017.

105. Other factors such as the rise of an NGO debt relief movement in support of Nigeria, Britain's 2005 "Year of Africa" initiative, and the important work of a Washington development think tank, the Center for Global Development (CGD), might also have played a role. See Callaghy, "Anatomy of a 2005 Debt Deal: Nigeria and the Paris Club," working paper, University of Pennsylvania, 2009. Ambassador Campbell also mentioned that the U.S. government wanted to prevent Nigeria from sliding back to military rule.

106. Beswick, "Managing Dissent in a Post-Genocide Environment: The Challenge of Political Space in Rwanda," *Development and Change* 41, no. 2 (2010).

107. Embassy Kigali to Department of State, "Rwanda Accepts 20 Million of USG Darfur Equipment," September 4, 2008. Document in possession of the author.

108. Foreign Military Training Joint Report to Congress, FY2006 and FY2007. Available at www.state.gov/t/pm/rls/rpt/fmtrpt (last accessed August 8, 2018).

109. Serafino, "Global Peace Operations Initiative." The ACOTA agreement asked beneficiary states to deploy to UN missions if the United States so requested

110. Embassy Cairo to Department of State, "Egypt: Darfur Troop deployment Highlights Intent to Maintain Significant Role," January 10, 2008. Document in possession of the author.

111. Ibid.

112. Author's interview with Andrew Natsios, U.S. special envoy to Darfur, February 2012.

113. Chanlett-Avery and Dolven, "Thailand: Background and U.S. Relations," Congressional Research Service, Washington, D.C., 2012).

114. Author's interview with John Blaxland, Australian military attaché to Thailand, November 2011.

115. Chanlett-Avery and Dolven, "Thailand."

116. See for instance Dorussen and Ward, "Intergovernmental Organizations and the Kantian Peace: A Network Perspective," *Journal of Conflict Resolution* 52, no. 2 (2008).

117. Author's interview with John Campbell, U.S. ambassador to Nigeria, March 2017.

118. Ibid.

6. FIGHTING FOR INDEPENDENCE IN EAST TIMOR

1. Durch, ed., *Twenty-First-Century Peace Operations* (Washington, DC: US Institute of Peace Press, 2006), 407.

2. Dupont, "Asean's Response to the East Timor Crisis," *Australian Journal of International Affairs* 54, no. 2 (2000): 167.

3. Coleman, *International Organizations and Peace Enforcement*, 253.

4. The UN Security Council publicly opposed the invasion, and the territory's nominal status in the UN remained "non-self-governing territory under Portuguese administration."

5. Nevins, *A Not-So-Distant Horror: Mass Violence in East Timor* (Ithaca, NY: Cornell University Press, 2005), 62; Wheeler and Dunne, "East Timor and the New Humanitarian Interventionism," *International Affairs* 77, no. 4 (2001): 809.

6. Durch, *Twenty-First-Century Peace Operations*, 394; White, "The Road to Interfet: Reflections on Australian Strategic Decisions Concerning East Timor, December 1998–September 1999," *Security Challenges* 4, no. 1 (2008): 71.

7. Connery, *Crisis Policymaking: Australia and the East Timor Crisis of 1999* (Canberra: ANU Press, 2010), 50.

8. Ibid., 18.

9. Howard, *Lazarus Rising*, 341.

10. Durch, *Twenty-First-Century Peace Operations*, 395. White reports that to this date it remains unclear to what extent Habibie's decision to hold a referendum was caused by Howard's letter. Habibie may well have been already contemplating fairly radical steps before he received it. He could presumably have reached that decision without Howard's intervention, but according to White, some anecdotal evidence suggests that a re-reading of Howard's letter in late January provided the final spur. White, "The Road to Interfet," 73.

11. Author's interview with Hugh White, deputy secretary for strategy and intelligence, Australian Department of Defence, December 2011.

12. Durch, *Twenty-First-Century Peace Operations*, 407.

13. White, "The Road to Interfet," 82. Internationally, Australia was also instantly perceived as the logical candidate to lead such an operation.

14. Author's interview with Chris Barrie, chief of the Joint Chiefs of Staff, Australian Department of Defence, December 2011.

15. White, "The Road to Interfet," 82.

16. Fernandes, "The Road to Interfet: Bringing the Politics Back In," *Security Challenges* 4, no. 3 (2008): 90.

17. Connery, *Crisis Policymaking*, 92; Kelly, *The March of Patriots*, 508.

18. Greenlees and Garran, *Deliverance: The Inside Story of East Timor's Fight for Freedom* (Crows Nest, Australia: Allen & Unwin, 2003), 240. The U.S. government viewed Indonesia as a potential counterbalance to Chinese power in Southeast Asia. Moreover, the United States had important business interests in Indonesia and a strong desire to see Indonesia's democratic experiment under Habibie succeed. If East Timor destabilized Indonesian democracy—or worse, precipitated the breakup of that ethnically, religiously, and geographically diverse nation—the costs could be astronomical.

19. Kelly, *The March of Patriots*, 508. Clinton's decision to send U.S. troops to Kosovo had cost him significant political capital in U.S. Congress. The eruption of the East Timor crisis came the same day the White House was about to send legislation authorizing $3.4 billion to cover the costs of the Kosovo deployment to a Republican-dominated Congress.

20. Greenlees and Garran, *Deliverance*; Howard, *Lazarus Rising*, 346.

21. Kelly, *March of Patriots*, 508.

22. Nevins, *Not-So-Distant Horror*, 125; Greenlees and Garran, *Deliverance*, 246; Fernandes, "Road to Interfet," 94.

23. Fernandes, " Road to Interfet," 94.

24. Author's interview with Francesc Vendrell, UN special envoy for East Timor, November 2011.

25. Greenlees and Garran, *Deliverance*, 245.

26. Fernandes, "Road to Interfet," 94; Nevins, *Not-So-Distant Horror*, 124.

27. Howard, *Lazarus Rising*, 347.

28. Ibid.; White, "Road to Interfet," 82. On several occasions, Indonesia had threatened that it would consider any international military operation an "invasion." Australia also feared that without Indonesia's consent, no UN Chapter VII mandate would pass the UN Security Council. For very long, Indonesia had been a highly respected member of the non-aligned movement. A foreign intervention would give the impression of being a "failed state"—a humiliating image that Indonesia refused to accept. Many of Indonesia's UN friends felt the same way.

29. Robinson, *"If You Leave Us Here, We Will Die": How Genocide Was Stopped in East Timor* (Princeton, NJ: Princeton University Press, 2010), 196; Howard, *Lazarus Rising*, 346. Fernandes, "Road to Interfet," 94. The United States instructed the World Bank to freeze $300 million that had been scheduled for disbursement to Indonesia the following week. Moreover, it told the IMF to postpone a mission to Indonesia for discussions on its economic recovery program.

30. White, "Road to Interfet," 83; Kelly, *March of Patriots*, 511.

31. Edwards and Goldsworthy, *Facing North*, 249.

32. DFAT, *East Timor in Transition 1998–2000: An Australian Policy Challenge* (Canberra: DFAT, Commonwealth of Australia, 2001), 84. Howard, *Lazarus Rising*, 346.

33. Author's interview with Mike Keating, director, INTERFET Strategic Branch, Australian Department of Defence, December 2011.

34. Coleman, *International Organizations and Peace Enforcement*, 257.

35. Kelly, *March of Patriots*, 507.

36. Ryan, *Primary Responsibilities and Primary Risks: Australian Defence Force Participation in the International Force East Timor* (Land Warfare Studies Centre, 2000), 54; Dupont, "Asean's Response to the East Timor Crisis," 166. Greenlees and Garran, *Deliverance*, 266; Coleman, *International Organizations and Peace Enforcement*, 258.

37. Once it became clear that INTERFET would deploy, Indonesian President Habibie also insisted that INTERFET would have a substantial ASEAN component. See Dupont, "Asean's Response to the East Timor Crisis," 166.

38. Author's interview with Steve Ayling, director, INTERFET strategic planning, Australian Department of Defence, December 2011. This is how Ayling described the attitude many Australian officials held in the early stages of the process.

39. Dupont, "Asean's Response to the East Timor Crisis," 164.

40. Author's interview with Steve Ayling, director, INTERFET strategic planning, Australian Department of Defence, December 2011.

41. Connery, *Crisis Policymaking*, 37.

42. Ibid., 38.

43. Author's interview with Steve Ayling, director, INTERFET strategic planning, Australian Department of Defence, December 2011.

44. Ryan, *Primary Responsibilities and Primary Risks: Australian Defence Force Participation in the International Force East Timor* (Land Warfare Studies Centre, 2000), 54; Dupont, "Asean's Response to the East Timor Crisis," 166. Greenlees and Garran, *Deliverance*, 266; Coleman, *International Organizations and Peace Enforcement*, 258.

45. Among others, Malaysia and Australia were allies under the Five Power Defense Arrangement and joint members of the British Commonwealth. Australia also regularly conducted military exercises with Malaysia.

46. Author's interview with Bob Cotton, Australian high commissioner to Malaysia, December 2011.

47. Connery, *Crisis Policymaking*, 38.

48. Author's interview with Bob Cotton, Australian high commissioner to Malaysia, December 2011.

49. Hwang, *Personalized Politics: The Malaysian State under Mahathir*, vol. 237 (Singapore: Institute of Southeast Asian Studies, 2003).

50. Edwards and Goldsworthy, *Facing North*, 251.

51. Dee, "'Coalitions of the Willing' and Humanitarian Intervention," 10.

52. Author's interview with Australian diplomat, December 2011.

53. Author's interview with John Howard, Australian prime minister, December 2011.

54. Author's interview with Steve Ayling, director, INTERFET Strategic Planning, Australian Department of Defence, December 2011.

55. Ibid.

56. Ibid.

57. Kelly, *March of Patriots*, 505–6.

58. Howard, *Lazarus Rising*, 345.

59. Kelly, *March of Patriots*, 509.

60. Author's interview with Mike Scrafton, director, East Timor Policy Unit, Australian Department of Defence, December 2011.

61. Author's interview with John Howard, Australian prime minister, December 2011.

62. Howard, *Lazarus Rising*, 347.

63. Ryan, *Primary Responsibilities and Primary Risks*, 40.

64. Coleman, *International Organizations and Peace Enforcement*, 253.

65. Connery, *Crisis Policymaking*, 38.

66. Ibid., 37.

67. Author's interview with Mike Keating, director, INTERFET Strategic Branch, Australian Department of Defence, December 2011.

68. Ryan, *Primary Responsibilities and Primary Risks*, 107.

69. Valdivieso et al., eds., *East Timor: Establishing the Foundations of Sound Macroeconomic Management* (Washington, DC: International Monetary Fund, 2000), 19.

70. Greenlees and Garran, *Deliverance*, 268. The key donors were Japan ($100 million) and Portugal ($5 million). Since the Japanese money first had to be approved by the Diet, Australia stepped in and agreed to meet the initial deployment cost of the various detachments. It also agreed to finance the entire Fiji and the Philippines deployments. Overall, Australia also donated AU$3.5 million in equipment to developing countries participating in INTERFET.

71. Kelly, *March of Patriots*, 509.

72. DFAT, *East Timor in Transition 1998–2000*, 141.

73. Dupont, "Asean's Response to the East Timor Crisis," 164. Thailand, like Indonesia, was similarly struggling with a potent separatist movement in its southern provinces.

74. Edwards and Goldsworthy, *Facing North*, 251.

75. Ryan, *Primary Responsibilities and Primary Risks*, 50–51.

76. Mishra, *The History of Thailand* (Santa Barbara, CA: Brentwood, 2010), 146. The crisis started on July 2, 1997, with the Bank of Thailand deciding to float the baht, the Thai currency. As a direct result of this decision, the baht dramatically lost value. By the end of 1997, fifty-six Thai financial institutions had shut down. By the end of 1998, two million people had lost their jobs, and Thailand faced the worst recession in its history. During 1998, private consumption went down by 15 percent, public consumption by 4.9 percent, private investment by 45.8 percent, and public investment by 19.6 percent. Export growth shrank by 6.4 percent and imports by 35.5 percent. In response to the Thai economy's rapid disintegration, the Thai business elites and the urban middle class quickly demanded the removal of Prime Minister Chavalit Yongchaiyudh. In November 1997, Chavalit resigned, and a reshuffling of the minor parties enabled Chuan Leekpai to rise to power. Unsurprisingly, Chuan's key promise was that he would better address the unfolding crisis and restore the health of the Thai economy. He was assisted in this endeavor by some of Thailand's most famous economists, such as Tarrin Nimmanahaeminda and Dr. Supachai Panitchpakdi. During 1998 and 1999, Chaun devoted all of his attention and resources to restoring Thailand's external balance, plugging capital outflows, and reviving confidence in the baht.

77. Ibid. This was only the second time in Thailand's history that a civilian had ever occupied this position.

78. DFAT, *East Timor in Transition 1998–2000*, 141.

79. The United States and Europe had proven to be very stingy in this regard. Other pledges received were from Japan ($4 billion), Hong Kong, Malaysia, and Singapore ($1 billion each), and Indonesia and Korea ($500 million each). Subsequently, China pledged $1 billion, and the World Bank and Asian Development Bank announced contributions of $1.5 billion and $1.2 billion, respectively.

80. Author's interview with Australian diplomat, December 2011.

81. Author's interview with Steve Ayling, director, INTERFET strategic planning, Australian Department of Defence, December 2011.

82. Ryan, *Primary Responsibilities and Primary Risks*, 50.

83. Cotton, *East Timor, Australia, and Regional Order: Intervention and Its Aftermath in Southeast Asia* (London: Routledge, 2004), 126.

84. Greenlees and Garran, *Deliverance*, 268.

85. "Thai Premier Defends Decision to Send Troops to ET," *BBC Monitoring Asia Pacific*, September 30, 1999.

86. Author's interview with David Coghlan, INTERFET planning staff, Australian Department of Defence, December 2011.

87. Ryan, *Primary Responsibilities and Primary Risks*, 50; Edwards and Goldsworthy, *Facing North*, 251.

88. Author's interview with Steve Ayling, director of INTERFET strategic planning, Australian Department of Defence, December 2011.

89. Author's interview with Alexander Downer, Australian foreign minister, December 2011; "FED—Downer to Visit Regional Interfet Partners, Australian Associated Press, November 12, 1999.

90. Ibid.

91. Bookmiller, "Abdullah's Jordan: America's Anxious Ally," *Alternatives: Turkish Journal of International Relations* 2, no. 2 (2003): 174.

92. Author's interview with Steve Ayling, director, INTERFET strategic planning, Australian Department of Defence, December 2011. Emphasis added.

93. Ibid.

94. Ryan, *Primary Responsibilities and Primary Risks*, 52.

95. Greenlees and Garran, *Deliverance*, 268.

96. Moreover, the Philippine military had very little surplus capacity because most of its forces were indeed deployed to domestic hotspots such as Minandao. See Ryan, *Primary Responsibilities and Primary Risks*, 52.

97. Dee, "'Coalitions of the Willing.'"

98. Connery, *Crisis Policymaking*, 93.

99. Coleman, *International Organizations and Peace Enforcement*, 274.

100. Howard, *Lazarus Rising*, 462.

101. Grunau, "The Limits of Human Security: Canada in East Timor," *Journal of Military and Strategic Studies* 6, no. 1 (2003).

102. Hataley and Nossal, "The Limits of the Human Security Agenda: The Case of Canada's Response to the Timor Crisis," *Global Change, Peace, and Security* 16, no. 1 (2004): 10.

103. Grunau, "The Limits of Human Security," 16. Canada's economic ties with Indonesia had been growing substantially over the course of the 1990s. According to the East Timor Alert Network, Canadian investments in Indonesia had tripled under the Chrétien government. Hataley and Nossal, "Limits of the Human Security Agenda," 14. Moreover, Indonesia was Canada's fourth largest military export market, totaling C$ 21.8 million in 1999. Grunau, "Limits of Human Security," 6.

104. As quoted in Hataley and Nossal, "Limits of the Human Security Agenda," 11.

105. Author's interview with John Howard, Australian prime minister, December 2011.

106. Ryan, *Primary Responsibilities and Primary Risks*, 56.

107. Author's interview with Steve Ayling, director, INTERFET strategic planning, Australian Department of Defence, December 2011.

108. Australian Department of Defence, "Coalition Building—INTERFET Lessons Learned," March 16, 2001. Document in possession of the author.

7. RESISTING REBELS IN CHAD AND THE CENTRAL AFRICAN REPUBLIC

1. Harvey, *Peace Enforcers: The EU Military Intervention in Chad* (Dublin: Book Republic, 2010), 47.

2. The Chadian population, like many other African societies, is still deeply fractured along ethnic lines. Déby had consolidated his power in Chad by privileging his ethnic tribe, the Zaghawas. The Zaghawas, however, represent only 2 percent of Chadian society. The majority of Zaghawas live in western Sudan, which includes Darfur. Many rebels involved in the Darfur uprising were in fact of Zaghawa origin. By May 2005, many of Déby's closest collaborators—all Zaghawas themselves—were insisting that Déby change course and support the Darfur rebellion against Khartoum.

3. Al-Bashir helped them get organized in camps on the Sudanese side of the border and also supplied them with all of the necessary equipment to overthrow Déby.

4. Chad—Complex Emergency Situation Report #1 (FY 2007) Revised. Available at http://reliefweb.int/report/central-african-republic/chad-complex-emergency-situation-report-1-fy-2007-revised (last accessed January 4, 2016).

5. OCHA, Consolidated Appeal Chad 2007. Available at www.unocha.org/cap/appeals/consolidated-appeal-chad-2007 (last accessed January 4, 2016).

6. United Nations Security Council, Resolution 1778 (2007). Available at www.undemocracy.com/S-RES-1778%282007%29/page_2 (last accessed February 10, 2010).

7. France singlehandedly wrote all UN draft resolutions pertaining to Chad-CAR and prodded numerous Security Council members to support the resolutions.

8. Mattelaer, "The Strategic Planning of EU Military Operations: The Case of Eufor Tchad/Rca" (Brussels: IES, 2008), 14. To launch an EU operation is indeed a difficult political task involving four distinct steps, all of which require the approval of all EU member states. These include (1) approval of a crisis management concept; (2) approval of military strategic options; (3) approval of joint action; and (4) approval of final military directives. France did not shy away from building winning coalitions for each single vote. On July 23, France managed to gain an official mandate from the EU General Affairs and External Relations Council (GAERC), a committee composed of all EU foreign ministers, suggesting that the EU Council Secretariat prepare a crisis management concept for Chad-CAR. France then worked tirelessly for the European Council to approve the latter concept by September 12. Next, France gained approval from the European Council not only to support the concept but also to recommend actual military action in Chad-CAR. The latter step was completed on October 15 when the European Council produced the Joint Action Mandate (2007/677/CFSP) formally establishing EUFOR Chad-CAR. Finally, on November 15, France was also successful in convincing members of the European Council to adopt final military directives for EUFOR Chad-CAR. The operation was then good to go.

9. In return, France was not only to provide defense against external threats but also to assist in maintaining internal security. In other words, Chad and the CAR could automatically request direct French intervention to ensure the security of their government in the face of insurgency or coup attempts. The French government, however, had the right to honor or refuse requests as it saw fit.

10. This location makes the base an extremely valuable strategic asset ideal for deploying French troops and aircraft rapidly all over Africa. Since 1986 France stationed approximately 1,200 soldiers permanently in N'Djamena under Operation Épervier—an operation initially conceived to discourage Libyan transgression of the 16th parallel, also known as the Aouzou Strip.

11. Etienne, "L'opération Eufor Tchad/Rca: Succès Et Limites D'une Initiative Européenne" (Paris: Terra Nova, 2009), 10. In addition to these strategic advantages, Chad also holds an almost mythical place in French collective memory. It was in Chad—then still a French colony—where the famed French General Philippe Leclerc, a military officer loyal to "La France Libre" under Charles de Gaulle and in opposition to Pétain's "Régime de Vichy," began assembling an African force mostly composed of Chadians to liberate France from German occupation. This force then successfully fought Fascist Italy in Libya and famously swore in Kufra on March 2, 1941, that their fight would not stop "until the French flag flies again over the cathedral of Strasbourg," an oath that was ultimately fulfilled largely by the same regiment on November 23, 1944.

12. With the exception of Djibouti, Chad is the country where the French military has been most involved in the postcolonial period. For example, to maintain control of Chad in the 1980s, the French army battled, directly and indirectly, the armies of Qaddafi and inflicted a bitter defeat upon them in 1987. See for instance Charbonneau, "France," in

The International Politics of Mass Atrocities: The Case of Darfur, ed. Black and Williams (London: Routledge, 2010), 217.

13. French government officials apparently came to this conclusion after the African Union Summit in Maputo in July 2003, when Déby collapsed and fell into a coma. Only a very fast reaction by French diplomats saved him. While convalescing in Paris, he is said to have offered various rewards and commitments to France that very much convinced Paris that he was the only statesman in Chad. See Marchal, "Understanding French Policy toward Chad/Sudan? A Difficult Task Part 1–3." Available at http://africanarguments. org/2009/06/06/understanding-french-policy-toward-chadsudan-a-difficult-task-3/ (last accessed August 8, 2018).

14. Until that date, the UN had only dealt with the massive refugee inflows into Chad from Darfur through OCHA and its refugee agency (UNHCR), not through its peace-keeping department (UNDPKO).

15. Etienne, "L'opération Eufor Tchad/Rca," 9–10.

16. As quoted in Mattelaer, "Strategic Planning of EU Military Operations," 15. The French also wanted to reaffirm their military supremacy in the region and thus deter other rebels from following the Chadian examples. Marchal, for example, writes, "the March offensive took the French army by surprise. It showed that despite French support for Déby, foreign rebels could reach the capital city in very few days." Marchal, "Understand-ing French Policy toward Chad/Sudan?"

17. The mission was initially scheduled for November or December 2007 but had to be aborted due to renewed threats of rebel attacks.

18. Seibert, "African Adventure? Assessing the European Union's Military Intervention in Chad and the Central African Republic" (Cambridge, MA: MIT Security Studies Work-ing Paper 2010), 10.

19. Novosselof and Gowan, "Security Council Working Methods and UN Peace Oper-ations: The Case of Chad and the Central African Republic, 2006–2010" (New York: New York University Center on International Cooperation, 2012), 11. Author's interview with Victor da Silva, UN special representative for MINURCAT, Brussels, February 2011.

20. In contrast to his predecessors, Sarkozy did not relish the Franco-Chadian rela-tionship, nor did he share their conception of "la France-Afrique," that France and Africa had a special and mutually indispensable relationship. In essence, Sarkozy considered the numerous French military bases and operations in Africa a waste of money. Thus, as soon as he acceded to power, he asked his advisors to cut costs and repatriate as many French military assets from Africa as possible. One of the most costly assets was indeed the French military base in Chad.

21. "A Statesman without Borders," *New York Times*, February 3, 2008.

22. Novosselof and Gowan, "Security Council Working Methods and UN Peace Oper-ations," 40.

23. Déby anticipated new rebel attacks with the arrival of the dry season starting in late October or early November of 2007.

24. Sarkozy wanted to demonstrate to the French citizens that whatever their political orientation, they would be able to identify with his new administration. See for instance Marchal, "Understanding French Policy toward Chad/Sudan?"

25. Author's interview with Bernard Kouchner, French foreign minister, Paris, February 2011.

26. Author's interview with Bernard Thorette, chief of staff of the French Army, Paris, February 2011.

27. Charbonneau, "France," 217.

28. Novosselof and Gowan, "Security Council Working Methods and UN Peace Oper-ations," 40; Seibert, "African Adventure?" 48–49. In 2004, the EU had set up the Athena

Mechanism—a permanent mechanism to administer the financing of common costs of EU military operations. The mechanism foresaw that in the case of an EU military deployment, the bulk of the operational common costs (such as the establishment of headquarters, transport costs, salaries of locally hired personnel, barracks and lodging/infrastructure, and the like) would be shared among all EU member states—not only those that participate in the operation. The breakdown of each EU member state's contribution would be determined in accordance with the GNP scale. All other "non-common" costs, however, had to borne by the participating EU member states (that is, coalition contributors would pay their own deployment costs).

29. France did involve the EU Council Secretariat and the Commission in the development of conceptual scenarios for the operation, though all key decisions were made in Paris and then "sold" to Brussels. See Bono, "The EU's Military Operation in Chad and the Central African Republic: An Operation to Save Lives?" *Journal of Intervention and Statebuilding* 5, no. 1 (2011): 32; Mattelaer, "Strategic Planning of EU Military Operations," 13–15.

30. Author's interview with French official, February 2012. See also Dijkstra, "The Military Operation of the EU in Chad and the Central African Republic," 4.

31. For details on the EU Battlegroup concept, see www.consilium.europa.eu/uedocs/cmsUpload/Battlegroups.pdf (last accessed August 8, 2018).

32. Mérand, *European Defence Policy: Beyond the Nation State* (Oxford: Oxford University Press, 2008).

33. "Finnish Government Considering Sending Troops to Chad instead of Darfur," *BBC Monitoring Europe*, August 15, 2007.

34. Author's interview with French official, February 2011.

35. Author's interview with John Biggar, director of security policy, Irish Department of Foreign Affairs and Trade, Dublin, Ireland, May 2011.

36. Author's interview with French official, February 2011.

37. Harvey, *Peace Enforcers*, 58.

38. Author's interview with French official, February 2011.

39. Mattelaer, "Strategic Planning of EU Military Operations," 13.

40. Author's interview with French official, February 2011.

41. Mattelaer, "Strategic Planning of EU Military Operations," 17.

42. Author's interview with Pat Nash, EUFOR operation commander, Cork, June 2011.

43. Author's interview with French official, February 2011.

44. Author's interview with French official, February 2011.

45. Embassy Paris to U.S. Secretary of State, "Chad/C.A.R.: French Views on Force Generation," November 16, 2007. Document in possession of the author.

46. Author's interview with French official, February 2011.

47. Author's interview with Pat Nash, EUFOR operation commander, June 2011. See also Engberg, *EU and Military Operations*, 99.

48. U.S. Mission to the EU to U.S. Secretary of State, "S/e Natsios urges EU to support Sudan sanctions and Peacekeepers for Chad," July 16, 2007. Document in possession of the author.

49. Embassy Paris to U.S. Secretary of State, "Chad/C.A.R.: French Views on Force Generation," November 16, 2007. Document in possession of the author.

50. Author's interview with French official, February 2011.

51. Author's interview with French official, February 2011.

52. Tardy, "CSDP: Getting Third States on Board," *Brief Issue*, European Union Institute for Security Studies, 2014, 3.

53. "Ahern to Seek Troop Safety Pledge," *Irish Times*, October 1, 2007.

54. "Officials Play Down Embarrassing Email," BBC News, April 28, 2008.

55. "Letters to the Editor—Debate on the Lisbon Treaty," *Irish Times*, February 1, 2008.

56. "Bertie's High-Risk Foreign Adventure," *The Phoenix*, February 8, 2008.

57. Author's interview with Dan Harvey, EUFOR spokesperson, May 2011.

58. Ahern, *Bertie Ahern: The Autobiography* (New York: Random House, 2009), 1.

59. Author's interview with Pat Nash, EUFOR operation commander, June 2011; author's interview with Michael Howard, secretary general, Irish Defense Ministry, May 2011; "Bertie's High-Risk Foreign Adventure," *The Phoenix*, February 8, 2008.

60. "Ireland, with Plain-Spoken 'Bertie' in Charge, Shines during EU Presidency," AP Newswire, June 30, 2004; "Ahern Had Backing of 21 EU Leaders for Top Job," *The Irish Examiner*, July 5, 2004.

61. Ahern, *Bertie Ahern*, 275.

62. Ibid.

63. Author's interview with Pat Nash, EUFOR operation commander, June 2011.

64. Blair, *A Journey* (New York: Random House, 2011), 653.

65. Author's interview with Derry Fitzgerald, deputy force commander MINURCAT, May 2011; author's interview with Dan Harvey, EUFOR spokesperson, May 2011; see also "Bertie's High-Risk Foreign Adventure," *The Phoenix*, February 8, 2008; "A Safe Pair of Hands Take Charge of EU Force in Chad," *The Irish Times*, January 29, 2008.

66. Author's interview with Michael Howard, secretary general, Irish Defense Ministry, May 2011.

67. "Army's African Mission Marks Watershed for EU," *The Irish Times*, September 28, 2007.

68. "Irish General to Command 3500 Troop Mission in Chad," *The Irish Times*, October 3, 2007; "Paris financera l'essentiel de l'operation Tchad-CAR," *Le Monde*, October 5, 2007.

69. "Government Set to Decide on Chad Deployment," *The Irish Times*, November 19, 2007.

70. Author's interview with French official, February 2011.

71. Author's interview with Pierre Séailles, liaison officer between EU Commission and EU Council during EUFOR Chad-CAR, February 2011.

72. Interview with Polish diplomat, Brussels, December 2009.

73. See for instance "Poland Sees No 'Room for Manoeuvre' at EU Treaty Summit," AFP, October 18, 2007; "Polish PM Brings World War Two into EU Vote Debate," Deutsche Welle, June 21, 2007.

74. "EU Elder Juncker Floats Compromise with Poland," Reuters News, June 21, 2007.

75. Interview with Polish diplomat, Brussels, December 2009. *The Krakow Post* provided an almost identical explanation in their issue of October 25, 2007. Available at http://www.krakowpost.com/article/664 (last accessed February 10, 2014).

76. "Polish Defence Minister Confirms Sending Troops to Chad, Pullout from Iraq," *BBC Monitoring Europe*, November 30, 2007.

77. "French Parliament Report on the Costs of Foreign Interventions," July 1, 2009. Available at www.assemblee-nationale.fr/13/rap-info/i1790.asp#P1848_59421 (last accessed May 19, 2015).

78. Author's interview with Finnish official, December 2009.

79. L'Europe peine à intervener autour du Darfour, *Le Figaro*, September 2007. See also Engberg, *EU and Military Operations*, 126.

80. OE24, "73 Prozent gegen den Tschad Einsatz." Available at www.oe24.at/oesterreich/politik/73-Prozent-gegen-den-Tschad-Einsatz/227424 (last Accessed July 16, 2012).

81. Interview with Undersecretary Hans Winkler, *Tiroler Tageszeitung*, August 25, 2007. The Austrian military and, in particular, its Special Forces had an interest in the Chad

operation. In their eyes, it constituted an interesting "training" opportunity in Africa, where they lacked any hands-on experience.

82. "Austria to Send 'up to 240' Soldiers to Chad for EU Mission," *BBC Monitoring Europe*, November 7, 2007.

83. Author's interview with Austrian diplomat, December 2009.

84. Author's interview with Austrian diplomat, July 2010.

85. Author's interview with Stefan Hirsch, spokesperson for the Austrian Defense Minister, July 2010.

86. Ibid.

87. Dijkstra, "Military Operation of the EU in Chad and the Central African Republic," 6.

88. "Russie Partenariats avec l'OTAN et l'UE," *Le Monde*, March 13, 2008.

89. "Moscou continue de coopérer avec l'OTAN sur l'Afghanistan et l'UE sur le Tchad," *Le Monde*, September 13, 2008.

90. "A Life Spent Keeping the Peace," *The Irish Times*, May 16, 2009.

91. "French Parliament Report on the Costs of Foreign Interventions," July 1, 2009. Available at www.assemblee-nationale.fr/13/rap-info/i1790.asp#P1848_59421 (last accessed May 19, 2015).

92. Embassy Paris to U.S. Secretary of State, "Chad/C.A.R.: French Views on Force Generation," November 16, 2007. Document in possession of the author.

8. POWER, DIPLOMACY, AND DIPLOMATIC NETWORKS

1. Moravcsik, *The Choice for Europe*, 62.

2. Milner, "International Theories of Cooperation among Nations: Strengths and Weaknesses," *World Politics* 44, no. 3 (1992): 469.

3. Goddard and Nexon, "The Dynamics of Global Power Politics," 8.

4. Scholars have put forward a catalogue of reasons that lead to such preference convergence. Some suggest that alliances matter: instances include Davidson, *America's Allies and War*; Weitsman, *Waging War*; Mousseau, "Democracy and Militarized Interstate Collaboration"; Von Hlatky, *American Allies in Times of War*; Corbetta and Dixon, "Multilateralism, Major Powers, and Militarized Disputes," *Political Research Quarterly* 57, no. 1 (2004). Others highlight the importance of financial incentives: for instance, Cunliffe, *Legions of Peace*; Bove and Elia, "Supplying Peace"; Gaibulloev et al., "Personnel Contributions to UN and Non-UN Peacekeeping Missions." Still others point to ideational and normative rationales: see Fung, "Global South Solidarity? China, Regional Organisations and Intervention in the Libyan and Syrian Civil Wars," *Third World Quarterly* 37, no. 1 (2016); Lebovic, "Uniting for Peace?". One group highlights the importance of civil-military relations, among them Kathman and Melin, "Who Keeps the Peace?"; Velazquez, "Why Some States Participate in UN Peace Missions While Others Do Not"; Sotomayor, *The Myth of the Democratic Peacekeeper*.

5. Ward and Dorussen, "Standing Alongside Your Friends," 406. Ward and Dorussen focus on peacekeeping operations.

6. Auerswald and Saideman, *NATO in Afghanistan: Fighting Together, Fighting Alone* (Princeton, NJ: Princeton University Press, 2014), 2; see also Krotz and Maher, "International Relations Theory and the Rise of European Foreign and Security Policy," *World Politics* 63, no. 3 (2011): 565.

7. See for instance Olson and Zeckhauser, "An Economic Theory of Alliances,"; Bobrow and Boyer, "Maintaining System Stability Contributions to Peacekeeping Operations"; Khanna, Sandler, and Shimizu, "Sharing the Financial Burden for UN and NATO Peacekeeping, 1976–1996"; Shimizu and Sandler, "Peacekeeping and Burden-Sharing, 1994–2000"; Passmore, Shannon, and Hart, "Rallying the Troops."

8. John Dreier to Miller, January 25, 1951, FRUS, 1951, Volume 2, 938.

9. See Risse, "'Let's Argue!'" 10–11.

10. De Dreu, Koole, and Steinel, "Unfixing the Fixed Pie"; O'Connor and Carnevale, "A Nasty but Effective Negotiation Strategy"; Olekalns and Smith, "Mutually Dependent"; Risse, "'Let's Argue!'" 21; Rathbun, *Diplomacy's Value*.

11. Weitsman, *Waging War*, 2.

12. Coleman, "Token Troop Contributions to United Nations Peacekeeping Operations," in *Providing for Peacekeepers*, ed. Bellamy and Williams (Oxford: Oxford University Press, 2013), 51.

13. I address some of these topics elsewhere. See Henke, "Great Powers and UN Force Generation"; "Why Did France Intervene in Mali in 2013? Examining the Role of Intervention Entrepreneurs," *Canadian Foreign Policy Journal* 23, no. 3 (2017).

14. See Fearon, "Bargaining, Enforcement, and International Cooperation," *International Organization* 52, no. 2 (1998). The notable exceptions regard this process as pre-bargaining. See for instance Bearce, Floros, and McKibben, "The Shadow of the Future and International Bargaining: The Occurrence of Bargaining in a Three-Phase Cooperation Framework," *Journal of Politics* 71, no. 02 (2009); Walter, *Committing to Peace: The Successful Settlement of Civil Wars* (Princeton, NJ: Princeton University Press, 2002), 300; Stein, *Getting to the Table: The Processes of International Prenegotiations* (Baltimore, MD: John Hopkins University Press, 1989); Druckman, "Prenegotiation Experience and Dyadic Conflic Resolution in a Bargaining Situation," *Journal of Experimental Social Psychology* 4, no. 4 (1968); Levenotoglu and Tarar, "Prenegotiation Public Commitment in Domestic and International Bargaining," *American Political Science Review* 99, no. 3 (2005); Ghosn, "Getting to the Table and Getting to Yes: An Analysis of International Negotiations," *International Studies Quarterly* 54, no. 4 (2010).

15. Fang and Ramsay, "Outside Options and Burden Sharing in Nonbinding Alliances," *Political Research Quarterly* 63, no. 1 (2010).

16. Wolford and Ritter, "National Leaders, Political Security, and the Formation of Military Coalitions," *International Studies Quarterly* 60, no. 3 (2016).

17. Coleman, *International Organizations and Peace Enforcement*; Hurd, "Legitimacy and Authority in International Politics," *International Organization* 53, no. 2 (2003).

18. Hawkins, *Delegation and Agency in International Organizations* (Cambridge: Cambridge University Press, 2006); Barnett and Finnemore, "The Politics, Power, and Pathologies of International Organizations," *International Organization* 53, no. 4 (1999): 707.

19. See for instance Keohane, *After Hegemony*, Moravcsik; "The Origins of Human Rights Regimes: Democratic Delegation in Postwar Europe," *International Organization* 54, no. 2 (2000); Simmons and Elkins, "The Globalization of Liberalization: Policy Diffusion in the International Political Economy," *American Political Science Review* 98, no. 1 (2004); Mansfield and Pevehouse, "Trade Blocs, Trade Flows, and International Conflict," *International Organization* 54, no. 4 (2000); Gartzke, Li, and Boehmer, "Investing in the Peace: Economic Interdependence and International Conflict," *International Organization* 55, no. 2 (2001); Russett and Oneal, *Triangulating Peace: Democracy, Interdependence, and International Organizations* (New York: Norton, 2001); Adler and Barnett, *Security Communities* (Cambridge: Cambridge University Press, 1998); Finnemore, "Norms, Culture, and World Politics: Insights from Sociology's Institutionalism," *International Organization* 50, no. 2 (1996); Johnston, "Treating International Institutions as Social Environments," *International Studies Quarterly* 45, no. 4 (2001); Checkel, "International Institutions and Socialization in Europe"; Haas, *When Knowledge Is Power: Three Models of Change in International Organizations* (Los Angeles: University of California Press, 1990); Chayes and Chayes, *The New Sovereignty: Compliance with International Regulatory Agreements* (Cambridge, MA: Harvard University Press,

1995); Ikenberry and Kupchan, "Socialization and Hegemonic Power," *International Organization* 44, no. 3 (1990): 283, 315.

20. In this literature, *networks* are generally defined as interconnected actors (also called *nodes*) that operate at different levels of analysis: intergovernmental organizations, national governments, nongovernmental organizations, or individuals. See Kahler, "Networked Politics: Agency, Power, and Governance," in *Networked Politics: Agency, Power, and Governance*, ed. Kahler (Ithaca, NY: Cornell University Press, 2009).

21. In this approach, network design is most often taken as a given. Network actors are generally assumed not to try to manipulate or change the structure. See ibid., 5, 7.

22. See for instance Wasserman and Faust, *Social Network Analysis: Methods and Applications* (Cambridge: Cambridge University Press, 1994), 4; Kahler, "Networked Politics," 13; Avant and Westerwinter, *The New Power Politics: Networks and Transnational Security Governance* (Oxford: Oxford University Press, 2016), 7; Hafner-Burton, Kahler, and Montgomery, "Network Analysis for International Relations," *International Organization* 63, no. 3 (2009); Hafner-Burton and Montgomery, "Power Positions"; Dorussen and Ward, "Intergovernmental Organizations and the Kantian Peace: A Network Perspective," *Journal of Conflict Resolution* 52, no. 2 (2008); Maoz, *Networks of Nations: The Evolution, Structures, and Impact of International Networks*, 1816-2001 (Cambridge, Cambridge University Press, 2011); Goddard, "Brokering Peace: Networks, Legitimacy, and the Northern Ireland Peace Process," *International Studies Quarterly* 56, no. 3 (2012).

23. Kahler, "Networked Politics."

24. See for instance Keck and Sikkink, "Transnational Advocacy Networks in the Movement Society," in *The Social Movement Society: Contentious Politics for a New Century*, ed. Meyer and Tarrow (Lanham, MD: Rowman & Littlefield, 1998); Slaughter, *A New World Order* (Princeton, NJ: Princeton University Press, 2004); Elkins, "Constitutional Networks," in *Networked Politics. Agency, Power, and Governance*, ed. Kahler (Ithaca, NY: Cornell University Press, 2009), 46; Eilstrup-Sangiovanni, "Varieties of Cooperation: Government Networks in International Security," in *Networked Politics: Agency, Power, and Governance*, ed. Kahler (Ithaca, NY: Cornell University Press, 2009).

25. In this sense, my approach comes closest to Macdonald, who also examines how social ties create constraints and opportunities that shape the strategies of aspiring conquerors. See Macdonald, *Networks of Domination: The Social Foundations of Peripheral Conquest in International Politics* (Oxford: Oxford University Press 2014).

26. See Kwon and Adler, "Social Capital"; Obukhova and Lan, "Do Job Seekers Benefit from Contacts"; Dika and Singh, "Applications of Social Capital in Educational Literature."

27. In this sense, these benefits come close to the notion of "social capital." In the existing literature, social capital has been analyzed at two different levels of analysis: (1) at the level of the collectivity taking on the form of a public good that helps solve collective action problems; and (2) at the level of the individual as a resource. I refer here to the second category. On the importance of the collectivity, see Putnam, *Bowling Alone: The Collapse and Revival of American Community* (New York: Simon and Schuster, 2001); foregrounding an emphasis on the individual are Macdonald, *Networks of Domination*; Bourdieu, "The Forms of Capital," in *Handbook of Theory and Research for the Sociology of Education*, ed. Richardson (New York: Macmillan, 1986).

28. Hafner-Burton and Montgomery conceive social power as prestige, which does not need to be activated but simply exists. See Hafner-Burton and Montgomery, "War, Trade, and Distrust: Why Trade Agreements Don't Always Keep the Peace," *Conflict Management and Peace Science* 29, no. 3 (2012); Hafner-Burton and Montgomery, "Power or Plenty: How Do International Trade Institutions Affect Economic Sanctions?" *Journal of Conflict Resolution* 52, no. 2 (2008); Hafner-Burton and Montgomery, "Power Positions."

29. Nexon, *The Struggle for Power in Early Modern Europe: Religious Conflict, Dynastic Empires, and International Change* (Princeton, NJ: Princeton University Press, 2009), 52.

30. I address these problems elsewhere. See Henke, "The Rotten Carrot."

31. See for instance Uzzi, "The Sources and Consequences of Embeddedness for the Economic Performance of Organizations: The Network Effect," *American Sociological Review* (1996).

32. See for instance Levitt and March, "Organizational Learning," *Annual Review of Sociology* 14, no. 1 (1988).

33. Carruthers and Babb, *Economy/Society: Markets, Meanings, and Social Structure*, 2nd ed. (Newbury Park, CA: Pine Forge Press, 2013), 78.

34. Pouliot, *International Security in Practice*, 15.

35. See Pouliot, "The Logic of Practicality: A Theory of Practice of Security Communities," *International Organization* 62, no. 2 (2008); Adler and Pouliot, "International Practices."

36. Lake, *Hierarchy in International Relations*; Tago, "Is There an Aid-for-Participation Deal"; Newnham, "Coalition of the Bribed and Bullied.".

37. See for instance Grieco, *Cooperation among Nations: Europe, America, and Non-Tariff Barriers to Trade* (Ithaca, NY: Cornell University Press, 1990); Gruber, *Ruling the World: Power Politics and the Rise of Supranational Institutions* (Princeton, NJ: Princeton University Press, 2000), 33.

38. McKibben, *State Strategies in International Bargaining*, 17–18.

39. Pouliot, *International Pecking Orders*.

40. Thompson, *Channels of Power*, 19.

41. Sidman, *Coercion and Its Fallout* (Boston, MA: Authors Cooperative, 1989), 196; Knorr, *Power of Nations: The Political Economy of International Relations* (New York: Basic Books, 1975); Baldwin, *Economic Statecraft* (Princeton, NJ: Princeton University Press, 1985); Mastanduno, "Economics and Security in Statecraft and Scholarship," *International Organization* 52, no. 4 (1998); Pape, "Soft Balancing against the United States," *International Security* 30, no. 1 (2005): 17; Thomas, *Ethics of Destruction*, 36.

42. Newnham, "More Flies with Honey: Positive Economic Linkage in German Ostpolitik from Bismarck to Kohl," *International Studies Quarterly* 44, no. 1 (2000).

43. Baldwin, "Thinking About Threats"; Mastanduno, "Economics and Security in Statecraft and Scholarship," 309. Compensation payments also often produce positive political ripple effects inside the participating country. Lobbying groups that benefit from the exchange push for further cooperation.

44. The book contributes to ongoing efforts to rethink how hegemony really works. See for example Pouliot, *International Pecking Orders*; Avant and Westerwinter, *The New Power Politics*; Goddard and Nexon, "Dynamics of Global Power Politics."

45. Rathbun, *Diplomacy's Value: Creating Security in 1920s Europe and the Contemporary Middle East*, 11; Bull, *The Anarchical Society: A Study of Order in World Politics* (London: Palgrave Macmillan, 1977), 158; Sharp, *Diplomatic Theory of International Relations*, 1.

46. See for instance Jönsson and Hall, "Communication," 24; Sharp, *Diplomatic Theory of International Relations*.

47. As quoted in Sending, Pouliot, and Neumann, *Diplomacy and the Making of World Politics*, 3.

48. Sharp, *Diplomatic Theory of International Relations*, 1.

49. Rathbun, *Diplomacy's Value*, 1. See also Fearon, "Domestic Political Audiences and the Escalation of International Disputes," *American Political Science Review* 88, no. 3 (1994); "Rationalist Explanations for War," *International Organization* 49, no. 3 (1995); Gartzke, "War Is in the Error Term," *International Organization* 53, no. 3 (1999).

50. See for instance Checkel, "International Institutions and Socialization in Europe"; Haas, *When Knowledge Is Power*; Chayes and Chayes, *New Sovereignty*; Lynch, "The Promise and Problems of Internationalism," *Global Governance* 5 (1999).

51. For a similar analysis in a non-IR-related context, see Granovetter, *Society and Economy*, 2017).

52. See for instance Bratt, "Explaining Peacekeeping Performance"; Findlay, *The Use of Force in UN Peace Operations*; Hultman, Kathman, and Shannon, "United Nations Peacekeeping and Civilian Protection in Civil War"; "Beyond Keeping Peace: United Nations Effectiveness in the Midst of Fighting," *American Political Science Review* 108, no. 4 (2014); Jett, *Why Peacekeeping Fails*; Jones, *Peacekeeping in Rwanda*; Kreps, "Why Does Peacekeeping Succeed or Fail?"

53. Scholars have argued that peacekeeping operations fail because the UN Secretariat is unable (or unwilling) to learn from past mistakes and UN officials apply cookie-cutter conflict resolution strategies and ignore the local context. See for instance Howard, *UN Peacekeeping in Civil Wars* (Cambridge: Cambridge University Press, 2008); Autesserre, *Peaceland: Conflict Resolution and the Everyday Politics of International Intervention* (Cambridge: Cambridge University Press, 2014).

54. Doyle, "The John W. Holmes Lecture: Building Peace," *Global Governance* 13, no. 1 (2007): 9.

55. Checkel, "International Institutions and Socialization in Europe: Introduction and Framework," 814.

56. See for instance Zürn and Checkel, "Getting Socialized to Build Bridges: Constructivism and Rationalism, Europe and the Nation-State," *International Organization* 59, no. 4 (2005); Hurd, "Legitimacy and Authority in International Politics," *International Organization* 53, no. 2 (1999).

57. See for instance Kelley, *Ethnic Politics in Europe: The Power of Norms and Incentives* (Princeton, NJ: Princeton University Press, 2004).

58. See Bellamy and Williams, *Providing Peacekeepers*, 19; Berman and Sams, *Peacekeeping in Africa: Capabilities and Culpabilities* (Geneva: UNIDIR, 2000), 256.

59. Cunliffe, *Legions of Peace*, 171.

60. Ricks, *Fiasco: The American Military Adventure in Iraq* (New York: Penguin, 2006), 34. Other explanations for these differences in patrolling behavior are (1) principal-agent theory; (2) different threat perceptions; (3) public opinion; and (4) strategic culture. See Auerswald and Saideman, *NATO in Afghanistan*.

61. Throughout history "hired forces" gained the reputation of having a sense of obligation and commitment that is less developed than other types of forces. They also have a record of being discouraged by setbacks and casualties and less willing to follow through when a situation goes sour. See for instance Singer, *Corporate Warriors*, 159–60.

62. Dwyer, "Peacekeeping Abroad, Trouble Making at Home," 217; Bhaskar, "Mutiny Reveals Bangladesh Chaos," *Aljazeera Online*, February 27, 2009.

63. Aning, "Unintended Consequences of Peace Operations for Troop-Contributing Countries from West Africa: The Case of Ghana," in *Unintended Consequences of Peacekeeping Operations*, ed. Aoi, De Coning, and Thakur (Tokyo: United Nations Press, 2007), 141; Levin, MacKay, and Nasirzadeh, "Selectorate Theory and the Democratic Peacekeeping Hypothesis"; Savage and Caverley, "When Human Capital Threatens the Capitol."

64. Levin, MacKay, and Nasirzadeh, "Selectorate Theory and the Democratic Peacekeeping Hypothesis"; Savage and Caverley, "When Human Capital Threatens the Capitol."

65. Singer, *Corporate Warriors*, 151–68.

66. United Nations, "Report of the Senior Advisory Group on Rates of Reimbursement to Troop Contributing Countries and Other Related Issues" (A/C.5/67/10), 13–14.

67. Granovetter, *Getting a Job*; Lin, *Social Capital: A Theory of Social Structure and Action*, Structural Analysis in the Social Sciences, vol. 19 (Cambridge: Cambridge University Press, 2002).

68. Uzzi, "Sources and Consequences of Embeddedness."

69. DiMaggio and Louch, "Socially Embedded Consumer Transactions."

70. Bush and Scowcroft, *A World Transformed* (New York: Knopf, 1998), 60.

71. James A. Baker Papers, box 172, folder 5, Series: The Politics of Diplomacy, Transcript: Baker 1993–1994; JAB, June 23, 1993, Tab 2, JAB May 1993, Seeley G. Mudd Manuscript Library, Princeton University, Princeton, New Jersey.

72. Coleman, *Foundations of Social Theory*, 302.

73. Pouliot, *International Pecking Orders*, 63; Cooley and Nexon, "Interpersonal Networks and International Security."

74. Neumann, *At Home with the Diplomats*, 35; Rozental and Buenrosto, "Bilateral Diplomacy," 230–32; Bull, *Anarchical Society*.

75. Cooley and Nexon, "Interpersonal Networks and International Security."

76. Macdonald, *Networks of Domination*, 54.

77. Das and Teng, "Between Trust and Control," 494; Leach and Sabatier, "To Trust an Adversary," 92.

78. Granovetter, "Problems of Explanation in Economic Sociology," 44.

79. Festinger, Back, and Schachter, *Social Pressures in Informal Groups*. Other scholars have also pointed out that diplomatic embeddedness allows naming and shaming third parties into compliance. See Hafner-Burton and Montgomery, "Globalization and the Social Power Politics of International Economic Networks," in *Networked Politics: Agency, Power, and Governance*, ed. Kahler (Ithaca, NY: Cornell University Press, 2009), 30–31.

80. Riker, *The Theory of Political Coalitions* (New Haven, CT: Yale University Press, 1962), 12.

81. Dupont, "Negotiation as Coalition Building," 51.

82. Coleman, *Foundations of Social Theory*, 313.

83. Halpern, *Social Capital* (Cambridge: Polity, 2005), 30. Such instrumentalization also needs to be measured. States who draw heavily on their diplomatic networks without putting much back will find their networks less productive over time.

Bibliography

Acheson, Dean. *The Korean War*. New York: Norton, 1971.

———. *Present at the Creation: My Years in the State Department*. New York: Norton, 1969.

Adebajo, Adekeye. "Nigeria." In *Providing Peacekeepers: The Politics, Challenges, and Future of United Nations Peacekeeping Contributions*, edited by Alex J. Bellamy and Paul Williams. Oxford: Oxford University Press, 2013.

Adler, Emanuel, and Michael Barnett. *Security Communities*. Cambridge: Cambridge University Press, 1998.

Adler, Emanuel, and Vincent Pouliot. "International Practices: Introduction and Framework." In *International Practices*, edited by Emanuel Adler and Vincent Pouliot, 3–35. Cambridge: Cambridge University Press, 2011.

Adler-Nissen, Rebecca, and Vincent Pouliot. "Power in Practice: Negotiating the International Intervention in Libya." *European Journal of International Relations* 20, no. 4 (2014): 889–911.

Ahern, Bertie. *Bertie Ahern: The Autobiography*. New York: Random House, 2009.

Ajayi, K. C. "Why Did Nigeria Go to Liberia? Nigeria and Sub-Regional Security: The Case of ECOWAS Monitoring Group—ECOMOG." Master's thesis, University of Ibadan, 2000.

Andersson, Andreas. "Democracies and UN Peacekeeping Operations, 1990–1996." *International Peacekeeping* 7, no. 2 (2000): 1–22.

Aning, Kwesi. "Unintended Consequences of Peace Operations for Troop-Contributing Countries from West Africa: The Case of Ghana." In *Unintended Consequences of Peacekeeping Operations*, edited by Chiyuki Aoi, Cedric de Coning, and Ramesh Thakur, 133–55. Tokyo: United Nations Press, 2007.

Aronow, Peter M., Cyrus Samii, and Valentina A. Assenova. "Cluster–Robust Variance Estimation for Dyadic Data." *Political Analysis* 23, no. 4 (2015): 564–77.

Auerswald, David P. "Explaining Wars of Choice: An Integrated Decision Model of NATO Policy in Kosovo." *International Studies Quarterly* 48, no. 3 (2004): 631–62.

Auerswald, David P., and Stephen M. Saideman. *NATO in Afghanistan: Fighting Together, Fighting Alone*. Princeton, NJ: Princeton University Press, 2014.

Autesserre, Séverine. *Peaceland: Conflict Resolution and the Everyday Politics of International Intervention*. Cambridge: Cambridge University Press, 2014.

Avant, Deborah, and Oliver Westerwinter. *The New Power Politics: Networks and Transnational Security Governance*. Oxford: Oxford University Press, 2016.

Axelrod, Robert. *The Evolution of Cooperation*. New York: Basic Books, 1984.

Aydin, Aysegul. *Foreign Powers and Intervention in Armed Conflicts*. Palo Alto, CA: Stanford University Press, 2012.

Baker, James Addison. *The Politics of Diplomacy: Revolution, War, and Peace, 1989–1992*. New York: Putnam, 1995.

Baker, Peter. *Days of Fire: Bush and Cheney in the White House*. New York: Anchor, 2013.

Baker, Wayne E., Robert R. Faulkner, and Gene A. Fisher. "Hazards of the Market: The Continuity and Dissolution of Interorganizational Market Relationships." *American Sociological Review* (1998): 147–77.

Baldwin, David A. *Economic Statecraft*. Princeton, NJ: Princeton University Press, 1985.
——. "Thinking about Threats." *Journal of Conflict Resolution* 15, no. 1 (1971): 71–78.
Baltrusaitis, Daniel F. *Coalition Politics and the Iraq War*. Boulder, CO: First Forum Press, 2009.
Barber, James, and John Barratt. "South Africa's Foreign Policy 1948–88: The Search for Status and Security." Cambridge: Cambridge University Press, 1990.
Barbieri, Katherine, and Omar M. G. Keshk. "Correlates of War Project Trade Data Set Codebook (Version 2.01)." 2012.
Barbieri, Katherine, Omar M. G. Keshk, and Brian M. Pollins. "Trading Data: Evaluating Our Assumptions and Coding Rules." *Conflict Management and Peace Science* 26, no. 5 (2009): 471–91.
Barnett, Michael N., and Martha Finnemore. "The Politics, Power, and Pathologies of International Organizations." *International Organization* 53, no. 4 (1999): 699–732.
Bayer, Resat. "Diplomatic Exchange Data Set, V2006.1." http://correlatesofwar.org (2006).
Bearce, David H., and Stacy Bondanella. "Intergovernmental Organizations, Socialization, and Member-State Interest Convergence." *International Organization* 61, no. 4 (2007): 703–33.
Bearce, David H., Katharine M. Floros, and Heather Elko McKibben. "The Shadow of the Future and International Bargaining: The Occurrence of Bargaining in a Three-Phase Cooperation Framework." *Journal of Politics* 71, no. 2 (2009): 719–32.
Bellamy, Alex J., and Paul Williams. *Providing Peacekeepers: The Politics, Challenges, and Future of United Nations Peacekeeping Contributions*. Oxford: Oxford University Press, 2013.
——. *Understanding Peacekeeping*. Cambridge: Polity, 2010.
Bennett, Andrew, Joseph Lepgold, and Danny Unger. *Friends in Need: Burden Sharing in the Persian Gulf War*. New York: St. Martin's Press, 1997.
Berman, Eric G. "The Provision of Lethal Military Equipment: French, UK, and US Peacekeeping Policies Towards Africa." *Security Dialogue* 34, no. 2 (2003): 199–214.
Berman, Eric, and Katie E. Sams. *Peacekeeping in Africa: Capabilities and Culpabilities*. Geneva: United Nations Publications UNIDIR, 2000.
Bernauer, Thomas, and Dieter Ruloff. *The Politics of Positive Incentives in Arms Control*. Columbia: University of South Carolina Press, 1999.
Beswick, Danielle. "Managing Dissent in a Post-Genocide Environment: The Challenge of Political Space in Rwanda." *Development and Change* 41, no. 2 (2010): 225–51.
Blackburn, Robert M. *Mercenaries and Lyndon Johnson's "More Flags": The Hiring of Korean, Filipino, and Thai Soldiers in the Vietnam War*. Jefferson, NC: McFarland, 1994.
Blair, Tony. *A Journey*. New York: Random House, 2011.
Bobrow, Davis B., and Mark A. Boyer. "Maintaining System Stability Contributions to Peacekeeping Operations." *Journal of Conflict Resolution* 41, no. 6 (1997): 723–48.
Bohlin, Thomas G. "United States–Latin American Relations and the Cold War, 1949–1953." PhD dissertation, Universiy of Notre Dame, 1985.
Bolton, John. *Surrender Is Not an Option: Defending America at the United Nations*. New York: Simon and Schuster, 2007.

Bono, Giovanna. "The EU's Military Operation in Chad and the Central African Republic: An Operation to Save Lives?" *Journal of Intervention and Statebuilding* 5, no. 1 (2011): 23–42.

Bookmiller, Robert J. "Abdullah's Jordan: America's Anxious Ally. *Alternatives: Turkish Journal of International Relations* 2, no. 2 (2003).

Borstelmann, Thomas. *Apartheid's Reluctant Uncle: The United States and Southern Africa in the Early Cold War.* Oxford: Oxford University Press, 1993.

Bosco, David. "Assessing the UN Security Council: A Concert Perspective." *Global Governance* 20, no. 4 (2014): 545–61.

Boulter, Roger Stephen. "FC Erasmus and the Politics of South African Defense 1948–1959." PhD dissertation, Rhodes University 1997.

Bourdieu, Pierre. "The Forms of Capital." In *Handbook of Theory and Research for the Sociology of Education,* edited by J. G. Richardson. New York: Macmillan, 1986.

Bourdieu, Pierre, and Loic Wacquant. *An Introduction to Reflexive Sociology.* Chicago: University of Chicago Press, 1992.

Bove, Vincenzo, and Leandro Elia. "Supplying Peace: Participation in and Troop Contribution to Peacekeeping Missions." *Journal of Peace Research* 48, no. 6 (2011): 699–714.

Bratt, Duane. "Explaining Peacekeeping Performance: The UN in Internal Conflicts." *International Peacekeeping* 4, no. 3 (1997): 45–70.

Brown, Cameron S. "The One Coalition They Craved to Join: Turkey in the Korean War." *Review of International Studies* 34, no. 1 (2008): 89–108.

Brysk, Alison. *Global Good Samaritans: Human Rights as Foreign Policy.* Oxford: Oxford University Press, 2009.

Bull, Hedley. *The Anarchical Society: A Study of Order in World Politics.* London: Palgrave Macmillan, 1977.

Burt, Ronald S. *Brokerage and Closure: An Introduction to Social Capital.* Oxford: Oxford University Press, 2005.

Bush, George, and Brent Scowcroft. *A World Transformed.* New York: Knopf, 1998.

Byman, Daniel, and Matthew Waxman. *The Dynamics of Coercion: American Foreign Policy and the Limits of Military Might.* Cambridge: Cambridge University Press, 2002.

Callaghy, Thomas M. "Anatomy of a 2005 Debt Deal: Nigeria and the Paris Club." Working paper, University of Pennsylvania, 2009.

Campbell, John. *Nigeria: Dancing on the Brink.* Lanham, MD: Rowman & Littlefield, 2011.

Carruthers, Bruce G., and Sarah L. Babb. *Economy/Society: Markets, Meanings, and Social Structure.* Newbury Park, CA: Pine Forge Press, 2000.

Chanlett-Avery, Emma, and Ben Dolven. "Thailand: Background and U.S. Relations." Congressional Research Service, Washington, D.C., 2012.

Charbonneau, Bruno. "France." In *The International Politics of Mass Atrocities: The Case of Darfur,* edited by David R. Black and Paul D. Williams. London: Routledge, 2010.

Chayes, A., and A. H. Chayes. *The New Sovereignty: Compliance with International Regulatory Agreements.* Cambridge, MA: Harvard University Press, 1995.

Checkel, Jeffrey T. "International Institutions and Socialization in Europe: Introduction and Framework." *International Organization* 59, no. 4 (2005): 801–26.

——. "Norms, Institutions, and National Identity in Contemporary Europe." *International Studies Quarterly* 43, no. 1 (1999): 84–114.

Coleman, James. *Foundations of Social Theory.* Cambridge, MA: Belknap Press, 1990.

Coleman, Katharina P. *International Organizations and Peace Enforcement: The Politics of International Legitimacy*. Cambridge: Cambridge University Press, 2007.

——. "The Legitimacy Audience Shapes the Coalition: Lessons from Afghanistan, 2001." *Journal of Intervention and Statebuilding* 11, no. 3 (2017): 339–58.

——. "The Political Economy of UN Peacekeeping: Incentivizing Effective Participation." New York: International Peace Institute, 2014.

——. "Token Troop Contributions to United Nations Peacekeeping Operations." In *Providing for Peacekeepers*, edited by Alex J. Bellamy and Paul D. Williams. Oxford: Oxford University Press, 2013.

Collier, David, Henry E. Brady, and Jason Seawright. "Outdated Views of Qualitative Methods: Time to Move On." *Political Analysis* 18, no. 4 (2010): 506–13.

Colman, Jonathan. *A "Special Relationship"? Harold Wilson, Lyndon B. Johnson and Anglo-American Relations "at the Summit," 1964–8*. Manchester: Manchester University Press, 2004.

Colman, Jonathan, and J. J. Widen. "The Johnson Administration and the Recruitment of Allies in Vietnam, 1964–1968." *History* 94, no. 316 (2009): 483–504.

Connery, David. *Crisis Policymaking: Australia and the East Timor Crisis of 1999*. Canberra: ANU Press, 2010.

Cooley, Alexander, and Daniel H. Nexon. "Interpersonal Networks and International Security: US-Georgia Relations during the Bush Administration." In *The New Power Politics. Networks and Transnational Security Governance*, edited by Deborah Avant and Oliver Westerwinter, 74–103. New York: Oxford University Press, 2016.

Cooley, Alexander, and Hendrik Spruyt. *Contracting States: Sovereign Transfers in International Relations*. Princeton, NJ: Princeton University Press, 2009.

Cooper, Andrew F. "The Changing Nature of Diplomacy." In *The Oxford Handbook of Modern Diplomacy*, edited by Andrew F. Cooper, Jorge Heine, and Ramesh Thakur. Oxford: Oxford University Press, 2013.

Cooper, Chester L. *The Lost Crusade: America in Vietnam*. New York: Dodd, Mead, 1970.

Corbetta, Renato, and William J. Dixon. "Multilateralism, Major Powers, and Militarized Disputes." *Political Research Quarterly* 57, no. 1 (2004): 5–14.

Cotton, James. *East Timor, Australia, and Regional Order: Intervention and Its Aftermath in Southeast Asia*. London: Routledge, 2004.

Cox, Lloyd, and Brendon O'Connor. "Australia, the US, and the Vietnam and Iraq Wars: 'Hound Dog, Not Lapdog.'" *Australian Journal of Political Science* 47, no. 2 (2012): 173–87.

Cranmer, Skyler J., Bruce A. Desmarais, and Elizabeth J. Menninga. "Complex Dependencies in the Alliance Network." *Conflict Management and Peace Science* 29, no. 3 (2012): 279–313.

Cumings, Bruce. *The Korean War: A History*. New York: Modern Library, 2011.

Cunliffe, Philip. *Legions of Peace: UN Peacekeepers from the Global South*. London: C. H. Hurst & Co., 2013.

Das, Tarun K., and Bing-Sheng Teng. "Between Trust and Control: Developing Confidence in Partner Cooperation in Alliances." *Academy of Management Review* 23, no. 3 (1998): 491–512.

Davidson, Jason W. *America's Allies and War: Kosovo, Afghanistan, and Iraq*. New York: Palgrave Macmillan, 2011.

Davis, Christina L. "International Institutions and Issue Linkage: Building Support for Agricultural Trade Liberalization." *American Political Science Review* 98, no. 1 (2004): 153–69.

——. "Linkage Diplomacy: Economic and Security Bargaining in the Anglo-Japanese Alliance, 1902–23." *International Security* 33, no. 3 (2008/9): 143–79.

De Dreu, Carsten K. W., Sander L. Koole, and Wolfgang Steinel. "Unfixing the Fixed Pie: A Motivated Information-Processing Approach to Integrative Negotiation." *Journal of Personality and Social Psychology* 79, no. 6 (2000): 975–987.

De Neuilly, Yves Buchet. "Devenir Diplomate Multilatéral." *Cultures and Conflicts* 75, no. 3 (2009): 75–98.

Dee, Moreen. "'Coalitions of the Willing' and Humanitarian Intervention: Australia's Involvement with Interfet." *International Peacekeeping* 8, no. 3 (2001): 1–20.

Devin, Guillaume. "Paroles de diplomates: Comment les négociations multilatérales changent la diplomatie." In *Négociations Internationales*, edited by Franck Petiteville and Delphine Placidi-Frot (Paris: Presses de Sciences Po, 2013)

DFAT. *East Timor in Transition 1998–2000: An Australian Policy Challenge*. Canberra: Department of Foreign Affairs and Trade, Commonwealth of Australia, 2001.

Dibb, Paul. "The Future of International Coalitions: How Useful? How Manageable?" *The Washington Quarterly* 25, no. 2 (2002): 129–44.

Dijkstra, Hylke. "The Military Operation of the EU in Chad and the Central African Republic: Good Policy, Bad Politics." *International Peacekeeping* 17, no. 3 (2010): 395–407.

Dika, Sandra L., and Kusum Singh. "Applications of Social Capital in Educational Literature: A Critical Synthesis." *Review of Educational Research* 72, no. 1 (2002): 31–60.

DiMaggio, Paul, and Hugh Louch. "Socially Embedded Consumer Transactions: For What Kinds of Purchases Do People Most Often Use Networks?" *American Sociological Review* (1998): 619–37.

Dockrill, Michael L. "The Foreign Office, Anglo-American Relations, and the Korean War, June 1950–June 1951." *International Affairs* 62, no. 3 (1986): 459–76.

Dodds, K. *Global Geopolitics: A Critical Introduction*. Upper Saddle River, NJ: Prentice Hall, 2005.

Dorussen, Han, and Hugh Ward. "Intergovernmental Organizations and the Kantian Peace: A Network Perspective." *Journal of Conflict Resolution* 52, no. 2 (2008): 189–212.

Douglas, Stinnett, Tir Jaroslav, Schafer Philip, and Gochman Charles. "The Correlates of War Project Direct Contiguity Data." *Conflict Management and Peace Science* 19, no. 2 (2002): 59–68.

Doyle, Michael W. "The John W. Holmes Lecture: Building Peace." *Global Governance* 13, no. 1 (2007): 1–15.

Dreher, Axel, Jan-Egbert Sturm, and James Raymond Vreeland. "Development Aid and International Politics: Does Membership on the UN Security Council Influence World Bank Decisions?" *Journal of Development Economics* 88, no. 1 (2009): 1–18.

Drezner, Daniel W. "The Trouble with Carrots: Transaction Costs, Conflict Expectations, and Economic Inducements." *Security Studies* 9, no. 1–2 (1999): 188–218.

Druckman, Daniel. "Prenegotiation Experience and Dyadic Conflict Resolution in a Bargaining Situation." *Journal of Experimental Social Psychology* 4, no. 4 (1968): 367–83.

Dumbrell, John. "The Johnson Administration and the British Labour Government: Vietnam, the Pound, and East of Suez." *Journal of American Studies* 30, no. 2 (1996): 211–31.

Dupont, Alan. "ASEAN's Response to the East Timor Crisis." *Australian Journal of International Affairs* 54, no. 2 (2000): 163–70.

Dupont, Christophe. "Negotiation as Coalition Building." *International Negotiation* 1, no. 1 (1996): 47–64.

Durch, William J., ed. *Twenty-First-Century Peace Operations*. Washington, D.C.: U.S. Institute of Peace Press, 2006.

Dwyer, Maggie. "Peacekeeping Abroad, Trouble Making at Home: Mutinies in West Africa." *African Affairs* 114, no. 455 (2015): 206–25.

Eayrs, James. *In Defence of Canada: Indochina: Roots of Complicity*. Toronto: University of Toronto Press, 1983.

Edwards, Peter, and Peter Goldsworthy. *Facing North: A Century of Australian Engagement with Asia*. Melbourne: Melbourne University Press, 2001.

Egerton, George. "Lester B. Pearson and the Korean War: Dilemmas of Collective Security and International Enforcement in Canadian Foreign Policy, 1950–53." *International Peacekeeping* 4, no. 1 (1997): 51–74.

Eggan, Fred. "The Philippines and the Bell Report." *Human Organization* 10, no. 1 (1951): 16–21.

Eichenberg, Richard C. "Victory Has Many Friends: US Public Opinion and the Use of Military Force, 1981–2005." *International Security* 30, no. 1 (2005): 140–77.

Eilstrup-Sangiovanni, Mette. "Varieties of Cooperation: Government Networks in International Security." In *Networked Politics: Agency, Power, and Governance*, edited by Miles Kahler. Ithaca, NY: Cornell University Press, 2009.

Elkins, Zachary. "Constitutional Networks." In *Networked Politics. Agency, Power, and Governance*, edited by Miles Kahler. Ithaca, NY: Cornell University Press, 2009.

Ellis, Desmond P. "The Hobbesian Problem of Order: A Critical Appraisal of the Normative Solution." *American Sociological Review* 36, no. 4 (1971): 692–703.

Ellis, Sylvia. *Britain, America, and the Vietnam War*. Westport, CT: Greenwood Publishing Group, 2004.

Engberg, Katarina. *The EU and Military Operations: A Comparative Analysis*. London: Routledge, 2013.

Erikson, Robert S., Pablo M. Pinto, and Kelly T. Rader. "Dyadic Analysis in International Relations: A Cautionary Tale." *Political Analysis* 22, no. 4 (2014): 457–63.

Estrada, Ernesto, and Francesca Arrigo. "Predicting Triadic Closure in Networks Using Communicability Distance Functions." *SIAM Journal on Applied Mathematics* 75, no. 4 (2015): 1725–44.

Etienne, Guillaume. *L'opération EUFOR Tchad/RCA : Succès et limites d'une initiative européenne*. Paris: Terra Nova, 2009.

Fang, Songying, and Kristopher W. Ramsay. "Outside Options and Burden Sharing in Nonbinding Alliances." *Political Research Quarterly* 63, no. 1 (2010): 188–202.

Farrar-Hockley, Anthony. *Official History: The British Part in the Korean War. Volume I: A Distant Obligation*. London: HMSO, 1990.

Fearon, James D. "Bargaining, Enforcement, and International Cooperation." *International Organization* 52, no. 2 (1998): 269–305.

——. "Domestic Political Audiences and the Escalation of International Disputes." *American Political Science Review* 88, no. 3 (1994): 577–92.

——. "Rationalist Explanations for War." *International Organization* 49, no. 3 (1995): 379–414.

Feaver, Peter D., and Christopher Gelpi. *Choosing Your Battles: American Civil-Military Relations and the Use of Force*. Princeton, NJ: Princeton University Press, 2004.

Ferejohn, John, and Charles Shipan. "Congressional Influence on Bureaucracy." *Journal of Law, Economics, and Organization* 6, no. 1 (1990): 1–20.

Fernandes, Clinton. "The Road to Interfet: Bringing the Politics Back In." *Security Challenges* 4, no. 3 (2008): 83–98.

Festinger, Leon, Kurt W. Back, and Stanley Schachter. *Social Pressures in Informal Groups: A Study of Human Factors in Housing*. Palo Alto, CA: Stanford University Press, 1950.

Findlay, Trevor. *The Use of Force in UN Peace Operations*. Oxford: Oxford University Press, 2002.

Finnemore, Martha. "Norms, Culture, and World Politics: Insights from Sociology's Institutionalism." *International Organization* 50, no. 2 (1996): 325–47.

——. *The Purpose of Intervention: Changing Beliefs about the Use of Force*. Ithaca, NY: Cornell University Press, 2003.

Fordham, Benjamin. *Building the Cold War Consensus: The Political Economy of US National Security Policy, 1949–51*. Ann Arbor: University of Michigan Press, 1998.

Fortna, Virginia P. *Does Peacekeeping Work? Shaping Belligerents' Choices after Civil War*. Princeton, NJ: Princeton University Press, 2008.

Friman, H. Richard. "Side-Payments Versus Security Cards: Domestic Bargaining Tactics in International Economic Negotiations." *International Organization* 47, no. 3 (1993): 387–410.

Funabashi, Yaichi. *The Peninsula Question: A Chronicle of the Second Korean Nuclear Crisis*. Washington, DC: Brookings Institutions Press, 2007.

Fung, Courtney J. "Global South Solidarity? China, Regional Organisations, and Intervention in the Libyan and Syrian Civil Wars." *Third World Quarterly* 37, no. 1 (2016): 33–50.

Gaibulloev, Khusrav, Justin George, Todd Sandler, and Hirofumi Shimizu. "Personnel Contributions to UN and Non-UN Peacekeeping Missions: A Public Goods Approach." *Journal of Peace Research* 52, no. 6 (2015): 727–42.

Gartzke, Erik. "The Affinity of Nations Index, 1946–2002." 2006.

——. "War Is in the Error Term." *International Organization* 53, no. 3 (1999): 567–87.

Gartzke, Erik, Quan Li, and Charles Boehmer. "Investing in the Peace: Economic Interdependence and International Conflict." *International Organization* 55, no. 2 (2001): 391–438.

George, Alexander L., and Andrew Bennett. *Case Studies and Theory Development in the Social Sciences*. Cambridge, MA: MIT Press, 2005.

Gerring, John. "Is There a (Viable) Crucial-Case Method?" *Comparative Political Studies* 40, no. 3 (2007): 231–53.

Ghosn, Faten. "Getting to the Table and Getting to Yes: An Analysis of International Negotiations." *International Studies Quarterly* 54, no. 4 (2010): 1055–72.

Gibler, Douglas M. "The Costs of Reneging Reputation and Alliance Formation." *Journal of Conflict Resolution* 52, no. 3 (2008): 426–54.

Gibler, Douglas M., and Meredith Reid Sarkees. "Measuring Alliances: The Correlates of War Formal Interstate Alliance Dataset, 1816–2000." *Journal of Peace Research* 41, no. 2 (2004): 211–22.

Gilligan, Michael, and Stephen J. Stedman. "Where Do the Peacekeepers Go?" *International Studies Review* 5, no. 4 (2003): 37–54.

Gilpin, Robert. *War and Change in World Politics*. Cambridge: Cambridge University Press, 1981.

Goddard, Stacie E. "Brokering Peace: Networks, Legitimacy, and the Northern Ireland Peace Process." *International Studies Quarterly* 56, no. 3 (2012): 501–15.

Goddard, Stacie E., and Daniel H. Nexon. "The Dynamics of Global Power Politics: A Framework for Analysis." *Journal of Global Security Studies* 1, no. 1 (2016): 4–18.

Granovetter, Mark. "Economic Action and Social Structure: The Problem of Embeddedness." *American Journal of Sociology* 91, no. 3 (1985): 481–510.

——. *Getting a Job: A Study of Contacts and Careers*. Chicago: University of Chicago Press, 1995.

——. *Society and Economy: Framework and Principles*. Cambridge, MA: Harvard University Press, 2017.

Granovetter, Mark S. "Problems of Explanation in Economic Sociology." In *Networks and Organization*, edited by Nitin Nohria and Robert G. Eccles, 29–56. Boston, MA: Harvard Business School Press, 1992.

——. "The Strength of Weak Ties." *American Journal of Sociology* (1973): 1360–80.

Greenlees, Don, and Robert Garran. *Deliverance: The Inside Story of East Timor's Fight for Freedom*. Crows Nest, Australia: Allen & Unwin, 2003.

Greenwood, Sean. "'A War We Don't Want': Another Look at the British Labour Government's Commitment in Korea, 1950–51." *Contemporary British History* 17, no. 4 (2003): 1–24.

Grey, Jeffrey. *The Commonwealth Armies and the Korean War: An Alliance Study*. Manchester: Manchester University Press, 1990.

Grieco, Joseph M. "Anarchy and the Limits of Cooperation: A Realist Critique of the Newest Liberal Institutionalism." *International Organization* 42, no. 3 (1988): 485–507.

——. *Cooperation among Nations: Europe, America, and Non-Tariff Barriers to Trade*. Ithaca, NY: Cornell University Press, 1990.

Gruber, Lloyd. *Ruling the World: Power Politics and the Rise of Supranational Institutions*. Princeton, NJ: Princeton University Press, 2000.

Grunau, Steve. "The Limits of Human Security: Canada in East Timor." *Journal of Military and Strategic Studies* 6, no. 1 (2003).

Guéhenno, Jean-Marie. *The Fog of Peace: A Memoir of International Peacekeeping in the 21st Century*. Washington, DC: Brookings Institution Press, 2015.

Haas, Ernst B. *When Knowledge Is Power: Three Models of Change in International Organizations*. Los Angeles: University of California Press, 1990.

Hafner-Burton, Emilie M., Miles Kahler, and Alexander H. Montgomery. "Network Analysis for International Relations." *International Organization* 63, no. 3 (2009): 559–92.

Hafner-Burton, Emilie M., and Alexander H. Montgomery. "Globalization and the Social Power Politics of International Economic Networks." In *Networked Politics: Agency, Power, and Governance*, ed. Miles Kahler (Ithaca, NY: Cornell University Press, 2009).

——. "Power or Plenty: How Do International Trade Institutions Affect Economic Sanctions?" *Journal of Conflict Resolution* 52, no. 2 (2008): 213–42.

——. "Power Positions: International Organizations, Social Networks, and Conflict." *Journal of Conflict Resolution* 50, no. 1 (2006): 3–27.

——. "War, Trade, and Distrust: Why Trade Agreements Don't Always Keep the Peace." *Conflict Management and Peace Science* 29, no. 3 (2012): 257–78.

Halaby, Charles N. "Panel Models in Sociological Research: Theory into Practice." *Annual Review of Sociology* 30 (2004): 507–44.

Hale, William M. *Turkish Foreign Policy since 1774*. London: Routledge, 2013.

Hall, Todd, and Keren Yarhi-Milo. "The Personal Touch: Leaders' Impressions, Costly Signaling, and Assessments of Sincerity in International Affairs." *International Studies Quarterly* 56, no. 3 (2012): 560–73.

Hamilton, Rebecca. *Fighting for Darfur: Public Action and the Struggle to Stop Genocide*. New York: Macmillan, 2011.

Hardt, Heidi. *Time to React: The Efficiency of International Organizations in Crisis Response*. Oxford: Oxford University Press, 2014.

Harvey, Dan. *Peace Enforcers: The EU Military Intervention in Chad*. Dublin: Book Republic, 2010.

Harvey, Frank P. *Explaining the Iraq War: Counterfactual Theory, Logic, and Evidence*. Cambridge: Cambridge University Press, 2012.

Hataley, Todd S., and Kim Richard Nossal. "The Limits of the Human Security Agenda: The Case of Canada's Response to the Timor Crisis." *Global Change, Peace, and Security* 16, no. 1 (2004): 5–17.

Hawkins, Darren G. *Delegation and Agency in International Organizations*. Cambridge: Cambridge University Press, 2006.

Henke, Marina E. "Buying Allies: Payment Practices in Multilateral Military Coalition-Building," *International Security* 43, no. 4 (2019): 128–62.

——. "Great Powers and UN Force Generation: A Case Study of UNAMID." *International Peacekeeping* 23, no. 3 (2016): 468–92.

——. "The Politics of Diplomacy: How the United States Builds Multilateral Military Coalitions." *International Studies Quarterly* 61, no. 2 (2017): 410–24.

——. "The Rotten Carrot: US-Turkish Bargaining Failure over Iraq in 2003 and the Pitfalls of Social Embeddedness." *Security Studies* 27, no. 1 (2018): 120–47.

——. "Why Did France Intervene in Mali in 2013? Examining the Role of Intervention Entrepreneurs." *Canadian Foreign Policy Journal* 23, no. 3 (2017): 307–23.

Hoekman, Bernard M. "Determining the Need for Issue Linkages in Multilateral Trade Negotiations." *International Organization* 43, no. 4 (1989): 693–714.

Hofmann, Stephanie C. "Overlapping Institutions in the Realm of International Security: The Case of NATO and ESDP." *Perspectives on Politics* 7, no. 1 (2009): 45–52.

Holmes, Marcus. "The Force of Face-to-Face Diplomacy: Mirror Neurons and the Problem of Intentions." *International Organization* 67, no. 4 (2013): 829–61.

Hopkins, Michael. "The Price of Cold War Partnership: Sir Oliver Franks and the British Military Commitment in the Korean War." *Cold War History* 1, no. 2 (2001): 28–46.

Howard, John. *Lazarus Rising*. Pymble, Australia: HarperCollins, 2010.

Howard, Lise Morjé. *UN Peacekeeping in Civil Wars*. Cambridge: Cambridge University Press, 2008.

Huber, John D., and Charles R. Shipan. *Deliberate Discretion? The Institutional Foundations of Bureaucratic Autonomy*. Cambridge: Cambridge University Press, 2002.

Huliaras, Asteris. "The Evangelical Roots of US-Africa Policy." *Survival* 50, no. 6 (2008): 161–82.

——. "Evangelists, Oil Companies, and Terrorists: The Bush Administration's Policy Towards Sudan." *Orbis* 50, no. 4 (2006): 709–24.

Hultman, Lisa, Jacob Kathman, and Megan Shannon. "Beyond Keeping Peace: United Nations Effectiveness in the Midst of Fighting." *American Political Science Review* 108, no. 4 (2014): 737–53.

——. "United Nations Peacekeeping and Civilian Protection in Civil War." *American Journal of Political Science* 57, no. 4 (2013): 875–91.

Hurd, Ian. *After Anarchy: Legitimacy and Power in the United Nations Security Council*. Princeton, NJ: Princeton University Press, 2007.

——. "Legitimacy and Authority in International Politics." *International Organization* 53, no. 02 (1999): 379–408.

——. "Legitimacy, Power, and the Symbolic Life of the UN Security Council." *Global Governance* 8 (2002): 35.

Hwang, In-Won. *Personalized Politics: The Malaysian State under Mahathir*. Singapore: Institute of Southeast Asian Studies, 2003.

Iida, Keisuke. "Involuntary Defection in Two-Level Games." *Public Choice* 89, no. 3–4 (1996): 283–303.

Ikenberry, G. John, and Charles A. Kupchan. "Socialization and Hegemonic Power." *International Organization* 44, no. 3 (1990): 283–315.

Iliffe, John. *Obasanjo, Nigeria, and the World*. Woodbridge, England: Boydell & Brewer, 2011.

Ingebritsen, Christine. "Norm Entrepreneurs: Scandinavia's Role in World Politics." *Cooperation and Conflict* 37, no. 1 (2002): 11–23.

Ingram, Paul, and Peter W. Roberts. "Friendships among Competitors in the Sydney Hotel Industry." *American Journal of Sociology* 106, no. 2 (2000): 387–423.

Jakobsen, Peter Viggo. "The Transformation of United Nations Peace Operations in the 1990s Adding Globalization to the Conventional 'End of the Cold War Explanation.'" *Cooperation and Conflict* 37, no. 3 (2002): 267–82.

Jentleson, Bruce W. "The Pretty Prudent Public: Post Post-Vietnam American Opinion on the Use of Military Force." *International Studies Quarterly* 36, no. 1 (1992): 49–73.

Jentleson, Bruce W., and Rebecca L. Britton. "Still Pretty Prudent: Post-Cold War American Public Opinion on the Use of Military Force." *Journal of Conflict Resolution* 42, no. 4 (1998): 395–417.

Jett, Dennis C. *Why Peacekeeping Fails*. New York: Palgrave 1999.

Johnson, Hilde F. *Waging Peace in Sudan: The Inside Story of the Negotiations That Ended Africa's Longest Civil War*. Long Island City, NY: Apollo Books, 2011.

Johnston, Alister I. "Treating International Institutions as Social Environments." *International Studies Quarterly* 45, no. 4 (2001): 487–515.

Jones, Bruce D. *Peacekeeping in Rwanda: The Dynamics of Failure*. Boulder, CO: Lynne Rienner, 2001.

Jönsson, Christer, and Martin Hall. "Communication: An Essential Aspect of Diplomacy." *International Studies Perspectives* 4, no. 2 (2003): 195–210.

Juncos, Ana E., and Christopher Reynolds. "The Political and Security Committee: Governing in the Shadow." *European Foreign Affairs Review* 12, no. 2 (2007): 127.

Kahler, Miles. *Networked Politics: Agency, Power, and Governance*. Ithaca, NY: Cornell University Press, 2009.

Kathman, Jacob D., and Molly M. Melin. "Who Keeps the Peace? Understanding State Contributions to UN Peacekeeping Operations." *International Studies Quarterly* 61, no. 1 (2016): 150–62.

Keck, Margaret E., and Kathryn Sikkink. "Transnational Advocacy Networks in the Movement Society." In *The Social Movement Society: Contentious Politics for a New Century,* edited by David S. Meyer and Sidney G. Tarrow, 217–38. New York: Rowman & Littlefield, 1998.

Kelley, Judith G. *Ethnic Politics in Europe: The Power of Norms and Incentives*. Princeton, NJ: Princeton University Press, 2004.

Kelly, Paul. *The March of Patriots: The Struggle for Modern Australia*. Melbourne: Melbourne University Publishing, 2009.

Keohane, Robert O. *After Hegemony: Cooperation and Discord in the World Political Economy*. Princeton, NJ: Princeton University Press 1984.

——. "The Big Influence of Small Allies." *Foreign Policy* 2 (Spring 1971): 161–82.

Keohane, Robert O., and Joe S. Nye. *Power and Interdependence: World Politics in Transition*. Boston, MA: Little and Brown, 1977.

Kesgin, Baris, and Juliet Kaarbo. "When and How Parliaments Influence Foreign Policy: The Case of Turkey's Iraq Decision." *International Studies Perspectives* 11, no. 1 (2010): 19–36.

Khanna, J., T. Sandler, and H. Shimizu. "Sharing the Financial Burden for UN and NATO Peacekeeping, 1976–1996." *Journal of Conflict Resolution* 42, no. 2 (1998): 176–95.

Kiszely, John. "Coalition Command in Contemporary Operations." London: RUSI, 2008.

Klare, Michael T. *Blood and Oil: The Dangers and Consequences of America's Growing Dependency on Imported Petroleum*. New York: Owl Books, 2005.

Knorr, Klaus E. *Power of Nations: The Political Economy of International Relations*. New York: Basic Books, 1975.

Krasner, Stephen D. "Global Communications and National Power: Life on the Pareto Frontier." *World Politics* 43, no. 3 (1991): 336–66.

Kreps, Sarah "Why Does Peacekeeping Succeed or Fail? Peacekeeping in the Democratic Republic of Congo and Sierra Leone." In *Modern War and the Utility of Force: Challenges, Methods, and Strategy*, edited by Jan Angstrom and Isabelle Duyvesteyn, 90–118. London: Routledge, 2010.

Kreps, Sarah E. *Coalitions of Convenience: United States Military Interventions after the Cold War*. Oxford: Oxford University Press, 2011.

Krieger, Miriam, Shannon L. C. Souma, and Daniel H. Nexon. "US Military Diplomacy in Practice." In *Diplomacy and the Making of World Politics*, edited by Ole Jacob Sending, Vincent Pouliot, and Iver B. Neumann. Cambridge: Cambridge University Press, 2015.

Krotz, Ulrich, and Richard Maher. "International Relations Theory and the Rise of European Foreign and Security Policy." *World Politics* 63, no. 3 (2011): 548–79.

Kwon, Seok-Woo, and Paul S. Adler. "Social Capital: Maturation of a Field of Research." *Academy of Management Review* 39, no. 4 (2014): 412–22.

Lake, David "Authority, Coercion, and Power in International Relations." Working paper, 2010.

Lake, David A. *Hierarchy in International Relations*. Ithaca, NY: Cornell University Press, 2009.

Lanz, David. "Save Darfur: A Movement and Its Discontents." *African Affairs* 108, no. 433 (2009): 669–77.

Lax, David A., and James K. Sebenius. *The Manager as Negotiator: Bargaining for Cooperation and Competitive Gain*. New York: Macmillan, 1986.

Lazarsfeld, Paul, and Elihu Katz. *Personal Influence*. Glencoe, IL: Free Press, 1955.

Leach, William D., and Paul A. Sabatier. "To Trust an Adversary: Integrating Rational and Psychological Models of Collaborative Policymaking." *American Political Science Review* 99, no. 4 (2005): 491–503.

Lebovic, James H. "Uniting for Peace? Democracies and United Nations Peace Operations after the Cold War." *Journal of Conflict Resolution* 48, no. 6 (2004): 910–36.

Leeds, Brett, Jeffrey Ritter, Sara Mitchell, and Andrew Long. "Alliance Treaty Obligations and Provisions, 1815–1944." *International Interactions* 28, no. 3 (2002): 237–60.

Levant, Victor. *Quiet Complicity: Canadian Involvement in the Vietnam War*. Toronto: Between the Lines, 1986.

Levenotoglu, Bahar, and Ahmer Tarar. "Prenegotiation Public Commitment in Domestic and International Bargaining." *American Political Science Review* 99, no. 3 (2005): 419–33.

Levin, Jamie, Joseph MacKay, and Abouzar Nasirzadeh. "Selectorate Theory and the Democratic Peacekeeping Hypothesis: Evidence from Fiji and Bangladesh." *International Peacekeeping* 23, no. 1 (2016): 107–32.

Levitt, Barbara, and James G. March. "Organizational Learning." *Annual Review of Sociology* 14, no. 1 (1988): 319–38.

Lin, Nan. *Social Capital: A Theory of Social Structure and Action.* Structural Analysis in the Social Sciences. Cambridge: Cambridge University Press, 2002.

Lippe, John M. "Forgotten Brigade of the Forgotten War: Turkey's Participation in the Korean War." *Middle Eastern Studies* 36, no. 1 (2000): 92–102.

Logevall, Fredrik. *Choosing War.* Berkeley: University of California Press, 1999.

Lynch, Cecelia. "The Promise and Problems of Internationalism." *Global Governance* 5 (1999): 83-101.

MacDonald, Paul K. *Networks of Domination: The Social Foundations of Peripheral Conquest in International Politics.* Oxford: Oxford University Press, 2014.

Mamdani, Mahmood. *Saviors and Survivors. Dafur, Politics, and the War on Terror.* New York: Doubleday, 2009.

Mansfield, Edward D., and Jon C. Pevehouse. "Trade Blocs, Trade Flows, and International Conflict." *International Organization* 54, no. 4 (2000): 775–808.

Maoz, Zeev. *Networks of Nations: The Evolution, Structures, and Impact of International Networks, 1816–2001.* Cambridge: Cambridge University Press, 2011.

March, James G., and Johan P. Olsen. "The Logic of Appropriateness." In *Oxford Handbook of Political Science*, edited by Robert E. Goodin. Oxford: Oxford University Press, 2011.

Marchal, Roland. "Understanding French Policy toward Chad/Sudan? A Difficult Task Part 1–3." *African Arguments Blog*, 2009.

Marshall, Monty G., Keith Jaggers, and Ted Robert Gurr. "Polity IV Data Series Version 2010," University of Maryland, College Park, Maryland. Retrieved from http://www.systemicpeace.org/polity/polity4.htm (2010).

Martin, Lisa L. *Coercive Cooperation.* Princeton, NJ: Princeton University Press, 1992.

Mastanduno, Michael. "Economics and Security in Statecraft and Scholarship." *International Organization* 52, no. 4 (1998): 825–54.

Mattelaer, Alexander. "The Strategic Planning of EU Military Operations—the Case of EUFOR Tchad/RCA." *IES Working Paper 5/2008* (2008).

Mayer, Frederick W. "Managing Domestic Differences in International Negotiations: The Strategic Use of Internal Side-Payments." *International Organization* 46, no. 4 (1992): 793–818.

McKibben, Heather Elko. *State Strategies in International Bargaining: Play by the Rules or Change Them?* Cambridge: Cambridge University Press, 2015.

Mearsheimer, John J. *The Tragedy of Great Power Politics.* New York: Norton, 2001.

Mérand, Frederic. *European Defence Policy: Beyond the Nation State.* Oxford: Oxford University Press, 2008.

Milner, Helen. "International Theories of Cooperation among Nations: Strengths and Weaknesses." *World Politics* 44, no. 3 (1992): 466–96.

Milner, Helen V. *Interests, Institutions, and Information: Domestic Politics and International Relations.* Princeton, NJ: Princeton University Press, 1997.

Mishra, Patit Paban. *The History of Thailand.* Santa Barbara, CA: Brentwood, 2010.

Mo, Jongryn. "Domestic Institutions and International Bargaining: The Role of Agent Veto in Two-Level Games." *American Political Science Review* 89, no. 4 (1995): 914–24.

Moravcsik, Andrew. *The Choice for Europe: Social Purpose and State Power from Messina to Maastricht.* Ithaca, NY: Cornell University Press, 1998.

——. "The Origins of Human Rights Regimes: Democratic Delegation in Postwar Europe." *International Organization* 54, no. 2 (2000): 217–52.

Morey, Daniel S. "Military Coalitions and the Outcome of Interstate Wars." *Foreign Policy Analysis* 12, no. 4 (2016): 533–51.

Morgan, T. Clifton. "Issue Linkages in International Crisis Bargaining." *American Journal of Political Science* 34, no. 2 (1990): 311–33.

Morrow, James D. "Alliances: Why Write Them Down?" *Annual Review of Political Science* 3, no. 1 (2000): 63–83.

——. "A Spatial Model of International Conflict." *American Political Science Review* 80, no. 4 (1986): 1131–50.

Moss, Todd J., Scott Standley, and Nancy Birdsall. "Double-Standards, Debt Treatment, and World Bank Country Classification: The Case of Nigeria." *Center for Global Development Working Paper*, no. 45 (2004).

Mousseau, Michael. "Democracy and Militarized Interstate Collaboration." *Journal of Peace Research* 34, no. 1 (1997): 73–87.

Mouw, Ted. "Social Capital and Finding a Job: Do Contacts Matter?" *American Sociological Review* 68, no. 6 (2003): 868–98.

Neumann, Iver B. *At Home with the Diplomats: Inside a European Foreign Ministry*. Ithaca, NY: Cornell University Press, 2012.

Nevins, Joseph. *A Not-So-Distant Horror: Mass Violence in East Timor*. Ithaca, NY: Cornell University Press, 2005.

Newnham, Randall. "Coalition of the Bribed and Bullied? US Economic Linkage and the Iraq War Coalition." *International Studies Perspectives* 9, no. 2 (2008): 183–200.

Newnham, Randall E. "More Flies with Honey: Positive Economic Linkage in German Ostpolitik from Bismarck to Kohl." *International Studies Quarterly* 44, no. 1 (2000): 73–96.

Nexon, Daniel H. *The Struggle for Power in Early Modern Europe: Religious Conflict, Dynastic Empires, and International Change*. Princeton NJ: Princeton University Press, 2009.

Novosselof, Alexandra, and Richard Gowan. "Security Council Working Methods and UN Peace Operations: The Case of Chad and the Central African Republic, 2006–2010." New York University Center on International Cooperation, New York, 2012.

O'Connor, Kathleen M., and Peter J. Carnevale. "A Nasty but Effective Negotiation Strategy: Misrepresentation of a Common-Value Issue." *Personality and Social Psychology Bulletin* 23, no. 5 (1997): 504–15.

Obukhova, Elena, and George Lan. "Do Job Seekers Benefit from Contacts? A Direct Test with Contemporaneous Searches." *Management Science* 59, no. 10 (2013): 2204–16.

Odell, John S. *Negotiating the World Economy*. Ithaca, NY: Cornell University Press, 2000.

Olekalns, Mara, and Philip L. Smith. "Mutually Dependent: Power, Trust, Affect and the Use of Deception in Negotiation." *Journal of Business Ethics* 85, no. 3 (2009): 347–65.

Olson, Mancur, Jr., and Richard Zeckhauser. "An Economic Theory of Alliances." *The Review of Economics and Statistics* 48, no. 3 (1966): 266–79.

Olson, M. *The Logic of Collective Action*. Cambridge, MA: Harvard University Press, 1965.

Ovendale, Ritchie. "The South African Policy of the British Labour Government, 1947–51." *International Affairs* 59, no. 1 (1982): 41–58.

Packer, George. *The Assassins' Gate: America in Iraq*. New York: Farrar, Straus and Giroux, 2005.

Paige, Glenn D. *The Korean Decision, June 24–30, 1950*. New York: Free Press, 1968.

Palmer, Glenn, Vito d'Orazio, Michael Kenwick, and Matthew Lane. "The Mid4 Dataset, 2002–2010: Procedures, Coding Rules and Description." *Conflict Management and Peace Science* 32, no. 2 (2015): 222–42.

Pape, Robert A. "Soft Balancing against the United States." *International Security* 30, no. 1 (2005): 7–45.

Passmore, Timothy J. A., Megan Shannon, and Andrew F. Hart. "Rallying the Troops: Collective Action and Self-Interest in UN Peacekeeping Contributions." *Journal of Peace Research* 55, no. 3 (2018): 366–79.

Pearson, Lester B. *Mike: The Memoirs of the Rt. Hon. Lester B. Pearson, Volume Two: 1948–1957*. Toronto: University of Toronto Press, 1973.

Pedersen, Rasmus Brun. "Bandwagon for Status: Changing Patterns in the Nordic States Status-Seeking Strategies?" *International Peacekeeping* 25, no. 2 (2018): 217–41.

Perkins, Richard, and Eric Neumayer. "Extra-Territorial Interventions in Conflict Spaces: Explaining the Geographies of Post-Cold War Peacekeeping." *Political Geography* 27, no. 8 (2008): 895–914.

Petiteville, Franck, and Delphine Placidi-Frot. *Négociations Internationales*. Paris: Presses de Sciences Po, 2013.

Pevehouse, Jon, Timothy Nordstrom, and Kevin Warnke. "The Correlates of War 2 International Governmental Organizations Data Version 2.0." *Conflict Management and Peace Science* 21, no. 2 (2004): 101–19.

Pilster, Ulrich. "Are Democracies the Better Allies? The Impact of Regime Type on Military Coalition Operations." *International Interactions* 37, no. 1 (2011): 55–85.

——. "Dyads Are Dead, Long Live Dyads! The Limits of Dyadic Designs in International Relations Research." *International Studies Quarterly* 60, no. 2 (2016): 369–74.

Pouliot, Vincent. *International Pecking Orders*. Cambridge: Cambridge University Press, 2016.

——. *International Security in Practice: The Politics of NATO-Russia Diplomacy*. Cambridge: Cambridge University Press, 2010.

——. "The Logic of Practicality: A Theory of Practice of Security Communities." *International Organization* 62, no. 2 (2008): 257–88.

Power, Samantha. "Dying in Darfur: Can Ethnic Cleansing in Sudan Be Stopped?" *The New Yorker*, August 30, 2004, 56–63.

Preston, Andrew. "Balancing War and Peace: Canadian Foreign Policy and the Vietnam War, 1961–1965." *Diplomatic History* 27, no. 1 (2003): 73–111.

Prince, Robert S. "The Limits of Constraint: Canadian-American Relations and the Korean War, 1950–51." *Journal of Canadian Studies* 27, no. 4 (1993): 129–52.

Putnam, Robert D. *Bowling Alone: The Collapse and Revival of American Community*. New York: Simon and Schuster, 2001.

——. "Diplomacy and Domestic Politics: The Logic of Two-Level Games." *International Organization* 42, no. 3 (1988): 427–60.

Quinlivan, James T. "Force Requirements in Stability Operations." *Parameters* 25, no. 4 (1995): 59.

Rana, Kishan S. "Embassies, Permanent Missions, and Special Missions." In *The SAGE Handbook of Diplomacy*, edited by Costas M. Constantinou, Pauline Kerr and Paul Sharp. London: Saye, 2016.

Rathbun, Brian C. "Before Hegemony: Generalized Trust and the Creation and Design of International Security Organizations." *International Organization* 65, no. 2 (2011): 243–73.

——. *Diplomacy's Value: Creating Security in 1920s Europe and the Contemporary Middle East*. Ithaca, NY: Cornell University Press, 2014.

——. *Partisan Interventions: European Party Politics and Peace Enforcement in the Balkans*. Ithaca, NY: Cornell University Press, 2004.

Recchia, Stefano. *Reassuring the Reluctant Warriors: US Civil-Military Relations and Multilateral Intervention*. Ithaca, NY: Cornell University Press, 2015.

Record, Jeffrey. *Wanting War: Why the Bush Administration Invaded Iraq*. Lincoln, NE: Potomac Books, 2010.

Regan, Patrick M. *Civil Wars and Foreign Powers: Outside Intervention in Intrastate Conflict*. Ann Arbor: University of Michigan Press, 2002.

Ricks, Thomas E. *Fiasco: The American Military Adventure in Iraq*. New York: Penguin, 2006.

Risse, Thomas. "'Let's Argue!': Communicative Action in World Politics." *International Organization* 54, no. 1 (2000): 1–39.

Risse-Kappen, Thomas. *Bringing Transnational Relations Back In: Non-State Actors, Domestic Structures, and International Institutions*. Cambridge: Cambridge University Press, 1995.

Robinson, Geoffrey. *"If You Leave Us Here, We Will Die": How Genocide Was Stopped in East Timor*. Princeton, NJ: Princeton University Press, 2010.

Rozental, Andres, and Alicia Buenrosto. "Bilateral Diplomacy." In *The Oxford Handbook of Modern Diplomacy*, edited by Andrew F. Cooper, Jorge Heine, and Ramesh Thakur. Oxford: Oxford University Press, 2013.

Rumsfeld, Donald. *Known and Unknown: A Memoir*. London: Penguin, 2011.

Russett, Bruce M., and John R. Oneal. *Triangulating Peace: Democracy, Interdependence, and International Organizations*. New York: Norton, 2001.

Ryan, Alan. *Primary Responsibilities and Primary Risks: Australian Defence Force Participation in the International Force East Timor*. Duntroon, Australia: Land Warfare Studies Centre, 2000.

Sandler, Todd. "The Economic Theory of Alliances: A Survey." *Journal of Conflict Resolution* 37, no. 3 (1993): 446–83.

Sarantakes, Nicholas Evan. "In the Service of Pharaoh? The United States and the Deployment of Korean Troops in Vietnam, 1965–1968." *Pacific Historical Review* 68, no. 3 (1999): 425–49.

Saunders, Elizabeth Nathan. *Leaders at War: How Presidents Shape Military Interventions*. Ithaca, NY: Cornell University Press, 2011.

Savage, Jesse Dillon, and Jonathan D. Caverley. "When Human Capital Threatens the Capitol: Foreign Aid in the Form of Military Training and Coups." *Journal of Peace Research* 54, no. 4 (2017): 542–57.

Schelling, T. C. *The Strategy of Conflict*. Cambridge, MA: Harvard University Press, 1980.

Schimmelfennig, F. "The Community Trap: Liberal Norms, Rhetorical Action, and the Eastern Enlargement of the European Union." *International Organization* 55, no. 1 (2003): 47–80.

Schmitt, Olivier. *Allies That Count: Junior Partners in Coalition Warfare*. Washington, DC: Georgetown University Press, 2018.

Seawright, Jason. *Multi-Method Social Science: Combining Qualitative and Quantitative Tools*. Cambridge: Cambridge University Press, 2016.

Seibert, B. H. "African Adventure? Assessing the European Union's Military Intervention in Chad and the Central African Republic." Cambridge, MA: MIT Security Studies Working Paper 2007.

Sending, Ole Jacob, Vincent Pouliot, and Iver B. Neumann. *Diplomacy and the Making of World Politics*. Cambridge: Cambridge University Press, 2015.

Serafino, Nina. *The Global Peace Operations Initiative: Background and Issue for Congress*. Washington DC: Congressional Research Service, 2007.

Shalizi, Cosma Rohilla, and Andrew C. Thomas. "Homophily and Contagion Are Generically Confounded in Observational Social Network Studies." *Sociological Methods and Research* 40, no. 2 (2011): 211–39.

Sharp, Paul. *Diplomatic Theory of International Relations*. Cambridge: Cambridge University Press, 2009.

Shimizu, Hirofumi, and Todd Sandler. "Peacekeeping and Burden-Sharing, 1994–2000." *Journal of Peace Research* 39, no. 6 (2002): 651.

Sidman, Murray. *Coercion and Its Fallout*. Boston, MA: Authors Cooperative, 1989.

Simmons, Beth A., and Zachary Elkins. "The Globalization of Liberalization: Policy Diffusion in the International Political Economy." *American Political Science Review* 98, no. 1 (2004): 171–89.

Singer, J. David, Stuart Bremer, and John Stuckey. "Capability Distribution, Uncertainty, and Major Power War, 1820–1965." In *Peace, War, and Numbers*, edited by Bruce Russett, 19–48. Beverly Hills, CA: Sage, 1972.

Singer, Peter Warren. *Corporate Warriors: The Rise of the Privatized Military Industry*. Ithaca, NY: Cornell University Press, 2003.

Siverson, Randolph M., and Harvey Starr. *The Diffusion of War: A Study of Opportunity and Willingness*. Ann Arbor: University of Michigan Press, 1991.

Skogmo, Bjørn. *UNIFIL: International Peacekeeping in Lebanon, 1978–1988*. Boulder, CO: Lynne Rienner, 1989.

Slantchev, Branislav L. "Feigning Weakness." *International Organization* 64, no. 3 (2010): 357–88.

Slaughter, Anne-Marie. *The Chessboard and the Web: Strategies of Connection in a Networked World*. New Haven, CT: Yale University Press, 2017.

——. *A New World Order*. Princeton, NJ: Princeton University Press, 2004.

Smith, Alastair. "Alliance Formation and War." *International Studies Quarterly* 39, no. 4 (1995): 405–25.

Snyder, Glenn H. *Alliance Politics*. Ithaca, NY: Cornell University Press, 1997.

——. "The Security Dilemma in Alliance Politics." *World Politics* 36, no. 4 (1984): 461–95.

Sotomayor, Arturo C. *The Myth of the Democratic Peacekeeper: Civil-Military Relations and the United Nations*. Baltimore, MD: John Hopkins University Press, 2014.

Stähle, Stefan. "China's Shifting Attitude Towards United Nations Peacekeeping Operations." *China Quarterly* 195 (2008): 631–55.

Stairs, Denis. *The Diplomacy of Constraint: Canada, The Korean War, and the United States*. Toronto: University of Toronto Press, 1974.

Stedjan, Scott, and Colin Thomas-Jensen. "The United States." In *The International Politics of Mass Atrocities: The Case of Darfur*, edited by David R. Black and Paul D. Williams. London: Routledge, 2010.

Stein, Janice Gross. *Getting to the Table: The Processes of International Prenegotiations*. Baltimore, MD: John Hopkins University Press, 1989.

Stojek, Szymon M., and Mwita Chacha. "Adding Trade to the Equation: Multilevel Modeling of Biased Civil War Interventions." *Journal of Peace Research* 52, no. 2 (2015): 228–42.

Stueck, William W. *The Korean War: An International History*. Princeton, NJ: Princeton University Press, 2005.

——. *Rethinking the Korean War: A New Diplomatic and Strategic History*. Princeton, NJ: Princeton University Press, 2002.

——. *The Road to Confrontation: American Policy toward China and Korea, 1947–1950*. Chapel Hill: University of North Carolina Press, 1981.

Tago, Atsushi. "Is There an Aid-for-Participation Deal? US Economic and Military Aid Policy to Coalition Forces (Non)Participants." *International Relations of the Asia-Pacific* 8, no. 3 (2008): 379–98.

——. "Too Many Problems at Home to Help You: Domestic Disincentives for Military Coalition Participation." *International Area Studies Review* 17, no. 3 (2014): 262–78.

——. "Why Do States Join US-Led Military Coalitions? The Compulsion of the Coalition's Missions and Legitimacy." *International Relations of the Asia-Pacific* 7, no. 2 (2007): 179–202.

Tardy, Thierry. "CSDP: Getting Third States on Board." Paris: European Union Institute for Security Studies, 2014.

Taylor, Charles. *Snow Job: Canada, the United States, and Vietnam (1954 to 1973)*. Toronto: House of Anansi Press, 1974.

Thomas, Ward. *Ethics of Destruction*. Ithaca, NY: Cornell University Press, 2001.

Thompson, Alexander. *Channels of Power: The UN Security Council and US Statecraft in Iraq*. Ithaca, NY: Cornell University Press, 2009.

Tierney, Dominic. "Multilateralism: America's Insurance Policy against Loss." *European Journal of International Relations* 17, no. 4 (2011): 655–78.

Tollison, Robert D., and Thomas D. Willett. "An Economic Theory of Mutually Advantageous Issue Linkages in International Negotiations." *International Organization* 33, no. 4 (1979): 425–49.

Tomz, Michael. *Reputation and International Cooperation: Sovereign Debt across Three Centuries*. Princeton, NJ: Princeton University Press, 2007.

Truman, Harry S. *Memoirs: Volume 2: Years of Trial and Hope, 1946–1952*. New York: Doubleday, 1956.

Turkmen, Fusun. "Turkey and the Korean War." *Turkish Studies* 3, no. 2 (2002): 161–80.

Uzzi, Brian. "Social Structure and Competition in Interfirm Networks: The Paradox of Embeddedness." *Administrative Science Quarterly* 42, no. 1 (1997): 35–67.

——. "The Sources and Consequences of Embeddedness for the Economic Performance of Organizations: The Network Effect." *American Sociological Review* 61, no. 4 (1996): 674–98.

Uzzi, Brian, and James J. Gillespie. "Knowledge Spillover in Corporate Financing Networks: Embeddedness and the Firm's Debt Performance." *Strategic Management Journal* 23, no. 7 (2002): 595–618.

Valdivieso, Luis, Endo Toshihide, Luis V. Mendonça, Tareq Shamsuddin, and Alejando López-Mejía, eds. *East Timor: Establishing the Foundations of Sound Macroeconomic Management*. Washington, DC: International Monetary Fund, 2000.

Van der Waag-Cowling, Noelle M. "South Africa and the Korean War: The Politics of Involvement." *Scientia Militaria: South African Journal of Military Studies* 44, no. 1 (2016): 224–37.

Vatahov, Ivan. "U.S. Recognises 'Functioning' Economy." *Sofia Echo*, March 6, 2003.

Velazquez, Arturo C. Sotomayor. "Why Some States Participate in UN Peace Missions While Others Do Not: An Analysis of Civil-Military Relations and Its Effects on Latin America's Contributions to Peacekeeping Operations." *Security Studies* 19, no. 1 (2010): 160–95.

Vickers, Rhiannon. "Harold Wilson, the British Labour Party, and the War in Vietnam." *Journal of Cold War Studies* 10, no. 2 (2008): 41–70.

Voeten, Erik. "Outside Options and the Logic of Security Council Action." *American Political Science Review* 95, no. 4 (2001): 845–58.

Voeten, Erik, Anton Strezhnev, and Michael Bailey. "United Nations General Assembly Voting Data." Harvard Dataverse, 2009.

Volman, Daniel. "US to Create New Regional Military Command for Africa: Africom." *Review of African Political Economy* 34, no. 114 (2007): 737–44.

von Hlatky, Stéfanie. *American Allies in Times of War: The Great Asymmetry*. Oxford: Oxford University Press, 2013.

von Hlatky, Stéfanie, and Jessica Trisko Darden. "Cash or Combat? America's Asian Alliances During the War in Afghanistan." *Asian Security* 11, no. 1 (2015): 31–51.

Vucetic, Srdjan. "The Anglosphere and US-Led Coalitions of the Willing, 1950–2001." *European Journal of International Relations* 17, no. 1 (2011): 27–49.

Wagner, R. Harrison. "Economic Interdependence, Bargaining Power, and Political Influence." *International Organization* 42, no. 3 (1988): 461–83.

Walt, Stephen M. "The Origins of Alliances." Ithaca, NY: Cornell University Press, 1987.

Walter, Barbara F. *Committing to Peace: The Successful Settlement of Civil Wars.* Princeton, NJ: Princeton University Press, 2002.

Ward, Hugh, and Han Dorussen. "Standing Alongside Your Friends: Network Centrality and Providing Troops to UN Peacekeeping Operations." *Journal of Peace Research* 53, no. 3 (2016): 392–408.

Wasserman, Stanley, and Katherine Faust. *Social Network Analysis: Methods and Applications.* Cambridge: Cambridge University Press, 1994.

Weisiger, Alex. "When Do States Abandon Coalition Partners During War?" *International Studies Quarterly* 60, no. 4 (2016): 753–65.

Weitsman, Patricia A. "Alliance Cohesion and Coalition Warfare: The Central Powers and Triple Entente." *Security Studies* 12, no. 3 (2003): 79–113.

——. *Waging War: Alliances, Coalitions, and Institutions of Interstate Violence.* Stanford, CA: Stanford University Press, 2014.

Welsh, Jennifer. "Authorizing Humanitarian Intervention." In *The United Nations and Global Security,* edited by Richard Price and Mark Zacher. London: Palgranve Macmillan, 2004.

Wheeler, Nicholas J. *Saving Strangers: Humanitarian Intervention in International Society.* Oxford: Oxford University Press, 2000.

Wheeler, Nicholas J., and Tim Dunne. "East Timor and the New Humanitarian Interventionism." *International Affairs* 77, no. 4 (2001): 805–27.

White, Hugh. "The Road to Interfet: Reflections on Australian Strategic Decisions Concerning East Timor, December 1998–September 1999." *Security Challenges* 4, no. 1 (2008): 69–87.

Wight, Colin, Lene Hansen, Tim Dunne, and Andrew Bennett. "The Mother of All Isms: Causal Mechanisms and Structured Pluralism in International Relations Theory." *European Journal of International Relations* 19, no. 3 (2013): 459–81.

Williams, Paul D. "Military Responses to Mass Killing: The African Union Mission in Sudan." *International Peacekeeping* 13, no. 2 (2006): 168–83.

Wilson, Harold. *A Personal Record: The Labour Government, 1964–1970.* Boston, MA: Little, Brown, 1971.

Wolford, Scott. *The Politics of Military Coalitions.* Cambridge: Cambridge University Press, 2015.

Wolford, Scott, and Emily Hencken Ritter. "National Leaders, Political Security, and the Formation of Military Coalitions." *International Studies Quarterly* 60, no. 3 (2016).

Wood, Herbert Fairlie. *Strange Battleground: The Operations in Korea and Their Effects on the Defence Policy of Canada.* Ottawa: R. Duhamel, Queen's printer, 1966.

Woodward, Peter. *US Foreign Policy and the Horn of Africa.* Burlington, VT: Ashgate 2006.

Worrall, Denis. *South Africa: Government and Politics.* Pretoria: Van Schaik (JL), 1980.

Yarhi-Milo, Keren. *Knowing the Adversary: Leaders, Intelligence, and Assessment of Intentions in International Relations.* Princeton, NJ: Princeton University Press, 2014.

Zartman, I. William, and Jeffrey Z. Rubin. "The Study of Power and the Practice of Negotiation." in *Power and Negotiation*, edited by Zartman and Rubin. Ann Arbor, MI: University of Michigan Press, 2002.

Zürn, Michael, and Jeffrey T. Checkel. "Getting Socialized to Build Bridges: Constructivism and Rationalism, Europe and the Nation-State." *International Organization* 59, no. 4 (2005): 1045–79.

Zyla, Benjamin. "NATO Burden Sharing: A New Research Agenda." *Journal of International Organization Studies* 7, no. 2 (2016): 5–22.

Index

Pages numbers followed by n indicate notes.